THE
IMPEACHMENT
AND TRIAL OF
PRESIDENT CLINTON

THE
IMPEACHMENT
AND TRIAL OF
PRESIDENT CLINTON

The Official Transcripts, from
the House Judiciary Committee Hearings
to the Senate Trial

Introduction by
Michael R. Beschloss

Edited by
Merrill McLoughlin

TIMES T BOOKS

Library of Congress Cataloging-in-Publication Data

Clinton, Bill
The impeachment and trial of President Clinton : the official
transcripts, from the House Judiciary Committee hearings to the
Senate trial.
p.   cm.
ISBN 0-8129-3264-1
1. Clinton, Bill, 1946—Impeachment.   2. Impeachments—United
States. I. United States. Congress. House. Committee on the
Judiciary. II. United States. Congress. Senate. III. Title.
KF5076.C57A2   1999b
342.73'062—dc21   99-25382

Random House website address: www.atrandom.com
Printed in the United States of America on acid-free paper

9 8 7 6 5 4 3 2

First Edition

The President, Vice President and all civil Officers
of the United States, shall be removed from Office
on Impeachment for, and conviction of, Treason, Bribery,
or other high Crimes and Misdemeanors.

CONSTITUTION OF THE UNITED STATES, ARTICLE II, SECTION 4

The House of Representatives shall … have the sole
Power of Impeachment.

ARTICLE I, SECTION 2

The Senate shall have the sole Power to try all Impeachments.
When sitting for that Purpose, they shall be on Oath or
Affirmation. When the President of the United States is tried,
the Chief Justice shall preside: And no Person shall be convicted
without the Concurrence of two thirds of the Members present.
Judgment in Cases of Impeachment shall not extend further
than to removal from Office, and disqualification to hold and
enjoy any Office of honor, Trust or Profit under the United States:
but the Party convicted shall nevertheless be liable and subject to
Indictment, Trial, Judgment and Punishment, according to Law.

ARTICLE I, SECTION 3

CONTENTS

PART IV   Appendices

INTRODUCTION

D ID WILLIAM Jefferson Clinton deserve to become the only elected president of the United States ever to be impeached—and then acquitted? Americans will be arguing well into the twenty-first century. When they do, this record of what an independent counsel, witnesses, prosecutors, defense lawyers, and members of Congress all said during twelve fierce weeks on Capitol Hill will be the place to start.

Thanks to Linda Tripp's secret taping of Monica Lewinsky's conversations about her private life with the president, the FBI's DNA tests on Lewinsky's blue Gap dress, her excruciatingly detailed grand jury testimony and the president's belated confession that he had publicly lied in denying an "inappropriate relationship" with her—all documented in the September 1998 report by Independent Counsel Kenneth Starr—there is no question that Clinton had private encounters in the West Wing of the White House with a young intern on his staff.

But here the consensus collapses. Did those encounters constitute "sexual relations" or not? Was the president committing perjury, as charged in Article I of the Bill of Impeachment, when he described them otherwise in a civil deposition and before a grand jury? Was he obstructing justice, as charged in Article II, when he spoke with his secretary Betty Currie and his friend Vernon Jordan about dealing with Lewinsky?

And if Clinton did commit perjury and/or obstruction of justice, did those crimes reach the constitutional threshold for the House to impeach him or the

Senate to expel him from office? Does breaking the law to conceal a private relationship show that a president is unfit to keep his job, or must the offense be a "crime against the state" like treason or bribery?

Clinton's impeachment and trial left Americans divided in other important ways. They differed over what kind of man the 42nd president was. Was Bill Clinton a "sociopath"—as columnist George Will called him—addicted to lying and cheating, respectful of only those rules he might be caught breaking, cutting corners in his presidential campaigns and, from the White House, using illegitimate means to enhance his power and cover up potential embarrassments?

Or was this a leader who, while he erred in getting involved with Monica Lewinsky and covering it up, got into trouble mainly by incurring the wrath of a "vast right-wing conspiracy"—as Hillary Rodham Clinton named it a week after the Lewinsky scandal burst into public view—that could not stand its failure to stop the election and reelection of the man it considered the image of the anti–Vietnam War generation, and which wanted him thrown out of the presidency by almost any means necessary?

By the laws of history, fifty or a hundred years from now, when political passions have cooled and we have far more information and hindsight than we do today, most historians and most Americans will have reached a common view on these and other questions.

For example, Clinton was impeached and acquitted almost precisely along party lines. Will that cast a shadow on the Republicans of the time? By this line of reasoning, a partisan majority in Congress was so driven by vengeance and desire to tarnish a popular president of the opposition party that it lowered the bar for impeachment and conviction and then failed to make a case strong enough to get a serious number of Democrats to vote against their president. Or will history find that the Democrats were so adamant to defend their own president that they turned a deaf ear to serious charges that should have moved some of them to demand his ouster?

A half century after Bill Clinton leaves the White House, if what we have learned from later sources suggests that this was an ethical man for whom the Lewinsky episode was one lapse, the multiple investigations of this president that began during his first spring in office will seem unfairly overzealous. But if new evidence suggests that the malfeasance of 1997–1998 was only the tip of the iceberg, the inquisition by Kenneth Starr and Republicans in Congress will be faulted mainly for failure to hit real paydirt.

By the middle of the next century, we will also know the answers to other mysteries. What will be the impact of the Clinton-Lewinsky scandal on the presidency? Have Clinton's deceptions about his private life reduced the moral authority of the office, making it more difficult for future presidents to persuade the American people and members of Congress to risk and sacrifice at moments of urgent national need?

Will the legal challenges to Clinton's assertions of executive privilege mean that future presidents will not feel comfortable seeking unvarnished advice from their aides or in the presence of Secret Service agents? Will the six-figure legal bills facing so many members of the Clinton entourage prevent future presidents from attracting first-rate talent?

The principal check on a president's daily exercise of power has always been Congress. By using the whip of impeachment, have the House and Senate of Henry Hyde and Trent Lott begun to tame the office that has been so powerful since Franklin Roosevelt fought the Great Depression and World War II? Are we about to enter a period like the one that began in 1869, after the last impeached president, Andrew Johnson? That was when the presidency was in eclipse, the office was filled by pygmies and Woodrow Wilson could write (in 1885) that the nation was under the spell of "Congressional government."

Years from now we will know whether the Clinton experience has made impeachment more commonplace. Are we in for a period in which impeachment is no longer a fire ax hauled out for extreme emergencies but a weapon of payback by one party against another, tantamount to a parliamentary vote of no confidence?

We will also know whether the events of 1998–1999 have helped to lower our expectations of presidents. Before Bill Clinton, most Americans demanded their chief executive to be not only an effective political leader but an example for their children—both monarch and prime minister.

But throughout the Clinton-Lewinsky scandal, about two-thirds of Americans told pollsters that they thought their president dishonest and untrustworthy at the same time two-thirds of Americans said they approved of his job performance. Are we getting into the habit of looking at presidents the way the French and Italians view prime ministers, asking only that our chief executives do a good job of running the economy and foreign policy, with little regard to their private lives and moral character?

After Watergate, the greatest scandal ever to afflict the presidency, Americans never again looked at their leaders or institutions with the same degree of respect. The Year of Monica Lewinsky was hardly Watergate, but by the end of Bill Clinton's Senate trial, polls showed that younger Americans were reacting the same way to what they took to be a sorry spectacle in Washington.

What will it mean that the first political memory for the 10-year-olds of our time will be not Franklin Roosevelt after Pearl Harbor, John Kennedy at the Cuban Missile Crisis or LBJ pushing Congress to pass the Civil Rights Act, but President Clinton insisting that he had "no sexual relationship" with Lewinsky, or the uglier moments of combat in the House and Senate documented in this book?

Historians must be optimists—especially historians of America, a country and system with almost infinite capacities for regeneration and healing. There is plenty of reason for optimism for the close reader of this volume. Whatever one's opinion of the outcome in the House and Senate, the most powerful man on earth was forced to confess that he had deceived the nation and the courts and, perhaps, to face some difficult truths about himself.

Throughout this book appear politicians of both parties taking political risks and operating above their mere selfish interests. The much-ballyhooed six-month Senate trial, which some claimed would paralyze the people's business and wreck foreign policy and the stock market, never materialized. Predictions that Washington would self-destruct in a war of all against all, waged with searing accusations and humiliating revelations about private lives, were not borne out.

In fact, when the whole ordeal ended on the 190th anniversary of Abraham Lincoln's birth, White House aides marveled that Bill Clinton seemed more focused and motivated than ever before to make something of his last two lame-duck years as president. Republican leaders pledged to put the bone-crushing experience behind them and work with the man they had so recently denounced as a common criminal. Senator after senator emerged to say that the trial had caused them to "bond together" as never before.

Just three months earlier, on Thursday, November 19, 1998, as Kenneth Starr unveiled his indictment before the House Judiciary Committee, who could have ever imagined such a denouement?

THE RISE OF THE INDEPENDENT PROSECUTOR

Starr's very existence as an independent prosecutor investigating the president was a singular feature of the late twentieth century. For most of American history, high-ranking members of the executive branch charged with grave offenses had been probed by the Justice Department.

Then came Watergate. In the spring of 1973, President Richard Nixon bowed to complaints that the charges against him could not be fairly investigated by Justice—especially because one of the key suspects in the scandal was Nixon's first attorney general and friend, John Mitchell. Archibald Cox, who had served as solicitor general for Nixon's old enemy, President John Kennedy, was appointed as a special prosecutor for Watergate.

That October, when Cox pressed too hard for access to the secret tapes Nixon had made of his private conversations, Nixon ordered his firing in the famous "Saturday Night Massacre." (Attorney General Elliot Richardson resigned rather than fire Cox. Nixon then fired Richardson's deputy, William Ruckelshaus, for refusing the same order. Finally, Solicitor General Robert Bork agreed to comply.) The outcry against Cox's firing in Washington and the nation fueled the drive for Nixon's impeachment and compelled him to appoint another special prosecutor, Leon Jaworski, a Houston lawyer who had been close to another Democrat, President Lyndon Johnson. When Nixon resigned in August 1974, many Americans believed that the Cox-Jaworski investigation deserved much of the credit for bringing the president to justice.

In 1978, Congress passed the Independent Counsel Act, designed to ensure that investigation of some future president or high appointee need not depend on another flukish decision like Nixon's to fashion an ad hoc special prosecution force. The law, which was subject to renewal, created the authority and procedure for appointing special counsels when serious charges were raised against high executive branch officials.

In the post-Watergate atmosphere, the public expected special prosecutors to be named when there was even a faint chance of misbehavior. Independent counsels were thus appointed to investigate charges of such varying magnitude as possible drug use by aides to President Jimmy Carter, possible Mafia ties of a Reagan cabinet member, and the Iran-*Contra* scandal, in which the Reagan administration traded arms to Iran for hostages and then diverted the proceeds to anticommunists in Nicaragua.

Congress kept renewing the act, with minor changes, because the public felt that it was working. By the late 1980s, however, it became clear that the statute had had several consequences that its authors had not fully anticipated.

One was the enormous power that the act gave a special prosecutor—open-ended budgets and freedom from the usual guidelines that Justice Department prosecutors have to observe. Former Judge Lawrence Walsh, who spent four years and $48 million investigating Iran-*Contra*, was criticized for both overzealousness and failure to nail any key figure for the offenses at the center of the scandal. (The Walsh investigation petered out on Christmas Eve 1992, when President George Bush, three weeks before leaving office, pardoned Reagan's defense secretary, Caspar Weinberger, and five other officials.)

The other was more profound. As long as the statute was in force, there was a greater chance than before 1978 that a president would suffer a serious investigation that could jeopardize or topple his presidency. This reduced presidential authority and tempted the more vehement opponents of a president like Reagan, Bush, or Clinton to demand such investigations in the hope that they would weaken or destroy a chief executive they did not like.

Were the act in force for earlier presidents, the course of history might well have been changed. Had a 1990s-style independent prosecutor investigated charges of serious corruption in the Bureau of Internal Revenue in 1952, for example, Harry Truman's presidency might be remembered for a major scandal that spread to the top of his Justice Department.

Had an independent counsel investigated President Dwight Eisenhower's chief aide, Sherman Adams, he or she would have discovered that Adams had taken not merely an Oriental rug or vicuna coat, as was publicly believed, but hundreds of thousands in cash from the New Hampshire businessman Bernard Goldfine. (Evidence of Adams's offenses was later discovered by the Justice Department of Robert Kennedy, who decided not to prosecute.) This would almost certainly have paralyzed Eisenhower during his last two years in office and tarnished his reputation.

Kenneth Starr, who had served as George Bush's solicitor general, was appointed by a three-judge panel in August 1994 to take over the investigation of possibly questionable business dealings by both Bill and Hillary Clinton related to the Whitewater land development venture. (Starr's predecessor was Robert Fiske, a New York lawyer whom Clinton's attorney general, Janet Reno, had appointed in January 1994 during a brief hiatus in the independent counsel statute.)

Starr's dominion would have been limited to Whitewater but for an Arkansas woman named Paula Corbin Jones, who charged that in 1991, then-Governor Clinton had sexually harassed her in a Little Rock hotel room. On January 15, 1997, five days before Clinton took the oath for his second term, the Supreme Court secretly decided that the case would be "unlikely to occupy any substantial amount of President Clinton's time" if allowed to proceed while he was still in office. (The ruling was publicly announced four months later.)

On Thursday, January 15, 1998, tipped off by Linda Tripp about Monica Lewinsky's relationship with the president, Starr's staff asked Attorney General Reno for permission to extend the independent counsel's investigation to possible obstruction of justice in the Jones case. The next day, after Reno agreed, they interviewed Lewinsky for almost ten hours at the Ritz-Carlton Hotel in Arlington, Virginia, threatening prosecution if she did not talk about her relationship with Clinton. On Saturday, January 17, 1998, in his scheduled sworn deposition in the Jones case, Clinton was startled to be asked in detail about Lewinsky and denied that their relationship was sexual.

On Wednesday, January 21, 1998, with a page 1 article in the *Washington Post*, the fourth great presidential scandal of the twentieth century (after Teapot Dome, Watergate, and Iran-*Contra*) burst into full public view.

HAULING OUT THE FIRE AX

After Election Day 1998, when Republicans nearly lost the House of Representatives and did more poorly than expected in the Senate, many supposed that the steam had gone out of impeachment. Polls showed that a majority of Americans thought the sanction was out of proportion to Clinton's alleged offenses.

For most of American history, the impeachment of a president had been virtually unthinkable. The one presidential impeachment—Andrew Johnson in 1868—suggested that the punishment be approached with caution. Charged with violating the Tenure of Office Act by firing Secretary of War Edwin Stanton, Johnson survived his Senate trial in May 1868 by one vote.

Most later scholars and other Americans came to believe that the Johnson impeachment was illegitimate. Not only was the statute he was accused of breaking later found to be unconstitutional (in 1926), but the congressmen and senators who pursued the 17th president were thought to be less concerned with looking for "high crimes and misdemeanors," as the Constitution prescribed, and more interested in finding some pretext for ousting a president whose leniency toward the defeated South they execrated.

Some in 1868 worried that an emboldened Congress would begin to use impeachment more frequently as a stick against presidents. But the hideousness of the Johnson impeachment and trial helped to ensure that the Congresses of the next 106 years would recoil from serious drives to impeach presidents unless there was supreme provocation. From time to time, angry representatives might demand that some president be impeached—the left-liberal Democrat Bella Abzug proposed such a bill against Nixon as early as 1971, in regard to the Vietnam War—but until Watergate, the fire ax was kept behind its pane of emergency glass.

Throughout Nixon's scandal, beginning in the spring of 1973, there was considerable consensus that if the 37th president could be proved to have abused power and obstructed justice, he would have committed clearly impeachable offenses and should be removed. The problem, as Nixon's defenders insisted, was finding sufficient evidence.

On Saturday evening, July 27, 1974, when the House Judiciary Committee began voting on five articles of impeachment, members still lacked access to the secret Nixon tapes that would seal his fate. Nevertheless, Nixon's accusers had made their case sufficiently strong that when the Democrat-dominated committee passed three articles (obstruction of justice, abuse of power, contempt of Congress for refusing to comply with the committee's subpoena for his secret tapes), members of his own party crossed the line to oppose him.

The same day that the committee began voting, the Supreme Court in *United States v. Nixon* demanded that the president give up his tapes. When the "smoking gun" conversations were revealed, most of Nixon's most vigorous defenders jumped to the other side. On Wednesday, August 7, when Republican House and Senate leaders John Rhodes and Hugh Scott joined Senator Barry Goldwater to see Nixon at the White House, they told him that impeachment by a wide margin was certain and that he could hope to get no more than a dozen votes to acquit him in a Senate trial.

Nixon escaped his certain fate by announcing that he would quit. Years later, in retirement, he insisted that Andrew Johnson's impeachment and trial would prove to be the last of an American president because, in the nuclear age, the country could not afford to have "a president in the dock" for six months or more.

The quandary for those members of Congress considering Bill Clinton's impeachment was almost the opposite of Nixon's. For most of Watergate, people did not argue that the accusations against Nixon did not met the constitutional threshold of impeachment, just that the president's guilt had not been proven.

In the Clinton case, as this book demonstrates, differences over the facts took a backseat to the argument over whether the president's alleged misbehavior met the constitutional standard. What would the outcome of the Clinton impeachment have been had Starr's referral to Congress not been limited to the president's cover-up of the Lewinsky affair but extended to other matters like Whitewater, the firing of White House travel office officials, campaign finance violations, and other areas in which the president stood accused?

THE MOOD IN THE WHITE HOUSE

During his impeachment and Senate trial, Andrew Johnson sat in the White House, ridiculing "the show" on Capitol Hill and after his acquittal thumbed his nose at his Radical Republican enemies in Congress one last time by vetoing two liberal Southern state constitutions and then pardoning Confederate President Jefferson Davis.

Like Johnson, Bill Clinton showed a propensity for roiling the hornets' nest. In August 1998, when the Gap dress and Lewinsky's testimony compelled him to confess their relationship on national television, Senate Judiciary Chairman Orrin Hatch of Utah encouraged the president to make a healing address, hinting that members of Congress might then relax their drive for his removal. After listening to Clinton's angry denunciation of Starr and of his pursuers, Hatch was heard to mutter, "What a jerk!"

After the surprise Democratic victories in November, reports soon surfaced that the president considered impeachment virtually a dead letter. Some Republicans on the House Judiciary Committee took his formal replies to the 81 questions sent him by Chairman Henry Hyde to be peremptory and insulting.

On Saturday afternoon, December 19, after Clinton's impeachment, the president made a defiant appearance at what was later called a "pep rally" in the White House Rose Garden. Democratic Senator Robert Byrd, who was thought to be wavering on conviction, called the event "an egregious display of shameless arrogance."

TRIAL IN THE SENATE

When the Senate began dealing with Andrew Johnson's impeachment in March 1868, the old chamber was turned into a near circus. For ten weeks, the house managers, the president's lawyers and forty witnesses droned on while professional gamblers in the gallery bet on Johnson's acquittal. Wavering senators were covertly offered money and women.

For those worried about the Senate's dignity, the trial of 1999 offered more horrifying possibilities—that dozens of people would be dragged onto the Senate floor to be interrogated about Clinton's relationship with Monica Lewinsky and its cover-up, capped by the woman herself, forced to testify about the most intimate details of what she had done with the president and whether this constituted sexual relations. Thanks to a compromise, senators agreed to keep the process from spinning out of control by opening the trial on Wednesday, January 6, hearing opening presentations by both sides, and then deciding what to do.

After both sides finished, the first option was adjournment; under the rules, at any time, a simple majority could decide to abort the trial. On Friday, January 22, Senator Byrd declared that two-thirds of the Senate was not likely to convict: "Lengthening this trial will only prolong and deepen the divisive, bitter, and polarizing effect that this sorry affair has visited upon our nation."

On Tuesday, February 2, Senator Hatch proposed in the *New York Times* that the Senate adjourn with a finding that Clinton gave "false and misleading testimony" and "impeded the justice system's search for truth," that he would be subject to prosecution after he left office, and that "the Senate acknowledges, recognizes, and accedes to the articles of impeachment passed by the House as Impeachment Without Removal, the highest form of condemnation other than removal." Denying Clinton acquittal would deny him "the result he craves for his own historic legitimacy."

The Byrd and Hatch gambits failed. The Senate authorized the House managers to depose Lewinsky, Vernon Jordan, and Clinton aide Sidney Blumenthal on videotape, from which excerpts were used by the prosecutors and the president's lawyers in their final presentations, shown on television screens on the Senate floor. Senators refused demands to change rules that required them to debate the president's removal in secret session. With a two-thirds vote to convict remaining unreachable, one choice remained.

Since the summer of 1998, many who considered Clinton's impeachment and conviction too brutal a sanction for his alleged offenses wished that the House and Senate would punish him with a resolution of censure. There was no certainty that such a punishment would be constitutional or that some future Congress would not expunge it from the record, just as the Senate did in the historical censure of President Andrew Jackson for his dealings with the Bank of the United States.

By the final week of the trial, the censure option was killed, mainly by Republicans, who reasoned that for Clinton to be the only elected president ever impeached would be a harsher punishment—and who wished to leave Democrats in the position of defending themselves in the year 2000 election as the party that had defended and tolerated Clinton's offenses.

WHAT PLACE IN HISTORY?

After fleeing the White House to escape impeachment, Richard Nixon privately predicted that fifty years later, when historians considered his presidency, Watergate would be a "footnote."

During the last nineteen years of his life, like the Ancient Mariner, Nixon conducted a campaign among journalists, historians, and the American people. He argued that his opening to China and other foreign policy achievements were more important than scandal and, more boldly, that perhaps he should never have been driven from office. After all, hadn't FDR abused federal agencies? Besides, Nixon argued, he was, like Roosevelt, a president operating in wartime. Had he not hired his Watergate "plumbers" to plug leaks of national security information, his diplomacy with China, the Soviet Union, and North Vietnam might have been endangered.

If Nixon hoped that the drive to bring him to justice would later be seen, as with Andrew Johnson, as a craven, last-ditch move by political enemies, he would be disappointed. Most Americans now believe that Nixon's offenses were amply proved and easily of the magnitude to demand his removal.

Bill Clinton will doubtless spend the rest of his life insisting that the three months on Capitol Hill in 1998–1999 were an unjust persecution. As early as the day after the impeachment vote, when asked by Elizabeth Shogren of the *Los Angeles Times* at a White House holiday dinner how it felt to be impeached, he replied, "Not bad," going on to add that in a decade or two history would view him more favorably.

The House managers and the others in Congress who pursued Clinton will have campaigns to run, too—first among voters who, in many cases, decried them for stalking a popular president at a moment of peace and prosperity. Then they, too, will try to sway the bar of history. At the time of both the House and Senate votes, member after member said that in historical terms, this would be the most important vote they would likely cast, short of a decision to go to war. Some Republicans in Congress insisted that they should be candidates for some new edition of John F. Kennedy's *Profiles in Courage,* which celebrated politicians who put principle ahead of ambition.

On the death in 1940 of Neville Chamberlain, the British prime minister who had tried to avert World War II by appeasing Hitler, the *Chicago Tribune* ran a cartoon showing a historian viewing niches of various sizes in a great pantheon of leaders, and wondering which size niche Chamberlain deserved.

Historians and future generations of Americans will judge President Clinton and his accusers. They will also have to decide where to locate his impeachment and trial in the American experience. On that debate, the curtain is now about to rise.

Michael R. Beschloss
April 1999

EDITOR'S NOTE

THE TASK of compressing into a volume of this size the millions of words that marked the impeachment proceedings and trial of President Clinton necessarily involves leaving a good many of those words on the cutting-room floor. In editing, my main goals were to be fair to all sides in presenting both the letter and the spirit of the debates, and to give readers who would never wish to wade through the many volumes of raw testimony a less daunting version that truly reflects the movement and the moment of these events. This edition also corrects spelling errors found in the original transcripts and includes explanatory footnotes where they might prove helpful.

The chief victims of the editing are rhetoric and repetition. Wherever possible, substance has trumped style, and judicious trimming has reduced what one witness before the House Committee on the Judiciary called "mind-numbing" reiteration of familiar issues. Another inevitable loss, sadly, is the formal phrasing and mannerly tradition that mark the deliberations of both chambers of the United States Congress, helping to sustain civility during even the most contentious times. An example: At one point during the fierce impeachment debate on the House floor, Wisconsin Republican Rep. F. James Sensenbrenner Jr. inquired, "Mr. Speaker, is the word *hypocrisy* in order on this floor?"

Apologies to any eloquent debaters who find their words missing from these pages; readers who seek the complete record should consult Appendix

IX in this volume. And thanks, too, to: Joseph D. McDonald, Publications Clerk of the House Judiciary Committee, for his help in finding transcripts that were not easily located; Luke Mitchell of Times Books for his patience and aid; and Michael Ruby for his incomparable advice and unwavering support.

Merrill McLoughlin
March 1999

PART I

THE HOUSE

*Inquiry by the Committee
on the Judiciary*

THE TESTIMONY
OF KENNETH STARR

In the same hearing room where the House Judiciary Committee had voted to impeach Richard M. Nixon in 1974, Chairman Henry J. Hyde of Illinois convened the committee[1] to consider the impeachment of President William Jefferson Clinton. The committee had previously heard testimony from an array of experts on impeachment—testimony addressing its history, its meaning, and the Congress's role.[2] But November 19 marked the opening of the real debate. The main business of the day was the presentation of his case against the president by Independent Counsel Kenneth Starr. After some sharply partisan skirmishing over the amount of time the president's lawyers would have to question Starr, the committee heard opening statements by Hyde and ranking Democrat John Conyers Jr. of Michigan.

Mr. Hyde: This morning, we commence our second public hearing in fulfillment of the mandate imposed on us in House Resolution 581.[3] While the business of impeachment is rare, and happily so, it becomes necessary from time to time, when circumstances require that it be exercised as a constitu-

[1] For a complete list of committee members, see Appendix I.
[2] For information on where to find documents and testimony not included in this book, see Appendix IX.
[3] For the full text of House Resolution 581, authorizing the committee's inquiry, see Appendix III.

tional counterbalance to allegations of serious abuse of presidential power. It is a part of the series of checks and balances that exemplify the genius of our Founding Fathers.

Throughout our history, we have had a number of impeachment inquiries, but this one represents a historical first. Never before has an impeachment inquiry arisen because of a referral from an independent counsel under Section 595(c) of the statute. For that reason, we have no precedent to follow on the involvement of the independent counsel in our proceedings. However, it seems both useful and instructive that we should hear from him, since he is the person most familiar with the complicated matters the House has directed us to review....

As we begin that search, we turn to one person, Judge Starr, who has a comprehensive overview of the complex issues we face. I thought we should have that overview before we hear from other witnesses.... In addition, we have yet to hear from the president, and I can assure my colleagues if and when the president would want to testify, he may have unlimited time to do so....

There are many voices telling us to halt this debate, that the people are weary of it all. There are other voices suggesting we have a duty to debate the many questions raised by the circumstances in which we find ourselves, questions of high consequence for constitutional government....

What is the significance of a false statement under oath? Is it essentially different from a garden variety lie, a mental reservation, a fib, an evasion, a little white lie, hyperbole? In a court proceeding, do you assume some trivial responsibility when you raise your right hand and swear to God to tell the truth, the whole truth, and nothing but the truth? And what of the rule of law? That unique aspect of a free society that protects you from the fire on your roof or the knock on the door at 3 a.m.? What does lying under oath do to the rule of law? Do we still have a government of laws and not of men? Does the law apply to some people with force and ferocity while the powerful are immune? Do we have one set of laws for the officers and another for the enlisted? ...

These are but a few questions these hearings are intended to explore—and just perhaps, when the debate is over, the rationalizations and the distinctions and the semantic gymnastics are put to rest, we will be closer to answering for our generation the haunting question asked 139 years ago in a small military cemetery in Pennsylvania, whether a nation conceived in liberty and dedicated to the proposition that all men are created equal can long endure.

Mr. Conyers: ... [W]e meet today for only the third time in the history of our nation to take evidence in an inquiry of impeachment against a president of the United States.

Today's witness, Kenneth W. Starr, wrote the tawdry, salacious and unnecessarily graphic referral that he delivered to us in September ... and now the majority members of this committee have called that same prosecutor forward to testify in an unprecedented desperation effort to breathe new life into a dying inquiry.

It is fundamental to the integrity of this inquiry to examine whether the independent counsel's evidence is tainted, whether conclusions are colored by improper motive. In short, it is relevant to examine the conduct of the independent counsel and his staff.... For example, the committee must determine whether Mr. Starr improperly threatened witnesses if they would not provide incriminating evidence against the president of the United States....

Let there be no mistake, it is not now acceptable in America to investigate a person's private sexual activity. It is not acceptable to force mothers to testify against their daughters, to make lawyers testify against their clients, to require Secret Service agents to testify against the people they protect, or to make bookstores tell what books people read. It is not acceptable for rogue attorneys and investigators to trap a young woman in a hotel room, discourage her from calling her lawyer, ridicule her when she asks to call her mother. But the record suggests, I am sorry to say, that is precisely how Kenneth W. Starr has conducted this investigation....

Is it just coincidence that even before he was appointed Independent Counsel Mr. Starr was ... in contact with lawyers for Paula Jones? Is it just coincidental that Mr. Starr, until recently, drew a $1-million-a-year salary from his law firm that represents the tobacco industry, which is fighting President Clinton's effort to deter teen smoking? ... Is it just a coincidence that the independent counsel failed to provide this committee with important exculpatory evidence in his referral ...?

Perhaps Mr. Starr will persuade us not to be concerned about these matters. But he surely carries the burden of showing us and the American people that these things did not affect his fairness nor his impartiality....

Finally, Mr. Chairman, I would be remiss ... if I did not observe that to date our committee process has not been bipartisan nor fair. All this committee has done since September 9 is to, in a partisan manner, dump salacious grand-jury material on a public that does not want it. It was you ... who said this process could not proceed unless it was bipartisan. We need to do better than 11th-hour unilateral decisions to subpoena witnesses having little to do with the underlying referral. We need to do better in offering the president a full and fair opportunity to participate....

Chairman Hyde then introduced the independent counsel, former U.S. solicitor general Kenneth Starr. "On August 5th, 1994, the Special Division of the United States Court of Appeals for the District of Columbia Circuit appointed Judge Starr to investigate what has become known as the Whitewater matter," Hyde noted. "Since that time, Attorney General [Janet] Reno and the Special Division added several other matters, including the White House Travel Office and the FBI files matters to Judge Starr's jurisdiction. After his submission of evidence, they further added what has become known as the [Monica] Lewinsky matter." To date, Hyde said, Starr's investigations had "led to the conviction of 14 persons, including a sitting governor of Arkansas ... the former number-three person in the United States Department of Justice and two former business partners of the president. Six other indictments are currently pending in the courts." After Starr was sworn in, Hyde asked him to proceed.

Mr. Starr: Thank you, Mr. Chairman....

Let me then begin with an overview. As our referral explains, the evidence suggests that the president made false statements under oath and thwarted the search for truth in *Jones v. Clinton.* The evidence further suggests that the president made false statements under oath to the grand jury on August 17 of this year.

That same night, the president publicly acknowledged an inappropriate relationship, but maintained that his testimony had been legally accurate. The president also declared that all inquiries into the matter should end because, he said, it was private. But shortly after the president's August 17 speech, Senators Lieberman, Kerrey and Moynihan[4] stated that the president's actions were not a private matter. In our view, they were correct....

The evidence suggests that the misuse of presidential authority occurred in the following ten ways:

First, the evidence suggests that the president made a series of premeditated false statements in his civil deposition on January 17, 1998. Those were

[4] Democrats Joe Lieberman of Connecticut, Bob Kerrey of Nebraska, and Daniel Patrick Moynihan of New York.

statements under oath.... By making false statements under oath, the president, the chief executive of our nation, failed to adhere to that oath and to his presidential oath to faithfully execute the laws.

Second, the evidence suggests that apart from making false statements under oath, the president engaged in a pattern ... of behavior during the *Jones* litigation to thwart the judicial process. the president reached an agreement with Ms. Lewinsky that each would make false statements under oath. He provided job assistance to Ms. Lewinsky at a time when the *Jones* case was proceeding and Ms. Lewinsky's truthful testimony would have been harmful. He engaged in an apparent scheme to conceal gifts that had been subpoenaed from Ms. Lewinsky. He coached a potential witness, his own secretary Mrs. Currie, with a false account of relevant events. Those acts constitute a pattern of obstruction that is fundamentally inconsistent with the president's duty to faithfully execute the law.

Third, the evidence suggests that the president participated in a scheme at his civil deposition in which his attorney, in his presence, deceived a United States district judge in an effort to cut off questioning about Ms. Lewinsky. the president did not correct his attorney's statement. A false statement to a federal judge in order to shortcut, and to prevent relevant questioning, is an obstruction of the judicial process.

Fourth, the evidence suggests that on January 23, 1998, after the criminal investigation had become public, the president made false statements to his Cabinet and used his Cabinet as unwitting surrogates to publicly support the president's false story.

Fifth, the evidence suggests that the president, acting in a premeditated and calculated fashion, deceived the American people on January 26 and on other occasions, when he denied a relationship with Ms. Lewinsky.

Sixth, the evidence suggests that the president, after the criminal investigation became public, made false statements to his aides and concocted false alibis that these government employees repeated to the grand jury sitting at the United States courthouse. As a result, the grand jury here in Washington received inaccurate information.

Seventh, having promised the American people to cooperate with the investigation, the president refused six invitations to testify before the grand jury. Refusing to cooperate with a duly authorized federal criminal investigation is inconsistent with the general statutory duty of all executive-branch employees to cooperate with criminal investigations. It also is inconsistent with the president's duty to faithfully execute the laws.

Eighth, the president and his administration asserted three different governmental privileges to conceal relevant information from the grand jury. The privilege assertions were legally baseless in these circumstances.... And they delayed and impeded the investigation.

Ninth, the president made false statements under oath to the grand jury on August 17, 1998.... The evidence demonstrates that the president failed to adhere to that oath and thus to his presidential oath to faithfully execute the laws.

Tenth, the evidence suggests that the president deceived the American people in his speech on August 17 by stating that his testimony had been legally accurate.

In addition to these ten points, it bears mention that well before January of 1998, the president used governmental resources and prerogatives to pursue his relationship. The evidence suggests that the president used his secretary, Betty Currie, a government employee, to facilitate and to conceal the relationship with Ms. Lewinsky. The president used White House aides and the United States ambassador to the United Nations in his effort to find Ms. Lewinsky a job at a time when it was foreseeable, even likely, that she would be a witness in the *Jones* case. And the president used a governmental attorney, Bruce Lindsey, to assist his personal legal defense during the *Jones* case.

In short, the evidence suggests that the president repeatedly used the machinery of government and the powers of his high office to conceal his relationship—to conceal the relationship from the American people, from the judicial process in the *Jones* case, and from the grand jury.

Let me turn, then, to the legal context in which these issues first arose. At the outset, I want to emphasize that our referral never suggests that the relationship between the president and Ms. Lewinsky in and of itself could constitute a high crime or misdemeanor.... The propriety of a relationship is not the concern of our office. The referral is, instead, about obstruction of justice, lying under oath, tampering with witnesses, and the misuse of power....

Paula Jones, a former Arkansas state employee, filed a federal sexual-harassment suit against President Clinton in 1994. The president denied those allegations. We will never know whether a jury would have credited the allegations.... When the president and Ms. Jones settled the case last week, the Eighth Circuit Court of Appeal in St. Louis was still considering the preliminary legal question whether the facts, as alleged, could constitute sexual harassment.

After the suit was first filed in 1994, the president attempted to delay the trial—or, more broadly, the proceedings—until his presidency had concluded. The president claimed a temporary presidential immunity from civil suit, and the case proceeded through the Court of Appeals to the Supreme Court of the United States.

At oral argument, the president's attorney specifically warned our nation's highest court that if Ms. Jones prevailed, her lawyers would be able to investigate the president's relationships with other women, as is common in sexual harassment cases. The Supreme Court rejected the president's constitutional claim of immunity and did so by a nine-to-zero vote. The court concluded that the Constitution did not provide such a temporary immunity from suit. The idea was simple and powerful: No one is above the law.

The Supreme Court sent the case back to trial with words that warrant emphasis. These are the words of our unanimous Supreme Court: "Like every other citizen who invokes" the District Court's jurisdiction, "Ms. Jones"—the words of the court again—"has a right to an orderly disposition of her claims."

After the Supreme Court's decision, the parties started to gather the facts. The parties questioned relevant witnesses in depositions. They submitted written questions. They made requests for documents.

Sexual harassment cases are often "he said/she said" kinds of disputes. Evidence reflecting the behavior of both parties can be critical—including the defendant's relationships with other employees in the workplace. Such questions can be uncomfortable, but they occur every day in courts and law offices across our country. Individuals in those cases take an oath to tell the truth, the whole truth and nothing but the truth. And no one is entitled to lie under oath simply because he or she does not like the questions or because he believes the case is frivolous or that it is financially motivated or politically motivated. The Supreme Court has emphatically and repeatedly rejected the notion that there is ever a privilege to lie....

During this fact-gathering process, Judge Susan Webber Wright in Little Rock followed standard principles of sexual harassment cases. Over repeated objections from the president's attorneys, the judge permitted inquiries into the president's relationships with government employees. On January 8, 1998, for example, Judge Wright stated that questions as to the president's relationships with other government employees... "are within the scope of the issues in this case."...

. . .

The key point about the president's conduct is this: On at least six different occasions from December 17, 1997, through August 17, 1998, the president had to make a decision. He could choose truth, or he could choose deception. On all six occasions, the president chose deception, a pattern of calculated behavior over a span of months.

On December 5, 1997, Ms. Jones' attorneys identified Ms. Lewinsky as a potential witness.

Within a day, the president learned that Ms. Lewinsky's name was on the witness list. After learning this, the president faced his first critical decision. Would he and Monica Lewinsky tell the truth about their relationship? Or would they provide false information—not just to a spouse or to loved ones, but under oath in a court of law?

Eleven months ago, the president made his decision. At approximately 2 in the morning on December 17, 1997, he called Ms. Lewinsky at her Watergate apartment and told her that she was on the witness list.... During this 2 a.m. conversation, which lasted approximately half an hour, the president could have told Ms. Lewinsky that they must tell the truth under oath. The president could have explained that they might face embarrassment but that, as a citizen and as the president, he could not lie under oath and he could not sit by while Monica did so. The president did not say anything like that.

On the contrary, according to Ms. Lewinsky, the president suggested that she could sign an affidavit in the case and use, under oath, deceptive cover stories that they had devised long ago to explain why Ms. Lewinsky had visited the Oval Office area. The president did not explicitly instruct Ms. Lewinsky to lie. He did not have to do so. Ms. Lewinsky testified that the president's suggestion that they use the pre-existing cover stories amounted to a continuation of their pattern of concealing their intimate relationship.

Starting with this conversation, the president and Ms. Lewinsky understood, according to Ms. Lewinsky, that they were both going to make false statements under oath.

The conversation between the president and Ms. Lewinsky on December 17 was a critical turning point. The evidence suggests that the president chose to engage in a criminal act—to reach an understanding with Ms. Lewinsky that they would both make false statements under oath. At that moment, the president's intimate relationship with a subordinate employee was transformed . . . into an unlawful effort to thwart the judicial process. This was no longer an issue of private conduct.

Recall that the Supreme Court had concluded that Paula Jones was entitled to an "orderly disposition" of her claims. The president's action on December 17 was his first direct effort to thwart [that] mandate. . . .

On December 23, 1997, the president submitted under oath a written answer to what lawyers call interrogatories. . . . The request stated, in relevant part, "Please state the name of federal employees with whom you had sexual relations when you were president of the United States." In his sworn answer, the president said, "None."

On December 28, the president faced a third critical choice. On that day, the president met Ms. Lewinsky at the White House. They discussed the fact that Ms. Lewinsky had been subpoenaed for gifts she had received from the president. According to Ms. Lewinsky, she raised with the president the question of what she should do with the gifts. Later that day, the president's personal secretary, Betty Currie, drove to Ms. Lewinsky's Watergate home. Ms. Lewinsky gave Mrs. Currie a sealed box that contained some of the subpoenaed gifts. Mrs. Currie then took the box and stored it under her bed at home.

In her written proffer on February 1, four weeks after the fact, Ms. Lewinsky stated that Mrs. Currie had called her to receive the gifts. If so, that necessarily meant that the president had asked Ms. Currie to call. It would directly and undeniably implicate him in an obstruction of justice. . . .

Ms. Currie, for her part, recalls Ms. Lewinsky calling her. But even if Ms. Lewinsky called Mrs. Currie, common sense and the evidence suggest some presidential knowledge or involvement. . . .

Let me add another point about the gifts. In his grand jury appearance in August, the president testified that he had no particular concern about the gifts in December of 1997 when he had talked to Ms. Lewinsky about them. And he thus suggested that he would have had no reason to take part in December in a plan to conceal the gifts. But there is a serious problem with the president's explanation. If it were true that the president in December was unconcerned about the gifts, he presumably would have told the truth under oath in his January deposition about the large number of gifts that he and Ms. Lewinsky had exchanged. But he did not tell the truth.

At that deposition, when asked about whether he had ever given gifts to Monica Lewinsky—and he had given her several on December 28th—the president stated, "I don't recall. Do you know what they were?" ... Meanwhile, the legal process continued to unfold, and the president took other actions that had the foreseeable effect of keeping Ms. Lewinsky "on the team." The president helped Ms. Lewinsky obtain a job in New York. His efforts began after the Supreme Court's decision in May of 1997, at a time when it had become foreseeable that she could be an adverse witness ... [and] intensified in December 1997, after Ms. Lewinsky's name appeared on the witness list.

Vernon Jordan, who had been enlisted in the job search for Ms. Lewinsky, testified that he kept the president informed of the status of Ms. Lewinsky's job search and her affidavit. On January 7, 1998, Mr. Jordan told the president that Ms. Lewinsky had signed the affidavit.

Mr. Jordan stated to the president that he was still working on getting her a job. The president replied: Good. In other words, the president, knowing that a witness had just signed a false affidavit, encouraged his friend to continue trying to find her a job. After Ms. Lewinsky received a job offer from Revlon on January 12, Vernon Jordan called the president and said "Mission accomplished."

As is often the situation in cases involving this kind of financial assistance, no direct evidence reveals the president's intent in assisting Ms. Lewinsky in her job efforts. Ms. Lewinsky testified that no one promised her a job for silence.

Of course, crimes ordinarily do not take place with such explicit discussion. But federal courts instruct juries that circumstantial evidence is just as probative as direct evidence. And here, the circumstantial evidence ... is strong. At a bare minimum, the evidence suggests that the president's job assistance efforts stemmed from his desire to placate Ms. Lewinsky so that she would not be tempted, under the burden of an oath, to tell the truth about the relationship. Monica Lewinsky herself recognized that at the time, saying to a friend, "Somebody could construe or say, 'Well, they gave her a job to shut her up. They made her happy.'"

... In mid-January, Ms. Lewinsky finalized her false affidavit with her attorney, who sent it to Judge Wright's court in Little Rock. The affidavit falsely denied a sexual relationship with the president and essentially recounted the cover stories that had been discussed during that middle-of-the-night conversation on December 17.

Let me turn to the president's January 17 deposition. Some have suggested that the president might have been surprised or ambushed at the deposition. Those suggestions are wrong. The president had clear warning that there would be questions about Monica Lewinsky. She had, again, been named on the December 5 witness list. On January 12, just five days before the deposition, Ms. Jones' attorneys identified Ms. Lewinsky as a trial witness.... Two days later, on January 14, the president's private attorney asked Ms. Lewinsky's attorney to fax a copy of the affidavit. During the deposition itself, the president's attorney stated that the president was, in his words, "fully familiar" with the affidavit.

At the outset of his January 17 deposition, therefore, the president faced a fourth critical decision. Fully aware that he would likely receive questions about Ms. Lewinsky, would the president continue to make false statements under oath, this time in the presence of a United States District judge...?

At the start of the deposition... [t]he president swore to tell the truth, the whole truth and nothing but the truth. As his testimony began, the president, in response to a question from Ms. Jones' attorneys, stated that he understood he was providing his testimony under penalty of perjury.

The president was asked a series of questions about Ms. Lewinsky. After a few questions, the president's attorney, Mr. Bennett, objected to the questioning about Ms. Lewinsky, referring to it as, in his words, "innuendo." Mr. Bennett produced Ms. Lewinsky's false affidavit. Mr. Bennett stated to Judge Wright that Ms. Lewinsky's affidavit indicated that, in Mr. Bennett's words, "there is absolutely no sex of any kind in any manner, shape, or form." Mr. Bennett stated that the president was "fully aware of Ms. Lewinsky's affidavit."

During Mr. Bennett's statement, the president sat back and let his attorney mislead Judge Susan Webber Wright. The president said not a word to the judge, or so far as we are aware, to his attorney.

Judge Wright overruled Mr. Bennett's objection. The questioning continued. In response, the president made false statements... about a whole host of matters. The president testified that he did not know that Vernon Jordan had met with Ms. Lewinsky and talked about the *Jones* case. That was untrue. He testified that he could not recall being alone with Ms. Lewinsky. That was untrue. He testified that he could not recall ever being in the Oval Office hallway with Ms. Lewinsky except perhaps when she was delivering pizza. That was untrue. He testified that he could not recall gifts exchanged between Ms. Lewinsky and him. That was untrue.

He testified, after a fourteen-second pause, that he was "not sure" whether he had ever talked to Ms. Lewinsky about the possibility that she might be asked to testify in the lawsuit. That was untrue. The president testified that he did not know whether Ms. Lewinsky had been served a subpoena at the time he last saw her in December 1997. That was untrue. When his attorney read Ms. Lewinsky's affidavit denying a sexual relationship, the president stated that the affidavit was "absolutely true." That was untrue....

The evidence suggests that the president directly contravened the oath he had taken, as well as the Supreme Court's specific mandate, in which the court had stated that Ms. Jones was entitled, like every other citizen, to a lawful disposition of her case.

As our referral outlines, the president's deposition did not mark the end of his scheme to conceal. During his deposition testimony, the president referred to his secretary, Betty Currie. The president testified, for example, that Ms. Lewinsky had come to the White House to see Ms. Currie, that Ms. Currie had been involved in assisting Ms. Lewinsky in her job search, and that Ms. Currie had communicated with Vernon Jordan about Mr. Jordan's assistance to Ms. Lewinsky. In response to one question at the deposition, the president said he did not know the answer and "you'll have to ask Betty."

Given the president's repeated references to Ms. Currie and his suggestion to Ms. Jones' attorneys that they contact her, the president had to know that Ms. Jones' attorneys might want to question Mrs. Currie. Shortly after 7 p.m. on Saturday, January 17 of this year—just two and a half hours after the deposition had concluded—the president attempted to contact Mrs. Currie at her home. The president asked Ms. Currie to come to the White House the next day, which she did.... According to Ms. Currie, the president appeared concerned and he made a number of statements about Ms. Lewinsky...:

"You were always there when she was there, right? We were never really alone."

"You could see and hear everything."

Ms. Currie concluded that the president wanted her to agree with him when he made these statements. Ms. Currie stated that she did in fact indicate her agreement, although she knew that the president and Ms. Lewinsky had been alone, and that she could not hear or see them when they were alone. Ms. Currie further testified that the president ran through the same basic statements with her again on either January 20th or the 21st.

...[A]t the time the president made these statements, he knew that they were false.... The president thus could not have been trying to refresh his recollection, as he subsequently suggested.... Is there a legitimate explanation for the president to have said those things in that matter to Mrs. Currie? The circumstances suggest not. The facts suggest that the president was attempting to improperly coach Mrs. Currie at a time when he could foresee that she was a potential witness in *Jones v. Clinton.*

The president's next major decision came in the days immediately after January 21st. On the 21st, the *Washington Post* reported the story of Ms. Lewinsky's relationship with the president.... [T]he president faced a decision: Would he admit the relationship publicly, correct his testimony in the *Jones* case and ask for the indulgence of the American people? Or would he continue to deny the truth?

... According to Dick Morris, the political consultant, the president and he talked on January 21st. Mr. Morris suggested that the president publicly confess. The president replied: "But what about the legal thing? ... You know, Starr and perjury and all?"

Mr. Morris suggested that they take a poll. The president agreed. Mr. Morris called with the results. He stated that the American people were willing to forgive adultery but not perjury or obstruction of justice. The president replied, "Well, we just have to win, then." ...

The first step was for the president to deny the truth publicly. For this, political polling led to Hollywood staging. The president's California friend and producer, Harry Thomason, flew to Washington and advised the president that the president needed to be very forceful in denying the relationship. On Monday, January 26th, in the Roosevelt Room, before members of Congress and other citizens, the president provided a clear and emphatic public statement denying the relationship. The president also made false statements to his Cabinet and to his aides. They then spoke publicly and professed their belief in the president.

The second step was to promise cooperation. The president told the American people on several television and radio shows on January 21st and 22nd that, in his words, "I'm going to do my best to cooperate with the investigation."

The third step was the president's refusal to provide testimony to the grand jury.... Refusing invitations to provide information to a grand jury in a federal criminal investigation ... was inconsistent with the January promise of the president to cooperate and with the general statutory duty of all government officials to cooperate with federal criminal investigations.

As a fourth step, the president ... authorized the use of various governmental privileges to delay the testimony of many of his taxpayer-paid assistants.... In the Lewinsky investigation, the president asserted two privileges—executive privilege and a government attorney-client privilege. A subordinate administration official, without objection from the president, claimed a previously unheard-of privilege that was called the protective function privilege. The privileges were asserted to prevent full testimony of several White House aides. They were asserted to prevent the full testimony of sworn law-enforcement officers of the Secret Service.

In asserting executive privilege, the president was plowing headlong into the Supreme Court's unanimous decision 24 years ago in *United States versus Richard Nixon*. There, the Supreme Court ruled that executive privilege was overcome by the need for relevant information and evidence in criminal proceedings. And thus, it came as no surprise that Chief Judge Norma Holloway Johnson ... rejected President Clinton's effort to use executive privilege to prevent disclosure of relevant evidence.

In asserting protective function and government attorney-client privileges, the administration was asking the federal courts to make up one new privilege out of whole cloth.... And thus it again came as little surprise that the federal courts rejected the administration's claims.... The Supreme Court refused to grant review of the cases notwithstanding the administration's two strongly worded requests, petitions for certiorari....

After Chief Judge Johnson ruled against the president, the president then dropped the executive privilege claim in the Supreme Court. And then, in August, the president explained to the grand jury why he had dropped the claim. The president stated, "I didn't really want to advance an executive privilege claim in this case beyond having it litigated." But this statement, made to the grand jury, was inaccurate. In truth, the president had again asserted executive privilege only a few days earlier. And a few days after his grand jury testimony, the president again asserted executive privilege to prevent the testimony of Bruce Lindsey....

When the president and the administration assert privileges in a context involving the president's personal issues ... when the president and the administration rebuff our office's efforts to expedite the cases to the Supreme Court; when the president contends in the grand jury that he never really wanted to assert executive privilege beyond having it litigated—despite the fact that he had asserted it six days earlier and would do so again 11 days afterwards, there is substantial and credible evidence that the president has misused the privileges available to his high office. And the misuse delayed and impeded the federal grand jury's investigation.

The fifth tactic was diversion and deflection. The president made false statements to his aides and associates about the nature of the relationship, as we have seen, with knowledge that they could testify to that effect to the grand jury sitting here in Washington. The president did not simply say to his associates that the allegations were false or that the issue was a private matter that he did not want to discuss. Instead, the president concocted alternative scenarios that were then repeated to the grand jury.

The final two tactics were related: to attack the grand jury investigation, including the Justice Department prosecutors who serve in my office . . . and to shape public opinion about the proper resolution of the entire matter. . . .

The president testified before the grand jury on August 17th. Beforehand, many in Congress and in the public advised that the president should tell the truth. . . . Senator Hatch[5], for example, stated that "So help me, if he lies before the grand jury, that will be grounds for impeachment." Senator Moynihan simply stated that perjury before the grand jury was, in his view, an impeachable offense.

The evidence suggests that the president did not heed this senatorial advice. Although admitting to an ambiguously defined inappropriate relationship, the president denied that he had lied under oath at his civil deposition. He also denied any conduct that would establish that he had lied under oath at that deposition. . . .

The president's answers have not been well received. Congressman Schumer, the senator-elect, for one, stated that "it is clear that the president lied when he testified before the grand jury." Congressman Meehan stated that the president engaged in a "dangerous game of verbal Twister."[6]

Indeed, the president made false statements to the grand jury and then that same evening spoke to the nation and criticized all attempts to show that he had done so as invasive and irrelevant. The president's approach appeared to contravene the oath that he took at the start of the grand jury proceedings. . . .

And thus ended the over-eight-month journey that had begun on December 5, 1997, when Monica Lewinsky's name appeared on the witness list. The evidence suggests that the eight months included false statements under oath, false statements to the American people, false statements to the president's cabinet and his aides, witness tampering, obstruction of justice,

---

[5] Republican Orrin G. Hatch of Utah.
[6] Democrats Charles E. Schumer of New York and Martin T. Meehan of Massachusetts, both members of the House Judiciary Committee.

and the use of presidential authority and power in an effort to conceal the truth of the relationship and to delay the investigation.

> *Starr then outlined for the committee how the Office of the independent counsel (OIC) had begun investigating the Lewinsky matter. On January 8, 1998, he said, one of his deputies had learned that Linda Tripp wanted to provide some information. Four days later, Tripp was debriefed on what she knew about Lewinsky's relationship with President Clinton and on the tapes she had made of her conversations with Lewinsky. Finding her information credible, the OIC contacted the Justice Department and "fully informed" Deputy Attorney General Eric Holder. "We stated that the Lewinsky investigation could be considered outside our jurisdiction as then constituted. We stressed that someone needed to work the case, the Justice Department or an independent counsel." On January 16, Attorney General Janet Reno decided to ask the three-judge panel that oversees the independent counsel's operations to expand Starr's jurisdiction. The request was granted. Starr continued:*

Seven months later, after conducting the factual investigation and after the president's grand jury testimony, the question we faced was what to do with the evidence. The chairman referred to Section 595(c) of the independent counsel statute, which requires an independent counsel investigating possible crimes to provide to the House of Representatives . . . "substantial and credible information that may constitute grounds for an impeachment." . . .

[A]s we understood the text of the Constitution, its history, and relevant precedents, it was clear that obstruction of justice in its various forms, including perjury, "may constitute grounds for an impeachment." . . . Even apart from any abuses of presidential authority and power, the evidence of perjury and obstruction of justice required us to refer the information to the House. . . .

Although perjury and obstruction of justice are serious federal crimes, some have suggested that they are not high crimes or misdemeanors when the underlying events concern the president's private actions. Under this theory, a president's obstruction and perjury must involve concealment of official actions. . . .

Justice Story[7] . . . stated in his famous "Commentaries" that there is not a syllable in the Constitution which confines impeachment to official acts. With all

---

[7] Justice Joseph Story of Massachusetts served on the U.S. Supreme Court from 1811 until 1845.

respect, an absolute and inflexible requirement of a connection to official duties appears, fairly viewed, to be an incorrect interpretation of the Constitution.

History and practice support the conclusion that perjury, in particular, is a high crime and misdemeanor. Perjury has been the basis, as the committee knows, for the removal of several judges.... In addition ... perjury seems to have been recognized as a high crime or misdemeanor at the time of the founding of our republic. And the House managers' report in the impeachment of Judge Walter Nixon, for perjury, stated, "It is difficult to imagine an act more subversive to the legal process than lying from the witness stand."

And finally, I note that the federal sentencing guidelines include bribery and perjury in the same guideline, reflecting the common-sense conclusion that bribery and perjury are equivalent means of interfering with the governmental process....

. . . The pattern of obstruction of justice, false statements and misuse of executive authority in the Lewinsky investigation did not occur in a vacuum. In August 1994, I—

At this point, Rep. Sheila Jackson Lee of Texas raised a point of order. She noted that the independent counsel's referral to the House had included no findings of guilt against President Clinton on issues stemming from Madison Guaranty Savings and Loan, Whitewater, or the controversies surrounding the White House travel office and the use of FBI files on White House personnel. "I believe Mr. Starr's remarks are now out of order," Ms. Jackson Lee objected. Chairman Hyde overruled the objection and allowed Starr to proceed.

[I]t was in August of 1994 that I took over the Madison Guaranty investigation from Robert Fiske. Over the ensuing years, I have essentially become independent counsel for five distinct investigations; for Madison Guaranty and Whitewater, for Foster-related matters, for the Travel Office, for the FBI files matter and for the Lewinsky investigation, as well as for a variety of obstruction and related matters that arose out of those five major investigations....

The center of all this, the core of our Arkansas-based investigation, was Madison Guaranty Savings and Loan. Madison was a federally insured savings and loan in Little Rock, Arkansas, run by Jim and Susan McDougal.... Mrs. Clinton and other lawyers at the Rose law firm in Little Rock performed legal work for Madison in the 1980s.

Madison first received attention in March 1992 when a *New York Times* report raised several issues about the relationships between the Clintons and the McDougals in connection with Madison Guaranty. Federal bank examiners examined Madison in 1992 and 1993, and the regulators sent criminal referrals to the Justice Department, and the Justice Department then launched a criminal investigation ... in November 1993.... Madison exemplified the troubled practices of savings and loans in the 1980s. The failure of the institution ultimately cost federal taxpayers approximately $65 million....

The McDougals' operation of Madison raised serious questions whether bank funds had been used illegally to assist business and political figures in Arkansas.... As to the Clintons, the question arose primarily because they were partners with the McDougals in the Whitewater Development Company....: Given Jim McDougal's role at the center of both institutions and given Whitewater's constant financial difficulties, there were two important questions: Were Madison funds diverted to benefit Whitewater? If so, were the Clintons either involved in or knowledgeable of that diversion of funds?

Those questions were not idle speculation. In early 1994, a Little Rock judge and businessman, David Hale, pled guilty to certain unrelated federal crimes. As part of his plea, David Hale told Mr. Fiske's team that he had received money as a result of a loan from Madison in 1986 and that his company loaned it to others as part of a scheme to help some members of the Arkansas political establishment. One loan of $300,000 went to Susan McDougal's make-believe company, which she called Master Marketing. Based on our investigation, we now know that some $50,000 of the proceeds of that loan went to benefit the Whitewater Corporation. David Hale stated that he had discussed the Susan McDougal loan with then-Governor Clinton....

In August 1994, when I first arrived in Little Rock ... we devised a plan. First, based on the testimony of David Hale and others, as well as documentary evidence, we would take steps.... if the evidence warranted, to seek an indictment of Jim and Susan McDougal and others involved in what clearly appeared to be criminal transactions. If a Little Rock jury convicted the McDougals or others, we would then ... determine whether they had other relevant information, including, of course, whether the McDougals possessed information that would either exonerate or incriminate the Clintons as to Madison and Whitewater matters....

We garnered a number of guilty pleas in my first year. One was from Webster Hubbell, who had worked at the Rose law firm and was knowledgeable about its work with Madison.... In addition, Robert Palmer, a real-estate appraiser, pled guilty to fraudulently doctoring Madison documents to deceive federal bank examiners. Three other associates of McDougal pled guilty and agreed to cooperate.

In August 1995 ... a federal grand jury in Little Rock indicted Jim and Susan McDougal and the then-sitting governor of Arkansas, Jim Guy Tucker. The case went to trial in March of 1996 amid charges by all three defendants and their allies that the case was a political witch hunt....

The president testified for the [Tucker] defense from the Map Room of the White House. During his sworn testimony, the president testified as a defense witness that he did not know about the Susan McDougal loan nor had he ever been in a meeting with Hale and McDougal about the loan. He also testified that he had never received a loan from Madison. This was important testimony. Its truth—or falsity—went to the core issues of our investigation.

On May 28, 1996, all three defendants were convicted—Jim McDougal of 18 felonies, Susan McDougal of four felonies and Governor Tucker of two felonies. Governor Tucker announced his resignation that day.

After his conviction, Jim McDougal began cooperating with our investigation.... He informed our career investigators and prosecutors that David Hale was accurate. According to Jim McDougal, President Clinton had testified falsely at the McDougal-Tucker trial. Jim McDougal testified that he had been at a meeting with David Hale and Governor Clinton about the Master Marketing loan. And Jim McDougal testified that Governor Clinton had received a loan from Madison....

Again, Ms. Jackson Lee questioned whether this line of testimony was germane or fair, in light of the fact that the independent counsel had not included Whitewater, Madison Guaranty, Travelgate, or Filegate in his referral. Again, Chairman Hyde overruled her point of order, observing that House Resolution 581 had deliberately given the committee's inquiry "wide-open range." He asked the witness to proceed.

In late 1997, we ... considered whether this evidence ... justified a referral to Congress.... But we concluded that it would be inconsistent with the statutory standard because of the difficulty of establishing the truth with a sufficient degree of confidence. We also weighed a prudential factor.... There were still two outstanding witnesses who might later corroborate, or contradict, the McDougal and Hale accounts: Jim Guy Tucker and Susan McDougal.

In 1998, we were finally able to obtain information from Governor Tucker.... He pled guilty in a tax-conspiracy case, and he ultimately testified before the Little Rock grand jury in March and April of this year. But he had little knowledge of the loan to Susan McDougal's fictitious company and the president's possible involvement in it.... Importantly ... Governor Tucker exonerated the president regarding long-standing questions whether the president and Governor Tucker had a conversation about the Madison referrals in the White House in October, 1993....

The remaining witness who perhaps could shed light on the issue was Susan McDougal.... Because the proceeds from the fraudulent loan that Susan McDougal received had benefited the Clintons—the proceeds were used to pay off obligations of the Whitewater Development Company for which the Clintons were potentially personally liable—Susan McDougal was subpoenaed to testify before the grand jury in Little Rock in August, 1996....:

Susan McDougal refused to answer any questions. District Judge Susan Webber Wright, in Little Rock, then held her in civil contempt, a decision later upheld unanimously by the United States Court of Appeals in St. Louis....

Starr then summed up a separate area of the original investigation, focusing on the Rose law firm's work for Madison during 1985 and 1986 and, in particular, on a "complicated real estate deal known as Castle Grande ... [which] was structured to avoid state banking regulatory requirements and involved violations of federal criminal law." In 1994 and 1995, grand jury subpoenas went to Rose and to the Clintons, seeking all documents related to Madison and Castle Grande.

But important evidence about Hillary Clinton's work—billing records and time sheets—were missing. They turned up "under unusual circumstances," said Starr, on January 5, 1996. Starr said that Webster Hubbell "may have additional information ... whether exculpatory or inculpatory, that we have been unable to obtain." Not only had he been at the Rose law firm at the time the work was done, but, Starr noted, after he was forced to resign from the Clinton Justice Department, Hubbell received payments of nearly $550,000 from several companies and individuals— many of them Clinton campaign contributors.

Among those who arranged consulting contracts for Hubbell was Vernon Jordan, who contacted MacAndrews & Forbes on his behalf—the same company that later offered Monica Lewinsky a job on Jordan's recommendation. Hubbell, Starr said, did "little or no work" for the $550,000. "This rush of generosity obviously gives *rise to an inference that the money was essentially a gift," said Starr. "And if it was a gift, why was it given?" Finally, Starr quoted taped conversations while Hubbell was in prison. In one, he had told his wife: "I won't raise those allegations—that might open it up on Hillary." The money he received and the comments he made, Starr said, "raise very troubling questions."*

Then the independent counsel turned to Travelgate and Filegate. The president had never figured at all in Starr's investigation of the former, he said. And a thorough inquiry into the latter had implicated no senior White House officials and had found "no evidence that information contained in the files of former officials was actually used for an improper purpose."

Finally, Starr returned to the Lewinsky matter:

[T]he Lewinsky investigation could not be properly conducted in a slapdash manner. It was our duty to be meticulous, to be careful. We were. And in the process, we uncovered substantial and credible evidence of serious legal wrongdoing by the president.... But bear in mind we submitted the referral, as we were required to do, to the House of Representatives and not to the public....

[A]s you know, by an overwhelming bipartisan vote, the House immediately disclosed our referral to the public. But I want to be clear, as a matter of fairness, that the public disclosure or nondisclosure of the referral and the backup materials was a decision that our office did not make and lawfully could not make. We had no way of knowing in advance...whether the House would publicly release both the report and the backup materials; would release portions of one or both; would release redacted versions of the report and backup documents; would prepare and release a summary...or would simply keep the referral and backup materials under seal, just as Special Prosecutor Leon Jaworski's submission in 1974 remained under seal.

As a result, we respectfully but we firmly reject the notion that our office was trying to inflame the public. We are professionals, and we were trying to get the relevant facts, the full story, to the House of Representatives....

In fact, the referral has served a good purpose. There has been virtually no dispute about a good many of the factual conclusions in the report.... A key reason, we submit, is that we insisted...that we be exhaustive in the investigation and that we document the facts and conclusions in our report.

I want to be absolutely clear on one point, however. Any suggestion that the men and women of our office enjoyed or relished this investigation is wrong, it is nonsense.... As I have said, our office was assigned a specific duty by the attorney general and the Special Division to gather the facts and then, if appropriate, to make decisions and report the facts as quickly as we possibly could.... Thirty years from now, not 30 days from now, we want to be able to say that we did the right thing....

I am not a man of politics, of public relations or of polls—which I suppose is patently obvious by now....

Rather, as a product of the law and of the courts, I have come to an unyielding faith in our court system—our system of judicial review, the independence of our judges, our jury system, the integrity of the oath and...the sanctity of the judicial process....

President Lincoln asked that..."reverence for the laws be proclaimed in legislative halls and enforced in courts of justice."

Mr. Chairman, Members, I revere the law. I am proud of what we have accomplished. We were assigned a difficult job. We have done it to the very best of our abilities. We have tried to be both fair and thorough....

After a recess, the committee returned for the questioning of Kenneth Starr. Under the rules, the minority and majority counsels would each have thirty minutes to ask questions. First up was Abbe Lowell, the Democratic counsel. Lowell began by asking Starr whether he agreed that there were "substantial differences" between his referral and the one sent by Watergate special prosecutor Leon Jaworski in 1974. Starr agreed that there were, explaining that the differences stemmed from the independent counsel law, which had not existed in 1974.

Mr. Lowell: On that point, Mr. Starr...this is how Mr. Jaworski's report has been characterized by Federal Judge John Sirica, who reviewed it in order to send it to Congress. Judge Sirica wrote: "Mr. Jaworski's report draws no accusatory conclusions. It contains no recommendations, advice or statements that infringe on the prerogatives of the other branches of government. It renders no moral or social judgments. It is a simple and straightforward compilation of information, and it contains no objectionable features."

This is how your report has been described: "It is a report that marshals and characterizes the information into an aggressive piece of legal advocacy. It is one where there are few of the factual assertions are left to speak for themselves. In short, it is a document with an attitude. It is notable for its failure to acknowledge that there might be more than one way to view at least some of the evidence." That was from the Supreme Court reporter of *The New York Times*, Linda Greenhouse, on September 12, 1998.

It cannot be your testimony, is it, Mr. Starr, that the 595(c) background material that you cite to this committee … required you to make the accusations, conclusions—in short, have a referral with an attitude—is it?

Mr. Starr: My opinion of the statute, or my reading and interpretation of the statute, Mr. Lowell, is that I am called upon to establish the reason that in the independent counsel's view the matters that I send before you may constitute a grounds for impeachment. That is a very serious and weighty matter and we approached it in a very serious and weighty manner.

I have the highest regard for the late John Sirica. I served with Judge Sirica. But he was addressing, in all fairness, a totally different set of circumstances. …

What we tried to do in this referral was to assemble in an organized form, rather than sending you simply truckloads of unorganized information, give it coherence, and then it is your judgment. And thus if it is the judgment that this referral has not, in fact, stood the test of your close examination—did we get the facts wrong?—then, of course, you should come to your own judgment and your own assessment.

But this reflects, just so the committee knows, the views of some of the most experienced prosecutors in the country. I stand behind it because it is mine. I stand behind each word of it. It is my ultimate judgment. …

Mr. Lowell: Whether it be your judgment, Mr. Starr, or the judgments of your entire staff, one thing I think you will agree with is that it was your and your staff's decision to include the words "premeditated," "concocted false alibis," "deceived," "pattern of obstruction," "lying under oath," "perjury"—which words you will never find in the report of Leon Jaworski when he was reporting the same kind of evidence to the Congress 24 years ago. Aren't I right about that?

Mr. Starr: … I am not taking issue with the fact that this document is no doubt in many respects different than the very kind of environment and legal standard under which Mr. Jaworski was operating.

But, Mr. Lowell … if our office is going to inform the House of Representatives that there may be substantial grounds for an impeachment, that is so weighty, that is so serious, that you need to have the benefit of our judgment and our assessment of the facts informed by our watching the witnesses, listening to the grand jury and the way the grand jury reacted to witnesses, the assessment of the grand jury, and then to give you our judgment. …

... This is only a tool for you to use as you see fit. But I don't think that it is fair to criticize my office for not following a pattern that was not governed by a statute. And Colonel Jaworski is not here to tell us what he would think if he went through the same process under the statutory regime that our professional colleagues went through.

Mr. Lowell: ... You have raised something that I think bears some note when you were talking about Mr. Jaworski not being here. But he did leave us his words.... In talking about... how to send material to Congress about the grave and serious matter of presidential wrongdoing, Mr. Jaworski wrote as follows... "The central key to the entire success was not accusing anyone. What we did is simply carried forward what the facts were, passed them on, not making an effort to interpret them, not making any sort of an effort to construe them or to say what we thought it showed, and let it be completely nonaccusative."

So we don't have Mr. Jaworski, but we do have his words, correct?

Mr. Starr: Absolutely.... We did go through an evaluative process, as I described. And while we did not have the benefit of Colonel Jaworski, except that which he has left us, I do think it is important for the committee to know that in light of the sober judgment—you're free to disagree with that judgment—but it's our professional judgment that the president engaged in abuse of his authority with respect to executive privilege.

We were guided by Sam Dash[8], who had very strong views on that... and who felt that we had to use certain kinds of language that I think, Mr. Lowell... you would disagree with.

Mr. Lowell: ... As I understand your testimony this morning, after the four years and however many dollars you have now spent... your office has not and is not sending an impeachment referral to the Congress on what has been affectionately or not so affectionately called Travelgate, nor on what has been called Filegate, and I think... you are not sending a referral on the original

---

[8] Samuel Dash served as counsel to the Senate Watergate Committee and as ethics adviser to the Office of the Independent Counsel; he resigned from the latter post the day after this hearing. He explained his resignation in a letter to Starr: "Against my strong advice, you decided to depart from your usual professional decision-making by accepting the invitation of the House Judiciary Committee to appear before the committee and serve as an aggressive advocate for the proposition that the evidence in your referral demonstrates that the president committed impeachable offenses."

Whitewater land deal, and pointed out in some of your investigation you have now learned that former Governor Tucker actually exonerated the president on some of the questions that you had.

Mr. Starr: Yes.

Mr. Lowell: The referral you sent, then, Mr. Starr, refers apparently only to the issues about the *Paula Jones* case and the questions of the president's conduct in dealing with that case. That is correct, is it not?

Mr. Starr: ... The referral does in other respects indicate the ties that we saw to earlier phases of our investigation and why we ... were choosing to assess this. But you're quite right; both with respect to the two matters you indicated, as well as the specific testimony by Governor Tucker, that those matters will, in fact, not be coming to you.

> *Lowell then turned to how the OIC had won jurisdiction over the Lewinsky matter. He reviewed Starr's testimony about how they had "fully informed" Deputy Attorney General Eric Holder about the matter under investigation. In order to rule on jurisdiction, he suggested, Starr and his office would have provided Justice Department officials "with all the information . . . needed to make that important choice." Starr's reply: "Certainly that which, in our judgment, was relevant to the decision."*
>
> *Lowell continued:*

Mr. Lowell: Mr. Starr, though, isn't it then true that, in fact, neither the deputy attorney general nor the attorney general had the facts that they needed because ... you did not ever mention the substantial contacts that you had already had in the *Paula Jones* case, the very subject about which you were seeking authority to investigate?

Mr. Starr: ... We did not go to the department, Mr. Lowell, to say we must have jurisdiction. We took to the department an issue ... to make jurisdictional decisions. . . .

[T]he information we had was there was inchoate criminality, which is a fancy way of saying something is afoot. It is breaking now. It is fast-moving, and we need to bring this to your attention, and you make the determination. We think there is a jurisdictional justification for what we have done thus far, but we think there are serious jurisdictional issues.

Now, it will be the attorney general's decision. Now, of what should the attorney general have been informed?

Mr. Lowell: ... [I]t appears that neither you nor any of the officials in your office told the attorney general that before you became the independent counsel, your law firm, Kirkland & Ellis, was actually contacted to represent Paula Jones and eventually helped her to find the lawyers she chose. That was not mentioned to the attorney general that day or at any other time that you were seeking jurisdiction ... was it?

Mr. Starr: Well, you're assuming that I had the benefit of all this information.

Mr. Lowell: Whether your law firm had been asked?

Mr. Starr: Yes ... because I certainly had had personal communications with Mr. Davis,[9] but I would have to reconstruct what others may have done in other offices. It is a large law firm. So if I could just say what I, in fact, knew at the time that this activity was underway, the reaching out to the attorney general ... I had, in fact, been contacted by, among others, Mr. Davis with respect to an amicus brief or some participation on the constitutional immunity issue in 1994, and those had been publicly reported....

Mr. Lowell: ... The question that I asked ... was not whether you had had contacts with Mr. Davis ... I asked whether you had, or any of your office members told the attorney general that your law firm, that you were still a member of and getting a salary from had indeed been sought out to be Paula Jones' lawyers....

Richard Porter, your partner, did not inform you that he had been asked to consider representing Paula Jones and had, in fact, assisted her in getting the attorneys she ultimately chose. Is that what you are saying?

Mr. Starr: Well, my best recollection is no. I know Richard Porter, I have had communications with him from time to time, but in terms of a specific discussion with respect to what the law firm may be doing or may not be doing, I'm not recalling that specifically, no.

---

[9] Gilbert Davis, one of Paula Jones' attorneys.

Mr. Lowell: You do recall, though, that...on at least six occasions you personally had had conversations with Paula Jones' attorneys over legal issues in the *Paula Jones* case.

Mr. Starr: ...I had had conversations with them....

My position on the constitutional immunity that the president enjoyed was very clear and was open. I was contacted, before I was appointed as independent counsel, by Bob Fiske. Bob Fiske was the independent counsel in Little Rock, Arkansas, and Mr. Fiske asked me whether I would be willing to consider writing an amicus brief on behalf of the Office of Independent Counsel...but no final decision was made....

It did not occur to me, that issue with respect to constitutional immunity...I never spotted the issue that my conversations with Bob Fiske, Gil Davis, my debating Lawrence Tribe on National Public Radio had the foggiest connection with issues that were unfolding at the time. Fault my judgment, if you will, but it just, frankly, did not occur to me....

Mr. Lowell: ...[D]id it not occur to you that you should tell the attorney general, who was making a decision about whether you were an independent counsel, that your law firm, Kirkland & Ellis, in addition to being asked to be Paula Jones' attorney, was providing legal advice, free legal advice, to a conservative women's group called the International Women's Forum, who were thinking about participating in the *Paula Jones* case itself?...

Mr. Starr: Well, again, it's not whether it occurs or not. I did have discussions with I think it's called the Independent Women's Forum as to whether they would, in fact, file an amicus brief again, strictly on the constitutional issue, not taking a position on the merits.

But the president, through his very able lawyers, had raised a very important question: Does the president of the United States enjoy immunity?...It was a matter of vigorous debate. And the fact that I had these discussions had all been...part of the public domain....[I]t was very clear that what we were investigating were serious crimes of perjury that had nothing to do with the constitutional immunity of the president.

Mr. Lowell: Mr. Starr, are you suggesting that when you told the deputy attorney general that he had to move with haste because this investigation was fast-moving, that you had no responsibility to also inform the attorney general about these contacts…which might make the attorney general, as you pointed out, have a choice to make between giving the investigation to you, or giving it to somebody whose independence, bias and involvement in the case was not questioned?

Mr. Starr: Well, I utterly disagree, with all respect, with your premise that to be involved on an issue of civil law and constitutional law in any way suggests a predisposition more generally. I would take the position that the president of the United States does not enjoy constitutional immunity from a suit, regardless of who the president is. It has nothing to do with the identity of the occupant of the office. It has everything to do with what the presidency is, and the nature of our relationship to one another as individuals, and whether we are all equal under the law.…

[O]ne factual correction.… I did not have conversations with the deputy attorney general. They were by others in my office, who were reporting to the deputy attorney general, on the information that was coming to us, and then saying what is your judgment?…

Next Lowell addressed Linda Tripp's discussions with Paula Jones' attorneys to "help them set up for the deposition of the president." He pressed Starr on why the OIC had not forbidden her to communicate with the Jones lawyers. At first, Starr replied, they didn't know Tripp was talking to the Jones camp. The OIC quickly found itself working "at cross purposes with the Jones attorneys" in order to protect its investigation—and, said Starr, "when it became obvious that [Tripp] was talking to someone in New York who apparently in turn was talking to someone at Newsweek," his office did tell her she must "protect the confidentiality of these matters."

Mr. Lowell: I am understanding you. But I am also understanding you to say that you're not contesting that on that day, she came in, she had the conversation, she showed you the tapes or told you about the tapes.… You had both the authority … to give her immunity and the authority to tell her not to talk. You did the first. You didn't do the second, did you?

Mr. Starr: Well, I would have to double-check to see exactly what we did tell her. But, no, what I am trying to make as clear as I possibly can is that what we were saying to Ms. Tripp: You have given us this remarkable information—allegations. They are extraordinarily explosive, that perhaps go to the president of the United States. We need backup. And she was coming to us as a witness. And this information was not, at the time that it was first coming to us, in the public domain. So... my colleagues, who were making these decisions on the spot, took the steps that we did. But if the suggestion is we wanted her to go public, the suggestion is absolutely wrong.

Mr. Lowell: ... I could well understand why people in Linda Tripp's position and your staff... didn't want the investigation to become public, but I could also understand why Linda Tripp wanted the information she had to go into the Paula Jones camp, and I could understand that you had the authority to stop that but didn't do it.

Mr. Starr: But what we did do, Mr. Lowell, in fairness... once it became clear that there was a following by the *Jones* lawyers of our investigation and the subpoenaing of witnesses... we took prompt remedial action. We went to Judge Susan Webber Wright, and we said stop it—please have them stop it. ...

Mr. Lowell: ... You are not suggesting that you and your staff that were talking to Linda Tripp—and then going to see the deputy attorney general—were not aware that on that following Saturday, January 17th, the president of the United States was already noticed for his deposition. You are not telling us that, are you?

Mr. Starr: No, we did know that. And indeed, the deputy attorney general and then the attorney general of the United States, Mr. Lowell, knew that there were serious allegations. This was days—several days—before the deposition. The deposition was on Saturday, the 17th. The attorney general made her decision knowing the information that we had. ...

Mr. Lowell: ... I know you don't disagree that independent counsels, although not in the Department of Justice, are required ... to follow the law that applies to federal Justice Department officials, prosecutors and investigators... Correct?

Mr. Starr: The statute speaks specifically to the question of the applicability of DOJ policies and practices and says to the fullest extent practicable.

Mr. Lowell: ... I would like to turn to the issue of your involvement with Monica Lewinsky on the first occasion... [D]on't you think your statement to the press, to the Congress and to the American people gave a very distorted picture of the facts of the night and the day that you first confronted Monica Lewinsky?

Mr. Starr: Well, I think not, and we can obviously discuss it—

Mr. Lowell: Well, let's do that line by line, because...I think it will be elucidative. If you look at the first line of your press statement, it states, "Monica Lewinsky consented to meet with several FBI agents." Do you see your statement that says that?

Mr. Starr: Yes, I do.

Mr. Lowell: In Monica Lewinsky's sworn testimony,...[s]he testified under oath that she was there to have lunch with Linda Tripp. She was then accosted by agents who flashed their badges at her, she asked to see her attorney, was told that that wasn't such a good idea. She was then asked to go upstairs to discuss how much trouble she was in...Do you think your statement that Monica Lewinsky consented to meet with several agents doesn't distort the picture of what really happened that day?

Mr. Starr: Well...it was consensual, that is, we made it clear that she was not under arrest and that she was, in fact, at liberty to make a decision as to what she wanted to do.

Mr. Lowell: ...[Y]ou said, "during the five hours while awaiting her mother's arrival, Miss Lewinsky drank juice and coffee, ate dinner at a restaurant, strolled around the Pentagon City Mall and watched television."...But your statement to the press, Mr. Starr, doesn't include the fact that Miss Lewinsky swore to that she was scared and was crying a lot of the time. When she asked to see her attorney, "she would not be able to help herself with her attorney there," she was told. She was threatened with going to jail for "27 years"; that she was not there for the 5 hours that your press statement says, but was there for over 10 hours; and that when she asked to call her mother to discuss what you were discussing with her, your deputy Jackie Bennett said, "You are 24. You are smart. You are old enough. You don't need to call your mommy." That wasn't in your statement to the press that day, was it?

Mr. Starr: No, it wasn't, Mr. Lowell, and let me explain what press statements are designed to do.... They are designed to respond to what we were, in fact, being accused of or charged with...improper conduct with a witness.

Now, the facts of the matter are these: We did, in fact, use a traditional technique that law enforcement always uses. We were waiting patiently for her mother to arrive. She chose not to make a decision before her mother arrived. And at the conclusion of her time with us, she had established a legal relationship, which we fully recognized and always honored, and she and her mother indicated—I was not there, but I am told they indicated their appreciation for the way in which she was being treated.

Now, this press statement was in response . . . to allegations that she was being subjected to the kinds of conditions that would overbear the will. . . . [T]he purpose of this was to say, here is, in fact, material that the public should . . . know. . . .

Mr. Lowell: When . . . you state in your press statement that she was repeatedly told she was free to leave and that she did so several times, do you not think it would have been a less distorted picture . . . to know that when she left the room, she was followed by agents, and that she swore under an oath that she "felt threatened that when she left, she would be arrested"? . . .

Mr. Starr: I think her perception was incorrect. We made it clear to the witness that she was, in fact, free to leave. And the Ritz-Carlton, shall I say, is a fairly comfortable and commodious place. We will show you—I am sure you have them—telephone records that indicate she reached out to Mr. Carter,[10] her attorney in a totally different matter, she called her mother, she, in fact, went for a walk, she went to a restaurant and the like. . . . And she didn't need to make a decision, because—here's the other side of the picture—she was encouraging others to join her in committing perjury. She was, as the information came to us, a felon in the middle of committing another felony.

Mr. Lowell: . . . You said you needed to do this because she was in the middle of committing a felony. You don't think she was going to leave the hotel room, go back and continue to do that which you brought her to the hotel room to do? You can't be meaning that.

Mr. Starr: Well, of course, . . . we had no way of knowing what she was going to do. What we did do is this: we had a consensual recording. We shared the results of that consensual recording with the Justice Department. We in-

---

[10] Frank Carter, a Washington, D.C., lawyer who had assisted Ms. Lewinsky in preparing an affidavit submitted in Paula Jones' lawsuit against President Clinton.

formed the Justice Department of what our intention was at the Ritz-Carlton. We then proceeded in a very professional way. And then we were being met, as is not atypically the case, with charges of improper conduct. We then said we should respond to that....

Mr. Lowell: As you are the deliverer to this committee of the principal evidence that the committee is going to get, and as you agreed with me that the choices you have made bear on the substantiality and credibility, my questions were trying to go to whether or not, when you make statements, when you provide information, you provide the complete picture....

One last point... Your statement to the press... indicated that when she was done with this ordeal... I think you said they thanked the FBI agents and attorneys for their courtesy. But you didn't put in... your referral that she thanked them for their courtesy after "they told me they were planning to prosecute my mother for the things that she had said she did"...

Mr. Starr: Mr. Lowell, the information that we had suggested that her mother may have been involved in serious activity, in serious criminal offenses. That was an issue. And she wanted to reach out to her mother, to discuss the questions with her mother. We honored that....

[T]he substance of what was being conveyed by the very loquacious Mr. Ginsburg[11] was that she was being held incommunicado. That was wrong....

The purpose of this press release... was to respond to specific allegations.... And I think in order fairly to assess this, you would have to say, "What was it that the independent counsel's office was having to respond to?" What we were responding to were allegations that were utterly unmeritorious....

Mr. Lowell: And those allegations, Mr. Starr... were that you were overbearing, that she wasn't free to make a decision on her own, that she was put in a position where her judgment would be questioned. And you are saying... the facts, as sworn to by Ms. Lewinsky, don't bear on whether or not those allegations were indeed exactly accurate?

Mr. Starr: Oh, Mr. Lowell, surely you don't think that a witness is going to say thank you, law enforcement, for finding out that I'm in the middle of com-

---

[11] William Ginsburg, a California attorney engaged by Ms. Lewinsky's father, Bernard Lewinsky, to represent her after she was confronted by Starr's office.

mitting a felony.... The reason that she was being approached ... was that she was trying to get Linda Tripp to commit perjury. And since you have inquired about this, her mother had made it clear that she was willing to help finance an operation for Linda Tripp so she could leave the jurisdiction and thereby avoid being confronted in the *Jones* deposition....

Could I say one other thing in fairness? The issues with respect to our conduct that evening have been litigated.... [U]sually if the witness believes that he or she has been mistreated ... there's a place to go and it's called the courthouse ... and they've been resolved favorably to us. We conducted ourselves professionally.

Mr. Lowell: ... Just so that the record's clear ... We know from the evidence that she contacted Mr. Ginsburg only after her mother arrived ... in the middle of the night. And the very first thing she said, when approached by your agents in the lobby, was, "I want to talk to my attorney, Frank Carter."

You don't mean to suggest to the committee that you and the agents ... were encouraging her to talk to her lawyer between the time she was first accosted and the time that she got on the phone with Mr. Ginsburg ...?

Mr. Starr: That is correct. We would not encourage someone who was involved in felonies, as we thought at the time, to in fact reach out to a lawyer, especially a lawyer who had assisted her in crafting a perjurious affidavit. Why would we possibly do that?

Mr. Lowell: Well, one reason would be because the rules of the Department of Justice, the law of the land, as decided by the Supreme Court and the Code of Federal Regulations require it.

Lowell asked a few more questions suggesting that Starr's deputies had not dealt fairly with Ms. Lewinsky that day on the question of whether she could consult a lawyer. Starr responded that because of the clear distinction between civil and criminal representation, they thought it proper not to encourage her to call Frank Carter. But, he added, "even if you disagree with that, Mr. Lowell, let me say these two things very briefly. One, she did, in fact, call, or we sought to call, Mr. Carter from the Ritz-Carlton.... Also, we tried to reach out to Legal Aid so that she could have counsel. She later got, of course, Mr. Ginsburg. So the idea that she was not, in fact, permitted the opportunity to try to consult with counsel is incorrect."

Mr. Lowell: ...I just want to...go through the principal charges that you made in bringing this matter before the committee.

[Y]ou say...that the president lied under oath on a variety of occasions having to do with the *Paula Jones* case.... [Y]ou spoke about Judge Webber Wright's rulings in the *Paula Jones* case. But in your testimony you did not also include, did you, that Judge Wright had ruled as to Monica Lewinsky's significance in the *Paula Jones* case...that the evidence "simply was not essential to the core issues of whether Paula Jones was the victim of a quid pro quo sexual harassment," and she finally threw out the case on the grounds that Ms. Jones had not proven what the law requires. And I wanted just the record to be complete, that when you talked about what Judge Webber Wright had ruled in your testimony, you never mention that on three occasions Judge Wright made ruling indicating that the significance of whatever it was between Monica Lewinsky and the president did not bear on her decision. That's a fact, isn't it?

Mr. Starr: Well, I disagree with the characterization of what she ruled.... We may have a different opinion of how she adjudicated the matter.

Mr. Lowell: And as to the issue of the false affidavit, which you state was something the president was complicit in to the extent that it was a ground for impeachment—your evidence also includes, does it not, Mr. Starr, that Ms. Lewinsky gave you a statement in which she said "neither the president nor Mr. Jordan or anyone on their behalf asked or encouraged her to lie"...?

Mr. Starr: Yes.

Mr. Lowell: You must be aware that she also said that she offered to show her affidavit to the president, but he did not even want to see it?...

Mr. Starr: Yes.

Mr. Lowell: You must also be aware that she explained to you that the president and she had obviously used cover stories from the beginning of their relationship long before she was ever listed as a *Paula Jones* witness...?

Mr. Starr: Yes, and our referral makes that point clear.

Mr. Lowell: As to the issue of whether or not she was given a job in some way to keep her happy, you know the evidence that you sent Congress includes the fact that the job search for her began long before she was listed as a *Paula Jones* witness, correct?

Mr. Starr: Yes, absolutely, and we make that clear in the referral.

Mr. Lowell: And you are also aware that she told the president in July... months before the *Paula Jones* case was an issue, that she was going to look for a job in New York?

Mr. Starr: Yes, she did.

Mr. Lowell: And you are aware as well that it was Ms. Tripp—not the president, Ms. Tripp—who suggested to Ms. Lewinsky that she bring Vernon Jordan into the process—you know the evidence says that, don't you?

Mr. Starr: I am aware of the evidence with respect to that...

Mr. Lowell: You're aware as well that the evidence you sent Congress indicates that on that crucial issue, as others have stated,... Ms. Lewinsky unequivocally, even though never asked the question, stated to you that no one ever asked her to lie, no one promised me a job for her silence. You understand she swore to that as well?

Mr. Starr: Yes. And, Mr. Chairman, may I respond? I'm trying to be brief, but Mr. Lowell, as you also know... we specifically say Ms. Lewinsky has stated that the president never explicitly told her to lie.

Mr. Lowell: I understand that you say *explicitly.* I'd say that Ms. Lewinsky's statement that "no one told me to lie, no one offered me a job for my silence," is not equivocal—would you?

Mr. Starr: I would say that it is utterly incomplete and grossly misleading.... Her entire testimony is to the effect... that the cover stories were in fact going to continue.... But, yes, no one explicitly said, you know, "You will lie," using the "I" word. Rather, it was we will continue with cover stories which are not true.

Mr. Lowell: I have one last question, Mr. Starr... When you suggested to the committee that what you did, the choices you made, have to be looked at to determine the substantiality and the credibility of the evidence, I want to ask you whether or not you don't now see ... that the manner in which you decided the referral as one with attitude, your contacts between you, your law firm and Paula Jones' attorneys, the questions that have been raised about whether or not you got into this case with proper jurisdiction, the way you dealt with Monica Lewinsky ..., whether your office has been responsible for leaks, and the contradictions in the evidence between your referral and the statements you agree are in the evidence—doesn't that undermine the substantiality and credibility of the evidence on something as weighty as impeaching a president of the United States?

Mr. Starr: Mr. Lowell ... with all respect, what you have done is go into characterizations as opposed to deal with the facts. The facts are as we have found them to be. And not one of your questions suggests that the president was not involved in serious offenses. ...

Next came questions from the committee, with five minutes allotted each member. Republicans essentially gave Starr a chance to elucidate and expand upon the points he had made in his presentation and to defend himself against the challenges posed by Lowell and committee Democrats; the Democrats further questioned Starr's motives, methods, and conclusions. After a recess, the committee reassembled. Next up was David E. Kendall of the law firm Williams & Connolly, counsel for the president.

Mr. Kendall: ... My task is to respond to the two hours of uninterrupted testimony from the independent counsel, as well as to his four-year, $45 million investigation, which has included at least 28 attorneys, 78 FBI agents and an undisclosed number of private investigators; an investigation which has generated, by a computer count, 114,532 news stories in print and 2,513 minutes of network television time, not to mention 24-hour scandal coverage on cable, a 445-page referral, 50,000 pages of documents from secret grand jury testimony, four hours of videotaped testimony, 22 hours of audio tape, some of which was gathered in violation of state law, and the testimony of scores of witnesses, not one of whom has been cross-examined. And I have 30 minutes to do this.

It is a daunting exercise, but let me begin with the simple but powerful truth that nothing in this overkill of investigation amounts to a justification for the impeachment of the president of the United States. ...

Would you turn to Tab 5, which is a press release which your office issued under your name on February 5, 1998.... [Y]ou're addressing the fact that you have not been able to talk to Ms. Lewinsky yet. And you say..., "We cannot responsibly determine whether she's telling the truth without speaking directly to her. We found that there is no substitute for looking a witness in the eye, asking detailed questions, matching the answers against verifiable facts and if appropriate, giving a polygraph test."...

Kendall then proceeded to establish that in the course of the investigation, Starr had never actually met the witnesses nor sat in on interviews, depositions, or testimony. By his count, the independent counsel's office had submitted to the House 115 grand jury transcripts, and Starr had been present only for the questioning of the president; the office had submitted 19 depositions and 134 FBI interviews, and Starr had been present for none.

Mr. Kendall: You're here really as an advocate for this referral, are you not?

Mr. Starr: ... [N]o, I think that's not right. I do believe in the referral.... But the reason that I should not be advocating is because it is this committee's judgment that they will come to by virtue of the submission of this in writing with the supporting materials.... Our... task was to put before them the information that we found met the statutory standard of substantial and credible information.

Mr. Kendall: In your testimony today you indicated that you had exonerated the president with regard to the travel office, if I heard you correctly. Is that correct?

Mr. Starr: Yes. What I indicated was that we had no information that related to his involvement, although I also made it clear that that investigation is continuing....

Mr. Kendall: Also, if I heard you correctly this morning you indicated that you had exonerated the president with respect to the FBI files matter which had arisen in 1996.... And today was the first time you have announced that with respect to these two matters, is it not, Mr. Starr?

Mr. Starr: Yes, it's the first time that we have viewed it as appropriate to speak to issues that are still, David, under investigation....

*Kendall then brought up a matter raised earlier by Democrat Robert Wexler of
Florida: charges that Starr's agents had looked into the adoption of an 8-year-old
from a Romanian orphanage by one reluctant witness, Julie Hiatt Steele. Starr said
that his "investigators work very hard and diligently to find relevant evidence," but
he didn't know for certain whether they had done as charged. He continued:*

Mr. Starr: I thought that what we were here today to discuss is a referral which
we believe contains substantial and credible information of potential impeachable offenses by the president of the United States. What a particular witness'
demeanor was or what a particular FBI agent asked is, to my mind, quite far removed from the sober and serious purposes that I thought brought us here together. And the final thing that I would say . . . Mr. Kendall, if there's an issue
with respect to the treatment of a witness, let's take it to court and have the court
resolve it in an orderly way, just as the Supreme Court of the United States said
that this particular individual is entitled to an orderly disposition of her claims.

*Kendall turned to the secrecy of the grand jury process. The two discussed the fact
that litigation was currently under way on 24 examples of information the president's lawyers argued must have originated with the OIC. Kendall said, "There has
been no case remotely similar to this in terms of the massive leaking from the prosecutor's office,"—to which Starr replied, "That's an . . . unfair accusation. I completely reject it." After some back-and-forth, Hyde informed Kendall that his time
was up. Kendall requested an hour more; Hyde granted 30 minutes.*

Mr. Kendall: . . . How this analysis was done, the campaign to disseminate information against the president, is very much a part of the fairness of the document which our committee is having to consider. . . . Is the analysis reliable, is
it fair? Does it present the facts? Have proper procedures been followed?

Mr. Starr . . . you did issue a press [statement] about Ms. Lewinsky's treatment at the Ritz-Carlton. That was a press release that was on the record.
Everybody knew you were saying that. You were accountable. . . .

But you also spoke frequently on background to the press. . . . you and those
around you, your subordinates.

Mr. Starr: Yes. Be careful when you say the "you," because I do not speak frequently or otherwise to the press.

Mr. Kendall: But did Professor Dash give you any advice as to what should be
on background, and what on the record?

Mr. Starr: ... I would have to search my recollection with respect to any specific observations that Sam gave us with respect to this. But let me say this. ... When you look at the information that we had in our office, and the FBI, as opposed to information that you had access to, it never, never entered the public domain.

For example, the dress, the DNA, the test results. Those were never in the public domain, because you did not have a witness in your joint defense arrangements, who you could debrief and tell you. ... You talked about fairness. It's time for some fairness with respect to all of these charges that keep being bandied around. ...

Mr. Kendall: ... I have never protested a press release which you have issued, have I? ... It's necessary to get the facts out, so that people are not misguided. But why speak off the record, on background? Why not be accountable?

Mr. Starr: ... [Y]ou're asking essentially press policy as opposed to constitutional issues that have brought us all here. And if this is an oversight hearing with respect to the press policy of the independent counsel's office, or if that is what the president's lawyer wants to spend his time doing, then that is your prerogative. So let me tell you then what our press policy is.

Mr. Kendall: Well, Mr. Starr, I have only got 30 minutes. ... [L]et me move on. You, yourself, executed an affidavit in the leaks investigation, did you not?

Mr. Starr: ... Why don't we allow that litigation to go forward instead of ... jumping to the conclusion that there has been a violation? ... And just to finish the point, when we had highly sensitive information that Mr. Kendall did not have—the DNA on the dress—that was held in our office and the FBI. There was no dissemination of that information. ...

Mr. Kendall: ... I think you have answered the question, and I would like to move on. ... One of the purposes [of Starr's deputies at the Ritz-Carlton] was to get Ms. Lewinsky to wear a recording device and surreptitiously record Mr. Jordan or the president, was it not?

Mr. Starr: It was not. ... She was ... given the opportunity, which she turned down, to be a cooperating witness. ... [W]e said one of the things that a cooperating witness can do is to assist us in consensual monitoring. We described that at a high level of generality. ...

Mr. Kendall: Could you turn to Tab 7 ... You may have read the *Time* magazine essay ... by Mssrs. Ginsburg and Speights in which they state the following: "The government didn't just want our client to tell her story. They wanted her wired. They wanted her to record telephone calls with the president of the United States, Vernon Jordan and others at their will." You're familiar with Mr. Ginsburg's charge?

Mr. Starr: Mr. Ginsburg is wrong.... He was wrong then, and it is a calumny to repeat that now....

Mr. Kendall: Mr. Starr, what is an FBI 302 Form?

Mr. Starr: An FBI 302 Form is a report of an interview by FBI agents with a witness.

Mr. Kendall: You categorically denied wanting to have Ms. Lewinsky wear a wire or secretly tape record the president or Mr. Jordan when the charge was made in the *Time* article; did you not? ... Let me direct you to Tab 12 in the volume. And this is ... your later letter to Steve Brill.... You say, "This is false. This office never asked Ms. Lewinsky to agree to wire herself for a conversation with Mr. Jordan or the president. You cite no source at all, nor could you, as we had no such plans." ...

Now ... you were not present at the Ritz-Carlton, were you?

Mr. Starr: No, I was not.

Mr. Kendall: Did you review, with Mr. Emmick,[12] say, what had happened there? ... [I]f you look at page 5 of that exhibit, it says—at 11:22 p.m.... "AIC Emmick talked to Bernard Lewinsky"—that is Ms. Lewinsky's father—"cooperation and interview, telephone calls, body wires, and testimony were mentioned." ... And then do you see down below ... Ms. Lewis has arrived on the scene—Ms. Lewinsky's mother—and ... she says, according to the FBI 302, "What if I partially cooperate?" That's as recorded by the FBI agent. "Marsha Lewis asked what would happen if Monica Lewinsky gave everything but did not tape anything?" Do you see that?

Mr. Starr: Yes, I do.

---

[12] Michael Emmick, one of Starr's deputies.

Mr. Kendall: It was in the grand jury that the events of Friday, January the 16th, were presented through the testimony of Ms. Lewinsky... [Y]our prosecutors had no more questions, and the grand jurors themselves began to inquire about the events that day.... And this elicited, then, from Ms. Lewinsky, who was under oath, a tearful description of what had happened to her. She asked Mr. Emmick to leave the room; did she not?

Mr. Starr: That's my recollection of the transcript; yes.

Mr. Kendall: And in fact, she said that she was told on Friday, January the 16th, by your agents, that she'd have to place calls or wear a wire to call Betty and Mr. Jordan and possibly the president.
   Question: "And did you tell them you didn't want to do that?"
   "Yes."
   Was that Ms. Lewinsky's testimony?

Mr. Starr: Yes, that is her testimony.

There followed an exchange in which Kendall sought to make it clear that the Office of the Independent Counsel had requested jurisdiction in the Lewinsky matter. Starr agreed that "We brought it to [the attorney general's] attention," adding that "we were concerned about whether any additional step could be taken properly within our jurisdiction." He elucidated:

Mr. Starr: At some point during the discussion,... we came to the view that we felt that because of the involvement... of Vernon Jordan, that this was related to our existing jurisdiction.... Here was Linda Tripp, who was a witness in the Travel Office matter, in the Vincent Foster documents matter and the Vincent Foster death matter, and she had come to us with information. And... she said, "I'm being asked to commit crimes. I'm being asked to commit perjury." We... did in fact send a letter indicating that we felt that this was related to our jurisdiction.... [T]he attorney general disagreed with that and said no, it's not related to your existing jurisdiction, but we think your office should investigate it; we can't because the president is implicated.

Mr. Kendall: ... Mr. Starr, when did you first learn, you yourself, that there might be an audiotape with a conversation involving the president and a young woman?

Mr. Starr:... If you are talking about Monica Lewinsky...the first I knew, to the best of my knowledge and recollection...was in January of 1998....

Mr. Kendall: Were you aware of how Ms. Tripp came to communicate with your office in January of 1988?

Mr. Starr:... I was at an American Bar Association Journal Board of Editors meeting when the initial contact was made with one of the associate independent counsels.... [T]hat was on January 8th—and I do not believe in that contact Linda Tripp's name was mentioned.... We were then called on January 12th by Linda Tripp...and I was made aware of the telephone call promptly thereafter....

Mr. Kendall: Were you aware that your partner, Richard Porter, had played a role in steering Ms. Tripp to your office?

Mr. Starr:... I have since read about what his role was. But I did not in any way have any involvement whatsoever, or participation in any way with whatever he did....

Kendall invoked the Ethics in Government Act, which he quoted as saying "that any independent counsel cannot have any person associated with a firm—not just a partner—represent in any matter any person involved in any investigation or prosecution under this chapter." He also cited an FBI report mentioning a conversation between Lucianne Goldberg and Richard Porter about Linda Tripp's nervousness over contacting the Office of the Independent Council.

Mr. Kendall: Did you...cause any check to be made...before you sought jurisdiction in the Lewinsky matter as to whether any person in your law firm had any kind of an association with the *Paula Jones* case?

Mr. Starr: No, I did not. But I must say what you pointed me to in the statute was representation. And I have read the 302 quickly for the first time...And the 302 does not talk about representation; it talks about calling a friend.

Mr. Kendall: It's possible, is it not, Mr. Starr, for the provision of legal advice of some kind to involve a representation, at least for conflict of interest purposes, even if there is no written retainer...?

Mr. Starr: Well, I am not sure I would readily agree with that.... [C]onflict of interest analysis is, as you well know ... very technical and very complicated, and very careful evaluation has to be made.... As you know, the issue of conflict is one that is at times ... very much a judgment call....

Mr. Kendall: Mr. Starr, can I direct your attention to exhibit at Tab 14 please? ... That is a *Washington Post* article from June of 1997 indicating that your investigators are now probing rumors about the president, is it not? ... And indicating that state troopers ... are being interviewed about rumors of affairs that the president had while he was governor of Arkansas....

Mr. Starr: That's what the story is about. But whether the story reflects the facts is obviously a different matter.

Mr. Kendall: Did you cause any investigation to be done as to whether, in fact, your investigators were asking witnesses about a list of 12 to 15 women by name, including Paula Corbin Jones?

Mr. Starr: ... [A]ll the attorneys were in Little Rock, as we were assessing a very important issue. And when we were in the midst of our discussions, we were receiving urgent inquiries from the *Washington Post* asking about interviews.... that had been conducted in February.... [I]n light of this, we then did make inquiries internally of the FBI ... and we said, "What kinds of questions are being asked? What is the purpose?"

And the purpose of the investigation was, ... we wanted to make sure, as investigators should do and as prosecutors should do, that we had reached out and interviewed anyone who might have relevant information....

Mr. Kendall: And ... did you go to the attorney general and seek an expansion of your jurisdiction to accompany this particular investigation?

Mr. Starr: ... This was the Whitewater phase of our investigation.... We're talking about Little Rock. We're not talking about activity in Washington. And we were, in fact, interviewing, as good ... investigators do, individuals who would have information that may be relevant to our inquiry about the president's involvement in Whitewater, in Madison Guaranty Savings & Loan and the like, and specifically a loan from Madison Guaranty that we had information on and which we were not able to secure as much information as we would like....

Mr. Kendall: Did you use private investigators to do this investigation into the 12 to 15 women?...Your GAO report...for the last three times has a line item of approximately...half a million dollars for, among other things, private investigators....

Mr. Starr: [W]e do hire retired FBI agents....

Chairman Hyde intervened. He promised Kendall that he would have plenty of chances to address the committee further and to present "whatever you want by way of evidence, witnesses, exculpatory material." Hyde then recognized David P. Schippers, chief investigative counsel for the committee.

Schippers opened by giving Starr an opportunity to rebut Kendall's charges of leaks from the Office of the Independent Counsel. He asked directly: "Do you have any information, evidence, or anything in your possession to indicate that anyone in your office has leaked anything?" Starr answered that he did not—but that he thought it important for the litigation over the alleged leaks to go forward.

Schippers also implicitly attacked Kendall's implications that Starr's agents had mistreated Monica Lewinsky and other witnesses. Even though Starr had not been present at all the interviews and depositions, he said, "You relied upon the integrity, the honesty and the decency of those agents and investigators, did you not?"

Finally, for the record, Schippers noted that with all the talk of "fairness," Starr had been questioned that day on the basis of a "two-and-a-half-inch" packet of material he had not seen before he sat down.

Then Schippers changed the subject:

Mr. Schippers: Now Judge Starr, you have been investigating President Clinton and the Monica Lewinsky matter and other matters involving perjury, obstruction of justice, conspiracy and so on for some seven or eight months.... Have you been...offered any exculpatory evidence or witnesses by the president in that time?

Mr. Starr: I don't believe that we have....

Mr. Schippers: Now, you have been pilloried and vilified in newspapers and magazines and here, unfortunately. Has the attorney general ever indicated that she had any thought of firing you for cause?

Mr. Starr: I'm not aware of any expression of any issue at all with respect to "good cause." There are—in fairness to the attorney general, because of the flurry of allegations that are just constant, there is a process of evaluation on her part. But no....

Mr. Schippers: ... Now all of these specific factors that various people have asked you if you reported to the attorney general when you met her on the ... 15th of January.... There was a litany of things that you apparently allegedly did not tell the attorney general at that meeting? ... But of course, shortly thereafter, all of that litany of information became available to the attorney general.

Mr. Starr: ... [T]hese were all in the public domain. As I said in response to questions ... earlier in the day, certain things did not occur to me as relevant or germane. It may be that others would say, "Gee, isn't it relevant that you were asked by Bob Fiske to consider preparing an amicus brief in the *Paula Corbin Jones* case?" I didn't view it as—well, it just didn't occur to me....

Now Schippers gave Starr a chance to defend the behavior of his deputies at the January 16 session at the Ritz-Carlton Hotel with Monica Lewinsky.

Mr. Starr: Well, I think that ... a fair assessment of the record will show that we wanted her cooperation, and we treated her with dignity and with respect. But we were prosecutors and we were investigators investigating crime; that's a serious matter, and we made it very clear to her she is in a serious situation....

Mr. Schippers: ... Now, sir, there was also some question as to why Ms. Lewinsky was not allowed to call Mr. Carter. Mr. Carter had been given to Monica Lewinsky by Vernon Jordan ... And the evidence available to you at that time, phone evidence, indicated that perhaps Mr. Jordan had been in telephonic contact with the president at the time he was getting her that lawyer, isn't that correct, sir?

Mr. Starr: That is correct.

Mr. Schippers: And in an abundance of caution, you did not want the president to know that Monica Lewinsky was talking to you, isn't that right?

Mr. Starr: That is correct....

Schippers established that, in any case, Lewinsky had ultimately chosen William Ginsburg, not Frank Carter, to represent her. He also said the evidence demonstrated that from January 16 on, "there was a three-day frenzy at the White House to try and find Monica Lewinsky by phone, by beeper, and that Mr. Jordan, Mr. Carter and Ms. Currie were in constant efforts to reach Monica Lewinsky," suggesting that "they were a little bit afraid of what Monica might say." And he stressed that until she was represented by counsel, she was never questioned about any criminal activity. Her first testimony before a grand jury, he noted, was seven months later; even if she had been upset on the night of January 16, he said, "she was sure as heck over it by August 6."

Turning to that grand jury testimony, Schippers read from the record:

Mr. Schippers: The first bullet says Monica Lewinsky testified before that grand jury that, "No one ever asked me to lie, and I was never promised a job for my silence." ... She also testified, "But nobody told me to tell the truth, either," ... didn't she?

Mr. Starr: Absolutely.

Mr. Schippers: Now, Monica Lewinsky also testified that she had a conversation with the president ... when she found out that she was on the witness list and the president told her, "You can make an affidavit." ... The affidavit, of course, would be for the purpose of avoiding testimony.... And in order to accomplish that purpose, both the president and Ms. Lewinsky were fully aware that that affidavit would have to be a lie. Isn't that right?

Mr. Starr: Yes.

Mr. Schippers: And it was the president's suggestion that she make that affidavit, according to her testimony?

Mr. Starr: According to her testimony, yes.

Schippers then declared that they would "talk a little bit about fairness." He established that Clinton had been permitted to give his grand jury testimony on videotape—a rare privilege; that he had been allowed to have his attorney present; that he had been permitted to read a statement before he testified. In addition, Schippers stressed, the president had been subpoenaed to testify after he had refused six invi-

*tations to do so voluntarily. Nonetheless, "as an accommodation to the president,"
Starr ultimately allowed him to appear "voluntarily."*

*Then Schippers turned to the grand jury. He got Starr to explain that the defense
never cross-examines witnesses before a grand jury, "because that's not the function
of the grand jury—it's to gather information and to determine whether there's probable cause to believe that a criminal offense may have been committed."*

Mr. Schippers: Now...the Constitution provides that the sole power of impeachment resides in the House of Representatives, isn't that correct?...And
that is in the nature of a grand jury proceeding which results in a charge, isn't
that right? So there should be no cross-examination at that stage of the proceeding either, should there?

Mr. Starr: That's entirely within your prerogative, but to the extent that you
are mirroring the grand jury there is no cross-examination.... I shouldn't be
advising the House of Representatives in terms of its prerogatives, but it
seems to me that under the Constitution you will have an extraordinary lati-
tude...to determine how to proceed. But you are quite right, the Constitution
contemplates the trial to be in the Senate...

Mr. Schippers: Now, Judge, there has been a lot of talk in the public domain...that all the president did was deny sex—deny a sexual relationship
with an intern. He went a lot further than that, didn't he, for example with Mr.
Blumenthal?...The president told Mr. Blumenthal that Monica made sexual
demands upon him which he rebuffed. Right? And that was not true, was it? He
also said that Monica Lewinsky threatened to claim an affair and he wouldn't
go along with it, that he had been threatened by Monica Lewinsky. Is that right?

Mr. Starr: Yes.

Mr. Schippers: Now, this is at a time when the president thought that it was a
one-on-one with Monica Lewinsky, didn't he?

Mr. Starr: I believe that that is what he thought at that time.

Mr. Schippers: And this would have been a perfect answer—she threatened
to say I had sex with her if I didn't do something for her. I didn't do something—therefore everything she's saying is a lie.

Mr. Starr: It would be a very good answer....

Chairman Hyde gave Schippers 15 extra minutes for his last few points. Schippers essentially posed a series of rhetorical questions aimed at underscoring crucial points in Starr's testimony—from the importance of perjury to the independent counsel's versions of the gift exchange and the alleged link between Lewinsky's job search and the signing of her affidavit, all aided by Vernon Jordan. Finally, he recited Starr's distinguished résumé and put it on the record that Starr had been "charged with unbelievable things of which you are incapable of being guilty," and all for doing a job—one he had never sought—to the best of his ability. He ended with a tribute: "I want to say I'm proud to be in the same room with you and your staff."

After Starr left the hearing room, the committee sparred over Republican efforts to subpoena three more witnesses: presidential lawyer Robert Bennett, attorney Daniel Gecker, and Nathan Landow, a major contributor to the Democratic Party. Gecker and Landow were both connected to the allegations of Kathleen Willey, who had claimed unwanted sexual advances by the president, and the Republican move provoked protests. "Everyone on this side of the aisle voted to limit the inquiry to the Monica Lewinsky referral," said Democrat Howard Berman of California. "The independent counsel has not made a referral on the Kathleen Willey case." Finally, the committee went into executive session to settle the matter.

THE QUESTION OF PERJURY

In his opening statement, Chairman Hyde explained that the day's testimony would be devoted to "perjury and related crimes like subornation of perjury, obstruction of justice, witness tampering, misprision and criminal contempt." All "thwart the proper workings of the justice system," he argued. "If citizens are allowed to lie with impunity, or encourage others to tell false stories, or hide evidence, judges and juries cannot reach just results."

John Conyers offered his view of what the committee had done so far: "dump salacious grand jury material onto the Internet . . . hearing an incredibly one-sided presentation from the prosecutor . . . deposing two witnesses[1] that have a peripheral relationship, at best, to the independent counsel's referral." He then protested that "once again, the committee is floundering into another unrelated area. Last evening, we were informed that the committee would now widen its investigation into campaign finance matters."[2] Just

---

[1] As decided in executive session after the November 19 hearing, the committee took closed-door depositions from attorney Daniel Gecker and from Nathan Landow, a prominent Democratic fund-raiser, both linked to the case of Kathleen Willey.

[2] On a party-line vote that infuriated Democrats, the committee had moved to compel testimony from FBI Director Louis J. Freeh and Charles G. La Bella, former head of the Justice Department task force investigating the 1996 campaign, and to subpoena documents from that investigation that included internal department memoranda and grand jury testimony.

ten days from an impeachment vote, Conyers said, the charges against the president were still unclear.

Chairman Hyde then introduced the morning's witnesses—two women who had been convicted of perjury for lying about sex.

The first, Pam Parsons of Atlanta, Georgia, had coached women's basketball at Old Dominion University and the University of South Carolina. In 1984, she pled guilty to a federal perjury charge stemming from a $75 million libel suit she had filed against Sports Illustrated after a 1982 article described her as a lesbian and quoted one of her assistants as saying she "recruited with sex in mind." During a 1984 trial, she denied sworn testimony that she had visited a gay bar with one of her former players. The jury found in favor of Sports Illustrated. But even so, the judge ordered an investigation into the conflicting testimony—and ultimately, Parsons pled guilty to perjury and served a four-month sentence in a federal prison.

The second of the morning's witnesses was Barbara Battalino of Los Osos, California, a doctor of osteopathic medicine, a psychiatrist, and a lawyer. In 1998, the Justice Department had brought charges against her after she falsely testified in a civil suit in which a former patient alleged malpractice and sexual harassment against Battalino, then a psychiatrist at a veterans' hospital in Idaho. She lost her job and her license, paid a $3,500 fine, and was sentenced to six months of home detention.

Of the two cases, Battalino's seemed somewhat more analogous to President Clinton's:

"The falsehood centered around my reticence to acknowledge the one act of consensual oral sex which occurred between myself and an unmarried male adult on Veterans Affairs premises. A civil suit was filed, complicated by the male party having secretly recorded phone conversations he and I had during the months an intimate relationship between us developed. These very tapes were instrumental in having the civil suit dismissed in September of 1998. . . .

"So how is it that I am a convicted felon? In early 1998, my attorney received word that the Department of Justice planned to indict me for perjury based on an untruthful response I gave to a question regarding whether anything of a sexual nature had occurred between myself and that individual on June 27th, 1991. . . . I justified in my own mind that this deception was warranted in order to protect my personal and professional self-interest. In an attempt to save myself and my family any further embarrassment and/or financial loss, I agreed to accept a negotiated disposition of the criminal case."

Toward the end of Battalino's testimony, she sounded the theme that the Republican majority wanted to underscore: "Because a president is not a king, he or she must abide by the same laws as the rest of us.... This nation must never let any person or people undermine the rule of law."

The afternoon session was also devoted to the subject of perjury. This time, the testimony came from a mixed group of experts:

Gerald B. Tjoflat, a U.S. circuit judge on the U.S. Court of Appeals for the 11th Circuit, who had served as chief judge for the 11th Circuit from 1989 until 1996.

Charles Wiggins, senior U.S. circuit judge on the U.S. Court of Appeals for the 9th Circuit, who had served as a U.S. Representative from California from 1966 to 1978 and had been a member of the Judiciary Committee during the Nixon impeachment.

Elliot Richardson, former secretary of Health, Education, and Welfare, secretary of Defense, attorney general of the United States, secretary of Commerce, and ambassador to the Court of St. James.

A. Leon Higginbotham Jr., professor of jurisprudence at Harvard and the John F. Kennedy School of Government, a former circuit judge and chief judge of the U.S. Court of Appeals for the 3rd Circuit.

Admiral Bud Edney, 37-year veteran of the U.S. Navy, whose assignments included command of a carrier air wing, command of the aircraft carrier USS Constellation, command of a carrier battle group; Edney also served as commander of all U.S. forces in the Atlantic and commandant of midshipmen at the U.S. Naval Academy.

Lt. Gen. Thomas Carney, 35-year veteran of the U.S. Army, who had served as commander of the Fifth Infantry Division, assistant commander of the 82nd Airborne Division and, just before his retirement, deputy chief of staff for personnel.

Alan Dershowitz, Felix Frankfurter professor of law at Harvard Law School.

Stephen Saltzburg, professor of trial advocacy, litigation and professional responsibility at the George Washington University Law School, formerly a deputy assistant attorney general for the Criminal Division and an associate independent counsel.

Jeffrey Rosen, associate professor of law at George Washington University Law School, legal affairs editor of The New Republic and staff writer for The New Yorker.

The first to testify was Judge Tjoflat.

Mr. Tjoflat: ... The system of justice depends on three things in order to function as its framers intended. The first thing is an impartial judiciary.... The second thing that is indispensable to the administration of justice is a bar of lawyers who are committed to adhering to the code of ethics at all times, in all matters. And the third thing that is indispensable to the administration of justice is the oath taken by witnesses.

Those three things together, under our system, produce justice. It is like a three-legged stool in a way. And if one of the legs or two of the legs break, then the stool collapses....

Now, today's hearing focuses on the third element, and that is the oath, in particular, what effect perjury has on the system of justice. One way to illustrate what perjury can do to the administration of justice is to imagine a pool of water, a pond, and you drop a pebble into the pond. The pebble is perjury, let us say, and it creates a ripple effect. The extent of the ripple effect depends on the extent to which the perjury is material, is important to the matter under inquiry, to the truth-seeking process.

Now, what happens with the ripple effect is that perjury of that sort implicates the judicial system.... [I]f it occurs in a case that is on trial, it may require a continuance of the case. It may require a mistrial. It may require more discovery.... If it's a pretrial proceeding of some sort, other machinery of the courts may have to be brought into play, because the natural tendency is to counteract perjury with other evidence in order to shed light on the truth.

And when that occurs, the courts are taxed in the sense that they cannot be made available to other litigants.... The courts have to expand themselves and their processes to accommodate the perjury, and that is called obstruction of justice. The perjury in that circumstance impedes the due administration of justice....

The next witness was Judge Wiggins, who explained that he was nearly blind and therefore unable to read his prepared remarks. But Henry Hyde asked him to address whether perjury and obstruction of justice were impeachable offenses. "That's an easy question to answer," said Wiggins. "Of course they are."

That said, however, Wiggins added that the House should be debating whether President Clinton himself had committed impeachable offenses of this kind. "I think there is little doubt that the president is vulnerable," Wiggins said. "But that does not preclude a second judgment by you as a member of the House to vote in the public interest on the question of whether the president should be impeached."

As Wiggins saw it, it might well make sense for the committee to present the impeachment question to the full House. But when the members were called upon to confront the question on the floor, he said, "Your standard should be the public interest. And I confess to you that I would recommend that you not vote to impeach the president."

The next witness was A. Leon Higginbotham.

Mr. Higginbotham: ... [L]et me give you, if I were teaching my class at Harvard, the hypothetical I would present to them. I would say, suppose that on January 17, 1998, and on August 17, 1998, which are the two dates on which President Clinton testified ... that his testimony was that when he was driving his automobile in a 50-mile-per-hour speed zone, he said he was going 49— but the record demonstrates, beyond a reasonable doubt, that he was going 55. And it would demonstrate that he knew that he was going 55.... Could the president of the United States, under those circumstances, be removed from office—because he gave a false statement about the speed of his car in a grand jury inquiry?

... I submit to you that perjury has gradations.... Some are serious, and some are less. And though I do not applaud the president for what he did, for impeachment purposes, there is not much difference between someone who testified falsely on a speeding incident, and someone who testified falsely about his relationship in a sexual matter voluntarily with a private person....

Now, let me press the doctrine a little more. [T]he two ladies who testified today, I respect them as decent human beings, who, like all of us, ... have frailties. And they were sentenced.

But what is the ... probative relevance of what they did, compared to impeaching a president—one who got 49 percent of the votes of the citizens of this nation? If they are sentenced, the presidency still holds up.... You cannot equate the president of the United States with a basketball coach from South Carolina. And that takes not a thing from her excellence, and the human empathy which we must have for her....

Next to speak was Elliot Richardson.

Mr. Richardson: ... As you have reminded us, Mr. Chairman, the principal focus of this hearing is on the consequences of perjury and related crimes.

That certainly has to be the area of your... primary concern. It does not follow, however, that there needs to be comparable emphasis on evidentiary matters. There is no material difference, indeed, between the Starr Report's allegations and the president's admissions. It is accepted that he did in fact, over a period of months, deny, withhold, and misrepresent the truth as to his relationship with Monica Lewinsky.

This committee, moreover, has no need to decide whether or not these lies constitute "perjury" as that term is defined by criminal law. Taking into account the number... and context of these lies, as well as the fact that they were deliberately intended to mislead bodies officially charged with pursuing the truth, you could reasonably regard them as warranting impeachment, even though they may not come within the definition of perjury.

But Article II, Section 4 of the Constitution specifies that on conviction by the Senate for an impeachable offense, the only available penalty is removal from office. To contemplate impeachment, therefore, is to raise the question of whether or not the circumstances justify so drastic a penalty.

The members of this committee, I submit, already have all the information they need on which to base their own individual answers to this question. If a majority of you conclude that the answer to this question should be no, it is obvious that the actual adoption by the House of Representatives of impeachment charges will be pointless. Worse, such action would automatically transmit those charges to the Senate for trial, thus indefinitely prolonging a final resolution to this matter. The Senate itself, meanwhile, would have no alternative but to convict or acquit....

This body, by contrast, is in a position, right now, to submit to the House as a whole its best judgment as to an intermediate course... censure or rebuke, with or without a formal acknowledgement of guilt....

To my mind, the intermediate course offers the most appropriate and least destructive solution. The initial wrongdoing was not criminal and did not, in contrast to that of Richard Nixon, entail the abuse of power. Given a president's unique status as the Chief Executive whose authority derives from a vote of the American people, his crimes or misdemeanors, should, in order to justify his removal, have to be higher than those that issue here....

Chairman Hyde recognized Admiral Bud Edney.

Adm. Edney: ... I will focus my remarks on the importance of ethics and integrity in the military chain of command of this great country. And at the top of that chain of command, as we all recognize, is our Commander-in-Chief.

We live in a society that more and more is transmitting a confused message on the subject of ethics and integrity.... Faced with this reality, the Armed Forces have concluded all personnel must be inculcated repeatedly with the requirement and expectation that military leadership must evolve from a foundation of trust and confidence. Ethics and integrity of our military leadership must be much higher than the society at large. And even the elected officials that serve that society.

Success in combat, which is our business, depends on trust and confidence in our leaders, and in each other. Ethics and integrity are the basic elements of trust and confidence....

So today, in our military, we are asking our people: What is right? Why do what is right?

... Our answer is, "Because the trust and confidence required of our profession, demands it." This trust and confidence must exist up and down the chain of command, where operations require execution of orders that endanger lives....

Leadership by example must come from the top. It must be consistent with the highest standards, and it must be visible for all to see. "Do as I say and not as I do" won't hack it in our military.

This country is firmly entrenched in the principle of civilian leadership of our military, and the authority of the president of the United States. Therefore, I believe those who hold that leadership position, to be credible, should meet the same standards.

America and her Armed Forces have always stood on the side of right and human decency. You do not throw these core values away, in the process of defending them.

You also do not lower the bar of ethical standards and integrity when individuals fail to live up to them. We must continue to remove those who fall short, and seek those who meet and exceed the requirements.... The cover-up of mistakes and responsibility by lying or obstruction, cannot be tolerated....

Lt. Gen. Thomas Carney was the next witness.

Gen. Carney: ... American servicemen and -women swear allegiance to the concepts embodied in a document. We do not swear allegiance to a king or a president, or to the motherland, or to the regiment. We swear to support and defend the Constitution of the United States against all enemies, foreign and domestic, and to bear true faith and allegiance to the same....

Of course, also included in that oath is that we will—and I quote—"obey the orders of the president and the officers appointed over me." That is in the oath, and that is not negotiable.... I will discuss the Army's in particular, with which I'm most familiar.

The first of those codes I encountered was the West Point motto, "Duty, Honor, Country," three simple words that I still study today. The boundless nature of the word "country" is best described in Article I of the Prisoner of War's Code of Conduct: "I am an American fighting man. I serve in the forces which guard my country and our way of life, and I am prepared to give my life in their defense."

The word "honor" includes all the chivalrous aspects of the word, including integrity. Integrity was very clearly delineated for us in the Cadet Honor Code: "A cadet does not lie, cheat or steal, nor associate with those who do." No one ever made a distinction about whether or not you were under oath or not.

The rationale for the code went beyond the notion that honorable men do not lie, cheat, or steal. It included the reality that battlefield reports impact decisions that affect the outcomes of battles, and the lives of soldiers. Consequently, soldiers do not want to serve with or around other soldiers that they don't trust.

... I am not so naive as so to think that the Army of a million men and women, active Guard and Reserve are void of weak leaders—certainly not—but the good news is that there are systems to weed them out in peacetime so that the terrible wartime consequences can be avoided.

Will soldiers follow weak leaders that don't abide by the standards I have attempted to describe? The answer is yes, they must, for they are bound by their oath to obey the orders of the president and the officers appointed over me. But the difference between an average unit and the best unit is most often its leaders—great leaders—men of character inspire soldiers to do extraordinary things. Conversely, a general malaise hangs over units whose leaders are weak. Soldiers want, indeed deserve leaders who are held accountable for the same standards that they are held to. The credibility of the system is at stake when that is not the case....

Alan Dershowitz spoke next.

Mr. Dershowitz: ... On the basis of my academic and professional experience, I believe that no felony is committed more frequently in this country than the genre of perjury and false statement crimes. Perjury during civil depositions and trials is so endemic that a respected appellate judge once observed that "experienced lawyers say that in large cities scarcely a trial occurs in which some witness does not lie." Police perjury in criminal cases ... is so pervasive that the former police chief of San Jose and Kansas City has estimated that hundreds of thousands of law enforcement officials commit felony perjury every year testifying about drug arrests alone.

But in comparison with their frequency, perjury crimes are among the most underprosecuted in this country.... Moreover, there is evidence that false statements are among the most selectively prosecuted of all crimes, and that the criteria for selectivity bear little relationship to the willfulness or frequency of the lies, the certainty of the evidence or any other neutral criteria relating to the elements of perjury.

Historically, I think we can all agree that false statements have admitted considerable variation and degree.... Clearly the most heinous brand of lying is the giving of false testimony that results in the imprisonment of somebody who is innocent. Less egregious, but still quite serious, is false testimony that results in the conviction of a person who may be guilty, but whose rights were violated in a manner that would preclude conviction if the police testified truthfully. There are many other points of this continuum, ranging from making false statements about income taxes to testifying falsely in civil trials. The least culpable genre of false testimony are those that deny embarrassing personal conduct of marginal relevance to the matter at issue in the legal proceeding.

I think it is clear that the false statements of which President Clinton is accused fall at the most marginal end of the least culpable genre of this continuum of offenses, and would never even be considered for prosecution in the routine cases involving an ordinary defendant....

Many judges who listen to or review police testimony on a regular basis agree with Judge Alex Kozinski of the 9th Circuit, who said it is an open secret long shared by prosecutors, defense lawyers and judges that perjury is widespread among law enforcement officials. Yet there is little apparent concern to remedy that serious abuse of the oath to tell the truth, even among those who now claim to be so concerned with the corrosive influences of perjury on our legal system....

A perfect example of the selective morality regarding perjury occurred when President George Bush pardoned the former secretary of defense, Caspar Weinberger, in 1992, even though the evidence was absolutely clear and convincing.[3]

The real issue is not the couple of convicted perjurers who appeared before this committee today, or the judges who condemn the evils of perjury, but the hundreds of thousands of perjurers who are never prosecuted and whom this committee does not seem to care about, many for extremely serious and calculated lies designed to undercut constitutional rights of unpopular defendants....
You could not fit into this room or into this building all of the people who testified more perjuriously than President Clinton and were not ever prosecuted....

On the basis of my research and experience, I am convinced that if President Clinton were an ordinary citizen he would not be prosecuted for his allegedly false statements....

Next to testify was Stephen Saltzburg.

Mr. Saltzburg: ... Is there a way to resolve the conflicts, condemn lying and deceit, affirm truth and limit the scope of impeachment at the same time? I think there is, and that is what I want to talk about. Judge Starr testified—accurately, in my view—that some of the answers that the president gave in the *Paula Jones* deposition were "not true" or were "false." This is very different from saying, as some have, that the president committed perjury in giving these answers.

An example will help to make my point. During the *Jones* deposition the president was asked to use a very carefully crafted definition of sexual relations. That definition defined certain forms of sexual contact as sexual relations, but for reasons known only to the *Jones* lawyers limited the definition to contact with any person for the purpose of gratification. It is not at all clear that the president's interpretation of the definition of "any person" as meaning other than himself was unreasonable. The question could have been worded much more clearly. And crass and unkind as it might be to suggest it, it is also unclear whether the president sought to gratify any person but himself. Thus his answers might in fact be true rather than false.

[3] Dershowitz was referring to the Iran-*Contra* scandal, in which Reagan administration officials secretly sold arms to Iran in exchange for the release of American hostages held by terrorists in Lebanon, then used proceeds from the sales to aid anticommunist rebels in Nicaragua. independent counsel Lawrence Walsh had charged Weinberger, Reagan's defense secretary, with lying to his prosecutors and to congressional investigators. President Bush pardoned Weinberger just before he left office.

Now, some of you will wince and say, "Aha, semantics—word-smithing." But you must face the fact that you cannot investigate perjury allegations without considering the state of mind and intent of the witness.... Indeed, once you recognize the difficulty of investigating perjury, the beginning of an answer emerges to my question of how to resolve the conflicts that divide you and the American people.

In considering past impeachments involving federal judges, who can be indicted while in office, the Congress generally has waited to let the criminal process work. Only after a judge was convicted of perjury did you consider impeachment. The president's unique constitutional role makes it unlikely that he can be indicted and/or prosecuted while in office, so you do not have the option of waiting. But you do have the option of deciding that allegations of perjury that do not involve corruption of or abuse of office should not give rise to an impeachment...because perjury is an elusive crime to prove, involves subjective judgments that are especially difficult to make in a politically charged environment. And when rising out of personal conduct, it is too attenuated from the official duties of the president....

You should be able to unanimously agree upon a resolution that condemns the president for doing what he obviously did, which was answering questions in the *Jones* deposition to deceive the court and the lawyers, to condemn the president for defending that conduct before the grand jury and to condemn him for lying to the American people. Such a resolution is perfectly consistent with your constitutional responsibilities. Nothing in the Constitution suggests that when a president engages in conduct that is reprehensible but not impeachable the Congress must be silent....

Each of you [also] has the right to communicate... your belief that Federal District Judge Susan Webber Wright should consider whether to impose sanctions on the president for his testimony in the *Paula Jones* case....

My speculation is that Judge Wright has stayed her judicial hand while this impeachment inquiry is ongoing, not wanting to intrude or have the judicial branch perceived as even slightly partisan. But if this committee ends its investigation, she should punish the president....

If she does, and you agree to censure his conduct, we will have resolved the conflicts that divide you. In doing so the government will teach the importance of truth and responsibility. We will condemn lying and deceit, and assure that consequences attach to witness misconduct. And we will carefully and properly reserve the political death penalty of impeachment for behavior more closely related to conduct of office than this president's.

The last member of the panel was Jeffrey Rosen.

Mr. Rosen: ... Because defendants have traditionally been viewed as inherently unreliable, their testimony, unlike that of witnesses, was not taken under oath until after the Civil War. Judges recognized that the instinct for self-preservation is so strong that a guilty defendant will naturally be tempted to lie to protect himself. And it was considered a form of moral torture to force an accused to choose between incriminating himself on the one hand and facing eternal damnation for betraying his oath to God on the other.

In *Clinton v. Jones,* the Supreme Court established that a sitting president can be sued and personally deposed and his private life subject to wide-ranging discovery, even about conduct that preceded his inauguration. In an increasingly partisan environment, any remotely plausible lawsuit against a president will find ample funding, and inevitably there will be a clash of testimony. Now in ordinary civil suits this is nothing to worry about. Assessment of credibility, after all, is the main function of a jury, and people who lie in civil depositions are ordinarily punished by losing the case rather than being prosecuted for perjury....

If this president is impeached for lying during civil discovery, however, every time a future president's testimony is contradicted under oath an impeachment perjury may have to be triggered. The country and president will again be distracted in ways whose costs are hard to measure.

The most serious allegation against President Clinton is that he may have committed perjury before the grand jury when he contradicted Ms. Lewinsky's assertion that he touched her breasts and genitals in an attempt to gratify her. It seems implausible, on the one hand, that the core of the president's defense to the charges against him is that he didn't intend to arouse or gratify Ms. Lewinsky when he touched her. But wouldn't it be equally implausible to impeach the president of the United States on the grounds that he committed perjury when he denied that he intended to arouse Ms. Lewinsky? ...

This is an indiscreet subject, but let me close with a call for prosecutorial discretion. Many of you are understandably concerned about establishing a double standard. Why should ordinary citizens be convicted of perjury for lying about sex while the president escapes punishment? But this concern is unfounded. If you exercise your discretion not to impeach the president, he will still be subject after he leaves office to precisely the same legal penalties as the witnesses who testified so movingly before us this morning.... Indeed, you may well choose to rebuke the president with a reputational sanction that no ordinary citizen faces, a congressional resolution of censure....

In the question-and-answer session, Judge Higginbotham urged the committee to reflect on the differences between the present case and the Nixon proceedings. Nixon "was attempting to obtain confidential information maintained by the IRS concerning political enemies...using the Federal Bureau of Investigation, the Secret Service and other executive personnel to undertake improper electronic surveillance and other investigatory techniques with regards to public enemies...creating and maintaining a secret investigative unit within the Office of the President, which utilizes the resources of the Central Intelligence Agency," said Higginbotham. "Is that comparable to this?"

Republican George W. Gekas of Pennsylvania questioned Higginbotham about the speeding-ticket analogy he had used in his opening statement. Suppose, he said, someone's child had been run over by the speeding defendant. Didn't that make the perjury more serious, since lying about his speed would have the effect of destroying the case of someone who insisted that speeding had caused great damage? And, if so, wasn't that analogous to the Paula Jones case—"if indeed the president and Monica Lewinsky testified falsely" to avoid damages or being found liable by a jury. "Doesn't it take on different connotations when rights are destroyed by the virtue of false statements under oath?" Gekas asked. Judge Higginbotham replied: "No doubt about it."

Democrat Rick Boucher of Virginia directed his question to the three academics. Would they agree, he asked, that even if the president were not impeached for his misdeeds, "the rule of law, and the principle that no person is above the law...is well served, in the event that he is vulnerable to prosecution, indictment and trial for any crimes that he commits while he holds the office of president"?

Dershowitz replied that while in theory the president could be prosecuted after leaving office, he would not be. For one thing, he said, "People who commit acts like the president's are never prosecuted for those acts." Second, he said "No prosecutor in his right mind would indict a president unless he were confident he would get a conviction. There would be no conviction in this case."

Saltzburg and Rosen thought there could be criminal prosecution. Saltzburg repeated his view that Judge Susan Webber Wright should be allowed to take over the case.

Democrat Jerrold Nadler of New York also had a question for the three professors. The independent counsel had given the committee a report, he said, "in which he characterized testimony that he received...[and] reached conclusions...of fact and conclusions of law." No witnesses were being called, he said, so "there is no evidence before the committee, since the prosecutors' opinions and conclusions are not evidence." What did the professors think of this process?

Dershowitz replied that the committee did need to hear evidence and that those who compared the committee to a grand jury, merely sending a charge along to a court for trial, made a badly flawed analogy: "To think that it's like an indictment, which could be handled on the basis of hearsay testimony...is to misunderstand the difference between a criminal case and a great constitutional crisis."

Saltzburg pointed out that in the Nixon case, there was no independent counsel who had done this sort of investigation. On some subjects, he thought, the committee needed to hear witnesses. The conflicting testimony about the president's gifts to Lewinsky, for instance, was highly confusing. But, he said, because of the OIC report, "You know what the president said. You heard his explanation. So...you know enough to make a judgment about whether...this is impeachable."

Rosen noted what he called "the one salutary effect of this particular hearing": that it vividly displayed the "deep constitutional problems with the independent counsel statute."

Hyde and Dershowitz sparred a bit over perjury and the rule of law. "There are all kinds of lies," said Hyde, defending the committee's work. "There are fibs, little white lies. There is hyperbole, exaggeration and mental reservations, evasions. But then there is swearing 'to God to tell the truth, the whole truth and nothing but the truth,' and then deliberately deceiving, lying.... And what becomes of the rule of law? What has happened to the oath? Has it been cheapened? And what does that mean for the rule of law?"

Dershowitz answered: "I think this committee is doing a terrible, terrible disservice to the rule of law and to the sanctity of the oath by trivializing the differences" among types of perjury. He went on: "What this committee is doing is trivializing the rule of law by only focusing on perjury because they want to get a president of the opposite party.... It's a sham."

Republican Ed Bryant of Tennessee addressed his question to Saltzburg and Rosen. He was coming to believe, he said, that the House could charge (impeach) the president, but only the Senate had the right to punish (remove, censure, or reprimand) him. What was the opinion of the scholars?

Rosen replied that he thought there would be no constitutional difficulty if the House and Senate passed joint resolutions "expressing your deep condemnation of the president's behavior."

Saltzburg essentially agreed. "If you say on balance we don't like this conduct but we don't think we'll vote impeachment, we don't think it rises to that level ... then I agree with Jeffrey that you have every right under the Constitution to pass a resolution, just as you would condemning Saddam Hussein, praising turkeys ... creating National Mother's Day."

Democrat William D. Delahunt of Massachusetts asked Wiggins to address much the same issue. Would he support a resolution "to censure or to sanction or to rebuke or condemn"? he asked. "Oh yes," Wiggins responded. In fact, he said, "I recommend that the president be sanctioned monetarily."

Republican Bob Goodlatte of Virginia said he rejected Dershowitz's contention "that this is simply about lying to cover up personal indiscretions." As Goodlatte put it: "The reason he lied—if the evidence supports that conclusion—is because he wanted to evade criminal prosecution for his previous efforts to obstruct justice, suborn perjury, and commit perjury in the Paula Jones lawsuit."

Dershowitz did not wholly disagree. The problem started, he suggested, "with an attempt to keep from the president's family a matter of personal interest. It then ... evolved and evolved." But Dershowitz felt strongly, he insisted, "that there is a difference between an impeachable crime of perjury and condemnable but not impeachable allegations." Dershowitz added: "I don't believe [the president] was completely forthright in his grand jury testimony, but I don't believe that he committed perjury in his grand jury testimony. And there is a big difference." If the record did demonstrate that perjury, "or if there were evidence of subornation of perjury, of the kind of cover-up that you describe, I think it would be a very, very different matter."

Democrat Steven R. Rothman of New Jersey pressed the point: Why did Dershowitz believe the president did not commit perjury before the grand jury? Dershowitz replied that perjury is very technical, very difficult to prove—and Clinton's testimony, he contended, "was not literally false—at least not literally false in any way that I have seen evidence to demonstrate beyond a reasonable doubt."

Georgia Republican Bob R. Barr's pursued the theme. Many of the witnesses seemed to be saying "perjury may be perjury, obstruction may be obstruction, but you have to look at the context—you have to look at whether it was really a serious offense." At first, Barr, said, this testimony depressed him. But, he went on, he had got over his depression because "there really are I think two Americas, and there is a real America out there. And I think our military witnesses understand that, and the two witnesses earlier today understood that.... And it is that America that I have great faith in, because it's that America that understands what perjury is." This "real America," said Barr, "understands that there ought to be a very high standard for our public officials. . . ."

Dershowitz responded with outrage. *"Whenever I hear the word "real Americans," that sounds to me like a code word for racism—a code word for bigotry—a code word—"* Barr interrupted: *"That's the silliest thing I have ever heard—"* But Dershowitz continued: *"We may have a disagreement about the merits of these issues, but I would no more impugn your Americanism than you should impugn mine, sir."*

At that point, Judge Higginbotham interjected, also taking issue with Barr's *"categorization of the 'real America.' "* *"Now let me put this in perspective,"* Higginbotham went on. In his prepared statement, he had cited some statistics. *"On page seven, I gave the fact that President Clinton got 379 electoral votes and 47,410,054 votes. I cited that because when you do an impeachment . . . you remove someone, Congressman Barr, who got elected by the real America."*

Clinton, Higginbotham continued, had opened the way for more pluralism on the federal bench. When you remove a president, he argued, *"you will be removing someone who may have some values which are as important as what you called perjury. . . . And I think that there's a real America which President Clinton took in terms of fairness. . . ."*

Barr responded that it was a *"very, very slippery slope"* to interject feelings about the particular policies of a president into the debate over whether he should be impeached for high crimes and misdemeanors. This, he argued, represented *"constitutional and legal relativism that I would certainly think a learned member of the bar . . . would not stray into."*

At the end of the session, Chairman Hyde thanked the witnesses. *"Even when you disagreed with us, which is most of the time, you helped us,"* said Hyde. *"You're here because you're darn good citizens and you want to contribute to this awful task we are grappling with, and you have made a great contribution."* The committee stood adjourned.

WITNESSES FOR THE DEFENSE

Chairman Hyde announced that the White House had provided a list of fourteen witnesses whose testimony it wanted the committee to hear—in addition to that of Gregory B. Craig, Special Counsel to the president, and White House Counsel Charles Ruff. The fourteen new witnesses, Hyde explained, would testify in four panels, on this day and the next. The third day, after presentations from Abbe Lowell and David Schippers, the committee members would make their own statements, then consider articles of impeachment.

John Conyers thanked Hyde for allowing the White House to present its witnesses, but added: "The independent counsel had four years to investigate the president. This committee has had four months. The White House is now getting two days." Conyers also took the opportunity to restate the position of many Democrats. "The legal case against the president is, in my judgment, a house of cards," he said. Yet the new Republican leadership would not allow the House to pursue what the public most wanted—"a meaningful way of censuring the president." He concluded: "If the American people ever wanted strong evidence that the extremists are still in control of this process, then that is it."

Chairman Hyde swore in the first panel, then introduced its members.

Mr. Hyde: Mr. Gregory Craig is assistant to the president and special counsel. The Honorable Nicholas Katzenbach is a former attorney general of the

United States under President Johnson, and undersecretary of state. He is also retired as senior vice president and chief legal officer of IBM. Professor Bruce Ackerman is the Sterling Professor of Law and Political Science at Yale University, and authority of Volume II, "We the People," which includes an historical and legal analysis of the impeachment of Andrew Johnson. Professor Sean Wilentz is the Dayton Stockton Professor of History and Director of Program and American Studies at Princeton University. Professor Wilentz is an expert and teacher of American history from the American Revolution through Reconstruction.... Professor Samuel H. Beer is the Eaton Professor of the Science of Government, emeritus, at Harvard University. He has written and lectured and taught about the American system of government for over 65 years.

Mr. Craig, you are recognized for a 15-minute statement.

Mr. Craig: ... During our presentation today and tomorrow we will show, from our history and our heritage, from any fair reading of the Constitution and from any fair sounding of our countrymen and women that nothing in this case justifies this Congress overturning a national election and removing our president from office. As we begin this undertaking, I make only one plea to you, and I hope it is not a futile one, coming this late in the process. Open your mind. Open your heart and focus on the record.... [Y]ou may already be determined to vote to approve some articles of impeachment against this president. That is your right and your duty, if you believe the facts and the law justify such a vote.

But there is a lot of conventional wisdom about this case that is just plain wrong. And if you are, in fact, disposed to vote for impeachment, in the name of a justice that is fair and blind and impartial, please do so only on the basis of the real record and on the real testimony....

By the close of tomorrow, all the world will see one simple and undeniable fact: Whatever there is in the record that shows that what the president did was wrong and blameworthy, there is nothing in the record in either the law or the facts that would justify his impeachment and removal from office....

Mr. Chairman, I am willing to concede that in the *Jones* deposition, the president's testimony was evasive, incomplete, misleading, even maddening, but it was not perjury.

On the allegation of perjury before the grand jury, which we all agree is the more serious offense, please look at the real record, not the referral's report of that record. Millions of Americans watched that testimony. They concluded, as I believe that you too will find, that in fact the president admitted to an improper, inappropriate and intimate relationship with Ms. Lewinsky....

When it comes to allegations that the president, with Ms. Lewinsky, Ms. Currie and Mr. Jordan, obstructed justice, we will show that the evidence presented in the referral is misleading, incomplete and frequently inaccurate. We will show that the president did not obstruct justice with respect to gifts, the job search or the affidavit, and we will show that the president did not seek wrongfully to influence Ms. Currie's testimony....

When it comes to allegations that the president abused his office, we will show that the president's assertions of executive privilege were perfectly proper and that the claims of attorney-client privilege were justified....

And when it comes to allegations that the president used the power of his office to mislead his aides—not ... for the purpose of protecting himself and his family, but, as alleged, to mislead the grand jury—we will show that false denials about an improper private relationship, whether those denials are made in private or before the entire world, simply do not constitute an abuse of office that justifies impeachment.

Finally, Mr. Chairman, ... let me just point out that in the course of this impeachment inquiry, the members of this committee have learned nothing new ... except that the president has finally, if belatedly, been cleared on the charges concerning Whitewater, the file matter, and the Travel Office. There has been no new evidence and there are no new charges. So ... if back in September when you received this referral, if back in October when you voted to conduct this inquiry, if back then you didn't think that the referral justified impeaching President Clinton, there is no reason for you to think so today....

Then Craig described the upcoming witnesses. The first panel, he said, would testify about the history of impeachment and constitutional standards. The second was made up of people who had served on the Judiciary Committee in 1974, during the proceedings against Richard Nixon. The third panel would address abuse of power and the fact-finding process. The last would discuss prosecutorial standards in perjury and obstruction-of-justice cases. Then White House Counsel Charles Ruff would sum up on behalf of the president.

Craig yielded to former Attorney General Nicholas Katzenbach.

Mr. Katzenbach: ... The process of impeachment is simply to remove from office upon conviction—not to otherwise punish the person involved. The Constitution provides the legislative branch—the Congress—with this means of removing from office the president, vice president and all civil officers upon conviction of treason, bribery, or other high crimes and misdemeanors. The threshold problem for the committee and the House is, of course, to determine what constitutes the "high crimes and misdemeanors" which would justify removal from office of an elected president. The phrase "high crimes and misdemeanors" is not a familiar one in modern American jurisprudence.

At common law it constituted a category of political crimes against the state.... In the United States, one of the Founders, James Wilson, made essentially the same point when he wrote that "impeachments are confined to political characters, to political crimes and misdemeanors, to political punishments." Or, as Justice Story observed, impeachment is "a proceeding purely of a political nature ... not so much designed to punish an offender as to secure the state against gross political misdemeanors." ...

If I am correct, then it seems clear to me the fundamental question is simply whether the president has done something which has destroyed the public's confidence in his ability to continue in office. If the public does not believe that what he has done seriously affects his ability to perform his public duties as president, should the committee conclude that his acts have destroyed the public confidence essential to that office? The only question, after all, is removal from office of an elected official. Is it the proper role of a partisan majority in Congress to conclude that the offenses are so serious as to warrant removal even if the public believes otherwise?

I do not find the arguments for this position persuasive.... I suggest that some perjury is more serious than others.... [A]ll perjury may be reprehensible, but it is still not of similar import when the ultimate issue is public confidence to perform the duties of office....

Second, the argument is made that the public's view as to what does or does not constitute a cause for impeachment is irrelevant because of the duty of the House to determine whether or not the president has committed a "high crime or misdemeanor." If this were a criminal trial, I would agree. If the president were extremely unpopular, as was Andrew Johnson, I would agree— simply because I would be unable to separate dislike for the president ... from lack of confidence based on "high crimes and misdemeanors." ...

This committee and this Congress are also faced with a totally new impeachment problem. Due to the existence of the independent counsel, the facts are publicly known and the areas of factual dispute relatively minor. Members of Congress have expressed concern over the evils of perjury and other alleged offenses and their serious nature. For whatever reason, the public remains unpersuaded....

Frankly, I can't see any constitutional basis for impeachment. To remove a popularly elected president requires, in my judgment, a showing of "great offenses" against the public weal sufficient to bring into question in the minds of reasonable people the capacity of the incumbent to continue to govern in a democracy with public support....

The next witness was Sean Wilentz of Princeton.

Mr. Wilentz: ... It is no exaggeration to say that upon this impeachment inquiry, as upon all presidential impeachment inquiries, hinges the fate of our American political institutions. It is that important. As a historian, it is clear to me that the impeachment of President Clinton would do ... great damage to those institutions and to the rule of law—much greater damage than the crimes of which President Clinton has been accused. More important, it is clear to me that any Representative who votes in favor of impeachment but who is not absolutely convinced that the president may have committed impeachable offenses—not merely crimes or misdemeanors, but high crimes and misdemeanors—will be fairly accused of gross dereliction of duty and earn the condemnation of history....

The scholarly testimony ... regarding the Constitution showed, at mind-numbing length, that there is disagreement over what constitutes grounds for presidential impeachment, as envisaged by the framers. Yet the testimony also showed that there is substantial common ground. Above all, the scholars agreed that not all criminal acts are necessarily impeachable acts. Only "treason, bribery, and other high crimes and misdemeanors," committed, in George Mason's explicit original language, "against the state" would seem to qualify....

A great deal of the disagreement among historians stems from a small but fateful decision made by the Constitutional Convention's Committee on Style. Before the Constitution reached that committee, Mason's original wording on impeachment was changed from "crimes against the state" to "crimes against the United States." The committee was charged with polishing the document's language, but with instructions that the meaning not be changed at all. By removing, in Article I, Section 4, the words "against the United States," the committee created a Pandora's box, which we have opened 211 years later....

The absence of that wording in the final document has persuaded some historians and constitutional scholars that the Constitution's phrase "high crimes and misdemeanors" embraces all sorts of private crimes. Yet many if not most American historians, including the nearly 500 who have now endorsed the widely-publicized statement deploring this impeachment drive... hold to the view that Mason's wording...best express[es] the letter and the spirit of what the framers had in mind. By that standard, the current charges against President Clinton do not, we American historians believe, rise to the level of impeachable offenses.

As further historical evidence, I would point to the fact that the only other occasions when presidential impeachment was pursued, against Presidents Andrew Johnson and Richard Nixon, plainly involved allegations of grievous public crimes that directly assaulted our political system.

Another pivotal piece of evidence...has to do with the Nixon impeachment. In 1974 the Judiciary Committee declined to approve a bill of impeachment connected to serious allegations that President Nixon had defrauded a federal agency, the Internal Revenue Service. The judgment was that because the allegations did not directly concern Nixon's public duties, they had no relevance to impeachment.

Without question, an occasion could arise when it would be necessary to expand on the framers' language, to cover circumstances they may have never contemplated, including truly monstrous private crimes. I would hope, for example, that any president accused of murder, even in the most private circumstances, would be impeached and removed from office. But not even the president's harshest critics, as far as I know, have claimed that the current allegations are on a par with murder.

Various Representatives, scholars and commentators have offered technically plausible...arguments, contending that the allegations against President Clinton rise to an impeachable standard under the definition of crimes against the state. There has been talk of a concerted attack on one of the coordinate branches of government, of a calculated presidential abuse of power (because President Clinton raised issues of executive privilege and because he lied to his aides) and of how perjury by a president, regardless of context, is a fundamental breach of trust that must be punished.... But these assertions rightly sound overwrought, exaggerated and suspicious to ordinary Americans....

Similar magisterial language was used in the impeachment proceedings against President Johnson and had considerable impact inside the Congress.... Since then, though, historians have looked behind the language at the actual facts of the case, as well as at the political context of the time. And in general they have concluded that the impeachment effort against Johnson was a drastic departure from what the framers intended, one that badly weakened the presidency for decades....

You may decide as a body to go through with impeachment, disregarding the letter as well as the spirit of the Constitution, defying the deliberate judgment of the people ... and in some cases, deciding to do so out of anger and expedience. But if you decide to do this, you will have done far more to subvert respect for the framers, for representative government and for the rule of law than any crime that has been alleged against President Clinton. And your reputations will be darkened for as long as there are Americans who can tell the difference between the rule of law and the rule of politics.

Samuel H. Beer of Harvard was the next witness.

Mr. Beer:... Removal from office, that grand and forbidding consequence of a successful impeachment, distinguishes this process radically from the judgment of a court. It resembles rather a vote of no confidence in a legislature, such as the British parliament.... Like a vote of no confidence, impeachment brings to an end a president's administration. Like a vote of no confidence, it relates not merely to some specific failure but is a judgment on his record and promise as a whole.... Because of these broad and weighty consequences, impeachment is primarily a political, not a judicial, act.

As a political act, impeachment, like a vote of no confidence, passes judgment on and enforces responsibility on the executive power. In the British system, that responsibility runs directly to the legislature.... For us, the responsibility of the president is essentially and directly to the voters. The legislature as a separate office, separately elected, likewise is held accountable by the voters. This separation of powers is fundamental in our constitutional design....

Where the ultimate sovereign is the people, the interference of one power, the legislature, in its exercise of such a dire responsibility as removal of a popularly elected president imposes severe duties on the legislators. The Congress...is acting in lieu of the people between quadrennial elections. At their best, the legislators will do what the people at their best would do, weighing the pluses and minuses of the record and the promise as a whole, asking, "Does the national interest require the removal from office of this president?" In the case of President Clinton, the American people have twice answered that question by electing him to the American presidency. And if we seek further light on the American mind, surveys of opinion continue to confirm that answer....

The failure to consider the whole record of Clinton's presidency in foreign and domestic affairs could have severe long-run costs. The removal of a president, thanks to such neglect in judgment, could substantially damage our democratic system. Consider the temptations which this precedent would excite in a Congress of a different party against a future president of a different party. As a great historian, Henry Adams, said when commenting on the failed attempt of the Jeffersonians to remove Justice Chase,[1] impeachment is not a suitable activity for party politics.

The last member of the first panel was Bruce Ackerman of Yale.

Mr. Ackerman: ... People seem to be assuming that once the present committee and the full House vote for a bill of impeachment, the stage will be set for trial in the Senate in the upcoming year. Nothing could be further from the truth.... When the 105th House dies on January 3rd, all its unfinished business dies with it.... [A] bill passed by the 105th House that is still pending in the 105th Senate on January 3rd cannot be enacted into law unless it once again meets the approval of the 106th House.

This is as it should be. Otherwise lame-duck Congresses would have a field day in situations like the present, where the old House majority has a setback in the polls....

Until the 20th Amendment was passed in 1933, a newly elected Congress ordinarily waited 13 months before it began its first meeting in Washington. In the meantime, lame ducks did the nation's business for a full session, often in ways that ran against the grain of the last election. This might have been an acceptable price to pay in the 18th century, when roads were terrible and it took time for farmer-representatives to arrange their business affairs. But over time, the operation of lame-duck Congresses proved to be an intolerable violation of democratic principles....

[The 20th Amendment] orders the new Congress to begin meeting as soon as possible after the elections—the text itself specifies January 3. In enacting

---

[1] Justice Samuel Chase of Maryland served on the U.S. Supreme Court from 1796 until 1811. A Federalist, he was impeached for partisan activities by the House in 1803 with the encouragement of President Thomas Jefferson, but the Senate found him not guilty.

it into our fundamental law, Americans believed they were reducing the lame-duck problem to vestigial proportions. Perhaps some grave national emergency might require decisive action, but the old Congress would simply fade away....

Generally, speaking, lame-duck Congresses have proved faithful to this expectation. For example, during the 65 years since the 20th Amendment became part of our higher law, no lame-duck House has ever impeached an errant federal judge, much less a sitting president. Such matters have been left to the judgment of Congresses that were not full of members who had been repudiated at the polls or who were retiring from office.

These proceedings, then, are absolutely unprecedented in the post-lame-duck era. Despite this fact, I don't question the raw constitutional power of the current lame-duck House to vote out a bill of impeachment. But I do respectfully submit that the Constitution treats a lame-duck bill of impeachment in precisely the same way it treats any other House bill that remains pending in the Senate on January 3. Like all other bills, a lame-duck bill of impeachment loses its constitutional force with the death of the House that passed it....

If this committee and the present House choose to go forward and vote in favor of a bill of impeachment, I respectfully urge the new speaker of the 106th Congress to do the right thing and remit the matter once again for consideration by the new House. Suppose, however, he does not do so. Suppose further that, if pressed, the Chief Justice upholds the continuing validity of the lame-duck impeachment despite the expiration of the 105th Congress. Even then, the new House of Representatives will not be able to escape the need for another up or down vote to determine whether a majority of members continue to favor impeachment.

To see why, consider that the House must select a group of its members, called impeachment managers, to present its case against the president at the Senate trial. Without the energetic prosecution of the case by the managers, the Senate trial cannot go forward. No managers, no trial, but only the new House can appoint the managers....

Thus, even if the new House leadership chooses to rely on a lame-duck impeachment, and refuses to allow another vote on a fresh bill before sending the matter to the Senate, there is no way it can avoid the need to test the majority sentiment of the new House. By voting against the slate of managers, a majority of the new House will be in a position to stop the impeachment process dead in its tracks....

To put my point in operational terms: If you don't believe that a bill of impeachment or that the election of impeachment managers will gain the majority support of the next House, the wise thing to do is to stop the process now. While it may be embarrassing to reverse gears after so much momentum has been generated in favor of a bill of impeachment, the leadership of the next House will confront a much more embarrassing situation if it becomes evident that its slender pro-impeachment majority has vanished over the Christmas recess.

During the question-and-answer session, Republican committee members returned again and again to the charges against President Clinton. Wisconsin's James Sensenbrenner, for instance, protested that "we've heard nothing from the president contradicting the fact witnesses and the grand jury testimony that Judge Starr sent over to us in 18 boxes worth of evidence." Craig replied that the White House had submitted three written responses to Starr's referral, taking issue with many of his specifics. And, he added, "We believe the president should be given a presumption of innocence, and that the burden should be on the committee to call fact witnesses." Other Republican members homed in on specific allegations of presidential perjury and obstruction of justice, underscoring their belief that these were serious attacks on the judicial system and challenging the president's defenders to argue them away. Pressed by Elton Gallegly of California on the president's testimony in the Jones civil deposition, Craig said: "He tried, I think, to answer accurately in a very narrow way. You may conclude, Congressman, that he did not succeed."

The Democrats, for their part, kept bringing the discussion back to the larger issues raised by the panel members. One after another lamented the party-line split on the matter, the fact that, in the words of Martin Meehan of Massachusetts, "It is a forgone conclusion that the majority of the members of this committee, on Saturday, will take the incredibly historic step of voting ... to impeach this president." Nothing the scholars could say, he added, would change that. Still, the White House witnesses didn't give up their argument that the Clinton case simply didn't warrant impeachment. In response to a question from California's Howard Berman, for instance, Katzenbach replied: "I am perfectly willing to take everything that Mr. Starr says and still conclude that that does not reach the level of high crimes and misdemeanors in this situation." The Democrats also repeatedly addressed the public distaste for the proceedings, and panel members agreed that the public attitude was important.

After a recess, Chairman Hyde welcomed the second panel of witnesses invited by the White House. All were former members of Congress: Elizabeth Holtzman from New York, Wayne Owens from Utah, and Robert F. Drinan, S.J., from Massachu-

setts. All three had been members of the House Judiciary Committee in 1974, during the Nixon impeachment hearings. After swearing in the panel, Hyde recognized each member for a ten-minute statement.

Ms. Holtzman: ... During Watergate, I spent many long hours poring over books and studies to understand the meaning of the term "high crimes and misdemeanors." The framers of the Constitution wrote the impeachment clause because they were fearful that the monarchy they had just overthrown in the revolution would return—that the newly created chief executive, the president, would become a tyrant.

But Independent Counsel Kenneth Starr's referral makes out no case of abuse of power, a subject I have been asked to address by the White House. In Watergate, the article of impeachment that charged abuse of power was, in a way, the most serious—and it was the one that received the largest number of Republican votes. Think of what presidential abuses we saw then: getting the CIA to stop an FBI investigation, getting the IRS to audit political enemies, illegally wiretapping members of the National Security Council staff and of the press, a special unit in the White House to break into the psychiatrist's office of a political enemy—and on and on.

By contrast, what does Mr. Starr point to as an "abuse of power" in his referral? Acts that do not in the farthest stretch of the imagination constitute any such abuse. Mr. Starr claims that the president did not voluntarily appear before a grand jury but had to be subpoenaed to appear. That is surely not an abuse of power.

Mr. Starr attacks the fact that the president authorized executive privilege to be claimed for a handful of staff members and required the independent counsel to prove his need for their testimony in court. Of course, once the court ruled that the testimony was required, then the president withdrew the claim. That too is not an abuse. Mr. Clinton's telling the American people that he did not have a sexual relationship with Monica Lewinsky is also not an abuse of power, although it was the wrong thing to do.

Parenthetically, I want to note that as one of the authors of the independent counsel statute, I believe that Mr. Starr overstepped his jurisdiction by arguing for impeachment on this ground or any ground. Both the referral and his appearance here go far beyond what the statute permits. We never intended to create a Grand Inquisitor for Impeachment. ...

I have heard it said that this committee views itself as a kind of grand jury and that it merely needs probable cause—not overwhelming evidence—to impeach. Instead, it is the Senate that must have substantial evidence to act. But if you use the analogy of a grand jury, then you should not be impeaching at all. No indictment would be sought by a prosecutor where there is no chance for conviction. And it is almost universally conceded that there are not enough votes in the Senate to convict President Clinton and remove him from office. In fact, federal prosecutors need to have a substantial likelihood of success before they can recommend indictment to the grand jury....

The same analogy holds true here. Impeachment should not be voted by the House unless there is a strong likelihood of conviction in the Senate. Impeachment is not a kind of super-censure, designed simply to besmirch a president's reputation. Impeachment is a tool to remove a president from office; it is a last resort to preserve our democracy. It must not be perverted or trivialized....

Robert Drinan, S.J., was the next to testify.

Father Drinan: ... The situation before the House Judiciary Committee today is entirely different from the scene in 1974. At that time, the country knew there was lawlessness in the White House. The documentation of appalling crimes was known by everyone. Abuse of power and criminality were apparent to the American people.... The procedure followed by the House Judiciary Committee at that time was, however, even-handed. Months of hearings took place with the president's lawyer, Mr. James St. Clair, always present and free to make comments and ask questions.

Today the scene is startlingly different. No investigation has been done by the House Judiciary Committee, nor have any fact-finding hearings been held. The 21 Republicans have no support whatsoever from the 16 Democrats. In addition, two-thirds of the nation continue to be opposed to impeachment.

In 1974, the members of the Democratic majority had constant conversation and dialogue with the Republican members.... The Democrats were aware of the intense problems that the Republicans had with the impeachment of a Republican president. But eventually, through the sheer force of the evidence, six or seven of the Republicans voted for one or more articles of impeachment. That was not a happy day when we voted for impeachment, and I remember well that Chairman [Peter] Rodino said to the press afterwards, when asked what was the first thing that he did ...: "I went to my office and cried."

Another difference: The House Judiciary Committee in 1998, unlike its predecessor in 1974, has allowed its agenda to be dictated by the calendar.

Strategy has been determined not by the need for thoroughness and fairness, but by the convenience of ending the process before Christmas of this year.

The House Judiciary Committee in 1974, furthermore, did not vote for all of the proposed articles of impeachment. A serious charge was made that President Nixon had back-dated his taxes in an effort to take advantage of an exemption that had been repealed. Only 12 members of the body voted for the proposition that this was an impeachable offense. Twenty-four members, including myself, voted that this misconduct, almost certainly a felony, was not impeachable....

Almost 70 percent of the nation and virtually every Democrat in the Congress are opposed to impeachment. These groups believe firmly that even if all the allegations in the Starr Report are true, there are no impeachable offenses. And I would anticipate, members of the committee, an explosion of anger like that that occurred after the Saturday Night Massacre... when people realize what you people anticipate you will do this Saturday...

The chair now recognized Wayne Owens.

Mr. Owens: ... I remember keenly this afternoon how I felt 25 years ago, when I learned, while deer hunting in the mountains of southern Utah, of the so-called Saturday Night Massacre, the forced resignation of Attorney-General Elliot Richardson and of Deputy Attorney General William Ruckelshaus, and then of Special Prosecutor Archibald Cox. I had been following the revelations of the Senate Watergate committee for six months. It was obvious that Sunday morning that the House would be required to pursue an impeachment investigation, and that my committee, the Judiciary Committee, would be called to conduct that investigation.

I think that I was initially in awe of the assignment, almost intimidated.... History would be looking over our shoulder, and we wanted, from Chairman Rodino on down, to be sure that we were careful, judicial, and bipartisan in all that we did. While we recognized that impeachment was a political process, we were determined that it would not be a partisan process, and we reported *unanimously* our recommendations to the House that the investigation go forward—all 21 Democrats and 17 Republicans—and it was accepted by the full House by a vote of 410 to four.

So, we are aware, I think, of your feelings as you approach the decisions you must make. Chairman Hyde indicated early on that the precedents of the Nixon impeachment would be followed closely, and my assigned task this afternoon is to argue to you that President Clinton's misdeeds do not reach the standard of impeachment which our committee established.

What was that standard? We defined impeachment in our final report as: "...a constitutional remedy addressed to serious offenses against the system of government." Ten Republican members of the committee, in a minority report, argued for a higher standard of judgment, saying: "...the president should be removable by the legislative branch only for serious misconduct dangerous to the system of government established by the Constitution."...

I want to recall for you briefly the circumstances surrounding the adoption of the so-called "Abuse of Power" article of impeachment in late July 1974. The committee had just passed the first article, referred to as the Obstruction of Justice article, by a solid vote of 21 Democrats and six of the 17 Republicans.

Proposed article of impeachment number two, after serious consideration and debate, was passed by an even larger majority. A total of seven Republicans joined 21 Democrats, finding that President Nixon had violated the constitutional rights of citizens, in five specific categories of abuse of his powers, and voted to report the article to the floor for full House consideration.

I urge you to consider carefully the gravity of those charges, which an overwhelming and bipartisan majority of the committee found to be sustained by not only clear and convincing evidence, but in fact, by evidence beyond a reasonable doubt, the test for conviction in the Senate.... President Nixon, it was clear, had:

1. Directed or authorized his subordinates to interfere with the impartial and non-political administration of the Internal Revenue law for political purposes,
2. Directed or authorized unlawful electronic surveillance and investigations of citizens and the use of information obtained from the surveillance for his own political advantage,
3. Permitted a secret investigative unit within the Office of the President to engage in unlawful and covert activities for his political purposes,
4. Once these and other unlawful and improper activities on his behalf were suspected, and after he knew or had reason to know that his close subordinates were interfering with lawful investigations into them, he failed to perform his duty to see that the criminal laws were enforced against those subordinates, and
5. He used his executive power to interfere with the lawful operations of agencies of the Executive Branch, including the Department of Justice

and the Central Intelligence Agency, in order to assist in these activities, as well as to conceal the truth about his misconduct and that of his subordinates and agents.

Today you are faced with a record of misdeeds by a president who carried on an illicit sexual affair, then publicly and privately misled others to protect his wife and daughter, and the public, from finding out about his infidelity. Personal, not official, misconduct, akin to President Nixon cheating on his taxes—improper and serious, but by nature personal misconduct and therefore not impeachable.

Your obligation, may I be permitted to point it out to you, is to put those powerful differences into perspective and to render a judgment based solely on the gravity of the offense, because there is little disagreement on the facts....

Questions for the second panel focused heavily on the differences between the Nixon impeachment hearings and the proceedings against President Clinton—and particularly on whether the charges in the present case measured up to those in the first. Largely with the concurrence of the panelists, the Democrats argued that the charges against Clinton were, in Conyers's words, "weak [and] puny." Barney Frank of Massachusetts described Starr's third count of perjury as a question of "What did the president touch and when did he touch it?"

The Republicans, by contrast, argued forcefully that the Clinton case was not about sex. Virginia's Bob Goodlatte put it this way: "I think the purpose of the president ... was to defeat the lawsuit, the sexual harassment lawsuit, to obstruct justice in that case, to coach witnesses and to bring forth a false affidavit from another individual. And those I think are very serious charges, very similar to the charges that the Watergate committee considered regarding President Nixon. . . ."

Democrats continued to lament the absence of direct witnesses and bipartisan spirit. Republicans continued to complain about the failure of the White House to directly address factual evidence against the president.

Chairman Hyde then introduced the third panel of White House witnesses: James Hamilton, who served as assistant chief counsel in the Senate Watergate Committee and as chairman of the legal ethics committee of the District of Columbia bar; and Richard Ben-Veniste, a former U.S. attorney who was assistant special prosecutor and chief of the Watergate task force from 1973 to 1975, and also served as minority chief counsel to the Senate Whitewater committee in 1995–1996. After swearing in the two, Hyde recognized Ben-Veniste.

Mr. Ben-Veniste:... The first Watergate Special Prosecutor, Archibald Cox, was fired on the orders of Richard M. Nixon when he refused to back down after subpoenaing Mr. Nixon's famously incriminating White House tape recordings. In response to the firestorm of public opinion following the "Saturday night massacre," President Nixon replaced Professor Cox with Leon Jaworski, a conservative Texan who vowed to continue the investigation with the independence and professionalism that had marked Mr. Cox's truncated turn at the helm. By all accounts, Leon Jaworski made good on his promise....

Upon his appointment, Mr. Jaworski immediately withdrew from his lucrative law practice and devoted himself entirely to his duties as Special Prosecutor. Even with President Nixon's unlawful firing of Archibald Cox, the Watergate cover-up case was investigated and prosecuted within 21 months of the creation of the Special Prosecutor's office.

The credibility of the Watergate special prosecutor's office was dependent upon the public perception of our investigation as professional, impartial and fair....

Mr. Starr has the unhappy distinction of being the first independent counsel to come under investigation himself for unethical and possibly illegal conduct. In addition to the 24 prima facie instances of improper leaks of grand jury material identified by Chief Judge Norma Holloway Johnson, there was the spin-leak of the Starr referral itself in the days leading up to its actual transmittal.... In addition, the aggressive and disproportionate tactics employed by Mr. Starr's office, sometimes in violation of Department of Justice guidelines, have left the public with a justifiable perception that Mr. Starr has conducted more of a crusade than an investigation—with the political objective of driving President Clinton from office....

Leon Jaworski took extraordinary care not to intrude beyond the proper boundaries of his office. Mr. Jaworski would be the last person to suggest that an attempt to pierce the president's attorney-client privilege, or to interfere with the time-honored protective function of the Secret Service, could be justified as an appropriate exercise of prosecutorial discretion....

Even 25 years ago, it was the practice of federal prosecutors not to subpoena the target of a grand jury investigation. On the other hand, it was considered unfair to deprive a target of an investigation of the opportunity to testify if he so desired. Accordingly, Mr. Jaworski extended an invitation to President Nixon to testify before the grand jury. When Mr. Nixon declined, Mr. Jaworski did not publicize the exchange—because to do so would have been an unfair comment on Nixon's decision not to testify. And again, there was no leak.

By comparison, Mr. Starr has aggressively pursued every opportunity to push the limits of legal boundaries.

Mr. Jaworski recognized that he had a responsibility to transmit to Congress important evidence bearing on the House Judiciary Committee's ongoing impeachment inquiry. At the same time, he was careful not to encroach on Congress's constitutional function of evaluating evidence and determining whether impeachment was warranted. Because the evidence was obtained through grand jury subpoenas, Mr. Jaworski first sought the grand jury's approval and then sought permission from Chief Judge John Sirica to transmit the material as an exception to Rule 6(c)...which would otherwise prohibit its dissemination. Judge Sirica reviewed the transmittal [and]...found that the transmittal rendered no moral or social judgments. He found that the grand jury had taken care to assure that the report had no objectionable features...and then he passed it along to the Judiciary Committee.

At the same time, Mr. Jaworski did *not* inform the House that the grand jury had voted to authorize him to name Richard Nixon as an unindicted co-conspirator in the upcoming Watergate cover-up trial. While the grand jury's action provided insight into *its* views of the evidence, the grand jury's decision was not itself evidence. And again, this explosive information was never leaked.

By comparison, Mr. Starr never submitted his proposed referral to Chief Judge Johnson for advance review, nor did he ask the grand jury to pass on its contents. Instead, we are told, he sought and received carte blanche permission from the three-judge special court which first appointed him to disseminate such information to the house as *he* deemed appropriate. Thus, no one but Starr and his subordinates reviewed the aggressively accusatory and gratuitously salacious referral before it was transmitted to the Judiciary Committee. Mr. Starr's ethics adviser resigned when he agreed to act as chief advocate for impeachment as a witness before this committee....

While I do not condone the president's conduct in his relationship with Ms. Lewinsky, or in the way he dealt with that issue in the *Paula Jones* deposition, it is clear to me that attempting to criminalize that conduct, much less make it the basis of articles of impeachment, would do a disservice to the Constitution and any notion of proportionality, moderation and common sense....

Chairman Hyde recognized James Hamilton.

Mr. Hamilton: ... The notion of "great and dangerous offenses" against the state captures the essence of what an impeachable offense should be. It must, as Alexander Hamilton said, "relate chiefly to injuries done to the society itself." A president should not be impeached to subject him to *punishment*, but rather to *protect* the state and society against "great and dangerous offenses" that might recur if he is allowed to remain in office.

I respectfully submit that the alleged abuses by President Clinton do not indicate that he is a danger to the nation.

Lying to the public and to his Cabinet and aides is disgraceful, but if we would impeach all officials who lie about personal or official matters, I fear that the halls of government would be seriously depleted. Other presidents—for example, Lyndon Johnson as to Vietnam—have not been candid in their public and private statements. There must be a higher bar for impeachment.

It is true that Article I of the impeachment resolution against Nixon charged that he misled the public about the scope of his administration's investigation of Watergate misconduct and the lack of involvement by administration and reelection committee personnel in this misconduct. But these statements involved lies about official actions and were part of a massive cover-up of government misdeeds. This is far different than lies about private consensual sexual conduct.

The claim that unsuccessfully asserting executive privilege to the grand jury is impeachable is extraordinarily thin. The president did so upon the advice of counsel, and the district court recognized that the president's conversations were presumptively privileged, although it found that the needs of the criminal justice system outweighed that privilege. At no time did the court suggest that the privilege was claimed in bad faith. ...

Neither the president's reticence to appear before the grand jury nor his failure to answer certain questions put by the prosecutors should constitute impeachable offenses. The president was well aware that he was facing a hostile prosecutor of whom he had much to fear. He was not under subpoena, and thus had no obligation to appear at a time certain. Moreover, Mr. Starr agreed to the rules that allowed the president to decline to answer certain questions in his grand jury depositions. In these circumstances, to brand his conduct as impeachable is untenable.

The claim that the president lied under oath, of course, is more troubling than these other allegations against President Clinton. But lying about private consensual sexual conduct seems more appropriately designated as a *low* crime rather than a *high* crime. While reprehensible, it is not a "great and dangerous offense against the state" that demonstrates the necessity of removing the president from office to protect the nation from further abuses.

I readily concede that lies under oath about treason, bribery, the break-in at the DNC or matters of national security could be high crimes and thus impeachable, but the conduct at issue seems of a different character....

Mr. Chairman, we must guard against turning our system into a parliamentary one where a national election can be negated by a legislative no-confidence vote. This is particularly true because the Congress has another tool with which to express its strong disapproval of the president's actions—a concurrent resolution of censure....

Some argue that a censure resolution would injure the presidency by setting a precedent that would censure commonplace. I have no doubt that censure resolutions, if judgment is not exercised and partisanship abounds, could be used unwisely to weaken the presidency. But how much more harm would be caused by impeaching a president for actions that, while deplorable, do not amount to "great and dangerous offenses" against the state or require his removal to protect the nation?...

The back-and-forth between committee members and witnesses covered mostly familiar ground. The Democrats attacked the process, Kenneth Starr's methods, and the all-or-nothing decision they were being forced to confront, while Republicans stressed that the president's defenders were not disputing the facts, and that in attacking the process, they were simply trying to divert attention from his misdeeds.

The evening's questioning did bring up a few new issues. Ben-Veniste, for instance, thought it very strange that Lucianne Goldberg had never been put before a grand jury, and he suggested, in response to a question from California Democrat Zoe Lofgren, that the committee should be looking hard at whether "somebody has set up something in motion to take [the president] down." Immediately following that testimony, Republican Bob Inglis of South Carolina asked Ben-Veniste about what he called a "regular," perhaps daily, conference call from the White House aimed at coordinating communications efforts. Had Ben-Veniste, Inglis asked, "participated in calls that sort of coordinated the attack on Ken Starr?" No, replied Ben-Veniste, he had not—although he had "on an irregular basis" been part of a conference call.

Virginia Republican Bob Goodlatte asked the witnesses to repeat something they had mentioned earlier: that they did not consider the standards in the Nixon im-

peachment to be a threshold for all impeachment. They agreed, in Hamilton's words, that the Nixon standards did not "set the bottom position of the bar," but that they "are indicative of the type of conduct we should look at." Goodlatte responded: "I think that the whole purpose of the White House's presentation today has been to try to raise the bar to that standard."

WITNESSES FOR THE DEFENSE, DAY TWO

Chairman Hyde swore in the last panel of witnesses invited by the White House, then introduced them to the committee:

Thomas P. Sullivan, a senior partner at Jenner & Block in Illinois, specializing in civil and criminal trial and appellate litigation, a former United States attorney for the northern district of Illinois.

Richard Davis, a partner with the New York law firm of Weil, Gotschal & Manges, an assistant U.S. attorney from 1970 through 1973 and task force leader for the Watergate special prosecution force, 1973–1975.

Edward S.G. Dennis Jr., a partner in the litigation section of the Philadelphia law firm of Morgan, Lewis & Bockius and former acting deputy attorney general of the United States.

William F. Weld, former Republican governor of Massachusetts, a counsel with the House Judiciary Committee during the Watergate inquiry and head of the criminal division at the Justice Department under Ronald Reagan, currently a partner in the Chicago law firm of McDermott, Will & Emery.

Ronald Noble, associate professor of law at New York University Law School, former undersecretary of the Treasury for enforcement and deputy assistant attorney general and chief of staff in the criminal division of the Department of Justice.

The chair recognized Thomas Sullivan.

Mr. Sullivan: ... In the federal criminal justice system, indictments for obstruction of justice and perjury are relatively rare. There are several reasons. One is that charges of obstruction and perjury are not substantive crimes but rather have to do with circumstances peripheral to underlying criminal conduct....

Second, charges of obstruction and perjury are difficult to prove, because the legislature and the courts have erected certain safeguards for those accused of these "ripple effect" crimes, and these safeguards act as hurdles for prosecutors.

The law of perjury can be particularly arcane, including the requirements that the government prove beyond a reasonable doubt that the defendant knew his testimony to be false at the time he or she testified, that the alleged false testimony was material and that any ambiguity or uncertainty about what the question or answer meant must be construed in favor of the defendant. Both perjury and obstruction of justice are what are known as specific intent crimes, putting a heavy burden on the prosecutor to establish the defendant's state of mind. Furthermore, because perjury and obstruction charges often arise from private dealings...the courts have required either two witnesses who testified directly to the facts establishing the crime or, if only one witness testifies to the facts constituting the alleged perjury, that there be substantial corroborating proof....

Responsible prosecutors do not bring these charges lightly.

There is another cautionary note.... Federal prosecutors do not use the criminal process in connection with civil litigation involving private parties. The reasons are obvious. If the federal prosecutors got involved in charges and counter-charges of perjury and obstruction of justice in discovery or trial of civil cases, there would be little time left for the kinds of important matters that are the major targets of the Department of Justice criminal guidelines....

The ultimate issue for a prosecutor deciding whether or not to seek an indictment is whether he or she is convinced that the evidence is sufficient to obtain a conviction—that is, whether there is proof beyond a reasonable doubt that the defendant committed the crime. This is far more than a probable cause standard, which is the test by which grand jury indictments are judged....

It is my opinion that the case set out in the Starr report would not be prosecuted as a criminal case by a responsible federal prosecutor.

Before addressing the specific facts...let me say that in conversations with many current and former federal prosecutors in whose judgment I have great faith, virtually all concur that if the president were not involved—if an ordinary citizen were the subject of the inquiry—no serious consideration would be given to a criminal prosecution arising from alleged misconduct in discovery in the *Jones* civil case, having to do with an alleged cover-up of a private sexual affair with another woman, or the follow-on testimony before the grand jury. This case ... would be declined out of hand.

... I would like to address several of the specific charges in the Starr Report. The first has to do with perjury in the president's deposition and before the grand jury about whether or not he had a sexual affair, relationship or relations with Ms. Lewinsky. The president denied that he did based on his understanding of the definition of the term "sexual relations" adopted by the court in the *Jones* case. That definition is difficult to parse ... but it is clear to me that the president's interpretation is a reasonable one, especially because the words which seem to describe directly oral sex were stricken from the definition by the judge. In a perjury prosecution, the government must prove beyond a reasonable doubt that the defendant knew when he gave the testimony that he was telling a falsehood; the lie must be knowing and deliberate. It is not perjury for a witness to evade, obfuscate or answer non-responsively. The evidence simply does not support the conclusion that the president knowingly committed perjury....

Let me turn to the issue of obstruction through delivery of the gifts [by] Ms. Lewinsky [to] Ms. Currie.... The evidence is that when talking to the president, Ms. Lewinsky brought up the subject of having Mrs. Currie hold the gifts, and the president either failed to respond or said "I don't know," or "I'll think about it." According to Mrs. Currie, Ms. Lewinsky called Mrs. Currie and asked Mrs. Currie to come to Ms. Lewinsky's home to take the gifts, and Mrs. Currie did so. Ms. Lewinsky testified that Mrs. Currie placed the call to Ms. Lewinsky. But the central point is that neither Mrs. Currie nor Ms. Lewinsky testified that the president suggested to Ms. Lewinsky that she hide the gifts, or that the president told Mrs. Currie to get the gifts from Ms. Lewinsky.

Under these circumstances, it is my view that a responsible prosecutor would not charge the president with obstruction, because there is no evidence sufficient to establish beyond a reasonable doubt that the president was involved. Indeed, it seems likely that Ms. Lewinsky was the sole moving force, having broached the idea to the president ... called Mrs. Currie to take the gifts, without the president's knowledge or encouragement. That is not the stuff of which an obstruction charge is made....

Time does not permit me to go through all of the allegations of misconduct in the Starr Report. Suffice it to say, that in my opinion, none of them is of the nature which a responsible federal prosecutor would present to a grand jury for indictment.

The chair now recognized Richard Davis.

Mr. Davis: ... Simply stated, no prosecutor should bring a case if he or she does not believe that based upon the facts and the law, it is more likely than not that they will prevail at trial. Cases that are likely to be lost cannot be brought simply to make a point or to express a sense of moral outrage....

I would respectfully suggest that the same principle should guide the House of Representatives as it determines to, in effect, make the decision as to whether to commence a "prosecution" by impeaching the president. Indeed, if anything, the strength of the evidence should be greater to justify impeachment than to file a criminal case.

In the context of perjury prosecutions, there are some specific considerations which are present when deciding whether such a case can be won.

First, it is virtually unheard of to bring a perjury prosecution based solely on the conflicting testimony of two people.... The inherent problems in bringing such a case are compounded to the extent that any credibility issues exist as to the government's sole witness.

Second, questions and answers are often imprecise. Questions sometimes are vague or use too narrowly defined terms, and interrogators frequently ask compound or inarticulate questions, and fail to follow up imprecise answers. Witnesses often meander through an answer, wandering around a question, but never really answering it.... [T]his makes perjury prosecutions difficult, because the prosecutor must establish that the witness understood the question, intended to give a false, not simply an evasive, answer and, in fact, did so. The problem of establishing such intentional falsity is compounded in civil cases by the reality that lawyers routinely counsel their clients to answer only the question asked, not to volunteer and not to help out an inarticulate questioner....

Third, prosecutors often need to assess the veracity of an "I don't recall" answer. Like other answers, such a response can be true or false, but it is a heavy burden to prove that a witness truly remembered the fact at issue....

I will now turn to the issue of whether, from the perspective of a prosecutor, there exists a prosecutable case for perjury in front of the grand jury. The answer to me is clearly no. The president acknowledged to the grand jury the existence of an improper intimate relationship with Monica Lewinsky, but argued with the prosecutors questioning him that his acknowledged conduct was not a sexual relationship as he understood the definition of that term being used in the *Jones* deposition. Engaging in such a debate ... simply does not form the basis for a perjury prosecution.

Indeed, in the end the entire basis for a grand jury perjury prosecution comes down to Monica Lewinsky's assertion that there was a reciprocal nature to their relationship in that the president touched her private parts with the intent to arouse or gratify her, and the president's denial that he did so. Putting aside whether this is the type of difference of testimony which should justify an impeachment of a president, I do not believe that a case involving this kind of conflict between two witnesses would be brought by a prosecutor. ...

A prosecutor would understand the problem created by the fact that both individuals had an incentive to lie—the president to avoid acknowledging a false statement at his civil deposition and Miss Lewinsky to avoid the demeaning nature of providing wholly unreciprocated sex. Indeed, this incentive existed when Miss Lewinsky described the relationship to the confidants described in the independent counsel's referral. Equally as important, however, Mr. Starr has himself questioned the veracity of his one witness capable of contradicting the president—Miss Lewinsky—by questioning her testimony that his office suggested she tape record Ms. Currie, Mr. Jordan and potentially the president. ...

It also is extraordinarily unlikely that in ordinary circumstances a prosecutor would bring a prosecution for perjury in the president's civil deposition in the *Jones* case. First ... with perjury prosecutions involving civil cases being rare, it would be even more unusual to see such a prosecution where the case had been dismissed on unrelated grounds and then settled, particularly where the settlement occurred after disclosure of the purported false testimony.

Second ... perjury prosecutions are generally filed where the false statement goes to the core of the matter under inquiry. Indeed, in order to prevail in a perjury prosecution, the prosecutor must establish ... that the purported false testimony was material. ...

Here, the *Jones* case was about whether then-governor Clinton sought unwanted sexual favors from a state employee in Arkansas. Monica Lewinsky herself had nothing to do with the facts at issue in that suit.... Given the lack of connection between these two events ... her purely consensual relationship with the president half a decade later would, I believe, not have even been admissible at any ultimate trial of the *Jones* case. While the court allowed questioning in the civil deposition about this matter, the judge did so under the very broad standard used in civil discovery. Indeed ... after the controversy about the president's relationship with Miss Lewinsky arose, the court considered this testimony sufficiently immaterial so as to preclude testimony about it at the trial.

Finally, the ability to prove the intentional making of false statements in the civil deposition is compounded by inexact questions, evasive and inconsistent answers, insufficient follow-up by the questioner, and reliance by the examiner on a definition of sexual relations rather than asking about specific acts.... This simply is not the stuff of criminal prosecution.

Turning to the issues of obstruction of justice involving the *Paula Jones* case, a prosecutor analyzing the case would be affected by many of the same weaknesses that are discussed above....

In August 1974, prior to the pardon, the Watergate Special Prosecution Force commenced the extraordinarily difficult process of determining whether to indict then former President Nixon.... I articulated two primary and competing considerations which I believed it appropriate for us ... to consider. The first factor was to avoid a sense of a double standard by declining to prosecute a plainly guilty person because he had been president. The second was that prosecutors should not proceed with even provable charges if they conclude that important and valid societal benefits would be sacrificed by doing so.... I believe today, 25 years later, that it is still appropriate for those deciding whether to bring charges to consider these factors....

Chairman Hyde next recognized Edward Dennis Jr.

Mr. Dennis: ... I am opposed to the impeachment of President Clinton. My opposition is grounded in part in my belief that a criminal conviction would be extremely difficult to obtain in a court of law due to weak proof of the criminal intent of the president, the questionable materiality of the Lewinsky affair to the proceedings in which it was raised and the probable sympathy a jury would have for any person charged with perjury for dancing around questions put to them that demanded an admission of marital infidelity....

Perjury and obstruction of justice are serious offenses. They are felonies. However, in my experience perjury or obstruction of justice prosecutions of parties in private civil litigation are rare.... The oath taken by witnesses demands truthful testimony at depositions and in grand jury proceedings. Nonetheless, imprecise, ambiguous, evasive and even misleading responses to questions don't support perjury prosecutions... Proof that a witness's testimony is untrue is not sufficient alone to prove perjury, and to prove that a witness is intentionally evasive or nonresponsive is not sufficient to prove perjury either. Courts are rigorously literal in passing on questions of ambiguity in the questions and the responses of witnesses under oath, and generally give the accused the benefit of any doubt....

I believe the question of whether there were sexual relations between the president and Ms. Lewinsky is collateral to the harassment claim in the *Jones* case. The president has confessed to an inappropriate relationship with Ms. Lewinsky. The *Jones* case was dismissed and is now settled. These circumstances simply would not warrant the bringing of a criminal prosecution, and a criminal prosecution would most likely fail....

The consequences of the impeachment of the president of the United States are far reaching. These consequences are grave, and impact the entire nation.... Where there is serious doubt, as there must be in this case, prudence demands that Congress defer to the electoral mandate....

The next witness was Ronald Noble.

Mr. Noble: ... When investigating a possible violation of the law, every federal prosecutor must heed the guidelines of the Department of Justice. DOJ guidelines recognize that a criminal prosecution "entails profound consequences for the accused and the family of the accused whether or not a conviction ultimately results." Career federal prosecutors recognize that "federal law enforcement resources and federal judicial resources are not sufficient to permit prosecution of every alleged offense over which federal jurisdiction exists." Federal prosecutors are told to consider the nature and seriousness of the offense, as well as available taxpayer resources.... Federal prosecutors "may properly weigh such questions as to whether the violation is technical or relatively inconsequential in nature, and what the public attitude is towards prosecution under the circumstances of the case." ...

Prosecutors are admonished not to "recommend in an indictment charges that they cannot reasonably expect to prove beyond a reasonable doubt by the legally sufficient evidence at trial." It is one of the most important criteria that prosecutors must consider. Prosecution should never be brought where probable cause does not exist, and "both as a matter of fundamental fairness and in the interest of the efficient administration of justice, no prosecution should be initiated against any person unless the government believes that the person will be found guilty by an unbiased trier of fact." ...

...As a general matter, federal prosecutors are not asked to bring federal criminal charges against individuals who allegedly perjure themselves in connection with civil lawsuits. As a rule, federal prosecutors on their own do not seek to bring criminal charges against people who perjure themselves in connection with civil depositions. This would open a floodgate of referrals. Parties by definition are biased, and it would be difficult to discount the potential bias. ...

Notwithstanding the reasons generally, there are 10 good reasons ... which support the view that a career federal prosecutor, asked to investigate allegations like those in the Clinton-Lewinsky matter, would not pursue federal criminal prosecution.

1. The alleged perjury occurred in a civil deposition and concerned private, lawful, sexual conduct between consenting adults.
2. The alleged perjured testimony was deemed inadmissible by the trial judge.
3. That evidence arguably was dismissed as immaterial by the trial judge.
4. In any event, the alleged perjured testimony was at most marginally relevant.
5. The alleged perjured testimony did not affect the outcome of the case.
6. The parties settled and a court dismissed the underlying civil lawsuit.
7. The settlement of the suit prevented the appellate court from ruling on a dismissal and on the materiality of alleged perjured testimony.
8. The theoretically harmed party knew of the alleged perjury prior to settlement.
9. Alleged political enemies of the defendant funded the plaintiff's suit.
10. A federal government informant conspired with one of the civil litigants to trap the alleged perjurer into perjuring himself.

...Even a prosecutor with exceptional judgment might be tempted by the challenge of bringing down a president. A prosecutor with unchecked power, unlimited resources and only one target might find the temptation even stronger. ...

For this reason, a prosecutor or a committee assigned such a case must strive to be objective—knowing that criticism of bias will be unavoidable. In the prosecutorial context, a 13-to-10 vote by the grand jury constitutes enough votes to proceed, but reflects that there must be, or might be, a serious problem with some aspect of the case. Similarly, a vote for impeachment based on a party-line vote or near party-line vote is a signal that something is wrong with the case and that the case may not be worth pursuing. This is particularly true where the overwhelming majority of Americans appear to be well-informed about the allegations and unbiased as a group, yet they do not want this president impeached. While indictments and impeachment proceedings are different, they carry at least two similarities: One, most of us know it when we see the clear cases for criminal conviction and for impeachment. Two, public confidence in the rule of law and our system of government would suffer if we regularly indicted cases or impeached presidents only to have juries or the Senate vote to acquit....

Chairman Hyde recognized the last panel member, William Weld.

Mr. Weld: ... I am no Tom Sullivan, but I have knocked around the criminal justice world a little bit. From 1986 to 1988, under President Reagan, I was the assistant attorney general in charge of the criminal division in Washington, which is relevant because that's the ... political appointment charged with ensuring the uniformity of charging decisions, decisions whether to seek an indictment around the country in various districts. Prior to that, for five years, I was the United States Attorney in Massachusetts, and I became familiar in the course of that seven years with the handbook, the *Principles of Federal Prosecution,* and with the United States Attorney's Manual and, when I was in Washington, with the practices and procedures that also have been developed over the years to try to ensure uniformity in charging decisions.

It so happens that in 1974, for nine months, I also worked for this committee under Chairman Rodino on the impeachment inquiry into President Nixon, and I worked on the constitutional and legal unit there, which was charged with reading every precedent ... having any relevance at all to what high crimes and misdemeanors means in the United States Constitution.

Like Mr. Sullivan, like many others, I do not consider myself an advocate here before you. I do have a couple of points of view that I would like to share with the members of the committee....

I do believe, Mr. Chairman, that during the Reagan administration, it was not the policy of the U.S. Justice Department to seek indictments solely on the basis that a prospective defendant had committed adultery or fornication.... It was also not the policy to seek an indictment based solely on evidence that a prospective defendant had falsely denied committing unlawful adultery or fornication....

Until this year, the policy of the Department of Justice was that in cases of false statements they would not seek an indictment solely on the basis of somebody denying that they themselves had committed misconduct. This is called the "exculpatory no" doctrine, and it was adopted in a lot of circuits. It was kicked out by the Supreme court in a decision by Justice Scalia early this year based on bad facts....

[O]n the law of impeachment, I am pretty well convinced that adultery, fornication or even a false denial...of adultery or fornication do not constitute high crimes and misdemeanors within the meaning of the impeachment clause of the U.S. Constitution. They are not offenses against the system of government. They don't imperil the structure of our government.

Impeachment, Weld argued, is a "prophylactic" remedy, not a punitive one. In his view, this case demanded something other than impeachment—but something more than censure. Among his suggestions: that the grand jury issue a detailed report on its findings; that the president acknowledge in writing his wrongdoing in language negotiated to make clear its gravity; that he pay a fine; and finally, that he be forced to "take his chances with respect to the criminal justice process" after leaving office.

The committee then turned to questions for the last panel of White House witnesses. John Conyers called it "one of the most important panels that we've had before us." And toward the end of the session, he cited what he saw as its primary lesson: "If no ordinary citizen would face a criminal prosecution based on these allegations, how can it be argued that to decline to vote for impeachment places the president above the law?" Even some Republicans remarked on the strength of the legal analysis. Charles Canady of Florida declared them "some of the best arguments in defense of this president."

But not all of his colleagues agreed. Bob Inglis of South Carolina continued his tally on the presentation of "facts": "The score now is zero to four; zero panels, zero witnesses dealing with facts. Everybody that we've heard from in these four panels has given conclusions, has given legal opinions. Not a single person has presented a fact."

Steven Rothman of New Jersey complained that the Republicans, too, had failed to call fact witnesses "to aid us in finding the truth." He also asked, rhetorically: "Should we...say the founders got it wrong, that they should have added 'evasiveness' as a high crime or misdemeanor...?"

And Republican Lindsey Graham of South Carolina ended with a rhetorical flourish of his own: "Governor Weld, you're the governor. There's a person out there that ... could hurt you legally and politically. If you used the resources of the governorship, if you got people in your office to plant lies, falsehoods, malicious rumors, and tried to use your office ... to trash out that potential witness against you, what should be your fate?" Mr. Weld's reply: "Well, in a clear enough case, my fate should be 'out of here.' "

After a half-hour recess, the committee returned to hear testimony from Charles F.C. Ruff, Counsel to the President—who, as Chairman Hyde pointed out, had also served as the final Watergate Special Prosecutor.

Mr. Ruff: ... [A]s counsel to the president, I appear before you today on behalf of the person who under our Constitution has twice been chosen by the people to head one of the three coordinate branches of government. Necessarily, I appear also on behalf of the man whose conduct has brought us to what for all of us is this unwelcome moment. Neither the president nor anyone speaking on his behalf will defend the morality of his personal conduct. The president had a wrongful relationship with Monica Lewinsky. He misled his family, his friends, his colleagues and the public, and in doing so, he betrayed the trust placed in him not only by his loved ones but by the American people.

The president knows that what he did was wrong. He has admitted it. He has suffered privately and publicly. He is prepared to accept the obloquy that flows from his misconduct, and he recognizes that, like any citizen, he is and will be subject to the rule of law. But ... the president has not committed a high crime or misdemeanor. His conduct, although morally reprehensible, does not warrant impeachment....

... I suggest to you that any fair-minded observer must conclude that the great weight of the historical and scholarly evidence leads to the conclusion that in order to have committed an impeachable offense, the president must have acted to subvert our system of government. And members of the committee, that did not happen....

... This committee has determined in its wisdom simply to accept at face value all of the conclusions reached in the independent counsel's referral and to look to whatever backup information was provided in support of those conclusions. But with that decision, I suggest to you, comes the obligation to look into that record and to ask what the witnesses really said....

What we tried to do in the submission that we gave to the committee yesterday, and what I will do much more briefly today, is to show you that your premise is wrong; that the very record on which you rely does not support the conclusion it purports to reach....

I need to stop here because I want to address an issue that probably has been heard bruited about more frequently than any other over the course of this committee's work, and it falls under the heading, I suppose, of legalisms.

What are they? Well, whatever they are, they have caused a great deal of pain to those of us engaged in trying to represent the president over the last many months. I and my fellow lawyers have been accused by the media and by some of you, heaven forfend, of actually employing legalisms in defending our client. And, Mr. Chairman, I have to plead guilty...on behalf of every lawyer who ever argued some point of law or nuanced fact to establish his client's innocence. But I am worried here...that our sometimes irresistible urge to practice our profession will stand in the way of securing a just result in this very grave proceeding for this very special client.

However, I do suggest that it is not legalistic to point out that the president did not say what some accuse him of saying. It is not legalistic to point out that a witness did not say what some rely on her testimony to establish. It is not legalistic to point out that a witness was asked poorly framed or ambiguous questions, and it is not legalistic to argue that a witness's answer was technically true, even if not complete. Yet, however proper it may be to make those arguments in a proceeding such as this one and for a witness such as the president, there is a risk that they will get in the way of answering the ultimate question: Did the president do something so wrong and so destructive of his constitutional capacity to govern that he should be impeached?

Even if we were successful, as I am confident we would be, in defending the president in a courtroom, that would not suffice to answer that question. For it is within your power...to decide that even though there is insufficient proof to establish that the president committed perjury, he nonetheless should be impeached. But I suggest to you that even then, our oft-criticized legalisms are relevant to you. They are relevant because they...reflect the judgments of lawyers, of judges, and, yes, legislators through the centuries that we must take special care when we seek to accuse a witness of having violated his oath.

Among the protections that the law has created...are the requirement that the witness intentionally testified falsely; that his testimony be material; the requirement that the question not be ambiguous; that the burden is on the questioner to ask the right question; and that the witness may be truthful but nonetheless misleading, without having violated the law....

The Office of Independent Counsel would have the committee believe that in three respects the president committed perjury in his testimony before the grand jury: first, by stating that his relationship with Ms. Lewinsky began in February 1996 rather than November 1995; second, by stating that he believed that a particular form of intimate activity was not covered by the definition of sexual relations approved by Judge Wright in the *Jones* case; and third, by stating that he had not engaged in specific types of sexual conduct, theoretically in order to conform his testimony to his civil deposition.

Now as to the first of these, you must begin your consideration with the proposition that the president acknowledged to the grand jury that he did have a wrongful intimate relationship with Ms. Lewinsky. What then might have led him to change by three months the date on which that relationship began? Well, the referral surmises, it must have been because although the president was prepared to make the most devastating admission of misconduct any husband and father could imagine, he still wanted to have the grand jury believe that when their relationship began, Ms. Lewinsky was a 22-year-old employee rather than a 22-year-old intern....

Well, putting aside for the moment the fact that under no circumstances would any reasonable prosecutor or any judge or jury find such a discrepancy material, there is absolutely no proof of any such purpose on the president's part. Not one witness, including Ms. Lewinsky, even suggested such a thing. The only proof the referral offers is...the contention that the president's concern about...Ms. Lewinsky's badge reflected concern about her status, that is as an intern, rather than, as was clearly the case, her ability to move freely in the West Wing of the White House....

As to the second of the three perjury allegations, the independent counsel would have the committee find that the president testified falsely because the independent counsel has concluded that the president's statement of his own belief in the meaning of the definition of sexual relations in the *Jones* case is not credible. At least here the independent counsel is candid enough to acknowledge that he has no evidentiary basis for that conclusion....

I suggest that those of you who have been prosecutors know as a matter of practical experience, and those of you who have not been prosecutors or even lawyers know as a matter of common sense, that no one could or would ever be charged with perjury because the prosecutor did not find credible a witness's statement of his personal belief, much less his personal belief about the meaning of a definition used in a civil deposition.

And so we come to the third. The referral alleges that the president lied when he admitted having one form of sexual contact with Ms. Lewinsky but denied having certain other forms of contact...in order to make his grand jury testimony consistent with the definition under which he testified in the *Jones* deposition. We will not drag the committee into the salacious muck that fills the referral. Instead, let each member assume that Ms. Lewinsky's version of the events is correct; and then ask, am I prepared to impeach the president because, after having admitted having engaged in egregiously wrongful conduct, he falsely described the particulars of that conduct?

Let each member even assume that the president testified as he did because he did not want to admit that in a civil deposition, confronted with a narrowly, indeed oddly, framed definition, he had succeeded in misleading opposing counsel; and then ask yourself, am I prepared to impeach the president for that?

The answer must be no.

...When one scrapes all the rhetoric, what one finds is this: The referral alleges that the president lied to a grand jury about the details of sexual conduct, not to conceal his wrongful relationship with a 22-year-old employee, but to avoid admitting in a civil deposition he misled plaintiff's counsel about an embarrassing matter that the court ultimately found immaterial.

Now, I do not in any sense, and nor would any of my colleagues, suggest that we take false testimony lightly.... What we do suggest is that if you were to conclude as to this aspect of their relationship that Ms. Lewinsky was telling you the truth and the president was not, you...should conclude that his conduct was wrong, deserving of severe condemnation; but you could not in good conscience and consistent with your constitutional responsibility conclude that the president should be impeached.

Surely the same result must follow to the extent that the referral alleges that the president committed perjury in the *Jones* deposition.

As any fair reading of the deposition must conclude, the questions were oddly and vaguely framed. The *Jones* counsel didn't follow up when they had the opportunity. Counsel were indeed invited, by the president's lawyer, to ask specific detailed questions and declined to do so. They decided to proceed on the basis of a truncated, artificial definition of sexual relations.

The president has said that he made no effort to be helpful, that he did not want to reveal his relationship, understandably. His answers were frequently evasive and incomplete, as my colleague, Mr. Craig, said yesterday, even maddening. They were misleading but they were not perjurious. And a fortiori, they cannot be the basis for an impeachment....

Let me just touch on two examples that demonstrate, I believe, how the committee can be misled by the referral into assuming a reality that does not exist.

First is the independent counsel's charge that the president conspired with Ms. Lewinsky to conceal gifts he had given her. The central events, as the independent counsel has described them, are these: that on Sunday, December 28th, 1997, Ms. Lewinsky visited the president at the White House. The independent counsel alleges ... "they discussed the fact that she had received a subpoena to testify in the *Jones* case and to produce any gifts that she had."

The president then gave Ms. Lewinsky a number of gifts because he believed she was moving to New York and it was Christmas time.

She went back to her apartment and sometime thereafter, on that day, according to the independent counsel, Betty Currie, the president's secretary, called and told Ms. Lewinsky that she understood that Ms. Lewinsky had something for her. Ms. Currie then drove to Ms. Lewinsky's apartment, took the gifts from her and put them under her bed....

[B]egin by noting that there is not one single suggestion anywhere in any testimony that the president suggested, brought up, hinted at the notion of Ms. Lewinsky's concealing these gifts....

Note as well that there is not one iota of proof that the president ever even mentioned Betty Currie in the context of this gift discussion. Note as well that Monica Lewinsky gave at least 10 ... versions of this event. The independent counsel chose one, the one ... most reflective of what that office believed to have been improper conduct.... They don't tell you about all of the ones in which Ms. Lewinsky doesn't mention the president saying anything to her or, at worst, says, "hmm, I will think about it."...

And if you move to the issue of who triggered the picking up of the gifts, you face a comparable problem. According to what I have to say is a simplistic summation by the Office of Independent Counsel, it is easy. Betty Currie called Monica Lewinsky; said, the president tells me you've got something for me to pick up, or I understand that you have something for me to pick up....

The problem is, Betty Currie says she never had such a conversation with the president. Betty Currie says, Monica Lewinsky called me. The president says he never had such a conversation with Betty Currie; didn't know anything about Betty Currie going to pick up gifts....

Indeed, presumably it is the independent counsel's theory that the reason for this transfer of the gifts from Monica Lewinsky to Betty Currie had directly to do with the *Jones* subpoena. The problem with that is that what Betty Currie says about her conversations with Monica Lewinsky is ... references to people asking about the gifts and, in particular, a reporter, Michael Isikoff....?

But let me point not to conflicting testimony.... Let me point to the actual events about which there is no conflict on December 28th. On that day, the president gave gifts to Ms. Lewinsky. The independent counsel would have this committee believe that on the very day in which the president and Ms. Lewinsky, and maybe Betty Currie, are conspiring to get rid of the gifts that she already had, the president added to the pile....

Let me just briefly suggest to you that a similar analysis on the issue of the job search leads to the same result. The referral would have you believe that there was an inextricable link between the assistance given to Monica Lewinsky in searching for a job and her role in the *Jones* case, either as a witness or in connection with her affidavit. It does so ... by offering a chronology that essentially focuses only on the events of late December and January.... [Y]ou will see that they talk about what happens on January 5th, Monica Lewinsky declines the U.N. job; January 7th, Monica Lewinsky signs the affidavit and Vernon Jordan informs the president that the affidavit has been signed. January 8th, the very next day, Ms. Lewinsky is interviewed by MacAndrews & Forbes, on Vernon Jordan's recommendation. Shortly thereafter, after it is reported that that interview did not go very well, Vernon Jordan calls Ron Perelman, and ultimately Ms. Lewinsky is reinterviewed and offered a job.

What could possibly be more incriminating?

Well, you might want to know, as I am sure you do if you have done your homework ... that Monica Lewinsky was looking for a job months before any of this ever happened. Mainly, candidly, she wanted a job in the White House....

Now, there was one person who I guarantee you ... could have gotten her a job in the White House. That's the president of the United States. It didn't happen; never pushed the button, never called anybody and said put her back in legislative affairs.... Strange.

Indeed if you look at the record, you will see that the president gave only limited assistance to Ms. Lewinsky in her job search, never put any pressure on anybody. Vernon Jordan has helped a lot of people in this town and he helped Monica Lewinsky, and he didn't do it because she was a witness in the *Jones* case or because she was going to file an affidavit....

You will search the referral in vain for an honest description of these events....

And one last piece on this subject. To the extent that it has been suggested that there was some linkage between the job search and the filing of her affidavit in the *Jones* case, I direct your attention to Ms. Lewinsky's interview with the FBI on July 27 in which she said, as clearly as anybody possibly could, there was no agreement to sign the affidavit in return for a job.... And there is, of course, Ms. Lewinsky's statement in the grand jury ... in response to a question from a conscientious grand juror ... "I think because of the public nature of how this investigation has been and what the charges have been that are aired, I would just like to say that no one ever asked me to lie. I was never promised a job for my silence."

. . . Now, one cannot read the independent counsel's description of what happened in the executive privilege area and come away, I think, with any true understanding of what happened. There is no indication of our efforts to accommodate, no indication that we understood the need to provide facts about the underlying conduct at issue, indeed no indication that we produced thousands and thousands of documents without ever once raising the issue of executive privilege.

Instead what happened is that the Office of Independent Counsel took the position that executive privilege simply didn't apply at all to his inquiry because it all arose out of the personal conduct of the president, and we litigated that issue ... on the ground that we weren't seeking to protect information about the president's personal conduct, what we were seeking to protect was the advice he was getting and the discussions that he was having among senior advisers with respect to ... his official business ...

We had state visits. We had the State of the Union Address. We had the core business of the president to worry about, and we told that to the judge, and guess what? Although you will never read it in the referral, the judge agreed with us. She said these conversations are presumptively privileged. And she instructed the independent counsel to ... demonstrate that their need for this information was greater than our interest in confidentiality, and only then did the independent counsel finally and reluctantly acknowledge that indeed executive privilege properly was asserted here. They made a showing to the judge.... The judge found that it overcame our interest in confidentiality, and that was the end of the assertion of executive privilege for Ms. Hernreich and Mr. Blumenthal,[1] the two non-lawyers involved. That all happened by March. There was no delay, no great hurdles to be overcome....

Now, if you ever had any question about the extent to which the independent counsel's referral sought to color, sought to paint the blackest picture of this insidious effort to assert a privilege... look to pages 207 and 208 of the referral.

...."The tactics employed by the White House have not been confined to the judicial process. On March 24, while the president was traveling in Africa, he was asked about the assertion of executive privilege. He responded, you should ask someone who knows. He also responded, I haven't discussed that with the lawyers, I don't know." And the referral said this was untrue. "Unbeknownst to the public, in a declaration filed in District Court on March 17, seven days before the president's public expression of ignorance, White House Counsel Charles F.C. Ruff"—that's me—"informed Chief Judge Johnson that he 'had discussed' the matter with the president, who had directed the assertion of executive privilege." ...

... [W]hat really happened was that I did, as my declaration says, consult with the president of the United States. He did authorize me to assert executive privilege. And... what really happened in March in Africa was not what the independent counsel said happened....

The actual exchange was this. Question by the press: "Mr. President, we haven't yet had the opportunity to ask you about your decision to invoke executive privilege. Why shouldn't the American people see that as an effort to hide something from them?"

The president: "Look, that is a question that is being asked and answered back home by the people responsible to do that. I don't believe I should be discussing that here."

Question: "Could you at least tell us why you think the First Lady may be covered by that privilege, why her conversation might fall under that?"

Answer...: "I haven't discussed it with the lawyers. I don't know. You should ask someone who does."

---

[1] White House aides Nancy Hernreich and Sidney Blumenthal.

By the way, the First Lady was found by Judge Johnson to be covered by the executive privilege, but it would have been nice, whatever argument the referral wanted to make, to at least put the full statement in the record....

. . . Only twice before has this committee ever voted out articles of impeachment against a president. Such a vote is not intended to say, well, we think there may be some reason to believe that William Clinton has done something wrong, but we will let the Senate sort out things at trial....

If there is any analogy to the grand jury, it is this, and you heard it from some of my former colleagues in the prosecution business.... For any professional prosecutor, the true test, and it is certainly true for serious cases, and one can conceive of no case more serious than this, is whether there is sufficient evidence on the basis of which a prosecutor could convince a jury beyond a reasonable doubt that an offense had been committed....

This is a matter of testing the charges that you're going to consider and asking yourself not would I win if I really litigated this in the Senate, but rather do I have enough evidence to justify putting the country through the horror that we all know will follow if, in fact, there is an impeachment.

In closing, I urge you to ask, as Senator Fessenden[2] asked 130 years ago, is the evidence before you of such character to commend itself at once to the minds of all right-thinking ... men as beyond all question an adequate cause for impeachment? And finally, ask what is best for our nation?

During the question-and-answer session, the Republicans repeatedly returned to the perjury charges, specifically, to whether the president had actually lied about his relationship with Monica Lewinsky in his Jones deposition, to the grand jury, to the American people. Each time the subject came up, Ruff repeated his view that while the president had knowingly made misleading statements, he had not really lied—and that, in any case, he had not committed perjury under the strict legal definitions of that offense.

In answer to a question from Elton Gallegly of California, Ruff explained: "[A]s misleading and evasive as the president's testimony in his deposition was, in my view, it represented, albeit perhaps an abortive effort to stay within some very narrow, strange boundaries and yet not to help—to be evasive." When Bob Inglis asked

---

[2] William Pitt Fessenden, U.S. Senator from Maine from 1855 to 1868, on the impeachment proceedings against President Andrew Johnson.

the difference between misleading and lying, Ruff replied: "Because he believed, rightly so in his own mind, that he was telling the truth, that he used the word 'sexual relations' to mean sexual intercourse and that he had not had sexual intercourse with Monica Lewinsky." But Charles Canady spoke for many Republicans when he said, "I am still frustrated by what I consider to be legal arguments that don't really meet the test of common sense and human experience." And Virginia's Bob Goodlatte repeated that when the president had denied "sexual relations with that woman" to the American people, his intent was "to avoid prosecution for a crime, that crime being perjury and obstruction of justice in the [Jones] case."

The Democrats, meanwhile, complimented Ruff on how clearly he had presented the president's case ("I think you have hit it out of the park," said Charles Schumer of New York). Texas's Sheila Jackson Lee pressed Ruff about how the Starr referral had misrepresented President Clinton's remarks about invoking executive privilege. Ruff explained that he believed the independent counsel had mistakenly relied upon an abbreviated account from the Washington Post, *which didn't give the full context of Clinton's comments, "So I don't attribute evil motive, but I do attribute error."*

At the very end of the session, Lindsey Graham read from the grand jury testimony of Clinton aide Sidney Blumenthal, in which Blumenthal recounted what the president had told him about Monica Lewinsky: "He said, 'Monica Lewinsky came at me and made a sexual demand on me.' He rebuffed her. He said 'I've gone down that road before, I've caused pain for a lot of people and I'm not going to do that again. She threatened me.' She said that she would tell people they had an affair and that she was known as the stalker among her peers and that she hated it and that if she had an affair or said she had an affair then she wouldn't be the stalker anymore."

Graham asked Ruff: "Do you agree with me that the president of the United States is telling an operative, for lack of a better word, that Monica Lewinsky was a sexual predator coming on to him?" Ruff replied that Graham's implication seemed to be "that this was somehow a directive to go out and trash Ms. Lewinsky or otherwise to denigrate her." He denied it. Graham then cited a number of media reports in the days and weeks following the Clinton-Blumenthal meeting—reports that attributed to White House sources comments critical of Ms. Lewinsky.

Graham voiced outrage. "This is something that is more than consensual sex," he said. "The president of the United States, I believe, planted stories that were false and shortly after those stories were planted, the White House operation went into effect, notifying the press that "if you ever hear anything about this witness, you need to know she's unreliable, she's a stalker, she's basically not a responsible person."

Ruff repeated his denial. "I absolutely reject the notion that the president of the United States either explicitly or implicitly authorized, directed, hinted at or caused any attack of the sort you describe."

Even as the White House witnesses were arguing their case, the Republican majority had been drafting four articles of impeachment. They charged the president with obstruction of justice, abuse of power, and two counts of perjury for statements about his relationship with Monica Lewinsky—in his civil deposition in the Jones case and before Starr's grand jury. Meanwhile, Democrats had been working on an alternative: a "sense of the Congress" resolution sharply censuring the president for his behavior. Hyde had agreed to allow a vote on the measure in the committee, and Democrats were lobbying House leaders for a vote by the full House.

After more than ten hours of testimony, the committee was adjourned.

THE SUMMATIONS

After a brief executive session, the committee heard the summations from Abbe Lowell, on behalf of the Democrats, and chief investigative counsel David Schippers, for the Republican majority. Lowell spoke first.

Mr. Lowell: ... There has been a lot of confusing talk about what an impeachment is. The minority staff has now pored over thousands of pages of constitutional history, legal articles and testimony, and we can begin this day, Mr. Chairman, explaining what an impeachment is not. Impeachment is not a means to punish the president. Impeachment is not a means to send a message to our children that the president isn't above the law. ...

Impeachment is not a penalty for the president not answering the 81 questions as some of you would have wished. Impeachment is not a form of rebuke or censure for the president's conduct. In fact, impeachment is not about the president's conduct. It is about Congress's conduct.

Just because the president might disgrace his office by his actions, and just because the independent counsel may have shown partiality and zeal in his investigation, this House can do better. The road to dishonor in office can end in this committee, in this room, on this very day. Because what an impeachment is, of course, is the single device to remove from the office the Chief Executive who you decide is constitutionally disqualified to serve, and by doing so overturn two national elections. ...

The public has been telling us for months and in every way they possibly can that they do not want to see a trial in the Senate where the issues will be about sex, and that they want there to be a censure or other alternatives to impeachment as the means to demonstrate that the president is not above the law. So before this week is out, I hope we listen to the wisdom of the nation as well....

We are not here to defend the president. He, better than anyone, has said that his conduct was not defensible, and he has apologized for it. We are here, however, to strenuously defend the requirements the Constitution poses on all of us before we would even consider the word "impeachment."...

Lowell then turned to some procedural concerns. He observed that the case against the president had been "something of a moving target": Kenneth Starr had originally proposed eleven grounds for impeachment; then, briefly, they had been "diced" by the majority counsel into fifteen grounds; finally, the evening before, the majority had produced four articles. "No matter how they are dressed up, redivided, renamed, reorganized or duplicated," said Lowell, "they all have the same central point: the president's improper relationship with Ms. Lewinsky, nothing more." And he protested, once again, that in the two articles charging perjury, "we cannot find... what statements the majority contends were lies." Then he turned back to the case:

For a week or more, the majority has stated that the president or the minority did not call fact witnesses. Mr. Inglis repeated that charge to White House counsel Ruff yesterday. But in America it should not have been our burden to do so. However, if it is fact witnesses you need, then it will be fact witnesses you get.

Mr. Chairman, on behalf of the minority, I now call to the stand Monica Lewinsky, Betty Currie, Vernon Jordan, Linda Tripp and the president of the United States. You see, their sworn testimony, contained in the same boxes on which majority counsel is relying to put forth articles of impeachment actually proves the president's case....

[I]f you truly want to go forward on impeachment based on what the president has admitted were strained and evasive answers to questions at the civil deposition, I thought you and the public should hear how this all first started.... I thought you should... hear the amazing exchange between three lawyers and a judge that went into the contorted definition of "sexual relations" at the *Paula Jones* deposition that has gotten us all here today....

Lowell then played the videotape of the president's deposition in the Jones case. In the segment, the lawyers for both sides and Judge Susan Webber Wright discuss the definition of "sexual relations" that Paula Jones's attorneys had chosen as the basis for their questions. The president's lawyer, Robert Bennett, repeatedly protests that the three-part definition is just too confusing. The Jones lawyers, says Bennett, should simply "ask the witness to describe as exactly as possible what occurred." But the Jones lawyers insist on the definition. The judge allows it, but strikes two parts of the definition on the ground that they are "just too broad." Bennett tries again: "[W]hat I don't want to do is . . . be asked questions and then we don't—we're all—we're ships passing in the night. They're thinking of one thing. He's thinking another. . . . He can ask the president: What did you do? He can ask him specifically in certain instances what he did. . . ." But the judge allows the definition, as amended, to stand.

Lowell continued:

Mr. Chairman . . . does anybody in this room, does anybody in the United States, have a clear conception of the definition of sexual relations, if those three people and that judge in that context had to spend that much time getting to the point? . . .

To those who would impeach the president and condemn him for not being more forthcoming in that deposition, put yourself in his position on that day. He was being set up by the *Paula Jones* attorneys and Linda Tripp, who had met with the Office of Independent Counsel just the day before. He knew that there was some collusion going on to embarrass him not about sexual harassment, but about a consensual affair. So his responses were an attempt to answer the questions evasively.

In the 20/20 hindsight of almost a year, we know he could have, should have, acted better. But are his responses to all those questions you put to White House counsel Ruff yesterday so hard to understand that you would impeach him for acting as anyone would in that circumstance?

In his grand jury appearance, the president explained his situation on that very day. And when you listen to what he is saying and put it in the context of what you now know was happening behind the scenes with Paula Jones and Linda Tripp and the attorneys, any fair-minded person would see that these were not impeachable reactions to that set-up predicament.

Lowell played a clip of the president's grand jury testimony. In it, Clinton explained that in the civil deposition, under attack by the Jones lawyers in what he viewed as a "bogus suit" and "unrelenting illegal leaks," he had "wanted to be legal without being particularly helpful." He added that Robert Bennett had invited the Jones lawyers to ask follow-up questions. "It now appears to me they didn't because they were afraid I would give them a truthful answer . . . and they were trying to set me up and trick me."

Lowell continued:

Despite this context, the majority staff has decided to include the civil deposition as a separate article for impeachment, perhaps to add the appearance of more wrongdoing. But . . . the context material we have just presented to the committee and to the public should put that attempt to rest and dispose of this article once and for all.

This would leave as the core of the perjury allegations the charge that the president lied under oath at his August 17th grand jury appearance. These are vaguely described in Article I.

Mr. Chairman, how did we get to perjury, which is what Article I suggests? Independent Counsel Starr's referral goes out of its way not to make a perjury charge, because that offense . . . is one of the hardest to prove. . . . And as all the federal prosecutors who testified here said, this would never be a real case in a real court. So if lawyers can conclude that this would not be charged as a crime, how do you as lawmakers allow it to be charged as a high crime?

. . . If it was President Clinton's lying about Ms. Lewinsky in the *Paula Jones* case that creates all of these impeachable offenses, then the committee and the House can resolve this issue by deciding the importance or impact of that statement in that specific case.

. . . When Judge Webber Wright . . . ruled on January 29th that the evidence about Ms. Lewinsky was "not essential to the core issues of the case" and "might even be inadmissible," when she made that same ruling on March 9, 1998, and when she ruled on April 1st that no matter what President Clinton did with Ms. Lewinsky, Paula Jones herself had not proven that she had been harmed, she gave this committee the ability to determine that the president's statements, whether truthful or not, were not of the grave constitutional significance to support an impeachment. . . .

But if reviewing the testimony in its proper context is not enough for the committee, and if it wants instead to go ahead with this article of impeachment, let us make sure that the committee, House Members who will voting on this on the floor, and the American people understand what will be the subject of a Senate trial.

[P]utting aside the majority's attempt to list as perjury charges that it makes in other places, there were three allegations of grand jury lies that I have to guess fit into the article's phrase about "the nature and details of the relationship." They are, first... the date when the relationship began; second, whether the president really believed that the term "sexual relations" did not include one type of sex; and third, whether the president touched Monica Lewinsky.

As to the date when the relationship began, the actual charge is that Monica Lewinsky testified that the affair began in November 1995, but the president said it started in February 1996. How can you in good faith ask this nation to endure a Senate trial to determine the difference between three months?...

The second allegation is that the president lied when he said his belief was that the phrase "sexual relations," as used in the *Paula Jones* deposition, did not include oral sex. When many in the majority asked how we can condone perjury in our society, this is the lie about which they are talking. How would you have a trial in the Senate to conclude whether the president was right about what he thought the phrase "sexual relations" meant? You heard and saw the gyrations that it took three lawyers and a judge to deal with this silly expression. So who would you call to determine that the president did not believe the interpretation? The answer is that you don't have to call anyone. You have enough information right now to conclude that such a trial is unnecessary....

But there is more. Listen to the witnesses, Monica Lewinsky and Linda Tripp, before the independent counsel confronted her, before she went back and forth over an immunity agreement, and before this became so important that the definition of sex will sink us into a constitutional quagmire. Listen to the woman who you would have the United States Senate call as a witness as she defines the term in the exact same way you now accuse the president of lying about:

[**Transcript of an Excerpt from One of Linda Tripp's Tapes**]
Ms. Lewinsky: We didn't have sex, Linda. Not—we didn't have sex.
Ms. Tripp: Well, what do you call it?
Ms. Lewinsky: We fooled around.
Ms. Tripp: Oh.
Ms. Lewinsky: Not sex.
Ms. Tripp: Oh, I don't know. I think if you go to—if you get a orgasm, that's having sex.
Ms. Lewinsky: No, it's not.

Ms. Tripp: Yes, it is.
Ms. Lewinsky: No, it's not. It's—
Ms. Tripp: It's not having—
Ms. Lewinsky: Having sex is having intercourse.

Where is the impeachable offense when the president's testimony and Ms. Lewinsky's are the same? Is this what you are going to bring to the floor of the Senate?

So the perjury that some in the majority have said tears at the fabric of our judicial system comes down to whether the president lied about whether he touched Ms. Lewinsky....

Finally, as to the article of perjury, some of the majority have now confused the three very precise allegations of lying in the referral with some general criticism of the president for stating that he didn't recall something or that he didn't remember the details of something. In fact, the majority staff has now included in Article IV the charge that the president abused his power by such statements in his answers to the 81 questions that were posed to him.

...Given statements from President Roosevelt's failure to remember that he promised military support for Panama in its conflict with Colombia over the canal, to President Reagan's failures to remember how funds flowed to the Contras, this committee should not make presidential lapses of memory into impeachable offenses or the office could go vacant forever....

As to Article III, alleging obstruction of justice, on October 5 we recognized that the charge, reminiscent to Watergate, was the most egregious of the four grounds alleged in the Starr referral.... [T]he charges are:

First, the president tried to have Miss Lewinsky submit a false affidavit;

Second, the president initiated a return of gifts he had sent Ms. Lewinsky so they would not be discovered in the *Paula Jones* case;

Third, the president sought to keep Miss Lewinsky quiet with a job; and

Fourth, the president sought to tamper with the testimony of Miss Currie.

Let me turn to each in order.... As to the claim the president [sought] to have Monica Lewinsky file a false affidavit,...both Miss Lewinsky and the president agreed with the very obvious point that she could have filed a completely truthful affidavit denying any sexual harassment and therefore avoided being called as a witness in the *Paula Jones* case.... What the president said was that Monica Lewinsky could file a completely honest and truthful affidavit in a suit about sexual harassment, saying she was not sexually harassed and by doing so, hopefully avoid having to be deposed. . . .

Then, members of the committee, read what Miss Lewinsky said the first time she ever came in to see the independent counsel, not after the sessions where they went over and over her testimony. She wrote in what the law calls a "proffer" the following statement: "Neither the president nor Mr. Jordan nor anyone on their behalf asked or encouraged me to lie." . . .

Add to your consideration Ms. Lewinsky's grand jury testimony about the affidavit when she stated that it could range between just somehow mentioning innocuous things to actually denying "sexual relations" as that term was defined.

If you want or if you need more evidence, you can find it in her August 6th grand jury appearance, when she was the one who admitted that she "would strongly resist" any attempt by President Clinton to make her reveal their relationship.

Do you want more evidence? Then consider that on this all-important issue of the president apparently, supposedly telling Ms. Lewinsky to file a false affidavit, she testified that when she asked the president if he wanted to see the affidavit, the president "told Ms. Lewinsky not to worry about the affidavit."

And finally, listen to Ms. Lewinsky, on December 22nd, 1997, give you the most important statement. . . . As to the president wanting or knowing about her lie, this is what she told Linda Tripp:

[Transcript of Audiotape]

Ms. Tripp: Mmm-hmm. He knows you're gonna lie. You've told him, haven't you?

Ms. Lewinsky: No.

. . . By the way, the witness, Ms. Lewinsky, also was uncontradicted in the 17 boxes of information that it was she, not President Clinton, who undertook each and every one of these steps that went beyond merely trying to deny their improper relationship. She invented the code names with Betty Currie; she, and no one else, was responsible for the talking points; she, with the prodding of Linda Tripp, not the president, decided to hide her dress; and it was her idea to delete e-mails and files from her computer.

For these acts, Ms. Lewinsky was given immunity, and the independent counsel and majority staff would have you vote that it was the president who obstructed justice. . . .

. . .

... Certainly the majority cannot claim to need a trial in the Senate for the issue of the gifts exchanged between the president and Ms. Lewinsky....

Ms. Lewinsky admitted that she raised the issue with the president, not vice versa. She offered sworn testimony describing this conversation on at least ten occasions. In seven of these, including the very first time she saw the independent counsel and the last time she saw the independent counsel, she indicated that the president never responded to this issue. In only two of all of her statements does she even state the outrageous lines leading to this article of impeachment, that all the president ever said on the subject of gifts, when she raised it about hiding them, giving them back, was "I don't know. Let me think about it." And then, Ms. Lewinsky said, "he left that topic."

This is hardly the stuff of obstruction. The independent counsel chose to state the president's response without bothering to tell you and the American people about the other nine times they asked Ms. Lewinsky the same question.

Well, let's call Betty Currie to the stand. Let her be the witness you want to hear from. She stated repeatedly that Ms. Lewinsky called her and raised picking up the gifts, and that the president never asked her to call Ms. Lewinsky. Here is her testimony.

She...said, "My recollection, the best I remember, is Monica calling me and asking me if I would hold some of the gifts for her. I said I would." The question was, "And did the president know you were holding these things?" Ms. Currie answered, "I don't know." Independent counsel asked, "Didn't he say to you that Monica had something for you to hold?" Ms. Currie answered, "I don't remember that. I don't."

Let me recall to the stand the president so that you can recall that it was he...who gave Ms. Lewinsky the proper advice.

[Transcript of Videotape from Clinton's Grand Jury Testimony]

Clinton: ... The reason I'm not sure it happened on the 28th is that my recollection is that Ms. Lewinsky said something to me like "What if they ask me about the gifts you've given me?"

That's the memory I have. That's why I question whether it happened on the 28th, because she had a subpoena with her—request for production. And I told her that if they asked her for gifts, she'd have to give them whatever she had; that that's what the law was.

... Finally, the evidence is uncontradicted as evidence could possibly be that on December 28, 1997 the president gave Ms. Lewinsky the most gifts he had ever given her on one day.... He did this after Ms. Lewinsky had been subpoenaed for gifts. And yet this charge, your article of impeachment, would have you believe that on December 28 he gave Ms. Lewinsky the gifts and a few hours later hatched some scheme and some conspiracy by asking Ms. Currie to go and retrieve the very gifts he had just given....

A damning allegation reminiscent of the worst of Watergate is when a president suborns perjury in another witness. That is what majority's proposed Article III suggests when it alleges that the president sought to influence the testimony of Betty Currie. But the actual evidence is not that the president was talking to Miss Currie as any potential witness, but that He was talking to his secretary about a media storm that was about to erupt....

On January 18, 1998, when the president called Miss Currie for a meeting ... the plain, uncontradicted and dispositive fact is simply this: Betty Currie was not listed as either a deposition or a trial witness ... and the article of impeachment is wrong to state the opposite....

Equally important ... President Clinton and Betty Currie, the only people involved in this event, both agree that the conversation on January 18 was not about testimony, was not intended to pressure her....

There has been so much misinformation about what was said between the president and Ms. Currie ... that perhaps it is best to let their own words speak for themselves. Let's recall the president to the stand first.

[Transcript of Excerpt of Clinton Testimony Before the Grand Jury]

(Unknown): How did you [happen to be] making this statement "I was never alone with her, right?"

Clinton: Well, first of all let's remember the context here. I did not, at that time, know of your involvement in this case. I just knew that obviously someone had given them a lot of information, some of which struck me as accurate, some of which struck me as dead wrong, but it led them to ask me a whole series of questions about Monica Lewinsky.

Then, on Sunday morning, "The Drudge Report" came out, which used Betty's name, and I thought that we were going to be deluged by press comments, and I was trying to refresh my memory about what the facts were.

...Let's call Ms. Currie to the stand and see what she would say.

She was asked the following question: "You testified that he wanted you to say 'right' at the end of those four statements, 'I was never alone'—you know, the four statements?" This is what Ms. Currie said: "I do not remember that he wanted me to say 'right.' I could have said 'wrong.' "

Independent counsel didn't like that answer, so asked: "Did you feel any pressure to agree with your boss?" She answered, "None." ...

...If there's no proof that the president had the wildest idea...that Betty Currie would ever be contacted, would ever become a witness, would ever be deposed, then you have no choice on the record but to see the obvious conclusion that it was the Drudge Report, the media inquiries and the president knowing that his deposition testimony was about to be leaked that caused all the events that you would impeach him over on a charge that does not exist.

As to the fourth allegation about the job search, how can the majority cause the crisis a Senate trial would incur based on an article of impeachment alleging obstruction of justice by trying to get Ms. Lewinsky a job? Each and every one of you know that there is no contradiction by any witness...that the job search began long before Ms. Lewinsky was even a dream to the *Paula Jones* attorneys....

...And finally, while it has been pointed out to the committee many times, it cannot be pointed out too often, because this statement by your witness, Monica Lewinsky, answers this charge about obstruction of justice and leaves this committee and the House with no proof. Ms. Lewinsky, even though never asked by the independent counsel, made sure she did not finish her grand jury testimony before stating, "No one asked me to lie, and I was never promised a job for my silence." ...

Mr. Chairman, Article IV raises the specter of abuse of power.... The term "abuse of power" does invoke the memory of President Nixon's offenses in 1974. Yet those who have appeared here as witnesses with Watergate knowledge.... all could tell you that the acts you are considering today are not the same....

As the committee takes up this proposal, keep focused that this was not an attempt by a president to organize his staff to spread misinformation about the progress of the war in Vietnam, or about a break-in in Democratic headquarters at the Watergate, or even about how funds from arms sales in Iran were diverted to aid the Contras. This was a president repeating to his staff the same denial of an inappropriate and extremely embarrassing relationship, the same denial that he had already made to the public. Does this article of impeachment envision that the president, having already made public denials, would have then gone inside the White House and told the staff something else?...

As to the ground for impeachment that the president had the audacity to assert privileges in litigation, White House counsel Ruff did a complete job of disproving any possible issue the committee could have. Let me only add one note: that it still remains shocking to me, as I hope it does to all the lawyers on this committee, that you would even consider as an article of impeachment an assertion of an evidentiary privilege by the president on the advice of his lawyers and the White House counsel that was found to exist by a judge, that that could ever been grounds for an impeachment.

I have heard the majority state that a president should not be above the law. And yet this proposed article would place him below the law that gives every American the right to assert legally-accepted privileges without fearing being thrown out of his job....

Again speaking to 1974, there is one more introductory thought I would like to make on this subject of burden and the requirements that you find proof by clear and convincing evidence.... [We have] suggested as a frame of reference that which is even more compelling today. That was the bipartisan vote against an article of impeachment for President Nixon's lying to the IRS about his taxes. Please be clear that the article proposed in 1974 included allegations that President Nixon's tax returns, like all filings with government agencies, had the import of an oath. Please also be clear that allegations included the fact that the lies in that matter were purposeful, included backdated documents and were about something important, the means by which our government is funded. Please also keep in mind ... that while some Members did justify their no votes because they felt the evidence was insufficient, that others, including the key Democrats ... did so because they said that it was not an impeachable offense.

With all of that in mind, let us ask what we asked you three months ago. If President Nixon's alleged lies to the Internal Revenue Service about his taxes were not grounds for impeachment in 1974, how then are the alleged lies by President Clinton about his private sexual relationship with Ms. Lewinsky grounds in 1998?

Just last week, you heard from someone who could help with the answer to that question, and I know we were listening when majority witness former

Watergate-era committee member and now federal Judge Charles Wiggins said: "I confess to you that I would recommend that you not vote to impeach the president. I find it troubling that this matter has grown to the consequences that it now occupies on the public screen."

... Both Watergate and today's inquiry started with a referral from a special prosecutor sending grand jury material to the Congress. But that is where the similarity ends. The Office of Independent Counsel today certainly hasn't acted like Mr. Jaworski's office did back then, and the two Judiciary Committees have not acted the same either. The Judiciary Committee in Watergate kept the evidence to itself, until it could be sure what was relevant and what was not. It did not dump the material into the public. The Judiciary Committee in Watergate had agreements on what witnesses to call and what evidence to gather.... The Judiciary Committee in Watergate heard from actual witnesses whose credibility could be assessed. It did not rely on the conclusions of a prosecutor.... And finally, the Judiciary Committee in Watergate took its actions, including the most important actions of voting articles of impeachment, with bipartisan votes....

... Alexander Hamilton stated that prosecutions of impeachment "will seldom fail to agitate the passions of the whole community and to divide it into parties more or less friendly or inimical to the accused. In many cases, it will connect itself with the pre-existing factions, and in such cases there will always be the danger that the decision will be regulated more by the comparative strength of the parties than by real demonstrations of innocence and guilt."...

Even though the majority has all the votes it needs to do as it pleases, we conclude today... by urging that we all listen to Hamilton's plea, by urging that we listen to each other, and by urging that we especially listen to the American people who are asking you to find a truly bipartisan way to avoid the course on which you are now embarked....

After a lunchtime recess and some other procedural business, Chairman Hyde announced that during the recess, "we called the White House counsel, Mr. Ruff, to invite him back if he wanted to, and he declined to come back, with thanks." Then he introduced chief investigative counsel David Schippers.

Mr. Schippers. ... Before we get into the president's lies and obstructions, it is important to place the events in their proper context....

Monica Lewinsky, a 22-year-old intern, was working at the White House during the government shutdown in 1995. Prior to their first intimate encounter, she had never even spoken to the president. Sometime on November 15th, 1995, Ms. Lewinsky made an improper gesture to the president.... Did the president immediately confront her or report her to her supervisors, as you would expect? Did he make it clear that such conduct would not be tolerated in the White House? No.... Instead, the president of the United States invited this unknown young intern into a private area off the Oval Office where he kissed her. He then invited her back later, and when she returned, the two engaged in the first of many acts of inappropriate conduct.

Thereafter, the two concocted a cover story. If Ms. Lewinsky was seen, she was just bringing papers to the president. That story was totally false. The only papers she brought were personal messages, having nothing to do with her duties or those of the president.

After Ms. Lewinsky moved from the White House to the Pentagon, her frequent visits to the president were disguised as visits to Betty Currie. Now, those cover stories are important because they play a vital role in the later perjuries and obstructions.

Over the term of their relationship, the following significant matters occurred. Monica Lewinsky and the president were alone on at least 21 occasions. They had at least 11 personal sexual encounters, excluding phone sex;... They had at least 55 telephone conversations, some of which, at least 17, involved phone sex. The president gave Ms. Lewinsky 24 presents, and Ms. Lewinsky gave the president 40 presents.

...During the fall of 1997, things were relatively quiet. Monica Lewinsky was working at the Pentagon and looking for a high-paying job in New York. The president's attempt to stall the *Paula Jones* case was still pending in the Supreme Court, and nobody seemed to care one way or another what the outcome would be. Then, in the first week of December, 1997, things began to unravel....

A few words of caution, if I may. The evidence and testimony must be viewed as a whole.... Remember, events and words that may seem innocent, or even exculpatory in a vacuum, may well take on a sinister or even criminal connotation when observed in the context of the whole plot.

For example, everyone agrees Monica Lewinsky testified, no one ever told me to lie. No one ever promised me a job. When considered alone,... this would seem exculpatory. In the context of the other evidence, we see this is...parsing words to give a misleading inference. Of course no one said, Monica, go in there and lie. They didn't have to. Monica knew what was expected of her. Similarly, nobody promised her a job. But once she signed that false affidavit she got one, didn't she?

Likewise, please don't permit the obfuscations and legalistic pyrotechnics of the president's defenders to distract you from the real issue here.... The real issues are whether the president of the United States testified falsely under oath, whether he engaged in a continuing plot to obstruct justice, to hide evidence, to tamper with witnesses, and to abuse the power of his office in furtherance of that plot.

The ultimate issue is whether the president's course of conduct is such as to affect adversely the office of the presidency by bringing scandal and disrespect upon it...and whether he has acted in a manner contrary to his trust as president and subversive to the rule of law and to constitutional government....

Schippers then described the events of Friday and Saturday, December 5 and 6, 1997. That Friday evening, Paula Jones' lawyers faxed a list of potential witnesses—including Monica Lewinsky—to the president's attorney. The next morning, Lewinsky went to the White House to deliver a letter and some gifts for the president to Betty Currie. A Secret Service officer told her that the president was not, as she thought, meeting with his lawyers; instead, Eleanor Mondale was with him. Furious, Lewinsky left the premises, called Currie from a pay phone, and went home. After the call, Currie told the Secret Service watch commander that the president wanted someone fired for disclosing his meeting with Mondale.

Lewinsky later spoke with the president on the phone, and he was very angry about her behavior. Then, in an abrupt about-face, he invited her to the White House, where she found him "sweet and affectionate." Currie, meanwhile, told some Secret Service officers that if they kept quiet about the Lewinsky incident, there would be no disciplinary action—and the watch commander later reported that the president told him "I hope you use your discretion."

According to Schippers, the president met with his lawyers at about 5 P.M., after Lewinsky had left. Robert Bennett had a copy of the witness list; the president later testified that he had heard about the witness list before he saw it. In other words, Schippers suggested, "It is valid to infer that hearing Ms. Lewinsky's name on the witness list prompted the president's sudden and otherwise unexplained change from very angry to very affectionate."

Schippers continued:

Now, to go back a little, Monica Lewinsky had been looking for a good-paying and high-profile job in New York since the previous July. She wasn't having much success.... In early November, Betty Currie arranged a meeting with Vernon Jordan.... On November 5th, Monica met for 20 minutes with Mr. Jordan. No action followed.... It was obvious that he made no effort to find a job for Ms. Lewinsky. Indeed, it was so unimportant to him that he actually had no recollection of an early November meeting....

During the December 6th meeting with the president, she mentioned that she had not been able to get in touch with Mr. Jordan and that it didn't seem that he had done anything to help her. The president responded by saying, oh, I'll take care of that. I will get on it, or something to that effect. There was obviously still no urgency to help Monica....

The first activity calculated to help Monica actually procure employment took place on December 11th. Mr. Jordan met with Ms. Lewinsky and gave her a list of contact names. The two also discussed the president.

By the way, that meeting Mr. Jordan remembered.

Vernon Jordan immediately placed calls to two prospective employers. Later in the afternoon he even called the president to give him a report of his job search efforts.... :

But why the sudden interest? Why the sudden change in focus?... Did something happen to remove the job search from a low to a high priority on that day?

Oh, yes, something happened. On the morning of December 11, 1997, Judge Susan Webber Wright ordered that Paula Jones was entitled to information regarding any state or federal employee with whom the president had sexual relations or proposed or sought to have sexual relations. To keep Monica on the team was now of critical importance.

... [O]n December 17, 1997, between 2 and 2:30 in the morning, Monica Lewinsky's phone rang unexpectedly... and it was the president of the United States. The president said that he wanted to tell Ms. Lewinsky two things: one, that Betty Currie's brother had been killed in a car accident; and second, he said that "he had some more bad news," that he had seen the witness list for the *Paula Jones* case, and her name was on it. The president told Ms. Lewinsky that seeing her name on the list broke his heart....

... Ms. Lewinsky asked what she should do if she were subpoenaed. The president responded, well, maybe you can sign an affidavit.

Now, both parties knew that the affidavit would need to be false and misleading in order to accomplish the desired result.

Then the president had a very pointed suggestion.... No, he did not say, go in and lie. What he did say is, you know, you could always say you were coming to see Betty or that you were bringing the papers....

So when the president called Monica at 2 a.m. on December 17th to tell her she was on the witness list, he made sure to remind her of those prior cover stories. Ms. Lewinsky testified that... she understood that the two would continue their pre-existing pattern of deception....

... [A]t this point he still had the opportunity to establish a non-sexual explanation for their meetings...because his DNA hadn't yet turned up on Monica Lewinsky's blue dress....

...Ms. Lewinsky's greatest fears were realized on December 19th, when Monica was subpoenaed to testify in a deposition to take place on January 23, 1998, in the *Jones* case. Extremely distraught, she immediately called the president's best friend, Vernon Jordan....

Mr. Jordan invited Ms. Lewinsky to his office, and she arrived shortly before 5 p.m., still extremely distraught.... Jordan called the president at about 5 on the 19th and told the president that Monica had been subpoenaed.

During the meeting,... which Jordan characterized as a disturbing meeting, she talked about her infatuation with the president. Mr. Jordan also decided that he would call a lawyer for her.... That evening, Mr. Jordan met with the president and relayed his conversation with Ms. Lewinsky. The details are extremely important, because the president, in his deposition, didn't recall that meeting.

Mr. Jordan told the president again that Ms. Lewinsky had been subpoenaed...that he was concerned about her fascination with the president, and that Ms. Lewinsky had even asked Mr. Jordan if he thought the president would leave the first lady after he left office. He also asked President Clinton if he had any sexual relations with Ms. Lewinsky.

Now, wouldn't a reasonable person conclude that this type of conversation would be locked in the president's memory?...

December 28, 1997, is a crucial date. The evidence shows that the president made false and misleading statements to the federal court, the federal grand jury and to the Congress of the United States about the events that took place on that date. It also is critical evidence that he obstructed justice.

Now, the president testified that it was possible, that is his word, that he invited Ms. Lewinsky to the White House for this visit. He admitted that he probably gave Ms. Lewinsky the most gifts he had ever given her on that date.... Among the many gifts the president gave Ms. Lewinsky on December 28th was a bear that he said was a symbol of strength.

The president forgot that he had given any gifts to Monica. Watch this from the deposition:

[Transcript of Videotape]
Question: Well, have you ever given any gifts to Monica Lewinsky?
Answer: I don't recall. Do you know what they were?
Question: A hat pin?
Answer: I don't, I don't remember. But I certainly, I could have.

Now, as an attorney, the president knew that the law will not tolerate someone who says "I don't recall" when the answer is unreasonable under the circumstances.... When asked in the grand jury why he was unable to remember, though he had given Ms. Lewinsky so many gifts only 2½ weeks earlier, the president put forth a lame and obviously contrived explanation: "I think what I meant there was I don't recall what they were, not that I don't recall whether I had given them."...

On December 28th, one of the most blatant efforts to obstruct justice and conceal evidence occurred. Ms. Lewinsky testified that she discussed with the president the facts that she had been subpoenaed and that the subpoena called for her to produce the gifts....

Ms. Lewinsky then suggested that she take the gifts somewhere or give them to someone, maybe to Betty. The president responded, "I don't know," or "Let me think about that."

Later that day, Ms. Lewinsky got a call from Ms. Currie, who said, "I understand you have something to give me," or "the president said you have something to give me." Ms. Currie has an amazingly fuzzy memory about this incident, but says that the best she can remember, Ms. Lewinsky called her. There is key evidence that Ms. Currie's fuzzy recollection is wrong....

Schippers showed the committee the log from Currie's cell phone, which recorded a telephone call at 3:32 P.M. on December 28, 1997, to Lewinsky's apartment. This, he said "proves conclusively" that it was Currie who called Lewinsky.

Why did Betty Currie pick up the gifts from Ms. Lewinsky? The facts speak for themselves. The president told her to.... If it was Ms. Lewinsky that called her, did Currie ask, like anyone would, why in the world would you want to give me a box of gifts from the president? Did she tell the president of this strange request? No.... She simply took the gifts and put them under her bed without asking a single question.

Another note about this. The president stated in his response to questions...from this committee that he was not concerned about these gifts. In fact, he said, he recalled telling Monica that if the *Jones* lawyers requested gifts, she should turn them over. The president testified that he is "not sure" if he knew the subpoena asked for gifts.

Why would Monica and the president discuss turning over gifts to the *Jones* lawyers if Ms. Lewinsky hadn't told the president that the subpoena called for gifts? On the other hand, if President Clinton knew the subpoena requested gifts, why would he give more gifts to Monica on December 28th? This does seem odd. Ms. Lewinsky's testimony, though, provides the answer. She said that she never questioned "that we were ever going to do anything but keep this private." That meant to, and this is a quote, "take whatever appropriate steps needed to be taken" to keep it quiet.

The only inference is that the gifts, including the bear, symbolizing strength, were a tacit reminder to Ms. Lewinsky that they would deny that relationship even in the face of a federal court subpoena.

Furthermore, the president at various times in his deposition seriously misrepresented the nature of his meeting with Ms. Lewinsky on December 28th. First he was asked, "Did she tell you she'd been served with a subpoena in this case?" The president answered, flatly, "No, I don't know she had been."

He was also asked if he ever talked to Monica Lewinsky about the possibility of her testifying. His answer: "I'm not sure." He then added that he may have joked to her that the *Jones* lawyers might subpoena every woman he had ever spoken to and that "I don't think we ever had more of a conversation than that about it."

Not only does Monica Lewinsky directly contradict this testimony, but the president himself also directly contradicted it when he testified before the grand jury. Speaking of his December 28th meeting, he said that he "knew by then, of course, that she had gotten a subpoena" and that they had a "conversation about the possibility of her testifying."

Remember, he had this conversation about her testimony only 2½ weeks before the deposition. Again, his version is not reasonable.

The president knew that Monica Lewinsky was going to make a false affidavit. He was so certain of the content that when Monica asked if he wanted to see it, he told her no, he had seen 15 of them.... Besides, he had suggested the affidavit himself, remember, and he trusted Mr. Jordan to be certain the mission would be accomplished....

On January 6th, Ms. Lewinsky picked up a draft of the affidavit from Mr. Carter's office. She delivered a copy to Mr. Jordan...in the belief that if Vernon Jordan gave his imprimatur, the president would also approve of the language. Ms. Lewinsky and Mr. Jordan...agreed to delete a paragraph inserted by Mr. Carter which Ms. Lewinsky felt might open a line of questions concerning whether she had actually been alone with the president.

Contrast this to the testimony of Mr. Jordan, who said he had nothing to do with the details of the affidavit. He admits, though, that he spoke with the president after conferring with Ms. Lewinsky about the changes that had been made in that affidavit.

The next day, January 7th, Monica Lewinsky signed the false affidavit. She showed the executed copy to Mr. Jordan that same day....

On January 8th, the next day, Ms. Lewinsky had an interview, arranged by Mr. Jordan, with MacAndrews & Forbes in New York. The interview went quite poorly, so Ms. Lewinsky was upset, called Mr. Jordan and told him. Vernon Jordan...then called the CEO of MacAndrews & Forbes, Mr. Perelman, to "make things happen, if they could happen." ... The next morning, Monica received her reward for signing the false affidavit; after a series of new interviews with MacAndrews & Forbes personnel, she was informally offered a job. When Monica called Mr. Jordan to tell him, he passed the good news on to Betty Currie. Tell the president, mission accomplished.

...After months of looking for a job...Vernon Jordan just so happened to make the call to the CEO the day after the false affidavit was signed....

Mr. Jordan was well aware that people with whom Ms. Lewinsky worked at the White House didn't like her.... Vernon Jordan asked if at "any point during this process you wondered about her qualifications for employment?" He answered: "No, because that was not my judgment to make." ... Mr. Jordan said that she had been hounding him for a job and voicing unrealistic expectations concerning positions and concerning salary. Moreover, she had narrated a very disturbing story about the president leaving the first lady, and how the president wasn't spending enough time with her. Yet none of that gave Mr. Jordan pause in making the recommendation. Do people like Vernon Jordan go to the wall for marginal employees? They do not, unless there is a compelling reason. The compelling reason was that the president told him this was top priority....

Now I'm going to read paragraph 8 of Ms. Lewinsky's affidavit. Here is what it says: "I have never had a sexual relationship with the president. He did not propose that we have a sexual relationship. He did not offer me employment or other benefits in exchange for a sexual relationship. He did not deny me employment or other benefits for rejecting a sexual relationship." ...

Schippers then described a flurry of phone calls between the president's counsel and Monica Lewinsky's lawyer in the days leading up to Saturday, January 17, the day the president was scheduled to be deposed in the Jones case. "Obviously, the president's lawyers needed that affidavit to be filed with the court to support his plans to mislead Ms. Jones' attorneys," Schippers argued. Carter filed the affidavit on January 17.

Meanwhile, Schippers noted, on January 15, Michael Isikoff of Newsweek *had called Betty Currie to ask about gifts sent to her, via courier, by Lewinsky. The president was out of town, so Currie told Lewinsky about the call and also reported it to Vernon Jordan. Jordan advised her to speak with White House aides Bruce Lindsey and Mike McCurry.*

The president also provided false and misleading testimony in the grand jury when he was asked about Mr. Bennett's representation in the *Jones* deposition that the president is "fully aware" that Lewinsky filed an affidavit saying that "there is absolutely no sex of any kind, in any manner, shape, or form with President Clinton."

President Clinton was asked about this representation made by his lawyer in his presence and whether he felt obligated to inform the federal judge, who was sitting there, of the true facts. The president answered that ... he didn't believe he "even focused on what Mr. Bennett said and the exact words he did until I started reading this transcript carefully for this hearing." ...

This last statement by the president is critical. First, he had planned his answers to the grand jurors. ... Second, he knew that he could only avoid that admission that he allowed a false affidavit to be filed by convincing the grand jury that he hadn't been paying attention. Take a look at this tape that is coming up, and you will see what the president of the United States doesn't want the people of the United States ever to see. Watch.

[Transcript of Videotape Excerpt from Clinton's Jones Deposition]
Robert Bennett: Your Honor—excuse me, Mr. President, I need some guidance from the court at this point. I'm going to object to the innuendo. I'm afraid, as I say, that this will leak. I don't question the predicates

here. I question the good faith of counsel, the innuendo in the question. Counsel is fully aware that Ms. Lewinsky has filed, has an affidavit which they are in possession of saying that there is absolutely no sex of any kind in any manner, shape or form, with President Clinton, and yet listening to the innuendo in the questions...

Do you think for one moment...that the president wasn't paying attention? They were talking about Monica Lewinsky, at the time the most dangerous person in the president's life. If the false affidavit worked, he was home free because they wouldn't be permitted to question him about her. Can anyone rationally argue that the president wasn't vitally interested in what Mr. Bennett was saying? Nonetheless, when he was asked in the grand jury whether Mr. Bennett's statement was false, he still was unable to tell the truth.... He answered with a now famous sentence: "It depends on what the meaning of 'is' is."...

But the president reinforced Monica's lie. Mr. Bennett read to him the paragraph...where she denied a sexual relationship—not sexual relations—sexual relationship with the president. Watch.

[Transcript of Videotape Excerpt from Clinton's Jones Deposition]
Question: ...Is that a true and accurate statement as far as you know it?
Answer: That is absolutely true.

"That is absolutely true." And at the time, the president knew that it was absolutely false....

By the time the president concluded his deposition, he knew that someone was talking. And he knew that the only person who could be talking was Ms. Lewinsky herself. The cover story that he and Monica had created and that he used liberally himself during the deposition was now in real jeopardy. It became imperative that he not only contact Ms. Lewinsky, but that he obtain corroboration from his trusted secretary, Betty Currie. So at about 7 p.m. on the night of the deposition, the president called Ms. Currie and asked that she come in the following day, which was a Sunday.... Sometime in the early morning hours of January 18, by the way, the president learned of a Drudge Report concerning Ms. Lewinsky that had been released earlier that day....

...At about 5 p.m., Ms. Currie met with the president. The president said that he had just been deposed and that the attorneys asked several questions about Monica Lewinsky. That, incidentally, was a direct violation of Judge

Wright's order prohibiting discussions about the deposition testimony. The president then made a series of statements to Ms. Currie:

I was never really alone with Monica, right?

You were always there when Monica was there, right?

Monica came on to me and I never touched her, right?

You could see and hear everything, right?

She wanted to have sex with me, and I can't do that.

During Betty Currie's grand jury testimony, she was asked whether she believed that the president wanted her to agree with that statement.

> **Question:** Would it be fair to say, then, based on the way he stated the five points and the demeanor that he was using at the time that he stated it to you, that he wished you to agree with that statement?
> **Answer:** I can't speak for him, but—
> **Question:** How did you take it? Because you told us at these meetings in the last several days that that is how you took it.
> **Answer:** (Nodding.)...
> **Question:** And you're nodding your head 'yes'; is that correct?
> **Answer:** That's correct....

When the president testified in the grand jury, he was questioned about his intentions when he made those five statements. The president stated: "I thought we were going to be deluged by press comments, and I was trying to refresh my memory about what the facts were. And what I wanted to establish was that Betty was there at all other times, in the complex. And I wanted to know what Betty's memory was about what she heard, what she could hear.... So I was not trying to get Betty Currie to say something that was untruthful. I was trying to get as much information as quickly as I could."...

Logic tells us that the president's plea, that he was just trying to refresh his memory, is contrived and false again. First, consider the president's options after he left his deposition: He could abide by Judge Wright's order to remain silent and not divulge any details of his deposition; he could choose to defy Judge Wright's orders, call Betty on the phone and ask her an open-ended question—for example, "what do you remember about Monica Lewinsky?"...or he could call Ms. Currie and arrange a Sunday afternoon meeting at a time when...the White House staff is at a minimum. The president chose the third option. He made sure that this was a face-to-face meeting.... He made sure that he had the meeting in his office, an area where he was comfortable and could utilize its power and its prestige to in-fluence future testimony....

Betty Currie could not possibly have any personal knowledge of the facts the president was asking about. How could she know if they were never alone? If they were, Ms. Currie wasn't there, right? So, too, how would she know that the president never touched Monica? No, this wasn't any attempt by the president to refresh anybody's recollection. It was witness tampering, pure and simple.

... [H]is attorneys have argued that those statements to her could not constitute obstruction because she had not been subpoenaed, and the president didn't know she was a potential witness at the time. This argument is refuted both by law and facts....

As discussed, the president and Ms. Lewinsky concocted that cover story that brought Ms. Currie into the fray.... True to the scheme, the president...invoked Ms. Currie's name frequently as a witness who could corroborate his false and misleading testimony about the Lewinsky affair in the deposition. For example, during that deposition when asked whether he was alone with Ms. Lewinsky, the president said that he was not alone with her or that Betty Currie was there with Monica.... Asked whether Ms. Lewinsky sent packages to him, he stated that Betty handled packages for him. Asked whether he may have assisted in any way with Ms. Lewinsky's job search, he stated that he thought Betty suggested Vernon Jordan talk to Ms. Lewinsky...

Of course Ms. Currie was a prospective witness, and the president clearly wanted her to be deposed as a witness....

Soon after her meeting with the president, Schippers recounted, Ms. Currie paged Ms. Lewinsky four times, all between 5:12 and 8:28 P.M.—and shortly after 11 P.M., the president called Currie at home to find out whether she had connected. The next morning, the unsuccessful calls continued. That afternoon, the president called Jordan, who joined the search.

At 4:54 P.M., Jordan heard from Frank Carter, whom he had enlisted in the search, that he had been told he was no longer Lewinsky's lawyer. Jordan relayed this news to the president.

Schippers continued:

Now why all this activity? It shows how important it was for the president of the United States to find Monica Lewinsky to learn to whom she was talking.... The president had just completed a deposition in which he'd provided false and misleading testimony about his relationship. She was a co-conspirator—"she" being Monica Lewinsky—in hiding this relationship from the *Jones* attorneys, and he was losing control over her....

On August 17, the last act of this tragedy took place. After six scorned invitations, the president of the United States appeared before a grand jury of his fellow citizens and took an oath to tell the truth. And we all now know what happened after that. The president equivocated, engaged in legalistic fencing, but he also lied. During the course of this presentation I discuss several of those lies specifically. Actually, the entire performance ... was calculated to mislead and to deceive the grand jury and eventually the American people. The tone was set at the very beginning. You recall Judge Starr testified that in a grand jury, a witness can either tell the truth, lie, or assert his privilege against self-incrimination. President Clinton was given a fourth choice. The president was permitted to read a statement....

Even that statement is false in many particulars. President Clinton claims that he engaged in wrong conduct with Ms. Lewinsky "on certain occasions in early 1996 and once in 1997." Notice he didn't mention 1995. There was a reason. On the three occasions in 1995, Monica was a 21-year-old intern. As for being on "certain occasions," the president was alone with Monica more than 21 times at least....

In addition, ... whenever the president was asked a specific question that could not be answered directly without either admitting the truth or giving an easily provable false answer, he said, "I rely on my statement." Nineteen times he relied on his statement—his false and misleading statement. Nineteen times, then, he repeated those lies....

Finally, Schippers addressed the president's responses to the eighty-one specific questions that had been submitted by the committee. In his answers, Schippers said, "the president elected to follow the pattern of selective memory, reference to other testimony, blatant untruths, artful distortions, outright lies and half-truths.... When he did answer, he engaged in legalistic hairsplitting in an obvious attempt to skirt the whole truth and to deceive this committee.

Now let's talk a little about abuse of power. As soon as Paula Jones filed her lawsuit, President Clinton, rather than confront the charges, tried to get it dismissed. To do so, he used the power and dignity of the Office of the president.... Remember, this was a private suit against the president in his private capacity. He argued that as president, he is immune from a lawsuit during his tenure in office; that is, that the president, as president, is immune from the civil law of the land....

More interesting is the rationale given by the president for his immunity ...: "The broad public and constitutional interests that would be placed at risk by litigating such claims against an incumbent president far outweigh the asserted private interests of a plaintiff who seeks civil damages for an alleged past injury."

... The president's lawyers are referring to the most basic civil rights of an American citizen to due process of law and to the equal protection of the laws—those same rights that President Clinton had taken an oath to preserve and protect....

But the president was just getting started. He employed the power and prestige of his office and of his Cabinet officers to mislead and to lie to the American people about the *Jones* case and the Monica Lewinsky matter. But even more ... the president has tried to extend the relatively narrow bounds of presidential privilege to unlimited, if not bizarre, lengths....

The whole plan was to delay, obstruct and detour the investigations, not to protect the presidency, but to protect the president personally.... With a single exception, every claim of immunity and every privilege has been rejected outright by the courts. Future presidents will be forced to operate within those strictures because one person assumed that the office put him above the law....

On Wednesday, January 21, 1998 the *Washington Post* published a story entitled CLINTON ACCUSED OF URGING AIDE TO LIE; STARR PROBES WHETHER PRESIDENT TOLD WOMAN TO DENY ALLEGED AFFAIR TO JONES LAWYERS. The White House learned the substance of the story on the evening of the 20th. After the president learned of the existence of that story, he made a series of telephone calls.

> The first call, Schippers said, was to Robert Bennett. Bennett was quoted in the Post the next morning, saying: "The president adamantly denies he ever had a relationship with Ms. Lewinsky, and she has confirmed the truth of that." After talking to Bennett, the president spoke with Bruce Lindsey—twice—and Betty Currie, then with Vernon Jordan. Finally, at 9 A.M., Schippers recounted, Clinton met with White House chief of staff Erskine Bowles and two of Bowles's deputies, John Podesta and Sylvia Matthews.

Erskine Bowles ... recounts the president's immediate words as he and two others entered the Oval Office: "And he looked up at us and he said the same thing he said to the American people. He said, 'I want you to know, I did not have sexual relationships with this woman, Monica Lewinsky. I did not ask anybody to lie, and when the facts come out you'll understand.' " After the president made that blanket denial, Mr. Bowles responded: "...Mr. President, I don't know what the facts are; I don't know if they're good, bad or indifferent, but whatever they are, you ought to get them out and you ought to get them out right now."...

Two days later, on January 23rd, Mr. Podesta had another discussion with the president: "...And he said to me that he never had sex with her, and that—and that he never asked, you know, he repeated the denial. But he was extremely explicit in saying he never had sex with her."

Then Podesta testified as follows:

Question: Okay. Not explicit in that sense, that he got more specific than sex, than the word "sex."

Answer: Yes, he was more specific than that.

Question: Okay, share that with us.

Answer: Well, I think he said—he said that there was some spate of, you know, what sex acts were counted, and he said he had never had sex with her in any way whatsoever.

Question: Okay.

Answer: That they had not had oral sex.

Later in the day on January 21st, the president called Sidney Blumenthal to his office. It is interesting to note how the president's lies become more elaborate and pronounced.... Remember that when the president spoke to Mr. Bowles and Mr. Podesta, he simply denied the story. But by the time he spoke to Mr. Blumenthal, the president had added three new angles: One, he now portrays Monica Lewinsky as the aggressor; two, he launches an attack on her reputation by portraying her as a stalker; and three, he presents himself as an innocent victim being attacked by the forces of evil....

...It is abundantly clear that the president's assertions to staff were designed for dissemination to the American people. But it is equally important to understand that the president intended his aides to relate that false story to investigators and grand jurors alike....

Schippers then recounted how President Clinton consulted his former adviser, Dick Morris. The two decided to take an overnight poll to assess public reaction. Morris reported "... *they're willing to forgive you for adultery, but not for perjury or obstruction of justice, or the various other things." The president's response, as recalled by Morris's testimony: "Well, we just have to win, then."*

"How do you do this?" Schippers asked—then answered his own question: "You employ the full power and credibility of the White House and the press corps . . . to destroy the witness." Schippers then cited a series of damaging reports about Monica Lewinsky, many ascribed to White House sources and allies. "Sound familiar?" asked Schippers. "It ought to, because that is the same tactics that were used to destroy Paula Jones. . . ."

Schippers then turned to the president's grand jury testimony on August 17, 1998. He went through testimony in which the president responded to various questions about what he had told his aides, and whether he knew his aides were likely to be called before the grand jury. Then Schippers summed up:

He stated that when he spoke to his aides, he was very careful with his wording. The president stated he wanted his statement regarding "sexual relations" to be literally true because he was only referring to intercourse. However, recall that John Podesta said that the president denied sex in any way whatsoever, including oral. . . .

And also take note of this fact: Seven days after the president's grand jury appearance, the White House issued a document, entitled "Talking Points, January 24, 1998." . . . This talking points document outlines proposed questions that the president may be asked in a press conference. It also outlines suggested answers to those questions. The talking points purport to state the president's view of sexual relations and his view of the relationship with Ms. Lewinsky. The talking points are as follows:

Question: What acts does the president believe constitute a sexual relationship?
Answer: I can't believe we're on national television discussing this. I'm not about to engage in an act-by-act discussion of what constitutes a sexual relationship.
Question: Well, for example, Miss Lewinsky is on tape indicating that the president does not believe oral sex is adultery. Would oral sex, to the president, constitute a sexual relationship?
Answer: Of course it would.

. . . [T]he president's own talking points refute his "literal truth" argument.

.   .   .

I would like to take a few moments to address some of the matters that have been put before you by the president's defenders over the past few days. Ever since this inquiry began, we've heard the complaint that no factual witnesses were being called by the majority. Actually, there are many factual witnesses: Monica Lewinsky, Vernon Jordan, Betty Currie, Sidney Blumenthal, Erskine Bowles, John Podesta, all of whom have testified one or more times, under oath, either in a formal deposition or before a grand jury....

Now, some members have suggested that none of these witnesses have been subjected to cross-examination. Well, the answer to that is twofold.

First, this is not, as some seem to believe, a trial. It is in the nature of an inquest. Any witnesses whose testimony is referred to in this proceeding will be subjected to full cross-examination if a trial results in the Senate.... As it stands, all of the factual witnesses upon whose testimony I have relied are uncontradicted and amply corroborated.

Second, if any member or the president's counsel had specific questions for any of these witnesses that I just named, he or she was free to bring them before the committee....

Although the president's lawyers admit that his actions in the *Jones* case and in the Lewinsky matter were immoral—and I think they used the term "maddening acts"—they argue that they don't rise to the level of criminal activity, and certainly not to the level of impeachable offenses.

They produced another gaggle of witnesses to testify that this really is not so bad, it's only lying about sex; that only private conduct is involved and really the Congress should just close up the book, slap the president on the hand.... Some even suggested that a prosecutor wouldn't even consider an indictment based upon the evidence available here. Well, that remains to be seen.

I doubt if any of those experts have read all the evidence that I have read, and we know that the prosecutors are in possession of that evidence, and perhaps much more. Whether to indict is their decision. And whether the offenses of President Clinton are criminally chargeable is of no moment whatever.... It is a fundamental precept that an impeachable offense need not be a criminal act....

Perhaps the most strident complaint from the president's supporters is what they perceive as the fundamental unfairness of this process. They have, however, been hard pressed to point with any degree of specificity to any unfair actions....

On the other hand, how fair have the president and his supporters been?...
How about employing every conceivable means, including perjury and obstruction, to defeat the legal rights of a woman who claimed she'd been
wronged?...

Was it fair to Monica Lewinsky to construct an elaborate lie that made it
appear that she was a predator who threatened to lie about a sexual encounter
if the president didn't succumb to her advances? By the way, if the dress had
not turned up, that story would have been President Clinton's defense today.
The stage had already been set. The scenery was in place and the actors had
been given their lines.

...And how about the constant trashing of anyone who had the courage to
criticize or to refuse to go along with the game plan? Is it fair to make misstatements about the independent counsel's referral and then use those misstatements as a basis to attack Judge Starr's credibility?...

This is a defining moment both for the presidency and especially for the
members of this committee.

For the presidency as an institution, because if you don't impeach as a consequence of the conduct that I have just portrayed, then no House of Representatives will ever be able to impeach again. The bar will be so high that only
a convicted felon or a traitor will need to be concerned....

It is likewise a defining moment for you, the members of this Judiciary
Committee.... These walls are infused with the honor and integrity that has
always prevailed in this chamber. Now it is your turn to add to or subtract
from that honor and integrity....

DEBATING THE ARTICLES

Each member of the committee had ten minutes for an opening statement. Most reviewed what the speaker considered the most salient points of the hearings and made clear where each member stood.

Mr. Sensenbrenner:...The evidence clearly shows that President Clinton lied to the grand jury fully seven and one half months after the president's relationship with Ms. Lewinsky hit the front pages. Those lies were told because the president was unwilling to admit he repeatedly lied in the Paula Jones deposition in January.... He then lied to his Cabinet and his staff so that they would unwittingly deceive the American public on this issue....

Mr. Clinton has recognized that his relationship with Ms. Lewinsky was wrong. I give him credit for that. But he has not owned up to the false testimony, the stonewalling, the obstructing the courts from finding the truth, and the use of taxpayer-paid White House resources to hide and perpetuate his lies. He has tried to use his apology for private misconduct to evade taking responsibility for the very grave public wrongs done to the judicial system's ability to find the truth...

Mr. Conyers:...The majority have simply rubber-stamped the unexamined, untested, double hearsay, yes, triple hearsay and conclusions of the independent counsel without conducting any factual investigation of its own....

My friends across the aisle, please let me remind you that it is you who are trying to overturn the results of two national elections, you who are attempting a legislative takeover of the executive branch, and you, not the president, who have the burden of coming forward with evidence....

If our hearings have made anything clear, it is that the distinction between personal misconduct and official misconduct has constitutional significance. The majority of our constitutional scholars have concluded that an offense is not impeachable unless it is political in nature.... Under our constitutional system of government, if the president misbehaves in a way that does not impact on his official duties, the remedy still lies in the voting booth....

Mr. McCollum: ... People who go to court in our system expect witnesses who are called to testify to tell the truth to the judge and the jurors. That's what we mean by the term "rule of law." Without truthful testimony, justice can't be rendered and the system doesn't work....

Under the Constitution, impeachable offenses are "treason, bribery and other high crimes and misdemeanors." ... Bribery and perjury both go to the same grave offense, the undermining of the administration of justice. And how could any person who fully understands and reflects on this fail to see that a president who gives perjurious, false and misleading testimony in a civil rights action brought against him and before a federal grand jury and encourages others to give perjurious, false and misleading testimony and uses the powers of his office to conceal the truth from the court and the grand jury and cover up his crimes should be impeached? ... If we tolerate such serious crimes as perjury and obstruction of justice by the president ... there will be grave, damaging consequences for our system of government....

Mr. Frank: After many years of investigations by every possible investigative tool of the federal government—congressional committees, the FBI under the command of the independent counsel, we have the following charge against Bill Clinton: He had a private consensual sexual affair and lied about it....

The fact is that previous cases of lying have called forth not only less than condemnation but congratulations from some of the members of this committee. That leads me to believe that what we are talking about with impeachment is an effort to get rid of a president who has been inconvenient, not a consistent application of a principle....

I am struck by those who have argued that censure is somehow an irrelevancy, a triviality, something of no weight. History doesn't say that. There are two members of this House right now who...were reprimanded for lying, myself and outgoing Speaker [Newt] Gingrich. We both were found to have lied, not under oath, but in official proceedings, and were reprimanded. I would tell you that having been reprimanded by this House of Representatives, where I'm so proud to serve, was no triviality....

Mr. Gekas: ... I say that a thousand historians and a swarm of political opinion polls and a gaggle of media programs and talk shows, nothing, none of those things, can change the vital facts in this case, and that is that falsehoods were uttered in a court proceeding under oath....

The Starr Report, which was full of tapes and Tripps and conspiracies and machinations of people behind the scenes and theories of executive privilege...put it together, package it all, and leaping out of that are the salient facts that the president uttered falsehoods under oath in the depositions and in grand jury, and later even to the 81 questions circulated by the Committee on the Judiciary....

And when coupled with the reality that every act of perjury strikes at the heart of the judicial system, endangers our individual rights to receive justice at the hands of our fellow citizens in the court system, then you can see that...perjury, falsehood under oath, has the capacity to destroy a branch of government, two branches of government, as a matter of fact all three branches of government.

If it is uttered by the president of the United States, he is diminishing the presidency, the executive branch. If he does so in a court of law, he is trampling against the walls of security that the court system provides all of us....

Mr. Schumer: ... Today we have four charges before us against the president: two perjury counts, obstruction of justice, and abuse of power. I would venture to say that if the obstruction and abuse charges were brought before an impartial jury of randomly selected American citizens and tried by competent lawyers on both sides, the president would be acquitted by a 12 to 0 margin....

So this case, this impeachment, boils down to two perjury charges. I agree that the president's testimony was misleading, maddening, evasive, prevaricating, and designed to shed as little light as possible on his embarrassing personal behavior. I have said so since September, that the president lied in his testimony and to the American people, but that he did so about a sexual relationship, not about matters of governance....

I believe that because [Kenneth] Starr knew that a case solely about sex and lying about sex would never pass muster with the American people, that he leveled the unsupportable charges of obstruction of justice and abuse of power. Many House Republicans, because of their hatred of President Clinton, were only too eager to accept the OIC's case without question....

Do you know, I think the American people still don't believe that we are foolish enough or partisan enough to do this. I think the American people are waiting for us to come to our senses and end this political game of chicken....

Mr. Coble: Much has been made about the absence of bipartisanship on this issue, and I want to reiterate my position on that. Do not point accusatory fingers at Republicans or Democrats because there is disagreement. Assuming we vote our consciences and exercise sound judgment, little else can be asked....

I represent a district far removed from the Beltway.... Here we are surrounded by Beltway advisers who demand fees in excess of $500 per hour. And many of these adept advisers, lawyers, counselors are spinmeisters. They attach their spin, and oftentimes confusion results.

But when I return to my district, I sometimes motor ... through the fox and the wine country of Virginia. And as I approach the North Carolina boundary line, my mind begins to clear, as I am at that point removed from the Beltway spin. All of sudden I am aware of the definition of sex. All of a sudden I know the meaning of "alone." I know what "is" is, as do the majority of my constituents....

Oliver Wendell Holmes said, "Sin has many tools, but the lie is the handle that fits them all." And the centerpiece to this scenario, I am convinced, ... is not sex; it is indeed perjury. It is the lie. It is the handle to the tool....

Mr. Berman: ... What is an impeachable offense? ... I find the best answer, albeit on a different subject, contained in the concurring opinion of Supreme Court Justice Potter Stewart ...: "The court was faced with the task of trying to define what may be indefinable. I shall not today attempt further to define the kinds of material I understand to be embraced, and perhaps I could never succeed in intelligibly doing so, but I know it when I see it." Justice Stewart was ruling on the definition of obscenity, not impeachment....

But as regards the basic concept of what constitutes an impeachable offense, for me the logic applies. I know it when I see it. And on balance, given the totality of the wrongdoing and the totality of the context, this isn't it....

There is something Alice-in-Wonderland-like watching someone so smart and so skilled, so admired by the American people for his intellect and his talents, digging himself deeper and deeper and deeper into a rabbit hole, and us along with him, and allowing him to escape accountability. This troubles me greatly, and I know it motivates many of the calls for impeachment....

That the president's conduct is not impeachable does not mean that society condones his conduct.... It just means that the popular vote of the people should not be abrogated for this conduct when the people clearly do not wish for his conduct to cause that abrogation....

Mr. Smith: ... By any common-sense measure, the president did not tell the truth, the whole truth, and nothing but the truth, as his oath required, when he testified before a judge and then before a grand jury ...

As committee witnesses have testified, many people have gone to jail for doing what the president did—lying or knowingly making false statements after swearing in court not to do so. However, others have not been punished for failing to tell the truth. So if the president were just an ordinary person ... it is not certain that he would be found to have committed a crime.

What then, makes this a case that rises to the impeachment level? I think there are two factors: the repeated and deliberate nature of the lies and the uniqueness of the office of the presidency....

The president consciously and persistently made an effort to deceive, give misleading answers, and tell lies. He made statements and engaged in actions designed to impede the investigation of the independent counsel. We already know the president still might be deceiving us today were it not for physical evidence that forced him to change his story.

As to the uniqueness of the office the president holds, he is a person in a position of immense authority and influence. He influences the lives of millions of Americans. He sets an example for us all....

My constituents often remind me that if anyone else in a position of authority, for example, a business executive, a military officer or a professional educator, had acted as the evidence indicates the president did, their career would be over....

Mr. Boucher: ... I have concluded that a statement by the Congress, formally censuring ... the president ... is more appropriate in these circumstances.

Of particular value to me in this analysis was the most recent congressional pronouncement on the proper use of the impeachment power. It is found in the report issued on a broad bipartisan basis by this committee in its 1974 proceeding in the Watergate inquiry....

To quote this committee's report, "Only that misconduct which is seriously incompatible with either the constitutional form and principles of our government or the proper performance of the duties of the presidential office will justify a use of the impeachment power."

... The facts now before this committee, which arise from a personal relationship and the effort to conceal it, simply do not arise to that standard. While the president's conduct was reprehensible, it did not threaten the nation, it did not undermine the constitutional form and principles of our government and it did not disable the proper performance of the constitutional duties of the presidential office....

I share the public's deep disdain for the actions of the president. And I am truly concerned that if Congress takes no action, many troubling...questions will remain with regard to the example that his conduct sets.

A resolution of censure passed by both houses of Congress requiring the signature of the president as an acknowledgement of the public's rebuke of his tawdry conduct is the preferable alternative....

Mr. Gallegly: ... I have carefully weighed the evidence, Mr. Chairman. I can only conclude that the president repeatedly lied under oath. His lies under oath I believe were intentional and premeditated....

The president, his delegates and my Democrat colleagues argue that even if these facts are provable, they do not rise to the level of impeachment. With all due respect, I believe they're wrong.... President Clinton's actions clearly fall under the heading of high crimes and misdemeanors. Our legal system, which protects the rights and liberties of all citizens, is dependent on people telling the truth under oath. The president is our chief law-enforcement officer and our chief magistrate. When he lies under oath, he undermines the integrity of our judicial system and threatens the rights and liberties of every one of us....

Before us is clear evidence that the president willfully and knowingly lied under oath, repeatedly and consistently. Those lies under oath are an attack on the rule of law against the very fabric of our society. He violated his oath of office and willfully sought to deny justice to another citizen. He violated the Constitution. To condone this would be to condemn our society to anarchy....

Mr. Nadler: ... Benjamin Franklin called impeachment a substitute for assassination. It is, in fact, a peaceful procedure for protecting the nation from despots by providing a constitutional means for removing a president who would misuse his presidential power to make himself a tyrant or otherwise to undermine our constitutional form of government....

Perjury is a serious crime, and if proven should be prosecuted in a court of law.... Perjury on a private matter, perjury regarding sex, is not a great and serious offense against the nation. It is not an abuse of uniquely presidential power. It does not threaten our form of government....

The American people have heard all the allegations against the president, and they overwhelmingly oppose impeaching him. The people elected the president. They still support him. We have no right to overturn the considered judgment of the American people.

There are clearly some members of the Republican majority who have never accepted the results of the 1992 or 1996 elections and who apparently have chosen to ignore the message of last month's election. But in a democracy, it is the people who rule, not political elites.... Some members of this committee may think the people have chosen badly, but it is the people's choice....

... The case is not there. The proof has not been put forward. The conduct alleged, even if proven, does not rise to the level of an impeachable offense. We should not dignify these articles of impeachment by sending them to the full House. To do so would be an affront to the Constitution....

Mr. Canady: ... I freely acknowledge that reasonable people can disagree about the weight of the evidence on certain of the charges. For example, I think there is doubt about the allegations that the president willfully lied concerning the date his relationship with Ms. Lewinsky began. But when we set aside any doubtful matters, we are still left with compelling evidence that the president made multiple false statements under oath, both in a civil rights case and before a federal grand jury, that he engaged in other conduct to corruptly influence the administration of justice and that he lied in sworn statements submitted to this very committee.

He did this not simply to avoid personal embarrassment.... On the contrary, he lied under oath and obstructed justice in a calculated effort to defeat the rights of a plaintiff in a federal civil rights case....

The Constitution does not authorize a censure of a president who is guilty of high crimes and misdemeanors. The Constitution provides for the impeachment of a president who has committed high crimes and misdemeanors....

William Jefferson Clinton must be called to account as the Constitution provides. He must be impeached and called before the Senate to answer for the harm he has ... caused by undermining the integrity of the high office entrusted to him by the people of the United States.

Mr. Scott: ... Since the beginning, a number of colleagues and I have called for a fair, expeditious and focused process. Such a process would have first specified the allegations. It would have then established a standard for determining which, if any, of those allegations constituted an impeachable offense. If any of the offenses ... might constitute an impeachable offense, the process would then have determined, with a presumption of innocence, whether those allegations were true by using cross-examination of witnesses and other traditionally reliable evidentiary procedures. If any such impeachable allegations were determined to be true, then we would judge whether they had the substantiality to justify the removal of the president from office....

Instead, we dumped mountains of salacious, uncross-examined and otherwise untested materials onto the Internet, then started sorting through boxes of documents to selectively find support for a foregone conclusion....

We have been warned repeatedly that these allegations are nowhere near what is necessary to overturn a national election.... Despite these cautionary flags, this committee has turned a deaf ear to hundreds of years of precedent and to the Constitution that has kept this country strong and unified....

And so here we are, on the verge of impeaching a United States president, overturning a national election, plunging our nation into constitutional crisis, in contradiction of everything the Founding Fathers labored to avoid, on a totally partisan basis....

Mr. Inglis: ... Most of us on this committee are lawyers and remember that Oliver Wendell Holmes sort of established the school of legal realism, which basically said let us abandon the search for truth and let us do relative justice between people because there is no truth out there to find. That ... set us on a significantly different course in our legal tradition than where we started at the foundation of the country....

President Clinton, I believe, is the culmination of that.... He is the epitome of someone who says there is no truth, everything is relative.... "We hold these relativistic moral assertions to be relativistically true. They work for me; see if they work for you." That's the way the White House spin machine would rewrite the preamble to the Declaration of Independence. But Mr. Jefferson said, "We hold these truths to be self-evident, that all men are created equal, that they are endowed by their creator with the right to life, liberty and the pursuit of happiness."...

I, for one, hope that we reassert here at the end of this millennium...that truth matters, that it matters whether the president of the United States lied or not. That, I believe, is the real question behind this....

[T]here are a lot of folks who would counsel, let's just move along. It is sort of the Clinton so-what defense. So what, I committed perjury. So what, I broke the law. Let's just move along.

I believe we have a constitutional obligation to act.... against the president of the United States and to punish his perjury and to act against his obstruction of justice and to say that we will not tolerate abuse of power....

Mr. Watt: ...I have seen the rule of law undermined in a number of different ways. I have seen it undermined by inequality of resources of people who come into the courtroom. I have seen it undermined by racism and bias.... I have seen it undermined by the lack of due process. I have seen the rule of law undermined by lying under oath....

But there is not a single way that the rule of law is undermined that is more disparaging and more important than a disregard for the law and the established standards of the law.... And that is why I was so outraged by the presentation by the majority counsel today....

[H]e said, "...if you don't impeach as a consequence of the conduct that I have just portrayed, then no House of Representatives will ever be able to impeach again." He went on to say "the bar will be so high that only a convicted felon or a traitor will need to be concerned."

My friends, that's what the rule of law says, that you can...impeach a president only when that standard is met....

Finally...he said these words, which I vigorously agree with: "One of the witnesses that appeared earlier likened the government of the United States to a three-legged stool...the legislative, the judicial and the executive. Remove one of those supports, and the state will totter. Remove two, and the structure will either collapse altogether or will rest upon a single branch of government. Another name for that is tyranny."

He is absolutely right. And where we are today is that we are trying to remove the executive of this country. We are about to tie up the judiciary and its chief justice in an impeachment trial in the Senate of the United States. And so the majority counsel would apparently have the legislative branch be the only standing leg of the stool....

Mr. Goodlatte: ... Many of the legal scholars testifying at the request of the president have admitted that the president lied in both the *Jones* case and before the grand jury, but argued that those offenses are not impeachable. If the committee were to adopt that position, however, it would create a double standard that places the president above the law. Virtually every public official in America, including our nation's governors, and virtually everyone in private employment would lose their job if they committed perjury or obstructed justice. In fact, many already have....

This same principle must also apply to the most powerful and privileged in our nation, including the president of the United States. To lose this principle devastates a legacy entrusted to us by our founding fathers and protected for us by generations of American families.

Some of my colleagues have decided that a resolution of censure is the only appropriate remedy for the president's actions. Their resolution admits that the president made false statements concerning his reprehensible conduct with a subordinate and wrongly took steps to delay discovery of the truth.... [I]f you truly believe the allegations contained in the censure resolution, how can you not vote to impeach? ...

Ms. Lofgren: ... We have finally reached the logical conclusion of what happens when a legislative chamber is obsessively preoccupied with investigating the opposition.... We now consider removing the president of the United States from the office to which he was twice elected ... for misconduct that is hardly a high crime or misdemeanor....

The people's will must not be overridden by those who ... believe they know what is best for the American people. The people's will may only be overridden and the government overthrown when the acts of the chief executive truly threaten our democratic institutions ... in other words, when the threat the president poses is so great that we can't wait until the next election to remove him....

Today I take my solace not in what we are about to do but in my belief that the American people get it. No, not every person knows the specific constitutional provisions at issue, but they know their government. They know what is important. They know the president they elected. They know what he has done. They know he has behaved badly, but they don't want him removed from office.... It's that simple....

For those who are out to get the president, shame on you. But beware: Next election, the voters will be out to get you. . . .

Mr. Buyer: . . . What are the consequences if this committee leaves a known perjurer in the Oval Office? First, perjury and obstruction of justice drive a stake in the heart of the rule of law. When the Constitution was ratified, it was christened as the grand American experiment. America stood alone in being governed by the rule of law as opposed to the rule of kings, tyrants, czars, monarchs, emperors, chiefs, sheiks, lords, barons and nobles. . . . We have an obligation to preserve the heritage of the rule of law. . . .

. . . If the president's verbal engineering prevails, then an evasive, incomplete, misleading and even maddening statement is not a lie. No one is ever really alone in the cosmos. "Is" is not a state of being. A person performing a sex act is having sexual relations, but the person receiving the sexual favor is not having sex. And a cover story is not a concocted rendition of an event with the willful intent to mislead others by lies, but instead a cover story is a simple, harmless revision of a historical event. . . .

C.S. Lewis called this technique "verbicide, the murder of a word." When plainspoken English language is twisted into the vague and ambiguous, society is devoid of trust. It undermines our social interactions, commerce, indeed, the rule of law and government itself. . . .

If this committee cannot bring itself to impeach a perjurious president, the bar will be raised for future circumstances that the House and this committee might face. Our children and grandchildren will face presidents who seek to flout the rule of law in a more ambitious manner. . . .

Ms. Waters: . . . I knew I would have to fight for the rights of minorities, women, the poor and the marginalized for the rest of my life. Never did I believe I would have to fight to protect the rights of the so-called most powerful individual of the free world.

This is a sad time in the history of this nation. We are on the brink of a Republican partisan impeachment of the president of the United States of America. The articles of impeachment are not based on his undermining of the Constitution, not based on actions that threaten the security of our nation, not based on treason, bribery, or a threat to our democracy but rather because of the blind, political determination of individuals who are philosophically . . . opposed to Bill and Hillary Clinton . . .

Mr. Starr's obvious bias and dislike of the president, his investigatory tactics and his flimsy case does not meet the constitutional standard for impeachment.... He has not made a credible case for perjury, obstruction of justice, or abuse of power. Finally, Mr. Starr has undermined his own investigation by his overzealous and unethical pursuit....

We have heard members of Congress describe the president's actions as "sickening," "reprehensible," and "unacceptable." However, the Constitution does not allow for the impeachment of a president because we are upset by his personal behavior....

Mr. Bryant: ... Some intimate that the Nixon case is the magic threshold, and anything less should not be considered for impeachment. That is simply, as the president's legal team put it, "a misleading statement." Analogize this situation to the prosecutor in a law court who fails to indict the bank robber who robbed five banks because the prosecutor had previously indicted a robber of 20 banks!

... Now we must use a common-sense approach to this evidence and look at the results of this series of calculations and incidents. Washington is a "wink and nod" community, where people do not need to say exactly what they want in order to get what they want done. Nor can we judge each act in a vacuum.... Just look at the time line, look at the actions and the results which all benefit the one person who says he had nothing to do with anything.

... Surely one cannot seriously argue perjury and obstruction of justice are not impeachable. They're paternal triplets of bribery, which is spelled out in the Constitution. Each of these have the same effect of thwarting the truth in our court system....

In conclusion, I would join the more than 100 newspapers and numerous other Americans to call upon the president to do the ... honorable thing: to resign from the office of the presidency.

Mr. Meehan: ... We have learned that [Bill Clinton] is more reckless in his private life than we even imagined—maddeningly reckless for someone with so much potential and so much to lose. We have learned that his instinct is to deceive when he's asked about his private recklessness, particularly when those doing the asking are linked to his political enemies. We have learned that this particular instinct to deceive carries into a judicial proceeding, though not without a competing instinct to act lawfully....

But can I conclude clearly, concretely and convincingly ... that he lacks the capacity to govern? Only if I willfully blind myself to the rule of life, a phrase I borrowed from Professor Lawrence Tribe. The rule of life teaches us that people are complex. They do wrong in certain contexts, yet forces behind that wrongdoing do not necessarily infect every context of their lives....

Branding a president who teetered on the edge of illegality in testifying about an illicit affair a tyrant or a traitor-in-waiting clearly defies the rule of life....

Yet... despite the awesome constitutional and practical significance of impeachment, we have been proceeding as if we are about to do anything but something exceptional.

Material witnesses? None to be found here, even though there are multiple instances of conflicting testimony on critical issues. We instead appear to have embraced a new theory of jurisprudence whereby the defense must prove its innocence to stave off punishment....

Accountable? Not us. We simply pass scandal on to the Senate, leaving it to the other body to do the dirty work of determining fact and meting out proportional punishment....

I say to my colleagues outside this committee... Please, save the Constitution from an overreach, save our nation from a prolonged Senate trial. Save... history from this committee's excesses.

Mr. Chabot: ... Back in 1972 I cast my first ballot in a presidential election. I was 19 years old, a college student. Like a majority of Americans that year, I voted for a Republican, Richard Nixon. Four years later, however, I voted for a Democrat, Jimmy Carter. That decision stemmed from my profound disappointment over Watergate.... Since that time I'd always hoped that our country would never again be confronted with an impeachment proceeding against an American president. But President Clinton's actions have again brought us to the brink of impeachment and he has no one to blame but himself....

The president of the United States, William Jefferson Clinton, has engaged in a pattern of cover-up and deceit. Standing alone, each individual offense is extremely serious. Collectively, they're overwhelming....

The historic record, the law and the Constitution tell us that the charges against the president do indeed rise to the level of impeachable offenses.

... Throughout these proceedings I have tried to keep an open mind, giving the president every opportunity to refute the facts that have been laid before our committee, but now all of the evidence is in and a decision is at hand. It has become apparent to me that impeachment is the only remedy that adequately addresses this president's illegal and unethical acts....

Mr. Delahunt:...Imagine you have been summoned to defend yourself in court. You don't know what you are charged with because there is no indictment. The prosecutor has spent four years investigating your financial dealings, but when you get to the courtroom, he only wants to talk about sexual indiscretions.

He sends the jury a 445-page report telling just his side of the story, and releases thousands of pages of secret grand jury testimony to the public. He calls none of the witnesses quoted in his report, so you can't challenge their accuracy. In fact, he calls only one witness, himself....

The judge allows new charges to be raised in the midst of the trial, but then drops them. He warns that you will be convicted if you do not offer a defense. Then, when you do so, he tells you not to hide behind legal technicalities.

The scene I have just described wasn't dreamed up by George Orwell or Franz Kafka;... In fact, it is similar to what is taking place here in America during the course of this impeachment inquiry....

We are about to impeach the president...on charges that never even would have been brought against an ordinary citizen....

Last year the House debated proposed term limits for members of Congress. One of the most respected leaders of the House led the fight against that legislation.... In his speech he said..."Our task today is to defend the consent of the governed, not to assault it. Do not give up on democracy. Trust the people."

The author of these eloquent words is my friend, the honorable Henry Hyde of Illinois. I remind him of these words today not to throw them back at him, but because it seems to me that the consent of the governed is once more under assault. And we sorely need such eloquence again....

Mr. Rothman:...I continue to hear from my Republican colleagues who say, why hasn't the president produced evidence exonerating himself? Well, look back at your law books, my friends. The accused is not required to prove his or her innocence. To put the burden of proof on the accused, in this case President Clinton, not only corrupts the Congress's impeachment power, but subverts 200 years of American justice.

...With no fact witnesses to prove the charges, with no opportunity to question them, with no opportunity to get to the truth, the prosecution here has not met its burden. Therefore, I am compelled and I will vote against the articles of impeachment...

But that does not end this matter. We must address the fact that in January of 1998, President Clinton wagged his finger and volunteered to us on television that he never had sexual relations with Monica Lewinsky.... He lied to us.

While that lie does not rise to the level of treason, bribery or other high crimes and misdemeanors, the president's lie and his...behavior with Ms. Lewinsky in the White House demands our punishment....

But I implore my colleagues to turn away from politics.... Impeachment was never meant to be a political tool, nor was it meant to be a punishment for immorality.... We must punish the president without punishing our system of government, our people or our great nation.

The committee adjourned, to resume opening statements the next morning, December 11:

Mr. Barr:... Sadly, I believe the case we are discussing today is but a small manifestation of President Clinton's utter and complete disregard for the rule of law. Throughout his presidency, his administration has been so successful at thwarting investigations and obstructing the work of Congress and the courts that it may be decades before history reveals the vastness of his abuse of power....

... You know, as children, all of us believed certain things with all of our hearts. We knew there was a difference between good and evil. We knew it was wrong to lie, and, equally important, that if we got caught, we would be punished....

In the short time I have served in Congress, I have learned that this place, this city, has an incredible power to complicate the simple. This staggering ability to muddle simple issues is perhaps best illustrated by the fact that much of the president's defense has hinged on defining common words in ways that shock most Americans who think they have a rather firm grasp on the meaning of words, such as "lie," "alone," "is," "perjury." ...

... [But] we are not locked in a strange parallel universe in which up is down, is becomes was, and being alone is a physical impossibility. We are not living in an alien world, we are living in America. We are living in an America in which we know that felons are prosecuted and are not allowed to remain in office. We live in an America in which rights prevail, wrongs must be righted, and indeed we have to stand up today, tomorrow, and forever, for the rule of law, the Constitution and accountability....

Ms. Jackson Lee:... I come here not angry at my Republican colleagues, but with a heavy heart.... I am sad, not only because the House is considering articles of impeachment for the president of the United States, but because I recognize that we are doing it without clear and convincing evidence. Nor are we using the standard outlined by our framers of the Constitution....

...There have been, including today, under 10 hearings by this committee that would decide the fate of this nation. There have been no fact witnesses brought by the majority, who...bear the heavy burden of proving that an impeachable offense has indeed been committed. And we have seen Mr. Starr...move from impartially referring the facts to being an advocate for the president's impeachment. Even worse, we have literally seen the prosecutor in this matter step away from his position as an officer of the court and step into the role of the witness-in-chief against the president of the United States. And this occurred to the horror of Mr. Starr's own ethics adviser, Sam Dash, who resigned because of it....

Mr. Chairman, we are morally bound to make our disapproval known. But we can best do it through censure, an act which would help us maintain constitutional integrity and to ensure that Lincoln's dream of the future will remain a constant reality; that we will continue to live in a nation where there is government of the people, by the people, and for the people....

Mr. Jenkins:...Throughout this proceeding many expressions of concern have been voiced about the presidency itself. I share these concerns and have for decades. Since 1960, one president has been tragically assassinated. One president was driven out of office and did not seek reelection. One president was caused to resign. Three good presidents were voted out of office after one full or a partial term of office. Only one president thus far in almost four decades has served two full terms in office. The presidency, I think, is under attack. But amid this concern there has been little mention that presidents themselves can strengthen the presidency by conducting themselves in a manner that brings pride and admiration and confidence to the minds of all our citizens....

If there is a vote to impeach, it will not be the end of our republic. Although our system is, indeed, fragile, it has survived impeachment, it has survived two world wars and numerous other conflicts, the Great Depression and a very bitter civil war. The country survived these things partly because we believe that we all, and the least among us, are entitled to a measure of dignity and to be dealt with fairly and to not be overwhelmed by the most powerful among us....

For those invested with great power and privileges, it seems to me that the simple code for them to follow is this: to whom much is given, much is expected in return.

Mr. Wexler: ... Wake up, America! They are about to impeach our president. They are about to reverse two national elections. They are about to discard your votes....

Before the Starr report was delivered to Congress, the Republicans said they would not even try to impeach the president over just the Monica Lewinsky affair. They promised grand White House conspiracies of misused FBI files, Whitewater land deals and travel office abuses.... They found nothing.

... Well, wake up, America. This elitist group has decided that they know better than you. This committee will vote straight down party lines to impeach and remove the president....

And what's it all about? Sex. They use criminal terms, like "perjury," but guess what the perjury is really about? ... [T]he impeachment of the president ... hinges on a tortured definition of sex. That's what the perjury in the grand jury is all about, folks, but they're going to impeach the president anyway.

The Republicans ... say the president tampered with witnesses. Well, you better wake up, America. You could be tampering with a witness and not even know it, because ... you can be guilty of witness tampering a person who is not a witness in any case. The facts clearly show that Betty Currie was not listed as a witness or a potential witness at the time of the alleged tampering, but they are going to impeach the president anyway.

They claim the president has obstructed justice, but ... Monica Lewinsky testified under oath that nobody, nobody, asked her to lie, and nobody offered her a job for her silence. But they are going to impeach the president anyway.

They claim the president abused his power. How? By asserting his constitutional rights and privileges pursuant to the advice of his lawyers. Well, wake up, America! Because if they can do it to the president, they can do it to you.... How un-American. But they are going to impeach him anyway....

... The president betrayed his wife. He did not betray his country.

Mr. Hutchinson: ... It is not for the president or his lawyers to determine who can or cannot seek justice, and if the president lied under oath in a federal civil rights case, then he took it upon himself to deny the right of a fellow

American ... equal access to relief in the courts. The president's lawyers have declared such a lie to be a small one, a small consequence, and therefore not impeachable. But I cannot see how denying the rights of a fellow citizen can be considered of small consequence. ...

There have been many criticisms of Judge Starr. ... In hindsight, I would have preferred that the attorney general had appointed a different independent counsel on the Lewinsky matter, that Judge Starr had been more actively involved in interviewing the witnesses, that he had not engaged in outside representation and that he had been less of an advocate and more of a conduit of the facts.

But ... despite these criticisms, the president had a decision to make when he testified in the civil deposition and in the grand jury; he could tell the truth, or he could lie. ... It is reminiscent of every criminal case that I have prosecuted to hear the president's lawyers attack the prosecutor, blame this committee, criticize the process ... I concede his lawyers that tactic. But I have also urged them to show me compelling facts rebutting the long trail of evidence suggesting that the president lied under oath and obstructed justice. This they have not done to my satisfaction. ...

Our nation has survived the failings of its leaders before, but it cannot survive exceptions to the rule of law in our system of equal justice for all. ... [I]magine a country where a Congress agrees the strong are treated differently than the weak, where mercy is the only refuge for the powerless, where the power of our positions govern all of our decisions. Such a country cannot long endure. ...

Mr. Barrett: ... Unfortunately, the president's conduct is not the only unsettling component to our present crisis. I am also deeply, deeply troubled by the events leading up to the president's deposition in the *Jones* case. There clearly was a channel of communication between Ken Starr's office and Paula Jones' attorneys through Linda Tripp, and I believe her motives and actions, in part personal, in part political, cannot be ignored here. If we are to set aside our only national election, we must be confident that political enemies or political motives did not set the stage for this political morality play, for if they did, then there is a potentially greater danger here to our democracy than lying about sex. ...

I want to thank you, Mr. Chairman, for your decision to permit a vote on our censure resolution here in committee. I agree with you that it will foster comity. But I have another request, not just to you, but to all my colleagues on this committee. I have listened as many, if not most members on the Republican side of the aisle have asserted that this is a vote of conscience....

So my request to you is a simple and straightforward one: Please let me vote my conscience both here in committee and on the floor. Please allow our censure resolution to move to the Rules Committee either on a positive or negative vote....

Mr. Pease: ... I do not believe that all of the allegations presented meet the standard of being proven by clear and convincing evidence. The final assessment of which meet what I believe to be the necessary higher standard of proof will depend in part on the form the articles take after the committee completes the amendatory process. Given what I know now, though, I anticipate that I will conclude this matter the way I began it, somehow managing to irritate virtually everyone in my district who holds an opinion...

Those who believe there's nothing here will be disappointed to know that I believe there is. Those who want me to do everything I can to vilify this president in every way possible will be disappointed to know that my assessment on the facts cannot allow me to do so....

As I conclude, Mr. Chairman, I would like to offer an observation about this committee. It has often been called one of the most polarized in the Congress.... There are members here with whom I strongly disagree. There are some I find annoying, even abrasive. But I believe all of the members of this committee are decent human beings who are honestly trying to do the right thing as they see it.

... I believe firmly that each of us has honestly, sincerely struggled to do what he or she believed must be done and that party affiliation was not the basis for decisions made here. Those who contend otherwise ... do a disservice to the members of this committee, to their work, and to the Congress.

Mr. Cannon: ... I believe profoundly that the behavior of this president is unacceptable because I agree with John Jay, one of our Founding Fathers, who said, "When oaths cease to be sacred, our dearest and most valuable rights become insecure." ...

We have heard much comparing this matter with Watergate. Nixon is said to have abused citizens through the IRS, the CIA, and the FBI. We do not have before us allegations that this president has done the same....

But we do want the president and those around him and future presidents and those around them to know that we will not allow weakness of character, willfulness, or any other trait of a president to undermine the sacredness of oaths....

Before the president committed the acts of perjury that we now confront, Alan Dershowitz, George Stephanopoulos and others warned the president that he would be impeached if he lied to the grand jury. It did not occur to them that it could be otherwise....

I'm not going to deal here with the facts of the case. They are compelling enough that even Democratic members of this committee and witnesses called by the president have acknowledged that the president lied under oath.... The fact is, the unwinding of this extraordinary constitutional system is inexorable if the president presents an example of perjury....

Mr. Rogan:... On the day George Washington became our first president, he pledged to our new country that the foundation of his public policies would be grounded in principles of private morality....

Most significantly, in his first presidential address, Washington presented himself not as a ruler of men, but as a servant of the law. He established the tradition that, in America, powerful leaders are subservient to the rule of law and to the consent of the governed....

There is no business of government more important than upholding the rule of law. A sound economy amounts to nothing beside it, because without the rule of law, all contracts are placed in doubt and all rights to property become conditional.

National security is not more important than the rule of law, because without it, there can be no security and there is little left defending....

Mr. Chairman, the evidence clearly shows that the president engaged in a repeated and lengthy pattern of felonious conduct, conduct for which ordinary citizens can and have been routinely prosecuted and jailed. This simply cannot be wished or censured away.... With a heavy heart, but with an unwavering belief in the appropriateness of the decision, I will cast my vote for articles of impeachment...

Mr. Graham:... We are going to have a partisan vote, but that is okay. You have parties, you have political thought, you have political differences. That is a good thing, not a bad thing. A lot of people have fought and died so you could have those differences....

I have asked the president on numerous occasions to reconcile himself with the law. I never meant for him to have to humiliate himself.... I merely want him to have the character and the courage to come forward and admit to criminal wrongdoing, that he violated his oath, that he engaged witnesses in an improper way.

I was willing to make sure, if I could in any fashion, that the whole affair would end then, that two years from now he need not have to face prosecution. I think the chances of that are almost zero. . . .

Should he be impeached? . . . The hardest decision I think I will ever make. Learning that the president lied to the grand jury about sex, I still believe that every president of the United States, regardless of the matter they're called to testify about before a grand jury, should testify truthfully, and if they don't, they should be subject to losing their job. . . .

And the most chilling of all things to me was the episode after he left the deposition, he told Mr. Blumenthal that Monica Lewinsky was basically coming on to him, he had to fight her off. He told Betty Currie, "She wanted to have sex with me and I couldn't do that." The most chilling thing was, for a period of time, the president was setting stories in motion that were lies. Those stories found themselves in the press to attack a young lady who could potentially be a witness against him.

To me, that is very much like Watergate . . . and every member of Congress should look at that episode and decide, is this truly about sex? . . . The president's fate is in his own hands. Mr. President, you have one more chance. Don't bite your lip; reconcile yourself with the law.

Ms. Bono: . . . [A]lthough the White House spin machine has tried to place the blame for these proceedings on Judge Starr or the committee majority . . . the reason we are here is because, unfortunately, the president of the United States lied to the American people and a federal grand jury and then he attempted to use the full power of the White House to cover it up. Then, instead of trying to present a credible defense that respected the intelligence of the American people, the White House and its allies used their spin machine to attack its opponents and destroy reputations.

. . . In the real world of everyday Americans, people who break the law face consequences. That is what our Founders intended when they drafted a Constitution and established the rule of law as the framework for our society. And when a president attempts to weave his way through the rule of law to cover up a lie, he puts the Constitution itself on trial. . . .

I know that the president is a very likeable man. I understand why people want this issue to just go away. But the issue we are facing is at the very core of our constitutional system, and while many people may like this president, I hope that they love their country more, because that is what I will base my vote on—my love for this country and on our Constitution....

Mr. Hyde: ... Perjury is not sex. Obstruction is not sex. Abuse of power is not about sex. It is important to understand that none of the proposed articles include allegations of sexual misconduct.... But when circumstances require you to participate in a formal court proceeding and under oath [you] mislead the parties and the court by lying, that is a public act and deserves public sanction....

What concerns me most deeply ... here is the significance of the oath. When the president performs the public act of asking God to witness his promise to tell the truth, the whole truth and nothing but the truth, that is not trivial. Whether it is a civil suit or before the grand jury, the significance of the oath cannot and must not be cheapened if our proud boast that we are a government of laws and not of men is to mean anything. I submit it means everything. It was purchased for us by the lives of countless patriots ...

Now, we seek impeachment, not conviction nor censure. Those are decisions for the ... Senate. We merely decide if there is enough for a trial. The accusatory body should not be the adjudicatory body.... That doesn't mean we don't take our responsibility seriously, but it means we have a different role.

We are told an impeachment trial would ... reverse two elections. We are not reversing any election. Bob Dole will not end up president of the United States if there is an impeachment. We are following a process wisely set down as a check-and-balance on executive overreaching, by our Founding Fathers.

This vote says something about us. It answers the question, just who are we, and what do we stand for? Is the president one of us, or is he a sovereign? We vote for our honor, which is the only thing we get to take with us to the grave.

The opening statements complete, Chairman Hyde announced a thirty-minute recess. Then the committee began the formal debate on the articles of impeachment. Under the rules, each of the four articles would be debated and voted on in turn.

Article I charged that President Clinton "willfully provided perjurious, false and misleading testimony" in his testimony before the federal grand jury.

In debate, Democrats homed in on a theme they had been sounding throughout the hearings: The article failed to provide specific quotes, did not single out the instances of false testimony that had given rise to the charge. In the words of Jerrold

Nadler: "It is basic that we should be told, before voting, the specific words that are alleged to be perjurious.... Could we have that? Could we have those words, please, so that we could discuss them as to whether they are perjurious and so that the Senate ... will know what the allegation is and the defense attorneys will know what they must defend against?"

Barney Frank suggested that the Republicans were avoiding specifics out of embarrassment. "I really believe the crux of this is that the three specific acts of grand jury perjury Kenneth Starr puts forward, you are embarrassed to take to the floor, you are embarrassed to try and unseat a twice-elected president on this degree of trivia and you have therefore used obfuscatory language to suggest a set of offenses that don't have specific support." Later in the debate, Frank said the Republicans "cannot be specific, because if they are specific, they are trivial. And if they want to be portentous, they have to be vague."

For their part, the Republicans argued that the draft language was merely a summary of a long and well-defined list of specific false testimony in the referral and attending documents. As George Gekas of Pennsylvania put it, "The article summarizes the allegation that is to go to the Senate and provides with it voluminous portions of records that sustain the main allegation in the article." The Judiciary Committee had done much the same in the Watergate case, they added. (To that point, the Democrats responded that perjury had not been the charge in 1974. "When you are dealing with perjury, it is the very words that constitute the crime," said Charles Schumer. "When you don't list the words that are allegedly perjurious, it is like alleging obstruction or subornation of a witness without mentioning the witness.")

Charles Canady took the time to recite a number of the president's grand jury statements that he believed to be lies, then said: "Now I understand that there are differences of opinion. I don't think that there is much room for a difference when you look at the whole weight of the evidence and all of this in context." And James Rogan declared: "This entire proceeding, from the day the Chairman first banged the gavel, has never been about the facts of the case in the eyes of the minority. It has been complaints about procedure."

In the end, the committee agreed to Article I on a straight party-line vote: 21 members, all Republicans, for; 16 members, all Democrats, against.

Article II charged that the president had "willfully provided perjurious false and misleading testimony" in the civil case brought against him by Paula Jones—both in answers to written questions in December 1997, and in his deposition on January 17, 1998.

The Democrats' main argument against Article II rested on materiality—that is, that even if the president lied about his relationship with Monica Lewinsky in the Jones' interrogatories and deposition, it was immaterial to Paula Jones' case. Lewinsky was a fully consensual partner in her relationship with President Clinton, the Democrats said, so the details of their affair were irrelevant to a sexual-harassment lawsuit of the sort brought by Jones. "To throw him out of office because he tried to conceal a consensual sexual relationship in a lawsuit in which it had no relevance," said Frank, "in fact would be a very grave error." The matter had been ruled on by the court, John Conyers added: "Judge Webber Wright made that clear in three separate rulings that testimony about the president's relationships with other women simply did not go to the core of the issues put in dispute by Ms. Jones." The Democrats also argued that the fact that Paula Jones' case had been dismissed—then settled before an appeal was heard—called into serious question the legitimacy of any article of impeachment based on it.

Republicans replied that what mattered was what the president had done at the time, when the case was very much alive. "The fact of the matter is that in this proceeding, the judge decided that the president would have to answer questions at the deposition concerning Ms. Lewinsky and other people that might have been in a similar position," said Canady. "Mr. Clinton didn't agree with that decision of the judge. I understand that. Mr. Clinton thought that was unfair. I understand that. But the judge decided he would have to answer those questions. Now, the judge having decided that, the president went in to the deposition and he lied. We all know that." And Gekas argued that because the president's false testimony was designed to thwart a suit brought against him by an American citizen, it "may be, in the context of the entire impeachment proceedings, more vital, more important and more worthy of our conscientious decision making than even the falsehoods uttered in the grand jury."

The vote on Article II was 20 ayes and 17 noes. It was along party lines, with one exception: Lindsey Graham of South Carolina joined the Democrats in voting against the article.

Article III charged that President Clinton had "prevented, obstructed and impeded the administration of justice, and has to that end engaged personally, and through his subordinates and agents, in a course of conduct or scheme designed to delay, impede, cover up and conceal the existence of evidence and testimony related to a Federal civil rights action brought against him." It enumerated seven alleged instances of obstruction of justice:

- *That Clinton had "corruptly encouraged" Monica Lewinsky to file a false affidavit in the Paula Jones case*

- *That he had urged her to lie if called as a witness in the case*
- *That he had "engaged in, encouraged or supported a scheme to conceal evidence" (i.e., the gifts he had given Lewinsky)*
- *That as events reached the crisis point, he had "intensified and succeeded" in an effort to find Lewinsky a job to keep her from testifying truthfully*
- *That at his deposition in the Paula Jones case, he allowed attorney Robert Bennett to cite Lewinsky's false affidavit on his behalf*
- *That he tried to influence the testimony of Betty Currie*
- *That he tried to influence the testimony of other staffers*

In the debate, one Republican explicated each of the seven. James Sensenbrenner, for instance, took the first. "[W]hen the president encouraged Monica Lewinsky to file an affidavit, he knew that it would have to be false for Ms. Lewinsky to avoid testifying," said Sensenbrenner. "If she filed a truthful affidavit, one acknowledging a sexual relationship with the president, she certainly would have been called as a deposition witness...." Asa Hutchinson was the spokesman on charge number 2; he cited the 2 A.M. phone call in which Clinton seemed to urge Lewinsky to use their longtime cover story if questioned about their relationship: "You can always say you were coming to see Betty or you were bringing me letters."

Most of the arguments both for and against the charges—both individually and collectively—had been raised repeatedly in the course of the hearings. The Republicans argued, with Steve Chabot, that all these individual events were connected in a "web and deceit and cover-up." The purpose "wasn't just to keep the president from being embarrassed," said Chabot. "It was to defeat a civil rights sexual harassment lawsuit.... This isn't about sex.... We are talking about the president of the United States engaging in cover-up, witness tampering and a well-planned effort to thwart our system of justice."

The Democrats, meanwhile, continued to protest that the charges were groundless and unfair—"a grab bag of allegations," said Nadler. Republicans, they argued, were basing their case on surmise and assumptions justified by no hard facts and were also willfully ignoring exculpatory evidence. Take the case of Lewinsky's affidavit, said Conyers: "Is there anyone here who doesn't know that she swore that no one ever asked her to lie and that the decision as to what the affidavit should contain was a decision made by her alone?" Or, said Schumer, consider the job hunt: "Yes, there was a job hunt. We all agree there was a job hunt. We all agree it started before there was any knowledge of a judicial process.... We all agree it was a very similar job search. And we all agree there are two plausible explanations after it became clear that there was a Paula Jones lawsuit and a deposition: One, to get Mon-

ica Lewinsky away from the scene to prevent the continuation of an illicit affair, and two, to keep Monica Lewinsky quiet before a judicial proceeding." The first, he suggested, made more sense.

Once again, the vote was along strict party lines: 21, all Republicans, yes; 16, all Democrats, no.

Article IV charged that President Clinton had "repeatedly engaged in conduct that resulted in misuse and abuse of his high office." It had four subsections, delineating the alleged instances of abuse: false statements design to deceive the public; false statements to aides and cabinet members so that they could disseminate the falsehoods; assertions of executive privilege to obstruct a federal criminal investigation, and lack of response or false responses to questions from the House of Representatives.

George Gekas opened the session by introducing an amendment that dropped the first three subsections altogether, leaving only the charge that the president had "willfully made perjurious, false and misleading sworn statements" in response to the Judiciary Committee's eighty-one questions.

"I have always valued the separation of powers and particularly with respect to executive privilege," Gekas explained, adding, "we ought to give, in my judgment and the judgment of many, the benefit of the doubt in the assertion of executive privilege." The president's counsel "was sure and certain in pointing out that in most of the executive privilege assertions by the president, he was advised by counsel"; in addition, "in the cases that wound up in court, the executive privilege itself, the right to assert it, was sanctified . . . permitted by the court." Thus he had persuaded his Republican colleagues that it would be best to leave out the first three charges. But, he said, "we feel just as strongly about leaving in number 4."

Most of the Democrats cautiously endorsed dropping the three charges, although Howard Berman called the move "an orchestrated dance to create an illusion of reasonability." And many agreed with Schumer that Gekas was moving the article "not from the ridiculous to the sublime, [but] from the very ridiculous to simply the ridiculous." Since Article IV, if so amended, would now be not about abuse of power, but about perjury, he returned to a theme the Democrats had sounded before: "What specifics? Which of the 81 questions rise to the level of impeachment? Do all of them? Do some of them? Does one of them?" Henry Hyde responded with ten specific examples. Even so, Jerrold Nadler rephrased Schumer's assessment, commending Gekas for changing "the absolutely indefensible to the still absolutely indefensible, but on fewer grounds."

The discussion then returned to broader subjects, particularly to the Democrats' ongoing complaint that the Republicans were trying to downplay the importance of the committee's course by arguing that a vote in the House for the articles of impeachment was not necessarily a vote to remove the president from office—that only the Senate had that power. There had been some suggestions that a committee member could vote for the articles of impeachment without believing that the president really ought to be removed.

Howard Coble of North Carolina said he understood all too well the gravity of the situation. "I have had knots in my gut all week because of this," he said. Frank alluded to that comment: "Why does he have knots in his stomach? Just because he is sending this over to the Senate to decide? He has knots in his stomach, as he courageously articulated, because he understands what we are doing. He understands that you are trying to undo the election."

Bob Barr reminded the committee, "the fact of the Constitution remains, impeachment is not removal from office. Impeachment is not removal from office."

Finally, the committee voted on Gekas's amendment: 29 ayes, 5 noes, and 3 present. All of the Republicans except Christopher Cannon voted in favor; four Democrats voted against, and three voted present.

Then they turned to Article IV itself, now reduced to the charge of lying to Congress. The vote was along straight party lines: 21 for, all Republicans, and 16 against, all Democrats.[1]

The last order of business was the censure resolution drafted by the Democrats.[2] As John Conyers observed, there was virtually no chance that the measure could pass in the committee, since not one of the Republicans was willing to vote for it. "So we will practice our arguments today and prepare them for a larger presentation" in the full House, said Conyers.

The terms of the debate were clear. Democrats argued, in the words of Rick Boucher of Virginia, that censure was simply the better route. "I have a deep disdain for the president's actions," said Boucher. "He deserves the admonishment and the censure and the rebuke of the Congress, and in adopting this resolution of censure, we will give voice to the widely held public view that the president should not be removed from office, but that he should be admonished by the Congress for his conduct."

Republicans credited the Democrats for the strength of the resolution's language. But they agreed with Lamar Smith of Texas: "The same reasons listed in this cen-

---

[1] For a full text of the four articles of impeachment sent to the House floor, see Appendix IV.
[2] For full text of the censure resolution, see Appendix V.

sure, in my judgment, justify an impeachment. There are three other reasons to ... oppose this censure. The first is that we don't know if it is constitutional.... The second reason is that it might be repealed by future Congresses. This is what happened with the previous censure back in 1834, when President Andrew Jackson was censured. The third reason ... is that it is contrary to precedent." It had been the Senate, not the House, he explained, that censured President Jackson.

Both sides cited constitutional experts. Both sides expressed grave reservations about the possibility that censuring a president would become a common way for Congresses to express political disagreements with chief executives. The Democrats observed that censure was the only truly bipartisan way out of the situation. Barney Frank: "Here's your choice: bipartisan censure, both parties, the majority of both parties saying we're appalled by what the president did, and we take this historical, unique opportunity to say so, or a narrow and crabbed bipartisan majority ..."

The final vote: 14 ayes, 22 noes (Democrat Robert Scott of Virginia voted with the Republican majority), and 1 present (Maxine Waters of California).

PART II

THE HOUSE

Floor Debate and Impeachment

Henry Hyde opened the session with the formal announcement: "Mr. Speaker, by direction of the Committee on the Judiciary, I call up a privileged Resolution (House Resolution 611) impeaching William Jefferson Clinton, president of the United States, for high crimes and misdemeanors, and ask for its immediate consideration." The clerk read the articles of impeachment, and after some procedural matters were disposed of, the debate was under way. The Speaker pro tempore for this debate was Ray LaHood of Illinois, widely regarded as one of the House's most accomplished parliamentarians.

Certain themes resurfaced again and again in the members' comments. Democrats protested the timing of the session: On the eve of the debate's scheduled opening, President Clinton had ordered American troops into action against Saddam Hussein's Iraq, and Democrats had wanted to postpone the debate until the hostilities ended; they succeeded in delaying the start by just one day. Minority whip David E. Bonior voiced his party's displeasure right at the start: "We do not believe this is a proper time to be debating removing the commander in chief, while thousands of men and women are fighting abroad." The question of censure, too, was much on the Democrats' minds; the House leadership refused to allow a vote on the floor. Finally, of course, questions of fairness and partisanship—ranging from the start of the Starr investigation to the very day of the debate—were at the forefront, as was the basic issue of whether President Clinton's conduct was truly impeachable.

Meanwhile, the Republicans repeated their core assertions that no one, including the president, is above the law; that the evidence amassed by Kenneth Starr proved conclusively that President Clinton had committed perjury and obstructed justice, thus impeding the judicial system and violating his oath of office, and that these offenses were eminently impeachable. Members of the Judiciary Committee took turns explicating the individual articles of impeachment. Many Republicans echoed the sentiments of Lamar Smith of Texas about the lessons the House would leave for posterity: "For the benefit of our country to set an example for our children, our grandchildren and future generations, we must maintain our high ideals. That the president has failed to meet the standard does not mean we should lower it."

Hyde led off the debate.

Mr. Hyde: ... The question before this House is rather simple. It is not a question of sex. Sexual misconduct and adultery are private acts and are none of Congress's business. It is not even a question of lying about sex. The matter before the House is a question of lying under oath. This is a public act, not a private act. This is called perjury....

[W]e must decide if a president, the chief law-enforcement officer of the land, the person who appoints the attorney general, the person who nominates every federal judge, the person who nominates to the Supreme Court and the only person with a constitutional obligation to take care that the laws be faithfully executed, can lie under oath repeatedly and maintain it is not a breach of trust sufficient for impeachment.

... The president's defenders in this House have rarely denied the facts of this matter.... They have admitted, in effect, he did it.

But then they have argued that this does not rise to the level of an impeachable offense. This is the "so what" defense whereby the Chief Executive, the successor to George Washington, can cheapen the oath, and it really does not matter. They suggest that to impeach the president is to reverse the result of a national election as though Senator Dole would become president....

As my colleagues know, we have been attacked for not producing fact witnesses, but this is the first impeachment inquiry in history with the Office of Independent Counsel in place, and their referral to us consisted of 60,000 pages of sworn testimony grand jury transcripts, depositions, statements, affidavits, video and audiotapes. We had the facts, and we had them under oath.... Now there was so little dispute on the facts they called no fact witnesses and have even based a resolution of censure on the same facts....

Let us declare, unmistakably, that perjury and obstruction of justice disqualify a man from retaining the presidency of the United States....

Richard Gephardt (D-Missouri): ... The actions of the majority, in my view, show a lack of common sense and decency.... [W]hen our young soldiers, men and women, are in harm's way, we should not be ... talking about removing our Commander in Chief....

We are now at the height of a cycle of the politics of negative attacks, character assassination, personal smears, of good people, decent people, worthy people. It is no wonder to me and to you that the people of our country today are cynical and indifferent and apathetic about our government and about our country. The politics of smear and slash and burn must end....

In this debate, we are being denied a vote as an alternative to impeachment for censure and condemnation of our president for the wrongful acts that we believe have been performed....

I know what you say. You say that the Constitution does not allow this vote of censure. Constitutional scholars in the hundreds ... have opined that ... the Constitution in no way prevents us from doing this.

What do I conclude? ... I can only conclude that some are afraid of this vote....

Asa Hutchinson (R-Arkansas): ... The first article is perjury before the grand jury.... The facts are that a federal civil rights lawsuit was filed by another citizen of the United States against the president. The Supreme Court said that lawsuit could proceed. In January of 1998, a deposition was taken, and the committee found that the president ... lied under oath in order to protect himself from that lawsuit. At that point, a criminal investigation was begun ... and as a result of that investigation, President Clinton agreed to testify before the federal grand jury investigating these allegations.

Prior to his testimony ... there was a uniform warning across this land ... Mr. President, whatever you do, do not lie to the grand jury.... Despite these warnings, the committee found that the president went before the grand jury, took an oath to tell the truth, and then intentionally provided false statements.... The article specifically charges the president lied about his relationship with a subordinate employee. He provided false statements about the truthfulness of his prior testimony. He falsely testified about statements made by his attorney in the previous lawsuit. False statements were made about his efforts to corruptly influence the testimony of witnesses....

The facts establish a pattern of false statements, deceit and obstruction, and by committing these actions, the president moved beyond the private arena of protecting personal embarrassing conduct and...invaded the very heart and soul of that which makes this nation unique in the world, the right of any citizen to pursue justice equally. The conduct obstructed our judicial system and at that point that became an issue...of national consequence....

Mr. Bonior (D-Michigan):...To force an impeachment vote is to completely ignore the will of the American people. The people of this country support the president...Why can we not stop right here and come to our senses?

The American people have made it very clear they oppose impeachment. They are looking for another solution, a just solution, a solution that condemns the president's wrongdoing yet enables America to put this sorry spectacle behind us and get on with the country's business.... Censure, this is the one option the Republican leadership refuses to consider. They will not even let us vote on it. President Ford supports censure, Senator Dole supports censure, Members on both sides of the aisle support censure. I dare say if it was made in order, it would pass. Yet the Republican leadership in this House is so angry, so obsessed, so self-righteous, that they are refusing us a true vote of conscience....

Barney Frank (D-Massachusetts): Mr. Speaker, this House is launched on a historically tragic case of selective moralizing....

When Ronald Reagan's Secretary of Defense was indicted for perjury by an independent counsel and pardoned by George Bush, Members on that side applauded the action. When Speaker [Newt] Gingrich was found to have been inaccurate 13 times in an official proceeding to the House Ethics Committee, he was reprimanded and simultaneously reelected Speaker with the overwhelming vote of Members on that side.

...The American people also believe censure is appropriate. Let me agree with those who say that simply because a large number of the voters believe something, we are not obligated to vote for it....

But while we have the right not to vote for something just because there is overwhelming public support, in a democracy, we have no right not to vote on it....

Chet Edwards (D-Texas):...History will surely judge this process as a combination of Kafka, To Kill a Mockingbird and Keystone Kops.

Mr. Speaker, if the Golden Rule were to be our guide, who among us... would want to be a defendant in a case where the rules of law and fairness were ignored, where secret grand jury testimony against us was released to the world, where there was not one direct witness, where your defense attorney was limited to one hour of cross-examining your chief accuser, where your attorney was forced to give your final defense even before one charge had been formally presented against you, where the charges of perjury against you were finally presented at the 11th hour and failed the test of decency which statements were allegedly perjurious?... We should not judge this president by that process....

George Gekas (R-Pennsylvania): Mr. Speaker, a loud lament has been heard about some deprivation of the right to vote one's conscience. But that is exactly why we are here today. All of us... must vote the ultimate sense of conscience....

The moment of truth for the president of the United States first faced him in December of 1997. It faced him in the nature of a legal document... interrogatories that were forwarded to him in pursuit by the *Paula Jones* attorneys of discovery proceedings in their case, a document... to be attested to under oath to answer certain questions. The president faced his moment of truth right there and then, the first item in the legal proceedings that have become the hallmark of these proceedings, and there under oath testified falsely....

But here is the important difference that Members must take into account.... The evidence is that when he signed these interrogatories... there was no parsing of definitions. There was no argument among the lawyers about meanings and definitions.... This was a straight interrogatory to which the president of the United States added perjurious and false answers.

In a single moment... he began the long chain of falsehoods that have led us to our moment of truth here today....

Rick Boucher (D-Virginia):... While the president's conduct was reprehensible, it did not threaten the nation. It did not undermine the constitutional form and principles of our government....

To misuse impeachment power in this case, as some are now prepared to do, will create a national horror. The divisions on this subject which now exist within our society will harden and deepen.... The president and the Congress will be diverted from their urgent national business while prolonged proceedings take place in the Senate. There will be a lowering of the standard for future impeachments with an inherent weakening of the presidential office....

John Lewis (D-Georgia):... America is sick. Her heart is heavy. Her soul is aching....

Almost 50 million people elected Bill Clinton as our president in spite of his... failings. They, the people, elected Bill Clinton President of the United States and they want him to remain the president of the United States. And yet some, some even in this Chamber, have never accepted the verdict of the people.... Instead they embarked on a crusade of personal destruction.

Our Constitution was never intended to be used as a hammer to destroy our political enemies....

What President Clinton did was wrong.... There is no disagreement, no debate. But how, how, my colleagues, should we respond? How we respond, how we act says as much about us and our character as it does about his.... Who among us has not sinned?

John Conyers (D-Michigan):... I want to remind my colleagues that I am witnessing the most tragic event of my career in the Congress, in effect a Republican coup d'état, in process....

Impeachment was designed to rid this nation of traitors and tyrants, not attempts to cover up extramarital affairs. This resolution trivializes our most important tool to maintain democracy. It downgrades the impeachment power into a partisan weapon that can be used with future presidents.... Now, I am personally outraged that we would decapitate the Commander in Chief at a time when we are at war abroad. Republicans sacrifice the national security by doing so....

Gerald Solomon (R-New York):... Mr. Speaker, the evidence is overwhelming, it is remarkably detailed, and it is corroborated at key points. It has also not been rebutted, in any meaningful way, by the president or his attorneys....

This notion of a world thrown into turmoil due to impeachment is completely false.

We are a resilient people, and we have endured depression and world wars in this century and a vicious civil war in the century before. After defeating fascism and communism in this bloody 20th century, are we to believe that we simply cannot survive without Bill Clinton?...

Bob Barr (R-Georgia):... Article III... lays out a case of obstruction of justice....

What is obstruction...? I respectfully direct the attention of each Member of this body to the United States Criminal Code, title 18, to those several provisions which set forth the principle that no man...shall tamper with witnesses, seek to hide witnesses, seek to hide evidence in a case, or seek to change, modify, or prevent testimony.

Yet there is in this report and in the accompanying 60,000 pages of evidence...evidence of a clear pattern of obstruction of justice...such things as making statements...with no other purpose than to influence the testimony of his secretary, who most assuredly would have been and was called as a grand jury witness, evidence such as the president calling...one of the most powerful attorneys in this city, Mr. Vernon Jordan, after it was found out that Monica Lewinsky would indeed be and had been subpoenaed as a witness to appear before the court and directed that she be found a job.

Evidence such as the president...picking up a telephone at 2 a.m....not by coincidence the very day that he found out that Ms. Lewinsky...would be a witness in the court case of Paula Jones and going over with her to reaffirm in her mind the stories, the cover stories, that they indeed had agreed to if just this calamity would befall them....

Sam Johnson (R-Texas): Mr. Speaker, we have heard the argument that our military forces are fighting. Do my colleagues know what they are fighting for? They are fighting to uphold the Constitution and the oath that we took and they took....

I believe the president violated the laws and beliefs he swore to uphold.... He chose to lie, cover up and evade the truth. His actions have made a mockery of the people who fought for this country and are fighting for this nation today, the Constitution and the laws we live under, and because of the president's actions Congress must act as dictated by the Constitution....

It is clear from the evidence that this president committed perjury. It is clear from the evidence that this president obstructed justice. It is clear from the evidence that this president abused the power of his office.

He systematically used his office and staff to protect his own personal interests....

Charles Schumer (D-New York):...What began 25 years ago with Watergate as a solemn and necessary process to force a president to adhere to the rule of law has grown beyond our control so that now we are routinely using criminal accusations and scandal to win the political battles and ideological differences we cannot settle at the ballot box.... We cannot disagree, it seems; we cannot forcefully advocate for our positions, without trying to criminalize or at least dishonor our adversaries....

I want to be clear. I am not pointing fingers at Republicans. The Democrats investigated John Tower for allegations not too dissimilar from allegations against the president. The gentleman from Georgia [Mr. Gingrich] led the investigation which brought down Speaker [Jim] Wright, and Speaker Gingrich was investigated and brought down as well. The ledger between the two parties is pretty much even.

Today we are upping the ante. The president could be removed from office over a matter that most Americans feel does not come close to the level of high crimes and misdemeanors as written in our Constitution....

Jerrold Nadler (D-New York):... The American people have heard the allegations against the president, and they overwhelmingly oppose impeaching him.... We have no right to overturn the considered judgment of the American people.

Mr. Speaker, this is clearly a partisan railroad job. The same people who today tell us we must impeach the president for lying under oath almost to a person voted last year to reelect the Speaker who had just admitted lying to Congress in an official proceeding....

Lindsey Graham (R-South Carolina):... What brought us here is not partisanship, but the conduct of one man who happened to be the president, who happened to be elected by the people and given the most solemn responsibility in the nation, to be the chief law enforcement officer of the land, and he failed miserably in that responsibility....

Here is what happened in Article IV. This House... authorized the Committee on the Judiciary to inquire into the allegations against the president.... Eighty-one questions were sent to flesh out the facts... and the president was asked under oath to give answers....

Mr. Speaker, unfortunately, the president lied in January to injure Paula Jones, he lied to the federal grand jury to injure the federal court system in this case, and I think the facts are overwhelming that he gave false, misleading and perjurious testimony to the Congress....

Article III of impeachment against Richard Nixon... was based on the idea that Richard Nixon as president failed to comply with subpoenas of Congress.... The day Richard Nixon failed to answer that subpoena is the day that he was subject to impeachment, because he took the power... over the impeachment process away from Congress...; and the day that William Jefferson Clinton failed to provide truthful testimony to the Congress... is the day that he chose to determine the course of impeachment....

Tom Barrett (D-Wisconsin): . . . Our Constitution does not allow us, no, it does not allow you, to remove a president from office because you cannot stand him. . . .

That is not an unfair allegation . . . because the vast majority of the people voting for impeachment today voted to reelect our Speaker, even though he had submitted information, false information, to the Committee on Standards of Official Conduct of this House, the judicial branch of this House. . . .

It is not an unfair allegation because when the Secretary of Defense under President Bush was duly indicted by a federal grand jury for perjury and he was pardoned by . . . George Bush, the silence on this side of the aisle was deafening. . . .

There is one difference, and only one difference, between the false allegations submitted by Speaker Gingrich and the perjury allegations against the Secretary of Defense and the president of the United States, and that difference is he is a Democrat. He is a Democrat, and so we are going to go after him. . . .

Charles Canady (R-Florida): . . . It is inaccurate to compare the situation involving the Speaker of the House with a case that is now before us. It is admitted that the Speaker submitted inaccurate information. . . . But the Committee on Standards of Official Conduct did not find that the Speaker was guilty of intentionally submitting false information. . . . In the case before us, there is overwhelming evidence that the president of the United States willfully, time after time after time, lied under oath. . . .

Steny Hoyer (D-Maryland): . . . If I believed that the conduct of this president had threatened our nation's security or undermined the operation of our government, or put at risk the principles of our democracy, I would vote to impeach. But I am absolutely convinced of the opposite. I have said that the president's conduct has defamed himself and his presidency. But it has not amounted to treason. It is not a case of bribery. And, as so many scholars of all political and philosophical stripes have testified, it does not amount to high crimes and misdemeanors. . . .

James Rogan (R-California): . . . Lawyers did not just show up one day and begin to question the president's personal lifestyle. The president was a defendant in a civil rights sexual harassment lawsuit, and just like every other defendant in those types of cases around the country, he was ordered by a federal judge . . . to answer under oath questions relating to his pattern of conduct . . .

Now, in a desperate last-ditch attempt to insulate this president from any constitutional accountability for his conduct, his defenders are forced to trivialize felony perjury. How trivial is perjury to the person who loses a child-custody case or goes to prison because perjured testimony was offered as a truth in a court of law? ...

Martin Meehan (D-Massachusetts): ... Here is how one prominent historian describes the impeachment of Andrew Johnson: "The impeachment was a great act of ill-directed passion, and was supported by little else. It was rather like an immense balloon filled with foul air, the most noisome elements of which were those most active."

... I fear that the words used to describe the Johnson impeachment will come to characterize what this House is about to do.... Will the House now have license to engage in free-wheeling speculation about how a president's private wrongs bear upon his or her capacity to govern, and then to pursue the removal of those whom it deems unfit? If so, I fear for the very concept that presidents are to be chosen directly by the people, not by the legislature....

Will an independent counsel's fact-finding be the sole record upon which the House votes to impeach a president? If so, I fear for future presidents of either party whose tenure in office might be threatened by the sort of overreaching that we have all accused independent counsels of at one time or another.

Will we now compel the ship of State in one direction while the rudder of popular opinion clearly points in the opposite direction? If so, I fear for the notion that consensus among the public counts for something when this House takes up the gravest of matters of State....

James Sensenbrenner (R-Wisconsin): ... I would like to quote from the book, *How the Good Guys Finally Won, Notes from an Impeachment Summer,* by Jimmy Breslin, published by Ballantine Books in 1975. This book quoted our former distinguished Speaker, Thomas O'Neill from Massachusetts, as follows: "O'Neill went down the hall, picking his way through the tourists, to attend the meeting at which John Rhodes, the Republican leader of the House, gave it one last try for Nixon. Rhodes said he wanted the impeachment resolution recommitted with instructions that there should be a vote on censuring the president. 'I am bitterly opposed to that,' O'Neill said. 'But you wouldn't be opposed to us having a vote on censure, would you?' Rhodes asked. 'Yes, I would,' O'Neill said."

I think that my friends on the other side of the aisle should listen to their former Speaker one last time, because on this one, he is right....

Sheila Jackson Lee (D-Texas):...I believe not one of us in these chambers...would ask for the resignation of a Member so charged.... Nevertheless, the majority is recklessly attempting to make impeachable offenses of purely private acts, in direct attack on the Framers' intent that impeachment was for great and dangerous offenses against the Constitution.

...The majority must allow us to vote on a freestanding censure resolution, constitutionally allowed, that acknowledges that the president was morally wrong, misled the American people and that the president, upon leaving office, will be subject to civil and criminal penalties. To do more lays the shredding of this Constitution at our feet....

Diana DeGette (D-Colorado):...We have divided this House with partisan politics, sowing mistrust and exposing the darkness in our own hearts. It started with the first vote of the 105th Congress to censure the Speaker, and it has continued to this day to the vote to impeach the president.

With all of the lost opportunities in between, it is no wonder we are losing the public's trust. After today, when the impeachment frenzy subsides, we will survey the damage to our own political system, we will have unnecessarily crippled the presidency for a generation to come. We will have wantonly weakened this House of Representatives, reaching a new low in partisan rancor. We will have substantially subverted the Constitution, which was designed to reflect the will of the people in a republic, not to promote a political party in what is slipping towards a parliamentary system....

Mr. Rogan:...Some of our friends on the other side have indicated that perjury is not an impeachable offense under the Constitution. I remind them of the testimony of the former Democratic attorney general of the United States, Griffin Bell.... General Bell referred to the legal authorities relied upon by our founders, such as Blackstone, in drafting the Constitution.

General Bell testified that Blackstone identified a series of..."crimes against justice," and those crimes included perjury. General Bell concluded, "I am of the opinion, my conclusion, is that those crimes are high crimes within the meaning of the impeachment clause."

Robert Wexler (D-Florida):...Impeachment is devastating. Impeachment is enduring.... If we dumb-down impeachment and make it easier for future Congresses to impeach presidents, we will forever weaken the institution of the presidency.

... To impeach for anything less than the highest of crimes is a distortion of the Constitution and hands a tremendous weapon to our present and future enemies.... That is why the Founding Fathers knew that... the strength of our national leader, the sovereignty of our nation trump all but the gravest of charges, those which subvert our government....

What have we become when we impeach a president over an extramarital affair and the lies to conceal it...? What have we become when we enter a new era of sexual McCarthyism...?... What have we become when our partisan warring does not stop at the water's edge but spills over and bestows upon Saddam Hussein the hope of a divided America? What have we become?

I fear, our own worst enemies.

Tom Campbell (R-California): Mr. Speaker... no speaker has refuted the facts. The facts are that the president did not tell the truth under oath on August 17 and on other occasions....

Let me address why that matters so much.... The August 17 incident... undermines my ability to trust this president whenever he says anything... if it is in his interest not to tell the truth. And that is what takes this conduct... to the level of a high crime and misdemeanor, because it incapacitates him from effectively serving as our president....

Today we are engaged in war in the Persian Gulf. I was assured by [Defense Secretary William] Cohen and by the Director of our Central Intelligence Agency that the timing was justified. Those two are honorable men. And because of their testimony, I believe the timing was justified. But I do not believe it was justified on the basis of what President Clinton has said, because I can no longer believe him. If it is in his interest not to tell the truth, he will not tell the truth....

Steven Rothman (D-New Jersey):... The Founding Fathers were clear. They created a strong presidency where the executive was elected for four-year terms. They did not want a parliamentary system where the Congress could remove the people's choice unless the president's conduct had threatened the very stability of the country.

The founders specifically rejected proposals to allow impeaching the president for poor character or for morally bad behavior.... The president can only be impeached for treason, bribery, or other high crimes or misdemeanors against the state....

Now, driven by their hatred and loathing of Bill Clinton and his policies, the Republican Party is about to take our constitutional balance of powers and permanently and irreparably and forever damage it....

Bill McCollum (R-Florida): ... Mr. Speaker, I simply want to respond to one of the comments the gentleman from New Jersey just made about the level to which it has to be for before we impeach a president.... It certainly does not have to be presidential powers only. If the president of the United States committed murder, if he committed a lot of other crimes, it seems to me that those would be perfectly impeachable, and if we are talking about perjury, which rises to the virtual level of bribery—in fact under the federal sentencing guidelines has a greater amount of sentencing...—it seems abundantly clear that perjury is impeachable.

Maxine Waters (D-California): ... This is indeed a Republican coup d'état.

... [T]he Republicans will couch this extremist radical anarchy in pious language which distorts the Constitution and the rule of law. Bill and Hillary Clinton are the real targets, and the Republicans are the vehicles being used by the right-wing Christian Coalition extremists to direct and control our culture.

... Yes, Bill Clinton is guilty of certain indiscretions in his private life. However, he did not commit high crimes and misdemeanors. Rather the president is guilty of being a populist leader who opened up government and access to the poor, to minorities, to women and to the working class. President Bill Clinton is guilty of not being owned by the good ol' southern boys or the good ol' eastern establishment. Mr. Speaker, President Clinton is guilty of being smart enough to outmaneuver the Republicans in the budget negotiations, electoral politics and the development and implementation of the people's agenda....

Mary Bono (R-California): ... The central issue is whether the president is above the law and whether sexual harassment and civil rights laws remain viable in effective protections for all Americans.... If Congress turns a blind eye to the president's behavior, then we are turning our back to ... victims of sexual harassment. Every person, including Paula Jones, is entitled to certain rights under our Constitution. This includes truthful testimony from all parties, and that is why we are here....

Vic Fazio (D-California): ... I am sad that a reckless president and a Republican Congress driven by blind animus for him have brought us to this moment in history....

Some of my colleagues obsess about Slick Willie in the same way that those on my side of the aisle used to about Tricky Dick. Robert Bork, Clarence

Thomas, Jim Wright, on and on; we do each other in in personal terms. Each one of us has been given a most precious gift, the right to represent some 600,000 American citizens... and yet when it comes time to be here for them we seem to lose track of the fundamental issues of our times and instead focus far too much on petty and partisan battles.... Sadly, it was the late Vince Foster who recognized in Washington peoples' lives are destroyed for sport....

Kevin Brady (R-Texas): Mr. Speaker, some Americans are not watching these proceedings. Instead, in hushed courtrooms across this country families slashed apart by violent crime and innocent people wrongly accused are staring intently at a witness stand, and they are praying. For many, their best hope... for justice depends upon that witness telling the truth, the full truth, under oath. Truth does matter, and if it is no longer the duty of the president to tell the truth under sworn oath, can we require it of any American? The answer is no, which is why justice, hope and the Constitution demand that today we vote "yes."...

Barbara Kennelly (D-Connecticut):... There is so much discussion now about what is a high crime. Let us think about what was not. Remember President Reagan and Iran-Contra?... Remember Harry Truman, taking over the steel mills, sending troops into Korea without letting the Congress telling him it was okay? Herbert Hoover and what happened there with the federal Reserve funds?

But there was no impeachment.... Collectively, our predecessors in this body understood fully both the necessity of impeachment as the ultimate bulwark against the potential tyranny of the executive, but also the very real threat impeachment presents to the structure of our government if... too readily used....

Zoe Lofgren (D-California):... The country is waiting for grownups to walk into this Chamber and stop this madness, but, alas, those Republicans with the maturity and judgment to ask that censure be utilized as an alternative... have been ignored by the majority in this House. The outcome appears clear: The Republicans will vote to impeach the president, whom they could not defeat at the polls....

The... public can see clearly what you are doing here today. You say that the president's dishonesty about sex has destroyed our constitutional form of government, but the people do not agree. They think that it is you who threaten our country by this cynical and political distortion of impeachment. As is generally the case, the American people have it right....

Mr. Canady: ... The question is not whether the president has destroyed our system of government. We know that that has not happened.... The question is whether by his conduct he has undermined the integrity of the law; whether by his conduct he has undermined the integrity of the high office that has been entrusted to him....

Joseph Kennedy (D-Massachusetts): ... [A]t its core, this is about an individual ... who had a wrongful affair. He lied about that affair, and he has asked for forgiveness....

There is only one group of people that ... cannot find that forgiveness, and that is people that had been locked in struggle over so many questions dealing with the future of this country against President Clinton's agenda....

The president has put the wood to the Republicans time and time again. He has taken away the issue of crime, he has taken away the issue of taxes. He has taken away so many of the issues that my colleagues in the past have had leadership roles on, and so they get angry at him. That is okay, they can get angry at him. But to dumb-down the impeachment process ... and allow this to be utilized in a partisan critical manner is an immoral act on the part of the Republican Party....

Peter King (R-New York): ... No one has a higher respect than I do for the gentleman from Illinois [Henry Hyde] ... and it causes me great pain to in any way differ from him.

But I feel I have no alternative. I strongly believe that for a president ... to be impeached, for an election to be undone, there must be a direct abuse of presidential power. There must be a president abusing the CIA, abusing citizens with the IRS or the FBI, a crime comparable to treason or bribery....

But there is even a larger issue here.... We are a nation consumed by investigations, by special counsels ... by scandal. We are driving good people from government. What we are talking about here in this case, the president's conduct, was illegal, it was immoral, it was disgraceful, it was indefensible, but the fact is, I don't believe rises to the level of treason or bribery....

Major Owens (D-New York): ... Our defendant is an outstanding citizen who has done great service for his people, for his government. On the basis of the charges before us, what prosecutor anywhere in America would press forward with this case and a demand for such a harsh punishment? ...

This defendant, this president, has been denied his basic rights.... This defendant is a victim of organized partisan persecution....

Mr. Rogan: ... The gentleman said that no reasonable prosecutor or judge would come forward on such an overwhelming case of perjury and bring this case before the court....

Under the Clinton Justice Department, since President Clinton became president, some 700 people have been tried and convicted for perjury and perjury-related crimes. As we speak today, Mr. Speaker, some 115 people sit in federal prisons as a result of their conviction on perjury charges....

Ed Bryant (R-Tennessee): ... One of the charges in this series of articles is obstruction of justice.... That involved this president of the United States ... causing additional innocent people to commit crimes. I cite to you the filing of a false affidavit by Monica Lewinsky, the hiding of evidence, the bringing of people, staff members, cabinet members into his office, telling them his version of the story, knowing that they would repeat that story when they were called to the grand jury....

Perjury is also very important in this case. This president did not have a lapse of judgment. On many occasions, through a pattern and practice he gave false testimony, in the grand jury, the deposition, in answering written interrogatories and to this very Congress ...

This president is a lawyer. He is a former law professor at the University of Arkansas. He is the former attorney general for the State of Arkansas, and he very well knows how important people telling the truth is in our court proceedings ... And yet he continues to parse his words. And his own lawyers ... say, yes, he misled, he evaded questions. He gave incomplete answers. That is their defense....

Because of the very events we are involved in today, many people call into question, is he giving us complete answers about what we are doing over in the Middle East? Is he evading questions? Is he misleading? ...

Tom Lantos (D-California): Mr. Speaker, I rise as the only Member in the history of the Congress who has lived under and fought against both fascism and communism. Every day I enter this hall I do so with a feeling of humility and pride, as one who has suffered the pain of living in a police state and now enjoys the exhilaration of living in a free society.

... Mr. Speaker, what distinguishes this House from the fake parliaments of police states is procedural fairness.... I ask that we have the opportunity to vote on a motion to censure the president. If the impeachment vote succeeds in this House, come January, President Clinton will be on trial in the Senate. But today, my friends, it is this House that is on trial.

Mr. Hutchinson: ... It is important to address that issue of censure. We discussed this in the committee and ... numerous constitutional experts ... addressed this. Stephen Presser, professor of legal history at Northwestern University School of Law, wrote a letter to the gentleman from Massachusetts [William Delahunt] ... saying that censure would not be constitutional. He said, "In my opinion, impeachment is the remedy for misconduct."

We go to the University of London, a similar response by Gary McDowell noted that censure ... would violate the separation of powers. And on to John Harrison, University of Virginia School of Law ... "My view at this point is that there are serious constitutional difficulties with congressional censure." ...

I think the gentleman's point was also on fairness. And, as has been read earlier today, going back to 1974 in this House, the Democrat Speaker refused to allow a vote on censure in reference to President Nixon; and so there is a precedent for what has transpired as well as constitutional considerations....

Mr. Lantos: Mr. Speaker, ... there is not a person in this body on either side who does not clearly understand that this body has every right to censure the president, and to hide behind these phony technicalities demeans this House. My colleagues know as well as I do that a censure vote could be taken, would be legal ... and would carry.

Mr. Hutchinson: Mr. Speaker, I appreciate the sincerity. But censure is being used in this case as a marketing tool to the American public to sell them on the idea that there is a simple, easy way to avoid our constitutional responsibility; and I think that we should stick with the Constitution.

Frank Riggs (R–California): Mr. Speaker, I just wanted to interject at this point in the debate ... in the last 48 hours I have spoken to both former President Ford and Bob Dole. Both men emphatically told me ... that they would vote to impeach, that ... barring a public acknowledgement, an admission of the president that he had lied under oath and perjured himself, it was the duty of the House to vote for the articles of impeachment.

Carrie Meek (D-Florida):... Too many of my colleagues have a "gotcha" syndrome. They want to do their best to get Mr. President. I saw it from the very beginning with every kind of gate there was in government reform. There was a tailgate, there was a post office gate. Every gate imaginable was brought before that committee long before this impeachment started, but it was the beginning of impeachment of William Jefferson Clinton.

My colleagues have not liked him from the very beginning....

Jesse Jackson Jr. (D-Illinois):... Essentially the same economic and political forces that drove the presidential impeachment process against Andrew Johnson in 1868 are driving the impeachment process 130 years later. There has been a role reversal. The Republicans of 1998 were the Democrats of 1868, but the underlying issue is essentially the same: Reconstruction. The first reconstruction was at issue in 1868; the second reconstruction is at issue in 1998....

Let us not be confused. Today Republicans are impeaching Social Security, they are impeaching affirmative action, they are impeaching women's right to choose, Medicare, Medicaid, Supreme Court Justices who believe in equal protection under the law for all Americans. Something deeper in history is happening than sex, lying about sex and perjury.

Mr. Canady:... It is claimed that the Committee on the Judiciary decided that tax fraud by President Nixon was not an impeachable offense.... It is true that the committee rejected an article of impeachment based on tax fraud against President Nixon, but it is equally clear that the overwhelming majority of the members of the committee who expressed an opinion... said that they were voting against that article because there was insufficient evidence to support tax fraud....

David Obey (D-Wisconsin):... To those who say censure has no bite, my response is this: I come from the State of Joe McCarthy. Tell him censure has no bite. It destroyed him....

Mr. Barr: Mr. Speaker, while I sincerely doubt that those who continue to bow down before the holy grail of censure will let the historical record of precedent interfere... I would direct their attention to a communication from President Andrew Jackson, the last president who was censured... "Censure, although it may have a place in certain procedures in the Congress, it has no place if it is used as a substitute for impeachment."...

Sidney Yates (D-Illinois): Mr. Speaker, I was elected to the House of Representatives for the first time in 1948.... For that reason, I am frequently asked by the press these days whether this Congress differs from the early ones to which I was elected.

I answer yes—there is a difference. There is a difference in the ambience...I have the impression that in the earlier Congresses Members were friendlier than now and I regret that. And they were friendlier towards the Presidency....

But that was prior to the special prosecutor law. That changed things and now we have...Mr. Starr, who investigated and found nothing to blame on Mr. Clinton on Whitewater, Travelgate, Filegate, his original charges. Then he stumbled on Monica Lewinsky. That gave him his chance.

Starr is determined to drive Mr. Clinton out of the Presidency—and...the Republicans are taking his recommendations to impeach him—as the *Chicago Tribune* said—for "low crimes and misdemeanors."...

Clifford Stearns (R-Florida):...If the opponents of impeachment wanted to avoid this process, they should have mounted a vigorous defense of the president by refuting the facts in the Starr report.... Those against impeachment have not contradicted one word of testimony contained in over 60,000 pages of sworn evidence, not one scintilla.

...Any military officer, from general to private, would be court-martialed. Any private citizen would risk prosecution. Any church leader, CEO of a Fortune 500 company, high school faculty member, or community leader, would not face censure, they would be fired for similar conduct....

Carolyn Kilpatrick (D-Michigan):... The Constitution is very clear. This is not a high crime or misdemeanor. It bothers me that some of my colleagues...have said we are using a marketing tool by asking for censure. Most of the American people want the president censured. Most of the American people, nearly 70 percent, do not want him impeached. Why, then, do we, who represent the people of these United States, come before the House with four articles of impeachment? I think it is a travesty....

Scott McInnis (R-Colorado):...I have read with interest the Democratic censure, and I quote parts from it: "...that the president violated the trust of the American people, lessened their esteem for the office of the president, and dishonored the office for which they have entrusted to him." It goes on, "The president made false statements concerning his reprehensible conduct with a subordinate, and took steps to delay discovery of the truth."

And they say to me, after they draft that kind of document, that that individual now qualifies for the position of the highest public trust?... There is not a schoolteacher in this country that would step into the classroom ever, ever again with this kind of conduct....

Edward Markey (D-Massachusetts):... We are permitting a constitutional coup d'état which will haunt this body forever. A constitutional clause intended to apply to a Benedict Arnold selling out his country will now be expanded to cover every personal transgression. Every future president, Democrat or Republican, will be subject to harassment by his political enemies....

When we talk to people... on the streets, they believe that the high crime against the Constitution is their families being cheated out of their government's ability to work on things that affect their families: Medicare, social security, the democratization of access to jobs and education....

GOP used to stand for "Grand Old Party." Now it just stands for "Get Our President."

Mr. Hutchinson: Mr. Speaker, I want to remind the gentleman from Massachusetts that it was the president's own Democrat attorney general who appointed this independent counsel, believing there was credible evidence that needed to be investigated. In regard to the high crimes and misdemeanors, the Constitution specifically mentions bribery.... [P]erjury and bribery are unique threats to the administration of justice, and that affects our society. That affects our government.

Nita Lowey (D-New York):... Unfortunately, there is a determined minority in America and in this Chamber who never accepted the legitimacy of this president. To them this episode is mere pretext to accomplish what they could not during two separate elections....

[M]ake no mistake, my colleagues, not all coups are accompanied by the sound of marching boots and rolling tanks. Some, like today, are wrapped in a constitutional veneer, softened by pious assertions of solemn obligation and duty....

Mr. Barr:... It is interesting to note, Mr. Speaker, that in the more than three months that the independent counsel's material, some 60,000 pages, have been over at the Ford Building there remain, I believe, four...Democrats on the Committee on the Judiciary that have not spent one minute reviewing that material; and even though arrangements have been made...to have other Members of both sides of the aisle not serving on the Committee on the Judiciary to review the material so they could answer any questions or look at the material firsthand, I believe there has been at most one Member on the Democrat side who has gone over to review the material.... [A]pparently, most Members on the other side are not interested in the evidence....

Mr. Conyers: Mr. Speaker, I have just been advised that the chairman of the House Committee on the Judiciary has unilaterally permitted Members other than committee members to visit the Ford Building to read other materials unbeknownst to me and we had not allowed any Democratic Members to go over there because we did not know that they were permitted...if they were not members of the Committee on the Judiciary. And I thank the gentleman from Georgia for pointing that out to us. It is an incredible violation of our democratic rights, and I am deeply offended by it.

Mr. Sensenbrenner:...Just so that all of the Members are clear, when the House passed House Resolution 525 in September, immediately after the receipt of the independent counsel's report, only members of the Committee on the Judiciary had access to the executive session material.... Then in October, when we passed our inquiry resolution, that superseded the previous resolution's provisions.... [T]hat meant that all Members of the House of Representatives had access to those executive session materials. That has been what the rule is since October 8....

Mr. Conyers: Mr. Speaker, I thank the gentleman from Wisconsin...for his explanation. The one thing it did not include, of course, was that only Members who were trying to have their minds made up...came over to the Ford Building that were not members of the Committee on the Judiciary two days before this proceeding on the floor. And I am glad to know now that everybody could have come over but nobody apparently availed themselves until this last minute twisting-of-arms took place.

Jim Greenwood (R–Pennsylvania):...Mr. Speaker, the gentleman from Michigan Mr. Conyers made reference...to last-minute arm-twisting of the undecided, and I feel compelled to comment.... I am one of the last few holdouts undecided in this debate, and it needs to be said that not once, not once in this entire ordeal, has a single member of my leadership, has a single colleague, has a single member of the Committee on the Judiciary, not only not asked me to vote one way, they have never even inquired as to how I would vote....

Ron Kind (D-Wisconsin):... In 1974, the House Committee on the Judiciary, when Congress was controlled by Democrats, drafted articles of impeachment against President Nixon based upon fraudulent tax returns. But the Committee on the Judiciary in a bipartisan fashion determined that it did not rise to the level of an impeachable offense because it was private as opposed to public misconduct.

Well, then, what is this all about...? If it is just about punishing and holding the president accountable and retribution, we can... punish President Clinton through censure and through private prosecution once the president leaves office....

Mr. Canady: Mr. Speaker, I want to make the point again which I made earlier today that in 1974 the Committee on the Judiciary did not, did not, determine that tax fraud is a unimpeachable offense. They simply determined that there was insufficient evidence that the president of the United States was in fact guilty of tax fraud.

Mr. Conyers: Could I point out to my friend, the gentleman from Florida, who took exception to why the income tax charge was not brought against Mr. Nixon in 1974, if he would read our report of the minority at page 10, he would learn that it was not for lack of evidence, it was because we determined that this was not a high crime or misdemeanor. And we were joined by Republican[s]....

Mr. Canady:... Is it not true, I ask of the gentleman from Michigan, as a member of the Committee on the Judiciary in 1974, that the gentleman voted in favor of the tax fraud article against President Nixon?

Mr. Conyers: Yes, Mr. Speaker, absolutely true.

Mr. Canady: Mr. Speaker, so the gentleman believes that tax fraud was an impeachable offense?

Mr. Conyers: Mr. Speaker, that is absolutely correct, and it does not contradict what I corrected the gentleman about.

Mr. Canady: I thank the gentleman very much.

Thomas Sawyer (D-Ohio): ... Perhaps no figure in our tradition of English law and history so well portrays an impeachment on the charge of perjury as Sir Thomas More. The author of "A Man for All Seasons" wrote that he was asked to testify in a form that required him to state that he believed what he did not believe and it required him to state it under oath.

Oliver Cromwell, accusing More of accepting a small gift in return for a favor said, "He is going to be a slippery fish. We need a net with a finer mesh. We will weave him one. It must be done by the law. It is just a matter of finding the right law. Or making one."

Cromwell, ... in seeking to entrap him, accused More of "perverting the law, of making smoky what should be clear light to discover his own wrongdoing." More replied, "The law is not a light for you or any man to see by, it is not an instrument of any kind; the law is a causeway upon which a citizen may walk safely."

But that was not to be the way of the court, and in his closing, More ... said, "What you have hunted me for is not my actions, but for the thoughts of my heart.... God help the people whose statesmen walk your road."

It matters little whether the motive was base or high. An entrapment is an entrapment. ...

Mr. Barr: ... Mr. Speaker, I would remind all of my colleagues ... that references to the word "entrapment" are rather misplaced. There is no such thing as entrapment for perjury or obstruction. It is a legal impossibility that is well settled law in federal courts and state courts as well. ...

Mr. Conyers: ... Mr. Speaker, the gentleman from Georgia announced a moment ago that the perjury trap is a legal impossibility. I refer him to the Ninth Circuit Court of Appeals decision, which said in 1991 that a perjury trap is created "... when the government calls a witness to testify for the primary purpose of obtaining testimony from him in order to prosecute him later for perjury." ...

Mr. Barr: ... Mr. Speaker, I would say to the distinguished ranking member on the Committee on the Judiciary that when President Clinton or any person appears before a grand jury or before a court, they have three—count them—and only three choices: They can tell the truth, they can take the fifth amendment, or they can lie. President Clinton chose the last option, he lied.

It is a legal impossibility for somebody to be forced to lie before a grand jury or in court, and that is the essence of what entrapment is. The president chose voluntarily to tell a lie; to conduct perjurious, misleading, and untruthful statements. He cannot be forced to do that....

Christopher Cannon (R-Utah):...Article III sets forth that the president willfully and deliberately allowed his attorney to make false statements to the court about the affidavit of Ms. Lewinsky. The president's defenders...have said he was not paying attention at the time when Mr. [Robert] Bennett raised the affidavit, but the videotape of the deposition shows otherwise....

The president's official defense was that he thought Ms. Lewinsky thought her affidavit was true, and he was just affirming her belief. First, the affidavit was not a statement of beliefs. It was a statement of the facts under oath. The president's response was evasive.

Second, in the affidavit Ms. Lewinsky stated she had not received any benefit from her relationship with the president. The facts are indisputable. There was an intense effort by Mr. Jordan on behalf of the president to get her a job.

Third, in the deposition, after reading from the affidavit, Mr. Bennett asked the president, "Is that a true and accurate statement, as far as you know it?" The president answered, "That is absolutely true." We know today that it was absolutely false.

President Clinton's deliberate effort to mislead Judge Wright is a clear obstruction of justice. Others have been prosecuted for less....

Bernie Sanders (I-Vermont): Mr. Speaker, I have never fully appreciated before just how out of touch this institution is with the needs of the American people.

Forty-three million Americans have no health insurance. Millions of senior citizens cannot afford their prescription drugs. And this House is going to vote to send to the Senate for a trial to go on month after month after month to discuss where Bill Clinton touched Monica Lewinsky....

Mr. Speaker, Bill Clinton acted deplorably.... But what the American people are saying loudly and clearly is, let's get on with the business of the American people....

Mr. Sensenbrenner:...We have heard all of these prophets of economic doom and gloom if the House discharges its constitutional duty today in impeaching the president. The NASDAQ hit an all-time high. I think the markets are smarter than some of the people who are making these accusations.

Patrick Kennedy (D–Rhode Island): Mr. Speaker, we have no right to stand here and debate the rule of law if we cannot even extend to the president of the United States that same right of due process as required by our Constitution.

The majority has replaced the notion of due process with a notion that if we just say something long enough it will become true....

Mr. Sensenbrenner:...Mr. Speaker, the gentleman from Rhode Island says the president was not given due process, and exactly the opposite is true. The chairman, the gentleman from Illinois [Mr. Hyde], gave the president a standing invitation to appear before the Committee on the Judiciary. He did not accept that offer....

Mr. Kennedy: Is not perjury a legal term? Has the gentleman defined perjury in a court of law, or is it just his constant repetition that the president has lied?

The Speaker pro tempore: The gentleman from Rhode Island is out of order.

Mr. Sensenbrenner: Mr. Speaker, the president's lawyers had up to 30 hours to present their defense. Mr. Starr had 12½ hours.... [T]he Democrats had almost two thirds of the witnesses before the committee. They called 28 witnesses, the Republicans called 15, and they shared two. The chairman, the gentleman from Illinois [Mr. Hyde], asked the White House to present evidence that would exonerate the president, and they did not.

Sherwood Boehlert (R–New York):...Much time has been spent during this prolonged ordeal comparing the situation to Watergate, only for most to conclude correctly that the two scandals have little in common. But they do have one aspect in common.... In a rare moment of personal insight, Richard Nixon concluded that he had destroyed himself by hating his enemies back. I am afraid that President Clinton fell into the same, all-too-human, trap. Blinded by his contempt for people who he thought were out to get him, the president forgot his larger obligations to his office, to the Constitution and to the American people....

Tim Roemer (D-Indiana): ... Mr. Speaker, this is our rule book. This is our sacred scripture in this body. There is nothing in here, Mr. Speaker, that prohibits a censure; there is no impediment in our Constitution to a censure. In fact we have censured and rebuked and criticized presidents three times, in 1834, in 1842, in 1860, and we have impeached a president once. There is precedent, Mr. Speaker. ...

Stephen Buyer (R-Indiana): Mr. Speaker, I have great respect for my colleague from Indiana and I would only respond by saying impeachment is the only power in the Constitution granted to Congress to address presidential criminal misconduct. ... The censure resolution that was offered the Committee on the Judiciary in fact has findings of guilt with a punishment. It is prohibited then as a bill of attainder and is therefore unconstitutional. ...

Mr. Nadler: Mr. Speaker, the gentleman from Indiana says that a censure resolution would be unconstitutional. The Congressional Research Service says that a censure resolution is an exercise of the implicit power of a deliberative right to express its views. The gentleman from Texas [Tom DeLay] offered House Resolution 433, disapproving the president's conduct with respect to campaign finances.

What is the distinction, why did the gentleman from Illinois [Mr. Hyde] make the censure resolution offered in committee in order? Was he exercising an unconstitutional prerogative?

Mr. Buyer: Mr. Speaker, I say that the censure resolution that was offered has specific findings of guilt and therefore makes it unconstitutional in its form.

Peter DeFazio (D-Oregon): ... The founders set an incredibly high bar for impeachment. ... The Republican majority has not raised and proven offenses that meet those standards. Rather they have met the standards set by Gerald Ford 25 years ago. He said an impeachable offense is anything 218 Members of the House will vote for. That is an unconstitutional and cynical standard. ...

Edward Pease (R-Indiana): ... After long debate, my conclusion on [censure] is simply this: If censure is intended as a punishment of the president, it is specifically constitutionally prohibited as a bill of attainder. If censure is not intended as a punishment of the president, it is meaningless.

I have not researched the options available to the Senate, but for the House, I am convinced that this option is not available.

Bob Clement (D-Tennessee): ... Mr. Speaker, when I listen to the majority party, it makes me wonder if they think the president had not been punished at all yet. The president has been punished. He has been humiliated. He has been embarrassed. He has paid a high price at home, as well as with the American people, as well as the people all across the world. ...

Ernest Istook (R-Oklahoma): Mr. Speaker, the president was given the opportunity to present witnesses or evidence which would dispute the facts. He did not. His legal hair-splitting defense could not alter the simple truth: The president lied, and lied under oath.

Here is what convinced me that this perjury is an impeachable offense and not simply a moral failure. These were not lies told under sudden pressure when he was unexpectedly asked embarrassing questions. The president's lies were planned well in advance. They were premeditated. He knowingly acted to block justice, even after a federal judge ruled his behavior was relevant and material. He orchestrated a deliberate scheme to tell multiple lies under oath on multiple occasions many months apart. ...

Mr. Meehan: ... The gentleman from Oklahoma just said that we gave the president an opportunity to call witnesses, to prove his innocence. Since when is the burden of proof in this country on the person being accused? You have the obligation to provide a case before the Committee on the Judiciary, and you did not provide a single material witness in this case. Not one witness. ...

Mr. Hutchinson: ... I want to respond to the gentleman from Massachusetts. He did have one thing right, and that is the burden of proof is on those going forward with impeachment. But that burden of proof was met with 60,000 pages of documents, an independent review by the Committee on the Judiciary, and ... there has not been one challenge to the evidence. ...

Mr. Meehan: Mr. Speaker, to respond to the gentleman from Arkansas [Mr. Hutchinson], every single charge that is made by the majority was responded to in our minority report. That is number one.

Secondly, only under this system, with the majority railroading this president, could we have a system where someone is accused of perjury, and they will not even tell us which words are perjurious. Nowhere in America could they ever charge someone with perjury and not tell them what they said.

Finally, there is no judicial proceeding anywhere in this country where we would not have a witness, a material witness, come before the bar, nowhere but under their majority.

Eni Faleomavaega (D-American Samoa): ... Mr. Speaker, I say to my friends in the majority, and they are my friends, when all of this is over, with blood all over this floor, my friends in the majority will have pounded and hammered some 218 nails on the flesh of this man. ...

Mr. Rogan: ... Mr. Speaker, [to] suggest that holding a president accountable after committing perjury in a criminal grand jury proceeding amounts to a coup d'état or will bring blood on the floor demeans the level of this debate. I quote from Dr. Larry Arnn[1]: "Elections have no higher standing under our Constitution than the impeachment process. Both stem from provisions of the Constitution. The people elect the president to do a constitutional job. They act under the Constitution when they do it. At the same time they elect a Congress to do a different constitutional job. The president swears an oath to uphold the Constitution. So does the Congress. Everyone concerned is acting in ways subordinate to the Constitution, both in elections and in the impeachment process. If a president is guilty of acts justifying impeachment, then he and not the Congress will have 'overturned the election.' He will have acted in ways that betray the purpose of his election. He will have acted not as a constitutional representative, but as a monarch, subversive of or above the law."

Mr. Nadler: Mr. Speaker, it is a coup d'état when you impeach a president for allegations that even if true, the overwhelming majority of constitutional scholars say are not impeachable offenses. It is a coup d'état when most of the prosecutors who testified in front of the committee said no prosecutor would seek an indictment because no jury would convict on the evidence we have. And it is a coup d'état when you seek to upset an election, to overturn an election without a broad consensus of the necessity for doing so against the majority of the American people. That describes a coup d'état, Mr. Speaker.

---

[1] Larry P. Arnn, President of the Claremont Institute, a conservative think tank in Claremont, California.

Corrine Brown (D-Florida):...Let me tell you what the real crime and high misdemeanor is, my fellow Americans. In 1994, the leaders announced their Contract on America. And today is the final agenda of that contract. They began their contract by attempting to cut school lunch, Head Start, food stamps, health care and Medicare for the elderly. These are the crimes that should be punished.

This is a modern day coup d'état, Mr. Speaker. It is the final piece of their contract. You can fool some of the people some of the time, but you cannot fool all of the people all of the time. And let me tell you, the American people are not fooled by your motives....

Mr. McCollum:...I just want to respond to...what the gentleman from New York [Mr. Nadler] said a while ago, that all the scholars we had before our committee said that these were nonimpeachable offenses, that prosecutors would not indict, that this would overthrow an election. The fact is, there is a wide division over the impeachment question. We had just as many scholars who said these are impeachable.

I happen to believe deeply perjury is equally grave or more grave than bribery and we in fact punish it more severely....

Mark Neumann (R-Wisconsin):...What do we know here? We know we have a 50-year-old married man, the most powerful man in the world, who had repeated sexual relations with a woman, a subordinate, 27 years his junior....

There is no walk of life in the United States of America where this behavior would be accepted. A college professor having consensual sex with one of his students would be dismissed. A CEO guilty of an office affair with an intern would be fired. A physician, a counselor, a pastor would lose their right to practice. A military officer would be dishonorably discharged....

William Delahunt (D-Massachusetts):...As we prepare to render our verdict on President Clinton, the American people and history itself are sitting in judgment on us and I believe they will judge us harshly because we have failed in our duty to the rule of law. We failed the rule of law when we abdicated our constitutional responsibility to an unelected prosecutor, when we rubber-stamped his conclusions and failed to conduct our own independent examination of a record replete with contradictions, inconsistencies and half truths. We failed the rule of law when we could not summon the political courage to call real witnesses to test their credibility....

We failed the rule of law when we informed the president's counsel of the precise charges only after he made his closing argument. That was unfair. We failed the rule of law when we put the burden on the president to prove his innocence....

James Traficant Jr. (D-Ohio): Mr. Speaker, I do not question anyone's motives. Both parties agree to some degree that the president broke the law. We disagree on the punishment....

Mr. Speaker, an impeachable offense should be one that threatens liberty, not chastity.... The president broke the law, we are sure of that, but I do not believe it requires the death penalty.

John Thune (R-South Dakota):... We are all subject to the same universal truth. We all fall short.... But to err repeatedly and willfully with impunity defies another universal truth, and that is the law of the harvest. In other words, one reaps what they sow, and the pattern of deception and dishonesty that acts as a body guard to this president strikes at the very core of his ability to lead....

If the president genuinely believes he is telling the truth, we are left with one of two equally miserable realities: Either the president chooses contempt and complete disregard for the truth, or his conscience is so diminished as to leave him unable to discern the truth from his lies. Both conclusions are ruinous to a constitutional republic, whose leaders must command the trust of those who lead....

Mr. Delahunt:... Mr. Speaker, I am particularly disturbed to hear speaker after speaker come here and speak to the issue of obstruction of justice and suborning of perjury. Let us listen to the testimony of the key witness, Monica Lewinsky, where she said clearly and unequivocally, "No one asked me to lie and no one promised me a job."

Listen to the evidence. Let us not make this a sham and a shambles. I beg you to listen to the evidence.

Charles Rangel (D-New York):.... What has this president done to cause so much hatred, so much animosity? And for those of you that say this is not about sex, I agree with you: This is about getting rid of the president of the United States....

You brought hatred to this floor. You can see it in the eyes, you can see it in the language, and people will walk lockstep and vote as Republicans and not as Members of the United States Congress.

Do you not think that as you keep talking about "no man is above the law," do you not understand that no Member here is above the will of the people of the United States of America? ... You have no right to get rid of him by saying "the rule of law," and then abuse the very rule of that law.

Mr. Buyer: ... Ms. Lewinsky's statements that no one told her to lie are not dispositive as to whether the president is guilty of obstruction. One need not directly command another to lie in order to be guilty of obstruction.... The statute prohibits elliptical suggestions as much as it does direct commands....

While Ms. Lewinsky and the president both testified "I never asked her to lie" and "he never asked me to lie," the circumstantial evidence is overwhelming. The statement was not necessary, because they concocted the cover story and they both understood the willful intent to conceal their relationship in order to impede justice in the *Jones versus Clinton* case.

Mr. McCollum: ... Mr. Speaker, I simply want to express concern over the gentleman from New York's statement that there was hatred over here on our side of the aisle with regard to the president. That is just not really true, in all honesty and sincerity.... I have personally talked with Members who have made their decisions only in the last few days after they have gone over the record who really truly did not want to impeach this president and have no hatred at all. It is an objective concern that perjury and obstruction of justice and the crimes are so overwhelming this president committed that they made that decision.

Mr. Delahunt: ... In response to my friend, the gentleman from Indiana [Mr. Buyer], let the record be clear. When Monica Lewinsky was confronted by Ken Starr in her proffer, she clearly and unequivocally stated that neither the president nor anyone in her behalf ever asked her to lie, and that is the evidence.

Richard Neal (D-Massachusetts): ... [W]hile we grapple with this issue tonight, we are all a bit uncertain about what this is all about, but we know what it is not about. It is not Watergate, it is certainly not Iran-Contra, and astonishingly enough, after the expenditure of $56 million and an investigation that has gone on longer than the Civil War, it is not about Whitewater....

What we have seen in this Congress really is the occurrence of two things: One, the rise of the Intimidator Caucus on the Republican side where they have intimidated moderate Republicans into voting for this impeachment proceeding. Secondly, we ask ourselves ... whatever happened to moderate Republicans?

Brian Bilbray (R-California): Mr. Speaker, I was not planning to address the body at this time, but a colleague, Mr. Neal, just impugned the moderates who have decided not to vote their way, as if we are somehow being pressured. I would challenge anyone on this floor to name the moderates who have come to you and said we have been pressured. I, for one, and my colleagues I have spoken to have said this is a vote of conscience and respect our vote of conscience as much as you are asking us to respect yours....

Ms. Jackson Lee: Mr. Speaker, we only want a fair shake at being able to convince our good friends about our case on the president.

I do not know if the gentleman from California would tell us if he has been able to see private showings of nonrelevant material in the secured room to influence their votes, and whether or not we have been given the same opportunity.[2] We do not mean they have been beaten, but we want to know whether or not the moderates have seen that. We have not had the opportunity to share the information that we have that suggests the president should not be impeached. This should be a fair process, Mr. Speaker.

Mr. Goodlatte: ... I would like to particularly call to the attention of the Members to Article III dealing with obstruction of justice.

The evidence shows that the president corruptly encouraged a witness in a federal civil rights action to execute a sworn affidavit in that proceeding that he knew to be perjurious, false, and misleading.

The evidence shows that the president corruptly encouraged a witness to give perjurious, false, and misleading testimony if and when called to testify personally in that proceeding.

---

[2] Republican members of the Judiciary Committee had urged other Republicans to review sealed FBI documents relating to a witness in the *Paula Jones* lawsuit. The documents had been submitted to Congress by the Office of the Independent Counsel, but were not made public and were only briefly referred to in Kenneth Starr's summary. They contained unsubstantiated allegations against President Clinton by a woman then identified only as "Jane Doe No. 5"; since then, the woman—Juanita Broaddrick—has gone public with her allegation that Clinton, when he was Arkansas' attorney general, sexually assaulted her in a hotel room.

The evidence shows that the president corruptly engaged in and encouraged or supported a scheme to conceal evidence. The evidence shows that the president corruptly prevented the truthful testimony of a witness in that proceeding at a time when the truthful testimony of that witness would have been harmful to him. And the evidence shows that the president corruptly allowed his attorney to make false and misleading statements to a federal judge....

Mr. Meehan: Mr. Speaker...let me refer to Monica Lewinsky's grand jury testimony: "No one asked me to lie, no one offered me a job for my silence."

You do not impeach a president because of guesswork, or inferences, or what he might have said, what he could have said, who might have said something. That is the evidence. You do not impeach a president based on this lack of evidence.

Mr. Nadler: Mr. Speaker, again, referring to the last gentleman, repeatedly saying an untruth does not make it true. I will remind the gentleman, the judge ruled that the Monica Lewinsky affair was not material to the *Paula Jones* case, and the president consequently did not deny her her day in court. Every prosecutor who came before the committee said there was not sufficient evidence for any of these perjury allegations.

Mr. Sensenbrenner:...Mr. Speaker, we have heard an awful lot about the transactions relative to what the president said at the deposition in the *Paula Jones* lawsuit relating to Monica Lewinsky's affidavit. I do not think the Members who thundered on denouncing what the gentleman from Virginia [Mr. Goodlatte] said have read page 63 of the committee report. I shall do so.

"After reading from the affidavit out loud, the president's attorney, Mr. Bennett, asked the president, 'Is that a true and accurate statement as far as you know it?' The president answered, 'That is absolutely true.' "....

During the same deposition, Robert Bennett, the president's attorney, stated, "Counsel is fully aware that Ms. Jane Doe No. 6 has filed, has an affidavit in which they are in possession of saying that there is absolutely no sex of any kind, any manner, shape or form with President Clinton."...

Now, a few months later, the grand jury testimony of Monica Lewinsky...confirmed that the contents of her affidavit were not true.

Question, Paragraph 8 of the affidavit says, "I have never had a sexual relationship with the president"; is that true?

Answer: "No."

Mr. Nadler: Mr. Speaker, with regard to the affidavit that the gentleman from Wisconsin referred to...

Monica Lewinsky testified that no one asked her to file a false affidavit. There is no evidence that the president asked her to file a false affidavit....

And finally, Monica Lewinsky's affidavit defined sexual relations in the way she clearly understood it, as we know from the tape of her conversation with Linda Tripp. After she was threatened by Mr. Starr and her mother was threatened, then she made an immunity deal, then she changed her testimony to what Mr. Starr wanted to hear. Starr admitted...that he chose when to believe her and when not to believe her. To get at the truth, she has to be cross-examined to determine...when she is telling the truth and when not.

Sander Levin (D-Michigan):...This debate here stands in stark contrast to the debate in 1991 on the Persian Gulf. The feelings were strong but it was nonpartisan and fair. Unlike today, the seats were filled and we came to deliberate, to exchange views, to listen to one another, not to pursue a set political agenda. In this decade, that was this House's finest hour. This is its worst....

What we learned growing up takes on new meaning today. Two wrongs do not make a right. The president was wrong, very wrong. To turn that today into impeachment is also wrong, very wrong.

Mr. Bryant: Mr. Speaker, the opposing side has made a point that Ms. Lewinsky said that the president never specifically told her to lie.... While the president did not expressly instruct her to lie, according to Ms. Lewinsky, he did suggest misleading cover stories....

...[T]he president suggested that if she was subpoenaed that she could file an affidavit to avoid being deposed. He also told her that she could say that she was working at the White House and she delivered letters to him and after leaving the White House, she sometimes returned to see Ms. Currie.

In the grand jury testimony of the president, he acknowledged that he and Ms. Lewinsky "might have talked about what to do in a nonlegal context to hide their relationship" and that he "might have said" that Ms. Lewinsky should tell people that she was bringing letters to him or coming to visit Ms. Currie. But he also stated that he never asked Ms. Lewinsky to lie. I think that is a classic example of the parsing of words that we have seen throughout this case....

Bobby Rush (D-Illinois):...Like never before, I have heard from senior citizens, the poor, and the working class, who have flooded my office with a steadfast refrain against these articles of impeachment. They have overwhelmingly supported and resoundingly pledged their support to President Clinton....

President Clinton has served as a ray of hope for forgotten Americans. As a consequence, this president continues to be bludgeoned by the Republican leadership because of his relationships with minorities, the working poor, and the disenfranchised of our nation, the very people who serve no useful purpose vis-à-vis the Republican agenda.

Mr. Speaker, this is wrong, wrong, wrong....

Mr. Goodlatte: ... [W]ith regard to Article III of the articles of impeachment, let the facts be known.

The evidence before this House indicates that the president engaged in a pattern of obstruction, while the *Jones v. Clinton* case was pending and while a federal criminal investigation into his alleged misconduct was pending, in order to thwart those proceedings.

The president encouraged Monica Lewinsky to file a sworn affidavit that he knew would be false in the *Jones v. Clinton* case. The president encouraged Monica Lewinsky to lie under oath if called personally to testify in the *Jones v. Clinton* case. The president related to Betty Currie, a potential witness in the *Jones v. Clinton* case, a false account of events relevant to testimony she might provide in the case.

The president told lies to White House aides who he knew would likely be called as witnesses before the grand jury investigating his misconduct, which these officials repeated to the grand jury, causing the grand jury to receive false information. The president intensified an effort to provide job assistance to Monica Lewinsky and succeeded in his efforts at a time when her truthful testimony in the *Jones v. Clinton* case would have been harmful to him.

The president engaged in a plan to conceal evidence that had been subpoenaed in the *Jones v. Clinton* case.

And the president at his deposition allowed his attorney to make a false representation to a federal judge in order to prevent questioning about Ms. Lewinsky.

I do not see how anyone, anyone, can deny the seriousness of these charges or the corrupting effect they have on the judicial system of this country if we allow them to go unaddressed.

Mr. Barrett: Mr. Speaker, the gentleman from Virginia said let the facts be known, so I think it is important that we let the facts be known.

With regard to Betty Currie, she was not a witness in the *Jones* case, she did not become a witness in the *Jones* case, she was never a witness in the *Jones* case. Yet they argue that somehow there is an obstruction of justice with the *Jones* case.

With regard to the job search, the record could not be clearer that Monica Lewinsky was looking for a job long before December and got a lot of assistance long before December.

Mr. Goodlatte: Mr. Speaker, with regard to the obstruction of justice, Article III, and the charge of suborning perjury or witness tampering with regard to Betty Currie, everyone here should understand that the issue is not whether or not Betty Currie was a witness. In fact, the law is very clear on that point. Title 18, Section 1512 of the United States Code with regard to witness tampering says that... an official proceeding need not be pending or about to be instituted at the time of the offense, and the courts have been clear on this....

So the issue was what did the president think was likely to occur with regard to Ms. Currie... and in a civil deposition he referred to her time and time and time again. So it is clear to me that he thought she likely to be a witness when he suggested to her that Ms. Lewinsky had come on to him, when he suggested to Ms. Currie that they were never alone, all of these statements intended to influence Ms. Currie's future testimony.

With regard to the issue of Ms. Lewinsky's employment, the question is whether the president's efforts in obtaining a job for Ms. Lewinsky were to influence her testimony or simply to help an ex-intimate without concern for her testimony. The fact of the matter is the president assisted Ms. Lewinsky in her job search in late 1997 at a time when she would have been a witness harmful to him in the Jones case were she to testify truthfully. The president did not act halfheartedly. His assistance led to the involvement of the Ambassador to the United nations, one of the country's leading business figures, Mr. Perelman, and one of the country's leading attorneys, Vernon Jordan.

I would suggest, Mr. Speaker, there is no coincidence between the fact that Ms. Lewinsky signed the false affidavit on the same day or the day after she received a job in New York.

Mr. Delahunt: Mr. Speaker, I think it is important to put on the record in response to my friend from Virginia Ms. Currie appeared before the grand jury on eight different occasions. On each occasion, she testified that in no way was she pressured to make any statement exonerating the president of the United States.

Joseph McDade (R-Pennsylvania): ... [A]fter reading the report of the Judiciary Committee, it is conclusive to me that the president violated his constitutional oath to the people of the United States. ...

However, I am gravely concerned about the tactics used by the independent counsel in this matter regarding the president. I am equally appalled by the tactics of another independent counsel in the case of former Secretary of Agriculture Mike Espy. ...

The tactics used by independent counsels are the same tactics used by regular federal prosecutors every day against American citizens. ... Nobody at the Justice Department raises any question about this type of conduct, which violates the Constitution. In my opinion, they contort the basic intent of the Constitution, which is to ensure the freedom of every citizen in this country. ...

Karen Thurman (D-Florida): Mr. Speaker, President Clinton, being merely human, gave in to lust. With the shame and embarrassment of that flaw being discovered, he deceived us. Those of us who voted for this man can forgive him. We can see what he has done, not only for this nation but across the world. We can see that this president has much more to give as a president.

But those on this floor who are calling for impeachment never voted for him, never supported him. They have pursued him relentlessly, and they cannot forgive or accept any imperfection in this man.

Just as lust and deceit are sins, so are hate and envy. Just two years ago, this House undertook disciplinary action against the Speaker for intentionally misrepresenting information to the House Ethics Committee. The Ethics Committee recommended and this House adopted on a bipartisan basis reprimand over censure, a penalty which allowed the Speaker to stand for reelection.

I do not know how to reconcile the hypocrisy of the House in holding the Speaker and the president to two different standards. ...

Dana Rohrabacher (R-California): Mr. Speaker, during the impeachment inquiry, many of those who have stood against the president have been targeted for personal vicious personal attack. The gentleman from Indiana [Mr. Dan Burton], the gentlewoman from Idaho [Mrs. Helen Chenoweth], the gentleman from Illinois [Mr. Henry Hyde], a Democrat, the gentleman from Pennsylvania [Mr. Paul McHale], and yesterday the gentleman from Louisiana [Mr. Bob Livingston] all have been made to suffer.[3]

What we have experienced on Capitol Hill is consistent with the threats and intimidation endured by each and every one of the women claiming to have been used and abused by the president of the United States....

Howard Berman (D–California): ... Those who argue that the institutions of government or the fabric of our society will be irreparably harmed by a failure to impeach the president seriously underestimate the American people. America is too strong a society, American parents too wise, the American sense of right and wrong is too embedded to be confused....

Impeachment is not a substitute for good parenting or personal moral values. I ask those who are open to a second thought to rethink this issue. Impeachment is not the proper vehicle for symbolic gestures....

Constance Morella (R–Maryland): ... No doubt the president's actions, in both words and deeds, have disgraced him, his family, his office. His legacy shall be indelibly scarred.

However, putting the country through the turmoil and the tumult of a Senate trial that could last months while the many important issues facing our nation go unaddressed is wrong. It is clear that the American people want us to close this sorry chapter in our history. I, therefore, plan to vote against the articles ...

Saturday, December 19 was voting day. Chairman Hyde had scheduled one last hour of debate before the vote itself. James Rogan of California led off, summing up for the majority: "The evidence is overwhelming. The question is elementary. The president was obliged under his sacred oath faithfully to execute our nation's laws. Yet he repeatedly perjured himself and obstructed justice, not for any noble purpose but to crush a humble lone woman's right to be afforded access to the courts. Now his defenders plead for no constitutional accountability for the one American

---

[3] In the heat of the impeachment process, these Members of Congress had been forced to admit marital infidelity. Speaker-designate Livingston had acknowledged past affairs because *Hustler* publisher Larry Flynt was threatening to reveal them. Flynt had offered a million-dollar reward for sexual revelations about top Republicans because, he told *The Washington Post,* "I just wanted to expose hypocrisy."

uniquely able to defend or debase our Constitution and the rule of law." A few other speakers followed, echoing the themes sounded on the previous day by their respective parties..

Then it was the turn of Speaker-designate Bob Livingston of Louisiana:

Bob Livingston (R-Louisiana):.... Our nation is founded on law, not on the whim of man. We are not ruled by kings or emperors, and there is no divine right of presidents. A president is an ordinary citizen, vested with the power to govern and sworn to preserve, protect and defend the Constitution of the United States. Inherent in that oath is the responsibility to live within its laws with no higher or lower expectations than the average citizen....

When the president appeared at the deposition of Ms. Jones and secondly before the federal grand jury, he was sworn to a second oath, to tell the truth, the whole truth and nothing but the truth, so help you God. This, according to witnesses to the Committee on the Judiciary and before the Special Counsel, he did not do. For this I will vote to impeach the president of the United States...

But to the president I would say:

Sir, you have done great damage to this nation over this past year, and while your defenders are contending that further impeachment proceedings would only protract and exacerbate the damage to this country, I say that you have the power to terminate that damage and heal the wounds that you have created. You, sir, may resign your post. And I can only challenge you in such fashion if I am willing to heed my own words.

To my colleagues, my friends and most especially my wife and family: I have hurt you all deeply, and I beg your forgiveness.

I was prepared to lead our narrow majority as Speaker, and I believe I had it in me to do a fine job. But I cannot do that job or be the kind of leader that I would like to be under current circumstances, so I must set the example that I hope President Clinton will follow.

Mr. Speaker, I will not stand for Speaker of the House on January 6, but rather I shall remain as a back bencher in this Congress that I so dearly love for approximately six months into the 106th Congress, whereupon I shall vacate my seat and ask my Governor to call a special election to take my place....

The Speaker-designate's announcement caused shock and consternation among his colleagues. As the last hour of debate wound down, many from both sides of the aisle addressed it. Pennsylvania Democrat Chaka Fattah said he hoped the Republicans recognized "that in their attempt to get Bill Clinton, they have at least lost one Speaker and one Speaker-to-be." Jerrold Nadler said that while he believed Livingston's resignation was "offered in good faith," it was a mistake: "It is a surrender ... to a developing sexual McCarthyism." Minority whip David Bonior echoed that sentiment: "The politics of personal smear is degrading the dignity of public office ... and the only way we will stop this vicious cycle is if we stand up and refuse to give in to it, whether it is Bill Clinton or Bob Livingston."

Several Republicans congratulated Livingston. As Tom Delay put it, "... he understood what this debate was all about. It was about honor and decency and integrity and the truth ... about relativism versus absolute truth." But Henry Hyde saw a different side to the story. "Something is going on repeatedly that has to be stopped," he said. "That is a confusion between private acts of infidelity and public acts, where as a government official, you raise your right hand and you ask God to witness to the truth of what you are saying. That is a public act. Infidelity, adultery ... is a private act."

Meanwhile, the members continued to sound the main themes of the debate. John Conyers summed up for the Democrats, taking the articles one by one. On Article I, he said, the Republican case came down to nothing more than "a lack of specificity ... in the president's testimony about who touched who and where and when it happened." Article II was unjustified because of the three rulings by a federal judge that Monica Lewinsky's allegations were not relevant to the core issues of Paula Jones's lawsuit. On Article III, Conyers argued, Lewinsky had testified the president never asked her to lie; Lewinsky, not the president, brought about the exchange of gifts, and the job search for Lewinsky had started long before she appeared on any witness list. As for Article IV, said Conyers: "The record shows the president answered the 81 questions completely, but that the alleged abuse of power lies in the fact that the majority disagrees with the answers."

Hyde spoke last for the Republicans. Most of the Democrats, he observed, were well aware that the president was a "serial violator of the oath." He went on: "Members recognize that problem because they want to censure him. That is impeachment lite. They want to censure him with no real consequences, except as history chooses to impose them." But censure, Hyde argued once again, was not a proper measure for the House to consider. Impeachment was the proper course. Hyde ended with a plea: "When the chief law enforcement officer trivializes, ignores, shreds, minimizes the sanctity of the oath, then justice is wounded, and Members on that side are wounded and their children are wounded. I ask Members to follow their conscience and they will serve the country."

After the Speaker pro tempore declared the debate closed, Democrat Rick Boucher of Virginia proposed, essentially, to amend the articles of impeachment in such a way as to substitute the censure resolution for them. It was a maneuver designed to force a vote on the measure, which Democrats were certain would pass with a bipartisan majority. But the House voted Boucher's amendment "not germane" to the question on the floor by 230 to 204.

It was finally time for the vote on the articles of impeachment. The results[4]:

Article I, charging that President Clinton willfully provided perjurious, false, and misleading testimony to the grand jury on August 17, 1998: yeas 228 (223 Republicans and 5 Democrats); nays 206 (5 Republicans, 200 Democrats, and 1 Independent); not voting 1.

Article II, charging that President Clinton willfully provided perjurious, false, and misleading testimony in the Paula Jones sexual harassment lawsuit: yeas 205 (200 Republicans and 5 Democrats); nays 229 (28 Republicans, 200 Democrats, and 1 Independent); not voting 1.

Article III, charging that President Clinton obstructed justice in the Jones case: yeas 221 (216 Republicans and 5 Democrats); nays 212 (12 Republicans, 199 Democrats, and 1 Independent); not voting 2.

Article IV, charging that President Clinton made perjurious, false, and misleading statements to Congress: yeas 148 (147 Republicans and 1 Democrat); nays 285 (81 Republicans, 203 Democrats, and 1 Independent); not voting 2.

Articles II and IV had not passed. Articles I and III were be sent on to the U.S. Senate for trial.

[4] See Appendix VI for a complete roll call.

PART III

THE SENATE
Trial

THE CASE FOR
THE PROSECUTION

Chief Justice William Rehnquist intoned the opening words: "The Senate will convene as a Court of Impeachment." After a prayer from the Senate chaplain, Sergeant at Arms James W. Ziglar made the proclamation that would be heard at the start of each day during the trial: "Hear ye! Hear ye! Hear ye! All persons are commanded to keep silent, on pain of imprisonment, while the Senate of the United States is sitting for the trial of the articles of impeachment exhibited by the House of Representatives against William Jefferson Clinton, president of the United States." Then the chief justice noted the presence of the House managers of the case against President Clinton and the president's defense team.[1] The managers, he said, would have twenty-four hours to present their case. "The Senate will now hear you," he said—and he recognized Henry Hyde.

"We are here, Mr. Chief Justice and distinguished Senators, as advocates for the rule of law, for equal justice under the law and for the sanctity of the oath," said Hyde, who then explained how the House managers would proceed. After an overview by James Sensenbrenner, he said, one team of managers would present the facts of the case. The next day, after a summary of the facts, a second team would address the law of perjury and obstruction of justice. On the third day, a third team would address constitutional law in relation to the case. Then there would be summations.

[1] For members of the President's defense team, see Appendix II.

Sensenbrenner previewed what the senators would be hearing from the teams of managers. He raised the issue of witnesses: "The House managers submit witnesses are essential to give heightened credence to whatever judgment the Senate chooses to make." He reviewed the question of whether perjury was, indeed, an impeachable offense—"Perjury is the twin brother of bribery," he said—and reminded the senators that "the three judicial impeachments of the 1980s were all about lies." And he summed up the case itself: "We are here today because William Jefferson Clinton decided to use all means possible—both legal and illegal—to subvert the truth about his conduct relevant to the federal civil rights suit brought against President Clinton by Mrs. Paula Jones." After telling the senators what the evidence would show, he addressed the bigger picture:

Within the walls of the Capitol and throughout this great country there rages an impassioned and divisive debate over the future of this presidency. This Senate now finds itself in the midst of the tempest.

We have all anguished over the sequence of events that have led us to this, the conclusive stage in the process. We have all identified in our own minds where it could have, and should have stopped. But we have ended up here, before the Senate of the United States, where you, the Senators, will have to render judgment based upon the facts. . . . Our legacy now must be not to lose the trust the people should have in our nation's leaders. Our legacy now must be not to cheapen the legacies left by our forebears. Our legacy must be to do the right thing based upon the evidence. . . ."

The chief justice recognized Rep. Ed Bryant of Tennessee.

Mr. Bryant: . . . Every trial must have a beginning and this trial begins on a cold day in January 1993. . . .

William Jefferson Clinton placed his left hand on the Bible in front of his wife, the Chief Justice and every American watching that day and affirmatively acknowledged his oath of office. . . . He became only the 42nd person in our nation to make the commitment to "faithfully execute" the office of the president and to "preserve, protect and defend the Constitution." . . .

William Jefferson Clinton is a man of great distinction. He is well-educated with degrees from Georgetown University and Yale Law School. He has taught law school courses to aspiring young lawyers. He served as governor and attorney general for the state of Arkansas. . . . The president now directs our great nation. He sets our agenda and creates national policy in a very public way . . .

President Clinton also serves as the nation's chief law enforcement officer.

It is primarily in this capacity that the president appoints federal judges. Within the executive branch, he selected Attorney General Janet Reno and appointed each of the 93 United States Attorneys who are charged with enforcing all federal, civil and criminal law in federal courthouses....

As protectors of our Constitution, the U.S. Attorneys and their assistants prosecute more than 50,000 cases per year.... Each and every one ... is dependent upon the parties and witnesses telling the truth under oath. Equally as important ... is that justice not be obstructed by tampering with witnesses nor hiding evidence....

Indeed, truth-telling is the single most important judicial precept underpinning this great system of justice we have, a system which permits the courthouse doors to be open to all people, from the most powerful man in America to a young woman from Arkansas.

On May 6, 1994, Paula Corbin Jones attempted to open that courthouse door when she filed a federal sexual harassment lawsuit against President Clinton.... The parties first litigated the question of whether Ms. Jones' lawsuit would have to be deferred until after the president left office. The Supreme Court unanimously ... allowed the case to proceed without further delay....

During the discovery phase, Judge Susan Webber Wright of the U.S. District Court for the Eastern District Court of Arkansas ordered the president to answer certain historical questions about his sexual relations with either state or federal employees....

Judge Wright validated Ms. Jones' right to use this accepted line of questioning in sexual harassment litigation.... Such standard questions are essential in establishing whether the defendant has committed the same kind of acts before or since—in other words, a pattern or practice of harassing conduct....

The "pattern and practice" witnesses whom Paula Corbin Jones was entitled to discover should have included ... Monica Lewinsky. But before I discuss the Ms. Lewinsky matter, I want to offer three matters of cause to each of you as jurors in this very important matter.

Number 1, I do not intend to discuss the specific details of the president's encounters with Ms. Lewinsky. However, I do not want to give the Senate the impression that those encounters are irrelevant or lack serious legal implications....

Number 2, the evidence and testimony in this proceeding must be viewed as a whole.... Remember, events and words that may seem innocent or even

exculpatory in a vacuum may well take on a sinister or even criminal connotation when observed in the context of the whole plot....

Number 3,...I ask you to pay particular attention to what I call the big picture. Look at the results of those various acts as well as who benefited....

I want to now rewind the clock back to November of 1995.... Ms. Lewinsky
has been working at the White House since July of 1995....

[F]rom...November 15 forward, remember that Ms. Lewinsky and the
president were alone in the Oval Office workplace area at least 21 times.,...
During that time, they had at least 11 of the so-called salacious encounters...Three in 1995, five in 1996, and three in 1997....

As Ms. Lewinsky's internship was ending that year, she did apply for and receive a paying job with the White House Office of Legislative Affairs. This
position allowed her even more access to the Oval Office area. She remained
a White House employee until April 1996, when she was reassigned to the
Pentagon....

After she began her job at the Pentagon in April, there was no further physical contact with the president through the 1996 election and the remainder
of that year. The two communicated by telephone and on occasion saw each
other at public events....

However...in 1997, Ms. Lewinsky was more successful in arranging visits
to the White House. This was because she used the discreet assistance of Ms.
Currie, the president's secretary.... Ms. Currie testified on one occasion when
Ms. Lewinksy told her, "As long as no one saw us—and no one did—then
nothing happened." Ms. Currie responded, "Don't want to hear it. Don't say
any more. I don't want to hear any more."

Early on during their secret liaisons, the two concocted a cover story to
use if discovered. Ms. Lewinksy was to say she was bringing papers to the
president....

Ms. Lewinksy stated that the president did not expressly instruct her to lie.
He did, however, suggest, indeed, the "misleading" cover story....

When she and the president both were subpoenaed in the *Jones* case, Ms.
Lewinksy anticipated that "as we had on every other occasion and every other
instance of this relationship, we would deny it."

In his grand jury testimony, President Clinton acknowledged that he and
Ms. Lewinsky "might have talked about what to do in a nonlegal context" to
hide their relationship and that he "might well have said" that Ms. Lewinsky

should tell people she was bringing letters to him or coming to visit Ms. Currie. He always stated that "I never asked Ms. Lewinsky to lie."

But neither did the president ever say that they must now tell the truth under oath....

Bryant turned to Lewinsky's attempts to return to the White House after the 1996 elections. Betty Currie had testified that the president asked her and Marsha Scott, deputy director of personnel, to help Lewinsky find a job. But in the spring of 1997, Lewinsky began to complain that there was no progress. On July 3, said Bryant, she wrote a note to the president mentioning some interest in working at the United Nations and threatening "that she might have to tell her parents about why she no longer had a job at the White House" if a job didn't materialize. The next day, the president scolded her that "it was illegal to threaten the president."

Then Linda Tripp said she had learned from a friend of hers on the White House staff that Lewinsky would never return to the White House. This, Lewinsky testified, was the "straw that broke the camel's back." She sent the president a letter asking for a job in New York.

During an October 11 meeting with the president, he suggested that she give him a list of New York companies which interested her. She asked if Vernon Jordan might also help. Five days later, she provided the president with her "wish list." ... [and] arrangements were made through the president and Ms. Currie for Ms. Lewinsky to meet with Mr. Jordan. On the morning of November 5, 1997, Mr. Jordan ... met with Ms. Lewinsky for the first time for about 20 minutes....

However, the evidence reflects that Mr. Jordan took no steps to help Ms. Lewinsky until early December of that year after she appeared on the witness list in the *Jones* case.... Then ... something happened which caused those interested in finding Ms. Lewinsky a job in New York to intensify their search. Within 48 hours of her signing this false affidavit in the *Paula Jones* case, Ms. Lewinsky had landed a job with a prestigious Fortune 500 Company.

... Unfortunately for your search for the truth in these proceedings, the president continues today to parse his words and use "legal hairsplitting" in his defense. I cite for your consideration his answer filed with this body just days ago. For instance:

1. Responding in part to the impeachment Article I, the president persists in a wrongheaded fashion with his legal hairsplitting of the term "sexual relations," which permits him to define that term in such a way that in the particular salacious act we are talking about here, one person has sex and the other person does not. . . .

2. Responding to both articles of impeachment, the president now would have you believe that he "was not focusing" when his attorney, Bob Bennett, was objecting during the deposition and attempting to cut off a very important line of questioning of the president by representing to Judge Wright that Ms. Lewinsky's affidavit proved that there is no need to go into this testimony about the president's life. . . .

3. In his further response to Article I, the president effectively admits guilt to obstruction. As I read this, . . . he states that he, the president, "truthfully explained to the grand jury his efforts to answer the questions in the *Jones* deposition without disclosing his relationship with Ms. Lewinsky." . . . Said another way, he intentionally answered questions to avoid the discovery of one of these female employees with whom he was sexually involved. That is precisely, folks, what impeding the discovery of evidence is. . . .

4. In his answer to Article II, the president "denies that he encouraged Monica Lewinsky to execute a false affidavit in the Jones case." When everything is said and done, Ms. Lewinsky had no motivation, no reason whatsoever to want to commit a crime by willfully submitting a false affidavit with a court of law. . . . [B]ut this 20-something-year-old young lady was listening to the most powerful man in the United States, whom she greatly admired, hearing him effectively instruct her to file a false affidavit to avoid having to testify about their relationship. And in order to do that, she had to lie about the physical aspects of their relationship. . . .

5. In an additional response to Article II, the president . . . asserts that "he believed that Ms. Lewinsky could have filed a limited and truthful affidavit that might have enabled her to avoid having to testify in the *Jones* case." That is an incredible statement . . . given the fact that the president knew firsthand of the extent of their sexual relationship, and he also knew that the *Jones* discovery efforts were specifically after that type of conduct. . . .

All Americans, including the president, are entitled to enjoy a private family life, free from public or governmental scrutiny. But the privacy concerns raised in this case are subject to limits. . . .

The first limit was imposed when the president was sued in federal court for alleged sexual harassment. The evidence in such litigation is often personal.... Nevertheless, Congress and the Supreme Court have concluded that embarrassment-related concerns must give way to the greater interest in allowing aggrieved parties to pursue their claims....

The second limit was imposed when Judge Wright required disclosure of the precise information that is in part the subject of this hearing today.... The fact that Judge Wright later determined that the evidence would not be admissible at trial, and still later granted judgment in the president's favor, does not change the president's legal duty at the time he testified....

The third limit is unique to the president.... As the head of the Executive Branch, the president has the constitutional duty to "take care that the laws be faithfully executed."...In view of the enormous trust and responsibility attendant to his high office, the president has a manifest duty to ensure that his conduct at all times complies with the law of the land.

In sum, perjury and acts that obstruct justice by any citizen—whether in a criminal case, a grand jury investigation, a congressional hearing, a civil trial or civil discovery—are profoundly serious matters. When such acts are committed by the president of the United States, those acts are grounds for conviction and removal from his office....

The chief justice recognized Rep. Asa Hutchinson of Arkansas.

Mr. Hutchinson:...I will be...focusing on the evidence that demonstrates obstruction of justice under Article II. You might wonder, well, why are we going to Article II before we have covered Article I on perjury? And the answer is that in a chronological flow, Article II, the obstruction facts, precede much of the perjury allegations....

Later on, there will be a full discussion of the law on obstruction of justice, but for our purposes, it is simply any corrupt act or attempt to influence or impede the proper functioning of our system of justice....

The obstruction, for our purposes, started on December 5, 1997...when the witness list from the *Paula Jones* case was faxed to the president's lawyers. At that point, the wheels of obstruction started rolling, and they did not stop until the president successfully blocked the truth from coming out in the civil rights case.

...Shortly thereafter, the president learned that the list included Monica Lewinsky. This had to be startling news to the president, because if the truth about his relationship with a subordinate employee was known, the civil rights case against him would be strengthened.... But to compound the problem, less than a week later, Judge Wright, federal district judge in Arkansas, on December 11, issued an order [directing] that the president had to answer questions concerning other relationships that he might have had....

The White House knew that Monica was on the witness list. The president knew that it was likely that she would be subpoenaed as a witness and that her truthful testimony would hurt his case.... What he had to do was he made sure that Monica Lewinsky was on his team and under control. And then on December 17, the president finally called Ms. Lewinsky to let her know she was on the list....

Now, what happened in the time between the president learning Monica Lewinsky was on the list and when he notified her of that fact ... is very important. The president ... talked to his friend, his confidant and his problem-solver, Vernon Jordan. Mr. Jordan ... was instrumental in securing consulting contracts for Mr. Webb Hubbell while Mr. Hubbell was under investigation by the independent counsel.... So the president was aware that Mr. Jordan had the contacts and the track record to be of assistance ... in delicate matters.

Now let's go back a little. Monica Lewinsky had been looking for a good-paying and high-profile job in New York since the previous July.... She was not having much success, and then in early November it was Betty Currie who arranged a meeting with Vernon Jordan, which was ultimately on November 5. At this meeting, Ms. Lewinsky met with Mr. Jordan for about 20 minutes....

... What happened as a result of this meeting? No action followed whatsoever. No job interviews were arranged and there were no further contacts with Mr. Jordan.... Indeed, it was so unimportant to him that he "had no recollection of an early November meeting" ...

And so look at the same exhibit 2 ... where it refers to Monica Lewinsky's grand jury testimony ... referring to a December 6 meeting with the president.

> I think I said that ... I was supposed to get in touch with Mr. Jordan the previous week and that things did not work out and that nothing had really happened yet [on the job front].

And the question was:

Did the president say what he was going to do?

The answer:

> I think he said he would—you know, this was sort of typical of him, to sort of say, "Oh I'll talk to him. I'll get on it."

So you can see from that that it was not a high priority for the president, either....

But then the president's attitude suddenly changed. What started out as a favor for Betty Currie dramatically changed after Ms. Lewinsky became a witness, and the judge's order was issued...on December 11....

...The witness list came in. The judge's order came in. That triggered the president to action. And the president triggered Vernon Jordan into action. That chain reaction here is what moved the job search along....

> *Here, Hutchinson cited testimony from Jordan to show that the president was intimately involved in the job search. When Jordan learned that Lewinsky had fired lawyer Frank Carter, he notified the White House. Asked why, he replied: "The president asked me to get Monica Lewinsky a job. I got her a lawyer. The Drudge Report is out and she has new counsel. I thought that was information that they ought to have." In another grand jury appearance, Jordan was asked why the president needed to know about Frank Carter. His response: "Information. He knew that I had gotten her a job, he knew that I had gotten her a lawyer.... He was interested in this matter. He is the source of it coming to my attention in the first place."*
>
> *Hutchinson continued:*

The next step in the obstruction is the false affidavit. This is directly related to the job mission. The president needed the signature of Monica Lewinsky on the false affidavit, and that was assured by the efforts to secure her a job....

...He gets the witness list. He could have called Monica Lewinsky immediately, but he needed seven days because he needed to make sure the job situation was in gear.... But she was notified on December 17. Between 2 and 2:30 a.m., her phone rang. It was the president of the United States. The president said that he had seen the witness list in the case and her name was on it. Ms. Lewinsky asked what she should do if subpoenaed, and the president responded, "Well, maybe you can sign an affidavit." Well, how would this work? Both parties knew that the affidavit would need to be false and misleading in order to accomplish the desired result....

... During that conversation, the president had a very pointed suggestion for Ms. Lewinsky ... that left no doubt about his purpose and the intended consequences. He did not say specifically, "Go in and lie." ... The president chose to give her the ideas as to what she could testify to that would be false.... So what he did say to her was, "You know, you can always say you were coming to see Betty or that you were bringing me letters." ...

It is interesting to note that the president, when he was asked by the grand jury whether he remembered calling Monica Lewinsky at 2 a.m. on that December 17th day, responded, "No, sir, I don't, but it is quite possible that that happened." When he was asked whether he encouraged Monica Lewinsky to continue the cover stories of coming to see Betty or bringing letters, he answered, "I don't remember exactly what I told her that night."

This is not a denial, and therefore I believe you should accept the testimony of Monica Lewinsky.... [Y]ou should ... give us the opportunity to present this witness so that you as jurors can fairly and honestly determine her credibility.

As expected, two days later, on December 19, Ms. Lewinsky received a subpoena to testify in the *Jones* case. This sets about an immediate flurry of activity.... Monica calls Jordan and Jordan immediately calls the president. Lewinsky meets with Jordan and requests that Jordan notify the president about her subpoena—this is at 4:47 p.m. Presumably in the middle of that meeting, at 5:01 p.m., the president of the United States telephones Mr. Jordan and Jordan notifies the president about Ms. Lewinsky's subpoena. Then that is whenever he arranged for Ms. Lewinsky's attorney ... and that night, Vernon Jordan goes to the White House to meet privately with the president on these particular issues.

Now, in that meeting ... Mr. Jordan told the president again that Ms. Lewinsky had been subpoenaed and related to the president the substance and details of his meeting with Ms. Lewinsky. It wasn't a casual consideration; the details were discussed, including her fascination with the president and other such issues.

This led Mr. Jordan to ask the president about his relationship with Ms. Lewinsky, and the response by the president of the United States was the first of many denials to his friends and aides....

Now, the subpoena had been delivered, but the testimony of Monica Lewinsky was not scheduled until January 23, and the president's deposition...was not scheduled until January 17. So the president and his team had some time to work....

Under the plan, Mr. Jordan would be the buffer; he would obtain an attorney—Mr. Carter—and that attorney would keep Mr. Jordan informed on the...general progress of the representation. All along the way, when Mr. Jordan gets information, what does he do with that? Mr. Jordan keeps the president informed...

The president knew that Monica Lewinsky was going to make a false affidavit. He was so certain of the contents that when Monica Lewinsky asked if he wanted to see it, he told her no, that he had seen 15 of them. Besides, the president had suggested the affidavit himself, and he trusted Mr. Jordan to be certain to keep things under control....

Now, let's go to the time when the false affidavit was actually signed, January 5, 1998.... Ms. Lewinsky meets with her attorney, Mr. Carter, for an hour. Carter drafts the affidavit for Ms. Lewinsky on the deposition.... Ms. Lewinsky telephones Betty Currie, stating that she needs to speak to the president...specifically, that she was anxious about something she needed to sign—an affidavit.... The president returns Ms. Lewinsky's call.

...Ms. Lewinsky mentions the affidavit she is signing and offers to show it to the president. That is where he says no, he had seen 15 others.

Hutchinson then summed up the events of January. Lewinsky picked up the affidavit and delivered it to Jordan. Then followed a series of phone calls between Jordan and Carter, Jordan and the White House, and Jordan and Lewinsky, who "agree to delete a portion of the affidavit that created some implication that maybe she had been alone with the president." Hutchinson's conclusion: "Mr. Jordan was very involved in drafting the affidavit." The following day, Lewinsky signed the affidavit, then delivered it to Jordan, who called the White House three times. Hutchinson continued:

The next day...January 8. After it is signed, what is important the next day? It was the other part of the arrangement, that she has the job interview...in New York.... The only problem was that it went poorly, very poorly. So at 4:48 p.m.... Ms. Lewinsky telephones Jordan....

What does Mr. Jordan do? He telephones Ron Perelman, the CEO of Revlon...to "make things happen if they could happen."...Mr. Jordan intercedes—and why? Because the false affidavit has been signed and he wants to make sure this is carried out....

Then on January 9 ... Lewinsky is offered the Revlon job in New York, and accepts.

Lewinsky telephones Jordan. And then, at 4:14, Jordan notifies Currie, calls Betty Currie, and says "Mission accomplished." and requests that she tell the president....

Let me ask you a question.... Would Mr. Jordan have pushed for a second interview without cooperation on the affidavit? Would Monica Lewinsky have received the support and secured the job if she had said "I don't want to sign an affidavit; I am just going to go in there and tell the truth; whatever they ask me, I am going to answer; I am going to tell the truth"? ...

Now the affidavit has been signed. The job is secure. Monica Lewinsky is on the team, and the president of the United States is armed for the deposition. So let's move there.

Just how important was Monica Lewinsky's false affidavit to the president's deposition? Let's look.... That false affidavit allowed Mr. Bennett ... when talking about the ... relationship between the president and Ms. Lewinsky—it allowed him to assert that "... there is absolutely no sex of any kind in any manner, shape or form with President Clinton." ...

I am sure it was the president's hope and belief that the false affidavit used in the deposition to bolster his own testimony would be the end of the matter. But that was not the case.... And so it is when we attempt to thwart the administration of justice—one obstruction leads to another....

By the time the president concluded his deposition, he knew there were too many details out about his relationship with Ms. Lewinsky. He knew that the only person who would probably be talking was Ms. Lewinsky herself. He knew the cover story that he had carefully created and that was converted into false statements in the affidavit was now in jeopardy and had to be backed at this point by the key witnesses, Monica Lewinsky and Betty Currie....

The president finishes testifying in the deposition around 4 p.m. At 5:38 p.m., the president telephones Mr. Jordan at home.... At 7:02, the president places a call to Mr. Jordan's office. And then, at 7:13, he gets Ms. Currie at home finally, and asks her to meet with him on Sunday....

[A]t 6:11 in the morning, the president had some more bad news. The Drudge Report was released....

But it was on that day that there was that critical meeting ... in the Oval Office between Betty Currie and the president of the United States.... Betty

Currie testified in the grand jury that the president said that he had just been deposed and that the attorneys had asked several questions about Monica Lewinsky....

The first: "I was never really alone with Monica, right?"

Second: "You were always there when Monica was there, right?"...

[T]he president is making those simple declaratory statements to her. There are three areas that are covered. First of all, the president makes a case that he was never alone with Monica Lewinsky. Second, he is making a point to her that "she was the aggressor, not me." The third point he is making, "I did nothing wrong."...

During Betty Currie's grand jury testimony...she was asked a series of questions, and she finally acknowledges that the president was intending for her to agree with the statements that were made....

When the president testified in the August 17 grand jury, he was questioned about his intentions when he made those five statements to Ms. Currie in his office on that Sunday....

The president: I thought we were going to be deluged by the press comments. And I was trying to refresh my memory about what the facts were.

Then he goes on to testify:

So, I was not trying to get Betty Currie to say something that was untruthful. I was trying to get as much information as quickly as I could.

Ladies and gentlemen of the Senate, you have to determine what the purpose of those five statements to Betty Currie were. Were they to get information, or were they to get her to falsely testify when she was called as a witness?...

...[H]e made short, clear, understandable, declarative statements telling Ms. Currie what the story was. He was not interested in what she knew. Why? Because he knew the truth, but he did not want Ms. Currie to tell the truth. The only way to ensure that was by telling her what to say, not asking her what she remembered....

...This was not any attempt for the president to refresh his recollection. It was witness-tampering, pure and simple.

Understanding the seriousness of the president's attempting to influence the testimony of Ms. Currie, his attorneys have tried to argue that those statements could not constitute obstruction of justice because she had not been subpoenaed and the president did not know that she was a potential witness at this time....

The law is clear that a person may be convicted of obstructing justice if he corruptly influenced the testimony of a prospective witness. The witness does not actually have to give testimony. The witness does not have to be under any subpoena. The witness does not have to be on any witness list....

Secondly, let's examine the defense in light of the facts. The president himself brought Ms. Currie into the civil rights case as a corroborating witness when he repeatedly used her name in the deposition, and just as significantly the president had to be concerned about a looming perjury charge against him in light of his false testimony in the deposition....

There is no question that Ms. Currie was a prospective witness, and the president clearly wanted her to be deposed as a witness as his "ask Betty" testimony demonstrates....

Now, remember, it was on a Sunday that Betty Currie was first called into the White House to go through these five statements, this coaching by the president. And then she testified to the grand jury:

Question: Did there come a time after that that you had another conversation with the president about some other news about what was going on? That would have been Tuesday or Wednesday—when he called you into the Oval Office?

Betty Currie's answer:

It was Tuesday or Wednesday. I don't remember which one this was, either. But the best I remember, when he called me in the Oval Office, it was sort of a recapitulation of what we had talked about on Sunday— you know, "I was never alone with her"—that sort of thing.
Question: Did he pretty much list the same—
Answer: To my recollection, sir, yes.
Question: And did he say it in sort of the same tone and demeanor that he used the first time he told you on Sunday?
Answer: The best I remember, yes, sir.

... This is more than witness-tampering. It is witness compulsion of false testimony by an employer to a subordinate employee.... At this point we are

The Case for the Prosecution 225

not talking about hiding personal facts from inquiring minds but an effort to impede the legitimate and necessary functioning of our court system.

Hutchinson briefly turned to the events of Monday, January 19, which was marked, he said, by a "frantic search" for Monica Lewinsky at the president's behest. "Why this flurry of activity?" asked Hutchinson. "Ms. Lewinsky was a co-conspirator in hiding this relationship from the federal court, and [the president] was losing control over her."

Then he addressed the subject of the gifts:

On December 28, another brick in the wall of obstruction was laid. It was the concealment of evidence. Ms. Lewinsky testified that she discussed with the president the fact that she had been subpoenaed and that the subpoena called for her to produce gifts....

> And then at some point I said to him [the president], "Well, you know, should I—maybe I should put the gifts away outside my house somewhere or give them to someone, maybe Betty." And he sort of said—I think he responded, "I don't know," or, "Let me think about that," and left that topic.

... Later that day Ms. Lewinsky got a call from Ms. Currie, who said, "I understand you have something to give to me," or, according to Ms. Lewinsky, "The president said you have something to give me." ...

And so, ladies and gentlemen, if you accept the testimony of Monica Lewinsky on that point, you must conclude that the directive to retrieve the gifts came from the president. I will concede that there is a conflict in the testimony on this point with the testimony of Betty Currie. Ms. Currie ... testified that, "the best she can remember," Ms. Lewinsky called her. But whenever she was asked further, she said that maybe Ms. Lewinsky's memory is better than hers on that issue. But there is helpful evidence to clear up this discrepancy.... Monica, you will recall, in her deposition said she thought ... that the call came from [Currie's] cell phone number.... The cell phone record was retrieved that showed ... that a call was made at 3:32, from Betty Currie to Monica Lewinsky. And this confirms the testimony of Monica Lewinsky that the follow-up to get the gifts came from Betty Currie. The only way she would know about it is if the president directed her to go retrieve the gifts....

We have presented to you a great amount of direct evidence, grand jury testimony, eyewitness testimony, documentary evidence. But juries can use circumstantial evidence as well.... So I think it is incumbent upon you to evaluate the circumstances very carefully in addition to the testimony.

Now, let's examine the key question for a moment. Why did Betty Currie pick up the gifts from Monica Lewinsky? Monica Lewinsky states that she did not request this and the retrieval was initiated by the call from Betty Currie. This was after the meeting with the president. Monica Lewinsky's version is corroborated by the cell phone record and the pattern of conduct on the part of Betty Currie. What do I mean by that? ... Betty Currie, a subordinate employee, would not engage in such activity on such a sensitive matter without the approval and direction of the president himself.

In addition, let's look further to the actions of Betty Currie. It becomes clear that she understands the significance of these gifts, their evidentiary value in a civil rights case, and the fact that they are under subpoena. She retrieves these items, and where does she place them? She hides them under her bed....

Now, let's look at the president's defense. The president stated in his response to questions ... submitted from the House to the president, he said he was not concerned about the gifts. In fact, he recalled telling Monica that if the *Jones* lawyers request the gifts, she should just turn them over to them. The president testified he is "not sure" if he knew the subpoena asked for gifts.

Now, why in the world would Monica and the president discuss turning over gifts to the *Jones* lawyer if Ms. Lewinsky had not told him that the subpoena asked for gifts? On the other hand, if he knew the subpoena requested gifts, why would he give Monica more gifts on December 28? ... Ms. Lewinsky's testimony reveals the answer. She said that she never questioned "that we were ever going to do anything but keep this private," and that means to take "whatever appropriate steps need to be taken." ...

Why would the president even meet with Monica Lewinsky on December 28 when their relationship was in question and he had a deposition coming up? Certainly he knew he would be questioned about it. Certainly if Monica became a witness she would be ... asked when was the last time you met with the president, and now they have to say December 28, if they were going to tell the truth.

The answer is, the president knew that he had to keep Monica Lewinsky on the team and he was willing to take more risks so that she would continue to be a part of the conspiracy to obstruct the legitimate functions of the federal court in a civil rights case.

It should be remembered that the president has denied each and every allegation of the two articles of impeachment, he has denied each element of the obstruction of justice charges.... This straightforward denial illustrates the dispute in the evidence and testimony. It sets the credibility of Monica Lewinsky, the credibility of Betty Currie, the credibility of Vernon Jordan, and others against the credibility of the president of the United States....

Now let's go forward, once again, to the time period in which the president gave his deposition in the *Paula Jones* case. The president testified under oath on January 17, and immediately thereafter, remember, he brought Betty Currie in to present a set of false facts to her, seeking her agreement and coaching her.

... There were no witnesses, and it boils down to a "he said, she said" scenario, and as long as that is the case, he believes he can win. If the president can simply destroy Monica Lewinsky's credibility... then he will escape the consequences for his false statements under oath and obstruction in the civil rights case. Now, remember, this viewpoint, though, is all before the DNA tests... on the blue dress....

In order to carry out this cover-up and obstruction, the president needed to go further. He needed not only Betty Currie to repeat his false statements, but also other witnesses who would assuredly be called before the federal grand jury and who would be questioned by the news media in public forums. And this brings us to the false statements that the president made to his... aides.

... First, the testimony of Sidney Blumenthal... about his conversations when the president called him in.... Mr. Blumenthal testified that "it was at that point that he"—referring to the president—"gave his account as to what happened to me and he said that Monica—and it came very fast. He said, 'Monica Lewinsky came at me and made a sexual demand on me.' He rebuffed her. He said, 'I've gone down that road before, I've caused pain for a lot of people and I'm not going to do that again.'... She threatened him. She said that she would tell people they'd had an affair, that she was known as the stalker among her peers, and that she hated it and if she had an affair or said she had an affair then she wouldn't be the stalker any more. And I said to him, I said, "When this happened with Monica Lewinsky, were you alone?' He said, 'Well, I was within eyesight or earshot of someone.' "

Let's go to John Podesta's testimony where he was called in the same fashion. The president talked to him about what is happening:

Question: Okay. Share that with us.
Answer: Well, I think he said—he said that—there was some spate of, you know, what sex acts were counted, and he said that he had never had sex with her in any way whatsoever.
Question: Okay.
Answer: —that they had not had oral sex.

...As the president testified before the grand jury, he knew these witnesses would be called before the grand jury.... The false statements to them constitute witness-tampering and obstruction of justice....

In this case, at every turn, he used whatever means available to evade the truth, destroy evidence, tamper with witnesses and took any other action required to prevent evidence from coming forward in a civil rights case that would prove a truth contrary to the president's interest....

...What did the president do that constitutes evidence of obstruction?

No. 1, he personally encouraged a witness, Monica Lewinsky, to provide false testimony.

No. 2, the president had direct involvement in assuring a job for a witness—underlining direct involvement. He made the calls, Vernon Jordan did, and it is connected with the filing of the false affidavit by that witness.

No. 3, the president personally, with corrupt intentions, tampered with the testimony of a prospective witness, Betty Currie.

No. 4, the president personally provided false statements under oath before a federal grand jury.

No. 5, by direct and circumstantial evidence the president personally directed the concealment of evidence under subpoena in a judicial proceeding.

No. 6, the president personally allowed false representations to be made by his attorney, Robert Bennett, to a federal district judge on January 17.

No. 7, the president intentionally provided false information to witnesses before a federal grand jury knowing that those statements would be repeated with the intent to obstruct the proceedings before that grand jury....

The seven pillars of this obstruction case were personally constructed by the president of the United States. It was done with the intent that the truth and evidence would be suppressed in a civil rights case pending against him. The goal was to win, and he was not going to let the judicial system stand in his way....

After a fifteen-minute recess, the chief justice recognized Rep. James Rogan of California.

Mr. Rogan: . . . On the afternoon of August 17, 1998, President Clinton raised his right hand and took an oath before the grand jury in their criminal investigation. . . . When the president made that solemn pledge, he was not obliging himself to tell the grand jury the partial truth, he was not obliging himself to tell the "I didn't want to be particularly helpful" truth; he was not obliging himself to tell the "this is embarrassing so I think I'll fudge on it a little bit" truth. He was required to tell the truth, the whole truth, and nothing but the truth, and he made that pledge in the name of God.

The attorneys for the Office of the Independent Counsel showed great deference to the president when they questioned him that day. The president's attorneys were allowed to be there with him during the entire proceeding. . . . [T]he attorney who questioned the president encouraged him to confer with his lawyers if there arose in the president's mind any reason to hesitate before answering a question. . . .

If a question was vague or ambiguous, the president could ask for a clarification. If he was unsure how to answer, or indeed whether to answer a question, he could stop the questioning, take a break, and consult privately with his attorneys who were present with him. If giving an answer would tend to incriminate him, he could refuse to answer the question by claiming his Fifth Amendment rights.

But if, after all of this, he decided to give an answer, the answer he gave was required to be the truth, the whole truth, and nothing but the truth. And it was no different than the obligation when he testified in the *Paula Jones* deposition—the same oath, the same obligation.

Let's look at how the president chose to meet his obligation. . . .

At his deposition in the *Paula Jones* case, the president was shown a definition approved by Judge Wright of what constitutes sexual relations. I am going to read the definition that was presented to the president. . . .

For the purposes of this deposition, a person engages in sexual relations when the person knowingly engages in or causes contact with the [certain enumerated body parts] of any person with an intent to arouse or gratify the sexual desire of any person.

Members of the Senate, just for clarification, I did not feel the need to actually relate to this body what those enumerated body parts are.

...After reviewing the definition, the president then denied that he ever had a sexual relationship with Monica Lewinsky.... But eight months after his deposition testimony...the tide had turned against his story. By August, Monica Lewinsky was now cooperating with the office of the independent counsel. If she was telling the truth in her sworn testimony, then the president's January denial in the *Paula Jones* case would have been a clear case of him committing perjury and obstructing justice.

Why? Because she was describing, in very graphic detail, conduct occurring between her and the president that clearly fit the definition of "sexual relations" as used in the *Paula Jones* deposition—conduct that he repeatedly denied under oath.

So by the time the president sat down for his grand jury testimony to answer these questions under oath, he had put himself in a huge box.... [C]ontinuing the lie was too risky a strategy even for the most accomplished of gamblers. But if he told the truth, his earlier perjury and obstruction of justice would have ended his presidency....

Remember that the president had actually authorized that a poll be taken for him by Dick Morris, and the poll wasn't just taken on whether the American people would forgive him for adultery; the president asked Dick Morris to poll...whether the American people would forgive him for perjury and obstruction of justice.... [H]e learned that the American people would forgive him for the adultery but they would not forgive him for perjury or for obstruction of justice.

Once he got the bad news from Dick Morris that his political career was over if he perjured himself, he told Dick Morris, "We'll just have to win." So at his grand jury testimony, once the first question was asked about his relationship with Monica Lewinsky, the president produced a prepared statement and read from it....

[Transcript of Videotape Presentation]

...When I was alone with Ms. Lewinsky on certain occasions in early 1996 and once in early 1997, I engaged in conduct that was wrong. These encounters did not consist of sexual intercourse. They did not constitute sexual relations as I understood that term to be defined at my January 17th, 1998 deposition. But they did involve inappropriate intimate contact.

These inappropriate encounters ended, at my insistence, in early 1997. I also had occasional telephone conversations with Ms. Lewinsky that included inappropriate sexual banter. I regret that what began as a friendship came to include this conduct. I take full responsibility for my actions. While I will provide the grand jury whatever other information I can, because of privacy considerations affecting my family, myself, and others, and in an effort to preserve the dignity of the office I hold, this is all I will say about the specifics of these particular matters. I will try to answer to the best of my ability other questions, including questions about my relationship with Ms. Lewinsky, questions about my understanding of the term of sexual relations, as I understood it to be defined at my January 17th, 1998, deposition, and questions concerning alleged subornation of perjury, obstruction of justice and intimidation of witnesses....

The president used that prepared statement as a substitute answer for specific questions about his conduct with Ms. Lewinsky 19 separate times during his testimony before the grand jury.... The evidence shows the president used this prepared statement in order to justify the perjurious answers he gave at his deposition which were intended to affect the outcome of the *Paula Jones* case....

For example, in that prepared statement, the president said his sexual contact with Ms. Lewinsky began in 1996, and not in 1995, as Ms. Lewinsky had testified. This was not a mere slip of memory over a meaningless time frame; there is a discrepancy in the dates for a reason. You see, under the president's version, in 1996 Monica Lewinsky was a paid White House employee. Under the facts as testified to by Ms. Lewinsky, when the relationship really began in 1995, ... she was a young, 21-year-old White House intern. The concept of a president having a sexual relationship in the White House with a young intern less than half his age was a public relations disaster.... It is clear that the president somehow viewed the concept as less combustible if he could take the "young intern" phrase out of the public lexicon....

The president's statement was intentionally misleading when he described being alone with Ms. Lewinsky only on certain occasions. Actually, they were alone in the White House at least 20 times and had at least 11 sexual encounters at the White House....

The president's statement was intentionally misleading when he described his telephone conversations with Monica Lewinsky as "occasional." In fact, there are at least 55 documented telephone conversations between the president of the United States and the young intern. And...the evidence shows that, at least on 17 of those occasions, those conversations included much more than mere sexual banter....

The most unsettling part of that statement was uttered near the close. Listen to what the president said: "I regret that what began as a friendship came to include this conduct."...The very day the president met and spoke with a young White House intern for the first time was the day he invited her back to the Oval Office to perform sex acts on him....

Thus, the president began his deposition testimony by reading a false and misleading statement to the grand jury. He then used that statement as an excuse not to answer specific questions that were directly relevant to allowing the grand jury to complete its criminal investigation....

It is important to remember that at the time the president testified that he never had sexual relations with Monica Lewinsky, this was not a risky perjury strategy. After all, he had successfully used Vernon Jordan to get Monica Lewinsky a good job in New York.... She had filed a false affidavit in the *Jones* case denying a sexual relationship with the president. She and the president had...agreed to comprehensive cover stories to deny the truth of their relationship.... And the bevy of gifts the president had given to Monica were now nestled safely under Betty Currie's bed....

...By the time of his grand jury testimony in August...things had changed drastically.... In light of Ms. Lewinsky's cooperation with the independent counsel, the impending FBI report on the DNA testing on the blue dress, and the president's decision not to confess to his crime, the president needed to come up with some excuse. Here is how the president, at his August grand jury appearance, tried to explain away his January deposition denial of engaging in sexual relations with Monica Lewinsky.

[Transcript of Videotape Presentation]

Q. Did you understand the words in the first portion of the [*Jones* deposition] exhibit, Mr. president, that is, "For the purposes of this deposition, a person engages in 'sexual relations' when the person knowingly engages in or causes—."? Did you understand, do you understand the words there in that phrase?

A. Yes...I can tell you what my understanding of the definition is, if you want...My understanding of this definition is it covers contact by the person being deposed with the enumerated areas, if the contact is done with an intent to arouse or gratify. That's my understanding of the definition.

Q. What did you believe the definition to include and exclude? What kinds of activities?

A. I thought the definition included any activity by the person being deposed, where the person was the actor and came into contact with those parts of the bodies with the purpose or intent of gratification, and excluded any other activity. For example, kissing's not covered by that, I don't think.

Q. Did you understand the definition to be limited to sexual activity?

A. Yes, I understood the definition to be limited to physical contact with those areas of the body with the specific intent to arouse or gratify. That's what I understood it to be.

Q. What specific acts did the definition include, as you understood the definition on January 17th, 1998?

A. Any contact with the areas that are mentioned, sir. If you contacted those parts of the body with an intent to arouse or gratify, that is covered.

Q. What did you understand ...

A. The person being deposed. If the person being deposed contacted those parts of another person's body with an intent to arouse or gratify, that was covered.

... What the president now was saying to the grand jury is that during their intimate relationship in the Oval Office, Monica Lewinsky had sexual relations with him; he didn't have sexual relations with her....

As if this ridiculous expansion of Judge Wright's definition of what constituted sexual relations wasn't enough, the president then decided to take his interpretation of the judge's definition one step further. He added a new element as to why he claimed the definition didn't apply to him....

[Transcript of Videotape Presentation]

A. As I remember from the previous discussion this was some kind of definition that had something to do with sexual harassment. So, that implies it's forcing to me. And I—there was never any issue of forcing in the case involving—well, any of these questions they were asking me. They made it clear in this discussion I just reviewed that what they were referring to was intentional sexual conduct, not some sort of forcible abusive behavior. So I basically—I don't think I paid any attention to it because it appeared to me that that was something that had no reference to the facts that they admitted they were asking me about.

...No reasonable interpretation of the president's testimony could be made that he fulfilled his legal obligation to testify to the truth, the whole truth and nothing but the truth. His statements were perjurious. They were designed to defeat Paula Jones' right to pursue her sexual harassment civil rights lawsuit against this president.

And by the way, in his testimony, the president conceded that if Monica Lewinsky's recitation of the facts was true, he would have perjured himself both in his deposition testimony and in repeating his denials before the grand jury. Listen to this.

[Transcript of Videotape Presentation]

Q. And you testified that you didn't have sexual relations with Monica Lewinsky in the *Jones* deposition under that definition, correct?

A. That's correct, sir.

Q. If the person being deposed touched the genitalia of another person, would that be in—with the intent to arouse the sexual desire, arouse or gratify, as defined in definition one, would that be, under your understanding, then and now, sexual relations?

A. Yes, sir.

Q. Yes, it would?

A. Yes, it would if you had a direct contact with any of these places in the body, if you had direct contact with intent to arouse or gratify, that would fall within the definition.

Q. So you didn't do any of those three things with Monica Lewinsky?

A. You are free to infer that my testimony is that I did not have sexual relations as I understood this term to be defined.

...Monica Lewinsky delivered consistent and detailed testimony under oath regarding many specific encounters with the president that clearly fell within the definition of sexual relations from the *Jones* deposition....

Monica Lewinsky's testimony is further corroborated through DNA testing and the testimony of her friends and family members, to whom she made near contemporaneous statements about the relationship.

Most importantly, Monica Lewinsky had every reason to tell the truth to the grand jury. She was under a threat of prosecution for perjury, not only for her grand jury testimony, but also for the false affidavit she filed on behalf of the president in the *Jones* case....

By way of contrast, the president was under obligation to give complete answers. Instead, he offered false answers that violated his oath to tell the truth, the whole truth and nothing but the truth....

... To dismiss this conduct with a shrug because it is "just about sex" is to say that the sexual harassment laws protecting women in the workplace do not apply to powerful employers or others in high places of privilege. As one wag recently noted, if this case is "just about sex," then robbery is just a disagreement over money.

Next, the president perjured himself before the grand jury when he repeated previous perjured answers he gave in the deposition of the *Paula Jones* case....

When the president testified in his January deposition, he knew full well that Monica Lewinsky's affidavit...was false. Yet, when this affidavit was shown to him at the deposition, he testified that her false claim was, in his words, "absolutely true."

He knew that the definition of "sexual relations" used in the earlier *Jones* deposition was meant to cover the same activity that was mentioned in Monica Lewinsky's false affidavit. Rather than tell the complete truth, the president lied about the relationship, the cover stories, the affidavit, the subpoena for gifts, and the search for a job for Ms. Lewinsky.

Later he denied to the grand jury in August that he committed any perjury during his January deposition. This assertion before the grand jury that he testified truthfully in the *Jones* case is in and of itself perjurious testimony because the record is clear he did not testify truthfully in January in the *Paula Jones* case....

Next, the president committed perjury before the grand jury when he testified that he did not allow his attorney to make false representations while referring to Monica Lewinsky's affidavit before the judge in the *Jones* case, an affidavit that he knew was false....

When Ms. Jones' attorneys attempted to question the president about his relationship with Ms. Lewinsky, the president's attorney, Mr. Bennett, objected to him even being questioned about the relationship...in light of Monica Lewinsky's affidavit saying that there was no sexual relationship between the two....

What did the president do during that exchange? He sat mute. He did not say anything to correct Mr. Bennett, even though the president knew that the affidavit upon which Mr. Bennett was relying was utterly false.

Judge Wright overruled Mr. Bennett's objection and allowed the questioning about Monica Lewinsky to proceed.

Later in the deposition, Mr. Bennett read to the president the portion of Ms. Lewinsky's affidavit in which she denied having a sexual relationship with the president. Mr. Bennett then asked the president, who was under oath, if Ms. Lewinsky's statement that they never had a sexual relationship was true and accurate.

Listen to the president as he responds.

[Transcript of Videotape Presentation]

Q. In paragraph eight of her affidavit, she says this, "I have never had a sexual relationship with the president, he did not propose that we have a sexual relationship, he did not offer me employment or other benefits in exchange for a sexual relationship, he did not deny me employment or other benefits for rejecting a sexual relationship." Is this a true and accurate statement as far as you know it?

A. That is absolutely true.

. . . When President Clinton was asked during his grand jury testimony eight months later how he could have sat silently . . . while his attorney made the false statement that "there is no sex of any kind," in any manner, shape, or form, to Judge Wright, the president first said that he was not paying "a great deal of attention" to Mr. Bennett's comments. . . .

This denial . . . simply does not withstand the test of truth. The videotape of the president's January deposition shows the president paying very close attention to Mr. Bennett when Mr. Bennett was making the statement about "no sex of any kind." . . .

Just in case the president's "I wasn't paying any attention" excuse didn't fly, the president, in his grand jury testimony, decided to try another argument on for size. He suggested that when Mr. Bennett made his statement about "there is no sex of any kind," the president was focusing on the meaning of the word "is."

He then said that when Mr. Bennett made the assertion that "there is no sex of any kind," Mr. Bennett was speaking only in the present tense, as if the president understood that to mean "there is no sex" because there was no sex occurring at the time Mr. Bennett's remark was made.

The president stated, "It depends on what the meaning of the word 'is' is." . . .

The president perjured himself when he said that Mr. Bennett's statement that there was no sex of any kind was "absolutely true," depending on what the meaning of the word "is" is.

The president did not admit to the grand jury that Mr. Bennett's statement was false, because to do so would have been to admit that the term "sexual relations" as used in Ms. Lewinsky's affidavit meant "no sex of any kind." Admitting that would be to admit that he perjured himself previously in his grand jury testimony and in his deposition. . . .

. . . Finally, the president committed perjury before the grand jury when he testified falsely about his blatant attempts to influence the testimony of potential witnesses and his involvement in a plan to hide evidence that had lawfully been subpoenaed in the civil rights action brought against him.

This perjurious testimony breaks down into four categories. . . . Let's look briefly at the first area.

The president made false and misleading statements before the grand jury regarding his knowledge of the contents of Monica Lewinsky's affidavit.

As we now know conclusively, Monica Lewinsky filed an affidavit in the *Jones* case in which she denied ever having a sexual relationship with the president, and that was a lie when it was filed. . . .

Monica Lewinsky later testified that she is "100 percent sure" that the president suggested she might want to sign an affidavit to avoid testifying in the case of *Jones versus Clinton*. In fact, the president gave the following testimony before the grand jury: "And did I hope she'd be able to get out of testifying on an affidavit? Absolutely. Did I want her to execute a false affidavit? No, I did not."

This testimony is false because it could not be possible that Monica Lewinsky could have filed a truthful affidavit in the *Jones* case, an affidavit acknowledging a sexual relationship with the president, that would have helped her to avoid having to appear as a witness in the *Paula Jones* case. . . .

Next, the president provided false testimony concerning his conversations with his personal secretary Betty Currie about Monica after he testified in the *Jones* deposition. . . . The president had just testified on January 17, 1998, in the *Paula Jones* deposition. He said he could not recall being alone with Monica Lewinsky and that he did not have a sexual relationship with her. . . .

Two and a half hours after he returned from the *Paula Jones* deposition, President Clinton called Ms. Currie at home and asked her to come to the

White House the next day.... At about 5 p.m. on Sunday, January 18, Ms. Currie went to meet with President Clinton at the White House.... According to Ms. Currie, the president then said to her in rapid succession:

> You were always there when she was there, right? We were never really alone. You could see and hear everything.
> Monica came on to me, and I never touched her, right?
> She wanted to have sex with me, and I can't do that.

Ms. Currie indicated that these remarks were "more like statements than questions." Ms. Currie concluded that the president wanted her to agree with him....

Ms. Currie said that she indicated her agreement with each of the president's statements, although she knew that the president and Ms. Lewinsky had in fact been alone in the Oval Office and in the president's study.

Ms. Currie also knew that she could not, and did not hear or see the president and Ms. Lewinsky while they were alone.

Ms. Currie testified that two or three days after her conversation with the president at the White House, he again called her into the Oval Office to discuss this. She described their conversation as, quote, "sort of a recapitulation of what we had talked about on Sunday—you know, 'I was never alone with her'—that sort of thing." ...

In his grand jury testimony, the president was asked why he might have said to Ms. Currie in their meeting on that Sunday "we were never alone together, right?" and "you could see and hear everything." Here is how the president testified:

> [W]hat I was trying to determine was whether my recollection was right and that she was always in the office complex when Monica was there, and whether she thought she could hear any conversations we had, or did she hear any—I was trying to—I knew ... to a reasonable certainty that I was going to be asked more questions about this. I didn't really expect you to be in the *Jones* case at the time. I thought what would happen is that it would break in the press, and I was trying to get the facts down. I was trying to understand what the facts were.

... The president also was asked about his specific statement to Betty Currie that "you could see and hear everything." He testified that he was uncertain what he intended by that comment:... "I'm not entirely sure what I meant by that, but I could have meant that she generally would be able to hear conversations, even if she couldn't see them. And I think that's what I meant."

The president also was asked about his comment to Ms. Currie that Ms. Lewinsky had "come on" to him, but that he had "never touched her."...

A. Now, I've testified about that. And that's one of those questions that I believe is answered by the statement that I made.

Q. What was your purpose in making these statements to Mrs. Currie, if it weren't for the purpose to try to suggest to her what she should say if ever asked?

A. Now, Mr. Bittman, I told you, the only thing I remember is when all this stuff blew up, I was trying to figure out what the facts were. I was trying to remember. I was trying to remember every time I had seen Ms. Lewinsky.... I knew this was all going to come out.... I did not know [at the time] that the Office of Independent Counsel was involved. And I was trying to get the facts and try to think of the best defense we could construct in the face of what I thought was going to be a media onslaught.

Finally, the president was asked why he would have called Ms. Currie into his office a few days after the Sunday meeting and repeated the statements about Ms. Lewinsky to her. The president testified that although he would not dispute Ms. Currie's testimony to the contrary, he did not remember having a second conversation with her along these lines....

These were false statements, and he knew that the statements were false at the time he made them to Betty Currie. The president's suggestion that he was simply trying to refresh his memory when talking to Betty Currie is nonsense....

Rogan next turned to the question of the gifts the president had given Monica Lewinsky. He reviewed the facts: On December 28, she met the president in the Oval Office and they discussed the fact that the gifts had been subpoenaed. Lewinsky testified that she had said "Maybe I should put the gifts away outside my house somewhere or give them to someone, maybe Betty," and that the president had replied, "I don't know" or "Let me think about that." When asked about this in his grand jury testimony, the president said, "I told her that if they asked her for gifts, she'd have to give them whatever she had.... I simply was not concerned about the fact that I had given her gifts. Indeed, I gave her additional gifts on December 28, 1997."

Rogan recalled how Betty Currie came to pick up the gifts and hide them under her bed, including the conflicts between Lewinsky and Currie over which of them had arranged the pickup; in light of the cell phone records, said Rogan, "the only logical conclusion" was that Lewinsky's version was correct: Currie must have initiated the pickup, and she would not have done so "unless the president told her to do it." He continued:

President Clinton perjured himself when he testified before the grand jury on this issue and reiterated to the House Judiciary Committee that he did not recall any conversation with Ms. Currie around December 28. He also perjured himself when he testified before the grand jury that he did not tell Betty Currie to take possession of the gifts that he had given Ms. Lewinsky....

Finally, the president gave perjurious testimony ... concerning statements he gave to his top aides regarding his relationship with Monica Lewinsky. Here is a portion of his grand jury transcript ...:

Question: Did you deny to them or not, Mr. President?

Answer: ... I did not want to mislead my friends, but I want to define language where I can say that. I also, frankly, do not want to turn any of them into witnesses because I—and sure enough, they all became witnesses.

Question: Well, you knew they might be witnesses, didn't you?

Answer: And so I said to them things that were true about this relationship. That I used—in the language I used, I said, there is nothing go[ing] on between us. That was true. I said, I have not had sex with her as I defined it. That was true. And did I hope that I would never have to be here on this day giving this testimony? Of course. But I also didn't want to do anything to complicate this matter further. So, I said things that were true. They may have been misleading, and if they were, I have to take responsibility for it, and I'm sorry.

The president's testimony that day that he said things that were true to his aides is clearly perjurious. Just as the president predicted, several of the president's top aides were later called to testify before the grand jury as to what the president told them. And when they testified before the grand jury they passed along the president's false account, just as the president intended them to do.

· · ·

The evidence reviewed by the House of Representatives and relied upon by our body in bringing articles of impeachment against the president was not political. It was overwhelming. He has denied all allegations set forth in these articles. Who is telling the truth? There is only one way to find out.

On behalf of the House of Representatives, we urge this body to bring forth the witnesses and place them all under oath. If the witnesses... that make the case against the president—who, incidentally, are his employees, his top aides, his former interns, and his close friends—if all of these people... are lying, then the president... deserves not just an acquittal, he deserves the most profound of apologies.

But, if they are not lying, if the evidence is true, if the Chief Executive Officer of our nation used his power and his influence to corruptly destroy a lone woman's right to bring forth her case in a court of law, then there must be constitutional accountability....

The Senate adjourned for the evening.

When the Senators reconvened the next day, the chief justice recognized Rep. Bill McCollum of Florida for a summary of the facts in the case. McCollum began by reviewing the court decisions that had given the Jones lawyers the right to question President Clinton about other relationships. He continued:

Mr. McCollum: ... On December 5, 1997, a year ago, about a week before Judge Wright issued her order making it clear that the president's relationship with Monica Lewinsky was relevant to the *Jones* case, Ms. Lewinsky's name appeared on the *Jones* witness list. The president learned this fact the next day, December 6. The president telephoned Monica Lewinsky at about 2 a.m. on December 17 and informed her about her name being on the witness list. That was about 10 days after he learned about it and about 5 days after Judge Wright's order. It was the order that made it clear that his relationship with Monica was discoverable by the *Jones* attorneys in that case....

During a telephone conversation on the 17th of December, the president told Monica she might be called as a witness, and he at that time suggested that she might file an affidavit to avoid being called... to testify in person in that case. In the same conversation, they reviewed these cover stories that they had concocted to conceal their relationship. He brought them up....

Why do you think they did that? In her grand jury testimony, Monica said the president didn't tell her to lie, but because of their previous understanding she assumed that they both expected that she would lie in that affidavit. In this context, the evidence is compelling that the president committed both the crimes of obstruction of justice and witness-tampering right then and there on December 17....

Now, let's look at... Monica Lewinsky's August 6 grand jury testimony,... where in the context of the affidavit she makes the now famous statement, "No one asked or encouraged me to lie." She did say that, but let's look at how she said that:

> For me, the best way to explain how I feel what happened was, you know, no one asked or encouraged me to lie, but no one discouraged me either.

... Later on, she says in her testimony...:

> ... [I]t wasn't as if the president called me and said, "You know, Monica, you're on the witness list, this is going to be really hard for us, we're going to have to tell the truth and be humiliated in front of the entire world about what we've done," which I would have fought him on probably. That was different. And by him not calling me and saying that, you know, I knew what that meant....
>
> Question: Did you understand all along that he would deny the relationship, also?
> Answer: Mm-hmm. Yes.
> Question: And when you say you understood what it meant when he didn't say, "Oh, you know, you must tell the truth," what did you understand that to mean?
> Answer: That—that—as we had on every other occasion and every other instance of this relationship, we would deny it.

After reading this, ... can there be any doubt that the president was suggesting that she file an affidavit that contains lies and falsehoods that might keep her from ever having to testify in the *Jones* case and give the president the kind of protection he needed when he testified?

And, of course, in that same December 17 conversation, the president encouraged Monica to use cover stories and tell the same lies as he expected her to do in the affidavit if and when she was called to testify live and in person.... Taken together,... these are counts 1 and 2 of the obstruction of justice charge....

Two days later, Monica Lewinsky was subpoenaed and contacted Vernon Jordan, who put her in touch with Attorney Frank Carter.... As we all know, this very false affidavit... was filed just before the president's deposition in the *Jones* case January 17. The record shows that... Jordan advised the president when Monica signed the affidavit on January 7.... Two days before, Monica says... she asked the president if he wanted to see the draft affidavit, he replied... that he didn't need to see it because he had already seen "15 others."

...I... would suggest to you that he was talking about 15 other drafts of this proposed affidavit since it had been around the horn a lot of rounds....

Here, McCollum reviewed the scene from the president's January 17 deposition in which Robert Bennett invoked Lewinsky's affidavit and the president failed to intervene.

Next, he turned to the exchange of gifts, reviewing the course of events on December 28, which ended with Betty Currie hiding them under her bed. In context, he asked, "How can anyone come to any other conclusion than that the president collaborated with Monica and Betty to hide these gifts?" McCollum predicted that the president's lawyers would argue that if he had been worried about the gifts, the president would not have given Lewinsky new ones on that very day. The explanation, he suggested, was that the president knew Lewinsky would keep them safely out of sight.

As for the job search, said McCollum, there was no question that Lewinsky had been looking for a job in New York long before December 1997: "The question is whether or not the president intensified his efforts to get her a job ... after it became clear to him that he would need her to lie, sign a false affidavit and stick with her lies in any questioning." Here again, he argued, the circumstantial evidence was overwhelming. The "full court press" by Jordan on Lewinsky's behalf began almost exactly as Judge Wright issued her order allowing the Jones lawyers to look into Clinton's other relationships, and it continued until, on the eve of the filing of her false affidavit and Clinton's Jones deposition, Lewinsky had a job in New York. The president, McCollum argued, was "keeping her happy so he could control her."

Finally, McCollum reviewed the president's sessions with Betty Currie, in which he made the declarative statements about his relationship with Lewinsky, and later explained that he had merely been trying to refresh his memory. McCollum continued:

Recognizing the weakness of their client's case on this, the president's attorneys have suggested that he was worried about what Ms. Currie might say if the press really got after her.... But common sense says he was much more worried about what Betty Currie might say to a court, after he had just named her several times and talked about her, if she were called as a witness....

Within four or five days of his *Jones* deposition, the president not only explicitly denied the true nature of his relationship with Monica Lewinsky to key White House aides, he also embellished the story when he talked with Sidney Blumenthal. To Sidney Blumenthal, he portrayed Monica Lewinsky as the aggressor, attacked her reputation by portraying her as a stalker and presented himself as the innocent victim being attacked by the forces of evil.... [H]e knew that the Office of Independent Counsel had recently been appointed to investigate the Monica Lewinsky matter....

In the context of everything else that he was doing to hide his relationship, it seems readily apparent that his false and misleading statements to his staff members, whom he knew were potential witnesses before any grand jury proceeding, were designed in part to corruptly influence their testimony as witnesses. In fact, the president actually acknowledged this in his grand jury testimony, that he knew his aides might be called before the grand jury....

Then McCollum reviewed the perjury charges. To begin with, he said, if Monica Lewinsky was to believed, it was clear that the president had lied to the grand jury about the "nature and details" of their relationship. He quoted from the president's testimony, which directly contradicted Lewinsky's own: "... I did not have sexual relations, as I understood this term to be defined. [Question]: Including touching her breasts, kissing her breasts, or touching her genitalia? [Answer]: "That's correct."

McCollum walked through a series of lies he contended the president had told the grand jury about whether he had lied in his Jones deposition. "If he lied in the deposition and then he told the grand jury that he didn't lie, he committed perjury in front of the grand jury," he explained. For example, said McCollum, the president had lied when he said, in the deposition, that he was never alone with Lewinsky except when she was delivering papers, when he said he could not recall gifts exchanged between the two of them and when he said he did not know that Vernon Jordan had met with Lewinsky and talked about the Jones case.

McCollum reviewed, once again, the president's silence when his attorney, Robert Bennett, cited Lewinsky's false affidavit as if it were true. And finally, he went over the lies the House managers contended had been told in the course of "the president's efforts to influence the testimony of witnesses and to impede the discovery of evidence in the Jones case."

Finally, McCollum summed up the perjury list:

The facts are clear that the president lied about having sexual relations with Monica Lewinsky even under his understanding of the definition of the *Jones* case if you believe Monica.

He lied when he said he gave truthful testimony in his *Jones* deposition.

He lied when he said he wasn't paying attention to his attorney's discussion of Monica Lewinsky's false affidavit during his deposition in the *Jones* case.

He lied when he said he told Monica Lewinsky she should turn over the gifts to the *Jones* lawyers if they asked for them.

He lied when he told the grand jury that he made the declaratory statements to Betty Currie to refresh his recollection.

And he lied when he told the grand jury that he only told the truth to his White House aides. In a couple of days the president's lawyers are going to have their chance to talk to you, and I suspect they will try to get you to focus on 10, 15, or 20 or 30, maybe even 100 specific little details. They are going to argue that these details don't square with some of the facts about this presentation. But I would encourage you never to lose sight of the totality of this scheme to lie and obstruct justice; never lose sight of the big picture. Don't lose sight of the forest for the trees....

After a brief break, the chief justice recognized Rep. George Gekas of Pennsylvania. Gekas explained that the task of the next panel was to discuss "the laws of our nation as they obtain to the facts that you now have well ingrained into your consciences."

Mr. Gekas: ... [W]e must begin ... with the Supreme Court of the United States, ... because the Supreme Court at one point in this saga determined in a suit brought by Paula Jones that indeed an average, day-to-day, ordinary citizen of our nation would have the right to have a day in court ... even against the president of the United States.... If perjury indeed was committed—and the record is replete that it in fact was—and if indeed obstruction of justice was finally committed by the president of the United States—as the evidence abundantly demonstrates—then we must apply the rights of Paula Jones to what has transpired....

It was an attempt, a bold attempt, one that succeeded in some respects, to obstruct the justice sought by a fellow American citizen.... That goes beyond saying that, "This is just about sex...."

> Gekas then focused on the interrogatories in the Jones case that the president had answered under oath on December 23, 1997, more than a month before his deposition in the case. They asked him to "name any persons with whom you have had sexual relations other than your wife" while he was governor of Arkansas or president of the United States. Clinton's answer: None. This, Gekas observed, was in the absence of any strained definitions; those came later, during the deposition. At this point, he contended, the president could be presumed to be using "the well-understood definition that everybody in America recognizes as being the true meaning of sexual relations, meaning sex of any kind."
>
> On January 15, Gekas continued, another interrogatory arrived—this one asking the president to submit anything pertaining to Monica Lewinsky—"notes, gifts, whatever," said Gekas. The president answered that there were none. These responses, Gekas argued, made it impossible for the president to "use the lawyer talk and judge banter and the ... definitions of sexual relations to cloud the answers that he gave at that time."

Obstruction of justice is obstruction of justice to an individual, to a family. You can take it from Paula Jones and telescope it upward to every community, in every courthouse, and every state and every community in our land, and there is a Paula Jones eager to assert certain rights and then confronted with someone who would tear it down by false testimony, by lies under oath.

That is what the gravamen of all this really is. One more thing. The counsel for the president have repeatedly ... asserted, as many of you have, that this is not an impeachable offense, for after all, they say, an impeachable offense is one in which there is a direct attack on the system of government; not perjury, not obstruction of justice.

So what, on those, they imply.... I must tell you that as an 8- or 9- or 10-year-old, I would accompany my mother to naturalization school three or four nights a week ... and she was so proud that she learned that the first president of the United States was George Washington, was prepared to answer that question if it was posed to her in naturalization court, and she was so proud when I was testing her, preparing. Each time I would say, "Mom, what are the three branches of Government?" And she would say, "The 'Exec' and the 'legislate' and the 'judish,' " in her wonderful, lovable accent. She knew the system of Government.... And she knew that one wall of the creed that protects our rights is the "judish." She knew that the courthouse and the rights of citizens which are advanced in that courthouse are the system of Government. Can anyone say that purposely attempting to destroy someone's case in the courthouse is not an attack on the system of Government of our country?

Mr. Chabot will elucidate on perjury.

Mr. Chabot: ... In the United States Criminal Code, there are two perjury offenses, ... in sections 1621 and 1623 of title 18 of the United States Criminal Code. Section 1621 is the broad perjury statute which makes it a federal offense to knowingly and willfully make a false statement about a material matter while under oath. Section 1623 is the more specific perjury statute which makes it a federal offense to knowingly make a false statement about a material matter while under oath before a federal court or before a federal grand jury....

There are four general elements of perjury. They are an oath, an intent, falsity, and materiality. I would like to walk you through each of those elements....

In this case, there has been no serious challenge made about the legitimacy of the oath administered to the president either in his civil deposition in the *Jones v. Clinton* case or before the federal grand jury....

The intent element requires that the false testimony was knowingly stated and described. This requirement is generally satisfied by proof that the defendant knew his testimony was false at the time it was provided....

So as you reflect on the president's carefully calculated statements ... ask a few simple questions: Did the president realize what he was doing, what he was saying? Was he aware of the nature of his conduct or did the president simply act through ignorance, mistake or accident? The answers to these questions are undeniably clear even to the president's own attorneys. In fact, Mr. Ruff and Mr. Craig testified before the Judiciary Committee that the president willfully misled the court. Let's listen to Mr. Ruff.

[Transcript of Videotape Presentation:]

Mr. Ruff: I'm going to respond to your question. I have no doubt that he walked up to a line that he thought he understood reasonable people— and you maybe have reached this conclusion—could determine that he crossed over that line and that what for him was truthful but misleading or nonresponsive and misleading or evasive was in fact false.

... The president's actions speak volumes about his intent to make false statements under oath. For example, the president called his secretary, Betty Currie, within hours of concluding his civil deposition and asked her to come to the White House the following day. President Clinton then recited false characterizations to her about his relationship with Ms. Lewinsky....

This is not the conduct of someone who believed he had testified truthfully. It is not the conduct of someone who acted through ignorance, mistake or accident. Rather, it is the conduct of someone who lied, knew he had lied, and needed others to modify their stories accordingly....

The next element of perjury is falsity. In order for perjury to occur in this case, the president must have made one or more false statements. Yesterday my colleagues went through the evidence on this matter in great detail and clearly demonstrated that the president did, in fact, make false statements while under oath.

... The test for whether a statement is material, as stated by the Supreme Court in *Kungys v. United States,* is simply whether it had a "natural tendency to influence" or was "capable of influencing" the official proceeding. The law also makes clear that the false statement does not have to actually impede the grand jury's investigation for the statement to be material.

... Because a grand jury's authority to investigate is broad, the realm of declarations regarded as material is broad. The president's false statements to the grand jury were material because the grand jury was investigating whether the president had obstructed justice and committed perjury in a civil deposition.

... The president's attorneys will try to distract you from the relevant law and facts in this case. To help you stay focused on the law, I would like to preview some of the arguments that may be made by the president's attorneys.

Legal smokescreen Number 1, the *Bronston* case. You will probably hear opposing counsel argue that the president did not technically commit perjury, and appeal to the case of *Bronston v. United States.* ... In the *Bronston* case, the Supreme Court held that statements that are literally truthful and nonresponsive cannot by themselves form the basis for a perjury conviction. This is the cornerstone of the president's defense....

So, when the president's counsel cites the *Bronston* case, remember the facts. Ask yourselves, are the president's answers literally true? And remember, to be literally true they must actually be true. It is also important to note that, consistent with the *Bronston* case, the response, "I don't recall" is not technically true if the president actually could recall.

The factual record in the case, consisting of multiple sworn statements contradicting the president's testimony and highly specific corroborating evidence, demonstrates that the president's statements were not literally true or legally accurate. On the contrary, the record establishes that the president repeatedly lied, he repeatedly deceived, he repeatedly feigned forgetfulness....

> *Here Chabot talked about several recent cases that limited the scope of the Bronston case. One appeals court ruling, for instance, had held that a defendant might be found guilty of perjury "if a jury could find beyond a reasonable doubt ... that the defendant knew what the question meant and gave knowingly untruthful and materially misleading answers ..."*
>
> *Chabot next addressed "smokescreen No. 2, the two-witness rule," which requires either two witnesses to a perjurious statement or one witness and corroborating evidence. The president's lawyers might try to invoke that rule, said Chabot, but he argued that it was explicitly not applicable under the perjury law pertaining specifically to grand jury testimony and that, in any case, "substantial evidence" satisfied the corroboration requirements under the other perjury section.*
>
> *Chabot continued:*

... Why is perjury such a serious offense? Under the American system of justice, our courts are charged with seeking the truth. Every day, American citizens raise their right hands in courtrooms across the country and take an oath to tell the truth. Breaking that oath cripples our justice system. By lying under oath, the president did not just commit perjury, an offense punishable under our criminal code, but he chipped away at the very cornerstone of our judicial system....

> *The chief justice recognized Rep. Christopher Cannon of Utah.*

Mr. Cannon: ... Article II specifies seven separate instances in which the president acted to obstruct justice.... [S]ection 1503.... often referred to as the general obstruction statute.... deems it criminal to use force or threats, or to otherwise act corruptly, in order to influence, obstruct, or impede the due administration of justice. Federal court rulings clarify that it is not necessary for a defendant to succeed in obstructing justice....

For the Government to prove a section 1503 crime, it must demonstrate that the defendant acted with intent. This can be shown through use of force, threats by the defendant, or by simply showing that the defendant acted "corruptly." ...

Under section 1503, the Government must also prove that the defendant endeavored to influence, obstruct or impede the due administration of justice....

The other federal crime which the president committed was witness-tampering under section 1512.... Sections 1503 and 1512 differ in an important way. There does not need to be a case pending at the time the defendant acts to violate the law under section 1512....

Putting it another way, a person may...commit the crime of witness-tampering...even before there is a case underway in which that person might be called to testify.

For the Government to prove the crime of witness-tampering, it must prove that the defendant acted...to influence, delay or prevent the testimony of any person in an official proceeding; or...acted to cause another person to withhold an object from an official proceeding. In the case before us, the evidence proves that the president endeavored to cause both of these results....

And the Government may show intent on the part of the defendant in several ways. It may prove the use of intimidation, physical force or threats; or it may prove intent by showing the use of corrupt persuasion or misleading conduct. In this case, the evidence shows that on several occasions the president acted corruptly to persuade some witnesses, and engaged in misleading conduct toward others, in order to...cause them to withhold evidence or give wrongful testimony....

...The difference between corruptly persuading a witness and engaging in misleading conduct toward the witness depends on the witness's level of knowledge about the truth of the defendant's statement.... If a defendant simply asks a witness to lie and the witness knows that he is being asked to lie, then the defendant is corruptly persuading the witness. In contrast, if a defendant lies to a witness, hoping the witness will believe his story, this is misleading conduct. They are different, but they are both criminal....

The focus of both statutes is on what the defendant believed. If the defendant believes that it is possible that some person might some day be called to testify at some later proceeding and then acted to influence, delay or prevent his or her testimony, the defendant commits the crime....

Whether attempting to persuade a person to testify falsely, or to ignore court orders to produce objects; whether suggesting to an innocent person a false story in hopes that he or she will repeat it in a judicial proceedings; or testifying falsely in the hopes of blocking another party's pursuit of the truth—all these acts obstruct justice; all these acts are federal felony crimes; all these acts were committed by William Jefferson Clinton....

After a recess, the chief justice recognized Rep. Bob Barr of Georgia.

    First, Barr addressed the different responsibilities of the House and Senate in the impeachment proceedings. The House's role, he said, was somewhat akin to that of a grand jury, while the Senate would function as the triers of fact. That helped explain why the House had called no witnesses in the case: "It is the more standard procedure," said Barr, "for the Government to present its case to the grand jury by way of summary witnesses."

    Second, Barr spoke about the two kinds of evidence, direct and circumstantial, emphasizing that "it is a principle of long and consistent standing in every federal court in our land ... circumstantial evidence ... shall not be afforded any less weight that direct evidence."

    Third, said Barr, there was the question of repetition. The House managers were not repeating facts and points of law simply because they thought the case would seem stronger if stated more often. Rather, he explained, "in a case such as this where you have two sets of laws alleged to have been violated ... each one of those has several different elements."

    Then Barr turned to his primary subject:

Mr. Barr: ... We believe the evidence presented clearly establishes that on December 17, 1997, the president encouraged a witness in a federal civil rights action brought against him, that witness being Monica Lewinsky, to execute a sworn affidavit in that proceeding which he knew to be perjurious, false, and misleading....

Barr reviewed the December 17 phone call from the president to Lewinsky, in which he told her she was on the Jones witness list and suggested she could file an affidavit to avoid testifying. Lewinsky had testified, he said, that "both she and the president understood . . . they would continue their pattern of covering up" and that she knew if she filed a truthful affidavit, the Jones lawyers would certainly depose her. The president, said Barr, denied asking Lewinsky to file a false affidavit. He sought only to have her execute an affidavit that would "get her out of having to testify." "While being factually correct," said Barr, "this statement reflects a legal impossibility."

He continued:

As Mr. Jordan's grand jury testimony corroborates, the president knew what Ms. Lewinsky planned to allege in her affidavit, yet the president took no action to stop her from filing it. As you have heard in earlier presentations, the president's lawyer, Mr. Robert Bennett, stated in court directly to Judge Wright when he presented the false affidavit, "There is absolutely no sex of any kind in any manner, shape or form," and that the president was "fully aware of Ms. Lewinsky's affidavit." The president took no action to correct his lawyer's misstatement.

As you have also heard, the president, in his grand jury testimony, tried to disingenuously dissect the words of his attorney to remove his conduct from further examination. . . . And he disavowed knowledge of his lawyer's representations by claiming he was not paying attention. . . .

Later in the deposition, when Mr. Bennett read to the president the portion of the affidavit in which Ms. Lewinsky denies their relationship and asked him "is that a true and accurate statement as far as you know it," the president answered, "That is absolutely true." This statement is neither credible nor true. It is perjury.

The inescapable conclusion from this evidence is that the president has lied, and continues to lie, about the affidavit. . . . Moreover, in engaging in this course of conduct, referring here to the words of the obstruction statute . . . the president's actions constituted an endeavor to influence or impede the due administration of justice in that he was attempting to prevent the plaintiff in the *Jones* case from having a "free and fair opportunity to learn what she may learn concerning the material facts surrounding her claim." These acts by the president also constituted an endeavor to "corruptly persuade another person with the intent to influence the testimony they might give in an official proceeding." . . .

In encouraging her to file an affidavit that would prevent her from having to testify, President Clinton was, of necessity, asking her to testify falsely in an official proceeding. He was attempting to prevent, and in fact did prevent, the plaintiff in that case from discovering facts which may have had a bearing on her claim against the president. His motive was improper in the language of the law, that is, corrupt. And his actions did influence the testimony of Ms. Lewinsky as a witness in the pending official proceeding in U.S. district court....

With regard to the issue of perjury before the grand jury concerning the affidavit,... when asked before the grand jury whether he had instructed Ms. Lewinsky to file a truthful affidavit, President Clinton testified, "Did I hope she would be able to get out of testifying on an affidavit? Absolutely. Did I want her to execute a false affidavit? No, I did not."

The evidence, however, clearly establishes that the president's statement constitutes perjury, in violation of section 1623 of the U.S. federal Criminal Code for the simple reason the only realistic way Ms. Lewinsky could get out of having to testify based on her affidavit would be to execute a false affidavit.... The president knew this. Ms. Lewinsky knew this. And the president's testimony on this point is perjury.... It was willful, it was knowing, it was material, and it was false.

... We, as managers, believe that the evidence presented to you also establishes that on December 17 the president encouraged a witness in a federal civil rights action brought against him to give perjurious, false and misleading testimony....

Throughout their relationship, the president and Ms. Lewinsky, understandably, wished to keep it secret, and they took steps to do that, steps that ultimately turned out to be and constitute criminal acts. For some time, in fact until Ms. Lewinsky testified under oath and under a grant of immunity, their efforts were remarkably successful....

Ms. Lewinsky testified later, after she left the White House job to work at the Pentagon, that phase two of the coverup went into effect. The two coconspirators began to use Ms. Currie as a source of clearance into the White House.... [O]n December 17, during that 2 a.m., or perhaps it was 2:30, telephone conversation... the president told her, "You know, you can always say you were coming to see Betty or that you were bringing me letters." Ms. Lewinsky testified that she understood this to be "really a reminder of things that they had discussed before." She said it was instantly familiar to her.... "I knew...exactly what he meant." And so, I respectfully submit, do all of us here know exactly what the president meant.

When the president, then, was questioned before the federal grand jury if he ever had said something like that to Ms. Lewinsky, he admitted that, well,

"I might...have said that. Because I certainly didn't want this to come out, if I could help it...."

The president knew that if Ms. Lewinsky were to testify that she only brought papers to the president or to see the president's secretary, her testimony would have been neither complete nor truthful. Yet, the president encouraged her to give that untruthful testimony and, in so doing, he broke the law of obstruction of justice. And, in lying about it, he compounded the problem by breaking the law of perjury....

Mr. Clinton's encouragement to Ms. Lewinsky to tell something other than the truth certainly would have influenced the discovery process in the *Jones* case.... And, as Mr. Cannon also made clear with regard to section 1512 of the federal Criminal Code, a person commits witness-tampering when he attempts to influence another person to give false testimony in an official proceeding.

Mr. Clinton did encourage Ms. Lewinsky to give false testimony about her reasons for being in the White House with the president. By encouraging her to lie, the president committed the crime of obstruction of justice under section 1503 and the crime of witness-tampering under section 1512 of the federal Criminal Code.

You have also, Members of the Senate, heard about the president's statements to Ms. Currie on January 18, and then again on the 20th or 21st....

As you have heard, Ms. Currie stated under oath she indicated her agreement with each of the president's statements, even though she knew that the president and Ms. Lewinsky had, in fact, been alone in the Oval Office and in the president's study. Prosecutors frequently see this pattern.... of agreeing to things that the person knows are not true, where you have a dominant person suggesting testimony to another person who is in a subordinate relationship. This, I submit, is yet another bright line between a private lie and public obstruction....

The president lied to the grand jury [in] mischaracterizing his earlier statements to Mrs. Currie, just as he tampered with her as a likely witness nine months earlier, in January.

The president's assertion—that he simply was trying to understand what the facts were—lacks even colorable credibility, when one considers that he had already testified. It was obviously too late to try to recollect what the "facts" were....

It was not only likely Ms. Currie would be called [as a witness], the president's own...deliberate testimony to the grand jury pretty much guaranteed that she would be called. He wanted her called so she could then buttress his false testimony. His actions clearly, we believe, violated both the general obstruction statute and the witness-tampering statute in these particulars in this regard.

... While the witness-tampering statute makes it a crime to attempt to influence the testimony of a person, it also makes it a crime to influence a person to withhold an object from an official proceeding; in other words, to tamper with evidence. The facts of this case, we as House managers believe, clearly show the president corruptly engaged in, encouraged, or supported a scheme with Monica Lewinsky and possibly others to conceal evidence that had been subpoenaed lawfully in the *Jones* case.

> *Barr reviewed, once again, the Lewinsky version of the gift exchange, in which Betty Currie called, said she understood Lewinsky had something to give her, then picked up the gifts—now under subpoena—and hid them under her bed.*

In his grand jury testimony, the president asserted he encouraged Ms. Lewinsky to turn over the gifts. Ms. Lewinsky's testimony directly contradicts that. Importantly, all other evidence of subsequent acts corroborates her testimony, not the president's....

While the president asserts he never spoke about this matter with Betty Currie, he would have us believe that his personal and confidential secretary would, on a Sunday, drive to the home of the woman with whom he was having an inappropriate intimate relationship, take possession of a sealed box which she believed to contain gifts given by the president, hide the box under the bed in her home, never question the person giving her the box, and never even mention to the president she had received the box of gifts.

The president's position...is not credible. It defies the evidence. It defies any reasonable interpretation or inference from the evidence.... And it stands in defiance of federal law....

Now, the president further points out that Ms. Currie has testified that Ms. Lewinsky called her to arrange to pick up the gifts, rather than the other way around. In fact, although Ms. Currie has testified inconsistently...she actually deferred to Ms. Lewinsky's superior knowledge of the facts....

Barr had two further points about the gifts. First, he addressed the president's "professed inability to remember" whether he knew, on December 28, that Lewinsky and the gifts had been subpoenaed. "The president, a man of considerable intelligence and gifted with an exceptional memory," Barr argued, had "a clear motive to state falsely to the grand jury that he could not recall" whether or not he knew about the subpoena; if he had admitted knowing, it "would have helped establish a motive on his part for orchestrating the concealment of the gifts."

Barr also said the president's lawyers might well argue that the president would not have given more gifts to Lewinsky that day if he had been worried about the evidence. It was more plausible, Barr argued, that "the additional gifts given that day demonstrated the president's continued confidence that Ms. Lewinsky would . . . conceal their relationship."

Now Barr turned to the job search:

. . . We believe, as managers, that the evidence shows that, beginning on or about December 7, 1997 . . . the president intensified and succeeded in an effort to secure job assistance for a witness in a federal civil rights case brought against him, in order to corruptly prevent the truthful testimony of that witness . . .

On December 6, the president became aware that Ms. Lewinsky had been named as a witness in the *Jones* case. . . . [A] mere 5 days later, Ms. Lewinsky, in fact, secured a second meeting with Mr. Vernon Jordan. But this time, unlike previously, this powerful Washington lawyer jumped for the former intern. He immediately placed calls to three major corporations on her behalf.

On December 11, Judge Wright ordered the president to answer Paula Jones' interrogatories. On December 17, the president suggested to Ms. Lewinsky she file the affidavit and continue to use their cover stories in the event she was asked about her relationship with the president. The next day she had two interviews in New York City arranged by Mr. Jordan. On December 22nd, Ms. Lewinsky met with an attorney at a meeting arranged by Mr. Jordan. The following day she had another job interview arranged by Mr. Jordan.

On January 7, Ms. Lewinsky signed the false affidavit and proudly showed the executed copy to Mr. Jordan. The next day, Ms. Lewinsky had an interview arranged by Mr. Jordan with MacAndrews & Forbes in New York City, an interview that apparently went poorly. [S]he called Mr. Jordan and so informed him. Mr. Jordan then called the CEO of MacAndrews & Forbes, Mr. Ron Perelman, to, in Mr. Jordan's words, "make things happen, if they could happen." After Mr. Jordan's call to Mr. Perelman, Ms. Lewinsky was called and told that she would be interviewed again the very next morning. That following day she was reinterviewed and immediately offered a job. She then called Mr. Jordan to tell him and he passed the information on to Ms. Currie. "Tell the president, mission accomplished."...

She gets the job. And what did the president get? The key affidavit to throw the *Jones* lawyers off the trail and possibly a witness outside the practical reach of the attorneys....

The president's efforts were designed to and did obstruct justice and tamper with a witness. And his actions, we submit, were criminal under both sections 1503 and 1512 of the federal Criminal Code.

The president's false statements to his senior aides. Here, too, the facts and the law come together and would form the basis, we respectfully submit, for a conviction on articles of impeachment. All that needs to be shown to prove a violation of the statute is that the defendant engaged in misleading conduct with another person to influence...testimony....

Then Barr summed up Bennett's allusion to the Lewinsky affidavit—and the president's silence—in the Jones deposition. Bennett, he noted, later wrote to Judge Wright to inform her that parts of the affidavit were "misleading and not true." Said Barr: "Sounds like perjury. Sounds like obstruction."

What we have before us, Senators and Mr. Chief Justice, is really not complex.... Virtually every federal or state prosecutor...has prosecuted such cases of obstruction before in their careers...involving patterns of obstruction, compounded by subsequent cover-up perjury. The president's lawyers may very well try to weave a spell of complexity over the facts of this case. They may nitpick over the time of a call or parse a specific word or phrase of testimony, much as the president has done. We urge you, the distinguished jurors in this case, not to be fooled....

At that point, Democratic Sen. Tom Harkin of Iowa addressed the chair. He objected to the "continued use of the word 'jurors' when referring to the Senate sitting as triers in a trial of the impeachment of the president of the United States." Harkin based his objection on the Constitution ("Article XIII...says the trial of all crimes, except in the cases of impeachment, shall be by jury") and on the Federalist

Papers: *"There will be no jury to stand between the judges who are to pronounce the sentence of the law and the party who is to receive or suffer it."*

The chief justice agreed: "The Chair is of the view that the objection of the Senator from Iowa is well taken, that the Senate is not simply a jury; it is a court in this case. Therefore, counsel should refrain from referring to the Senators as jurors."

The Senate was adjourned. The following morning, the chief justice recognized Rep. Stephen Buyer of Indiana.

Buyer recited, once again, the House managers' litany of the facts of the case, from the Supreme Court's ruling, in May 1997, that Paula Jones could pursue her case against the president to the president's testimony before the grand jury on August 17, 1998.

Then Buyer turned to the central question: whether the offenses charged were actually impeachable. In this case, he argued, the facts "are indefensible" and there was little argument on the law. So the president's defenders, he suggested, had obtained, from "political allies and friends in the academic world, signatures on a letter saying the offenses as alleged ... do not rise to the level of an impeachable offense." The managers, he declared, disagreed.

He continued:

Mr. Buyer: ... Lying to one's spouse about an extramarital affair is not a crime; it is a private matter. But telling that same lie under oath before a federal judge, as a defendant in a civil rights sexual harassment lawsuit, is a crime against the state and is therefore a public matter.... Our law has consistently recognized that perjury subverts the judicial process. It strikes at our nation's most fundamental value, the rule of law.

In "Commentaries on the Laws of England," Sir William Blackstone differentiated between crimes that "more directly infringe the rights of a public or commonwealth taken in its collective capacity, and those which, in a more peculiar manner, injure individuals or private subjects." This book was widely recognized by the Founding Fathers, such as James Madison.... Within a subcategory denominated "offenses against public justice," Blackstone included the crimes of perjury and bribery. In fact, in his catalog of public justice offenses, Blackstone placed perjury and bribery side by side....

... [H]ypothetically, if, when William Jefferson Clinton sat at the table in the civil deposition in the *Jones v. Clinton* case, and ... if he had then offered Judge Susan Webber Wright a cash bribe, there would be no question in this body what we must—what you must do. But what I am saying ... is that there is no difference...between a cash bribe or sitting before a federal judge and perjuring one's self.... Perjury and bribery are side by side....

The framers took significance of the oath very, very seriously. The crime of perjury was among the few offenses that the first Congress outlawed by statute as they met...

Today, perjury is punishable by up to five years imprisonment in a federal penitentiary.... Likewise, the Supreme Court has repeatedly noted the extent to which perjury subverts the judicial process and, thus, the rule of law....

Buyer now quoted from rulings in four cases to demonstrate that modern courts take perjury just as seriously as did the founding fathers. Then he turned to the subject of obstruction of justice:

... "Black's Law Dictionary" defines "obstruction of justice" as "[i]mpeding or obstructing those who seek justice in a court, or those who have duties or powers of administering justice therein." It is very clear. Not only is obstruction of justice, on its own, a crime in the federal Code, but, in addition, the federal sentencing guidelines...increase the sentence of a convicted defendant who has "willfully obstructed or impeded, or attempted to obstruct or impede, the administration of justice during the investigation, prosecution, or sentencing" of his offense. The commentary on the guidelines specifically lists as examples of obstruction actions the House alleges that President Clinton has committed, including "committing, suborning, or attempting to suborn perjury" and "destroying or concealing or directing or procuring another person to destroy or conceal evidence that is material to an official investigation or judicial proceeding...."

It is no exaggeration to say that our Constitution and the American people entrust to the president singular responsibility for the enforcing of the rule of law. Perjury and obstruction of justice strike at the heart of the rule of law. A president who has committed these crimes has plainly and directly violated the most important executive duty. The core of the president's constitutional responsibilities is his duty to "take care that the laws be faithfully executed." And because perjury and obstruction of justice strike at the rule of law itself, it is difficult to imagine crimes that more clearly or directly violate this core presidential constitutional duty....

You may hear arguments that perjury and obstruction don't really have much consequence in this case because it was a private matter and, therefore, not really a serious offense. I would like to arm you with the facts. The courts do not trivialize perjury and obstruction of justice.

According to the U.S. Sentencing Commission, in 1997, 182 Americans were sentenced in federal court for committing perjury. Also in 1997, 144 Americans were sentenced in federal court for obstruction and witness-tampering.... Where is the fairness to these Americans if they stay in jail and the president stays in the Oval Office? ...

If the president's lawyers try to tell you that this case is simply about an illicit affair, I believe that it demeans our civil rights laws.... If the evidence-gathering process is unimportant in federal civil rights sexual harassment lawsuits ... what message does that send to women in America?

... Are sexual harassment lawsuits, which were designed to vindicate legitimate and serious civil rights grievances of women across America, now somewhat less important than other civil rights? Which of our civil rights laws will fall next? Will we soon decide that the evidence-gathering process is unimportant with respect to vindicating the rights of the disabled under the Americans with Disabilities Act? Will the evidence-gathering process become unimportant with respect to vindicating the voting rights of those discriminated against based on race or national origin? ...

... I think it is important to pause here and reflect upon the constitutional duties of the president of the United States. I agree with the defense argument that this has not been alleged as a dereliction of the president's exercise of executive powers. So let me talk about his executive duties.

The president is reposed with a special trust by the American people. The president is a physical embodiment of America and the hope and freedom for which she stands. When the president goes abroad, he is honored as the head of a sovereign nation; our nation is acknowledged, not just the individual who occupies the Office of the presidency....

The president has a constitutional role as Commander in Chief.... [A]s the "single hand" that guides the actions of the armed services, it is incumbent that the president exhibit sound, responsible leadership and set a proper example ... In order to be an effective ... effective military leader, the president must exhibit the traits that inspire those who must risk their lives at his command. These traits include honor, integrity and accountability....

... America, again, is a Government of laws, not of men. What protects us from that knock on the door in the middle of the night is the law. What ensures the rights of the weak and the powerless against the powerful is the law

What provides the rights to the poor against the rich is the law. What upholds the rightness of the minority view against the popular but wrong is the law. As former President Andrew Jackson wrote, "The great can protect themselves, but the poor and the humble require the arm and shield of the law."...

I will leave you with the words of the first president of the Senate and the second president of our nation, John Adams. He said:

> Facts are stubborn things; and whatever may be our wishes, our inclinations, or the dictates of our passions, they cannot alter the state of facts and evidence.

I believe John Adams was right. Facts and evidence. Facts are stubborn things. You can color the facts. You can shade the facts. You can misrepresent the facts. You can hide the facts. But the truthful facts are stubborn; they won't go away....

After a brief recess, the chief justice recognized Rep. Lindsey Graham of South Carolina.

Mr. Graham:...I voted against Article II in the House, which was the deposition perjury allegations against the president standing alone. I think many of us may have thought that...he got caught off guard, and he started telling a bunch of lies that maybe I would have lied about...because it is personal to have to talk about intimate things; and our human nature is to protect ourselves, our family....

But...what he stands charged of in this Senate happened eight months later, after some members of this body said..."Mr. President, if you go into that federal grand jury and you lie again, you're risking your presidency."...Legal commentators said that. Professor Dershowitz and I probably don't agree on a lot....[E]ven he said that if you go to a grand jury and you lie as president, that ought to be a high crime....

Human failings exist in all of us. Only when it gets to be so premeditated, so calculated, so much "my interest over anybody else" or "the public be damned," should you really, really start getting serious about what to do. That happened in August, in my opinion, ladies and gentlemen....

...The Senate has spoken before about perjury and obstruction of justice and how it applies to high Government officials. And those Government officials were judges....

Now, in Judge Claiborne's trial they seized upon the language, "Judges shall hold their office during good behavior." And the defense was trying to say, unlike the president and other...high Government officials, the impeachment standard for judges is "good behavior." That is the term. It's a different impeachment standard.... And you said "Wrong." The good behavior standard doesn't apply to why you will be removed. It is just a reference to how long you will have your job.... What gets you out of office is whether or not you violate the constitutional standard for impeachment, which is treason, bribery, or other high crimes and misdemeanors.

So as I talk to you about these cases and what you as a body did, understand we are using the same legal standard, not because I said so, but because you said so. Judge Claiborne, convicted and removed from office by the Senate, 90–7. For what? Filing a false income tax return under penalties of perjury. One thing they said in that case was, "I'm a judge and filing false income tax returns has nothing to do with me being a judge and I ought not lose my job unless you can show me or prove that I did something wrong as a judge." They were saying cheating on taxes has nothing to do with being a judge.

You know what the Senate said? It has everything to do with being a judge. And the reason you said that is because you didn't buy into this idea that the only way you can lose your job as a high Government official under the Constitution is to engage in some type of public conduct directly related to what you do every day. You took a little broader view, and I am certainly glad you did.... This is a country based on character, this is a country based on having to set a standard that others will follow.

This is Manager Fish[2]:

> Judge Claiborne's actions raise fundamental questions about public confidence in, and the public's perception of, the federal court system. They serve to undermine the confidence of the American people in our judicial system...Judge Claiborne is more than a mere embarrassment. He is a disgrace—an affront—to the judicial office and to the judicial branch he was appointed to serve.

That is very strong language. Apparently, you agreed with that concept because 90 of you voted to throw him out....

[2] The late Rep. Hamilton Fish, Jr., Republican of New York, who served in Congress from 1969 to 1995.

Now we will talk more about public versus private. Senator Mathias[3] ...:

> Impeachable conduct does not have to occur in the course of the performance of an officer's official duties. Evidence of misconduct, misbehavior, high crimes, and misdemeanors can be justified upon one's private dealings as well as one's exercise of public office.... It would be absurd to conclude that a judge who had committed murder, mayhem, rape or perhaps espionage in his private life, could not be removed from office by the U.S. Senate.

The point you made so well was that we are not buying this. If you are a federal judge and you cheat on your taxes and you lie under oath—it is true that it had nothing to do with your courtroom in a technical sense, but you are going to be judging others and they are going to come before you with their fate in your hands, and we don't want somebody like you running a courtroom because people won't trust the results.

Judge Walter Nixon, convicted and removed from office for what? Perjury before a grand jury. What was that about? He tried to fix a case for a business partner's son in state court.... When they investigated the matter, he lied about ... doing anything related to trying to manipulate the results. He was convicted and he was thrown out of office by the U.S. Senate.

I guess you could say, what has that got to do with being a federal judge? It wasn't even in his court. It has everything to do with being a high public official because if he stays in office, what signal are you sending anybody else that you send to his courtroom or anybody else's courtroom? ...

Judge Hastings: This federal judge was convicted and removed from office by the U.S. Senate. But do you know what is interesting ...? He was acquitted before he got here. He was accused of conspiring with another person to take money to fix results in his own court. He gave testimony on his own behavior. The conspirator was convicted but he was acquitted.

You know what the U.S. Senate and House said? We believe your conduct is out of bounds and we are not bound by that acquittal. We want to get to the truth and we don't want federal judges that we have a strong suspicion or reasonable belief about that are trying to fix cases in their court.

So the point I am trying to make, you don't even have to be convicted of a crime to lose your job in this constitutional Republic if this body determines

[3] Charles Mathias, Republican of Maryland, a U.S. Senator from 1969–1987.

that your conduct as a public official is clearly out of bounds in your role. Thank God you did that, because impeachment is not about punishment. Impeachment is about ... restoring honor and integrity to the office. ...

If we can do nothing else for this country, let us state clearly that this conduct is unacceptable by any president. These are in fact high crimes. They go to the core of why we are all here as a nation and to the rule of law, the rules of litigation. ...

... I think the evidence will be persuasive that he is guilty. The logic of your past rulings and just fundamental fairness and decency, and helping the Supreme Court enforce their rules, if nothing else, will lead you to a high crime determination.

But we are asking you to remove a popular president. ... To set aside an election is a very scary thought in a democracy. I do not agree with this president on most major policy initiatives. I did not vote for this president. But he won; he won twice. To undo that election is tough. ...

Remember how you felt when you knew you had a perjurer as a judge, when you knew you had somebody who had fundamentally run over the law that they were responsible for upholding. Remember how you felt when you knew that judge got so out of bounds that you could not put him back in court ... because you would be doing a disservice to the citizens who would come before him. A judge has a duty to take care of the individuals fairly who come before the court. The president, ladies and gentlemen of the Senate, has a duty to see that the law applies to everyone fairly ... a higher duty in the Constitution.

Ladies and gentlemen, as hard as it may be, for the same reasons, cleanse this office. The vice president will be waiting outside the doors of this Chamber. ... If that vice president is asked to come in and assume the mantle of Chief Executive Officer of the land and chief law enforcement officer of the land, it will be tough, it will be painful, but we will survive and we will be better for it. ...

The chief justice recognized Rep. Charles Canady of Florida.

Mr. Canady: ... Who can seriously argue that our Constitution requires that a president guilty of crimes such as murder, sexual assault, or tax fraud remain in his office undisturbed? Who is willing to set such a standard for the conduct of the president of the United States? Who can in good conscience accept the consequences for our system of government that would necessarily follow? Could our Constitution possibly contemplate such a result? What other crimes of a president will we be told do not rise to the level of "high crimes and misdemeanors"? These are grave questions that must be addressed by this Senate. The president's defense requires that these questions be asked and answered.

Contrary to the claims of the president's lawyers, there is not a bright line separating official misconduct by a president from other misconduct of which the president is guilty. Some offenses will involve the direct and affirmative misuse of governmental power. Other offenses may involve a more subtle use of the prestige, status and position of the president to further a course of wrongdoing. There are still other offenses in which a president may not misuse the power of his office, but in which he violates a duty imposed on him under the Constitution.

Such a breach of constitutional duty—even though it does not constitute an affirmative misuse of governmental power—may be a very serious matter. It does violence to the English language to assert that a president who has violated a duty entrusted to him by the Constitution is not guilty of official misconduct....

As we have been reminded repeatedly, the Constitution imposes on the president the duty to "take care that the laws be faithfully executed." The charges against the president involve multiple violations of that duty. A president who commits a calculated and sustained series of criminal offenses has—by his personal violations of the law—failed in the most immediate, direct, and culpable manner to do his duty under the Constitution.

... There is no principled basis for contending that a president who interferes with the proper exercise of governmental power—as he clearly does when he commits perjury and obstruction of justice—is constitutionally less blameworthy than a president who misuses the power of his office....

Although neither the Senate nor the House has ever adopted a fixed definition of "high crimes and misdemeanors," there is much in the background and history of the impeachment process that contradicts the narrow view of the removal power advanced by the president's lawyers....

The truth is ... that treason and bribery may be committed by an official who does not abuse the power of his office in the commission of the offense.

A president might, for example, pay a bribe to a judge presiding over a case to which the president is an individual party. Or a judge might commit an act of treason without exercising any of the powers of his office in doing so. By the express terms of the Constitution those offenses would be impeachable. And there is no reason to impose a restriction on the scope of "other high crimes and misdemeanors" that is not imposed on treason and bribery....

To properly understand the purpose of the impeachment process under our Constitution, consideration must be given to use of impeachment by the English Parliament.... Through impeachment, Parliament acted to curb the abuses of exalted persons who would otherwise have free rein. Impeachment was used by the Parliament to punish a wide range of offenses: misapplication of funds; abuse of official power; neglect of duty; corruption; encroachment on the prerogatives of the Parliament; and giving harmful advice to the Crown....

During the impeachment of Lord Chancellor Macclesfield in 1725, Sergeant Pengelly summed up the purpose of impeachment. It was, he said, for the "punishment of offenses of a public nature which may affect the nation." He went on to say that impeachment was also for use in "instances where the inferior courts have no power to punish the crimes committed by ordinary rules of justice ... or in cases ... where the person offending is by his degree raised above the apprehension of danger from a prosecution carried on in the usual course of justice...."

As the British legal historian Holdsworth has written, the impeachment process was a mechanism in service of the "ideal ... [of] government in accordance with law." ...

Those who were impeached and called to account for "high crimes and misdemeanors" were those who by their conduct threatened to undermine the rule of law.

This English understanding of the purpose of impeachment serves as a backdrop for the work of the Framers of our Constitution....

Here, Canady summed up the debates at the Constitutional Convention and during the ratification conventions in the states—particularly the discussions of grounds for impeachment. "Maladministration" was rejected as too vague. "Making a bad treaty" came up often. In Virginia, "misbehavior" and "dishonesty" were considered. One of the most extended discussions, said Canady, was in North Carolina, where James Iredell, later a justice of the U.S. Supreme Court, spoke at length: "... According to these principles, I suppose the only instances in which the president would be liable to impeachment would be where he had received a bribe, or acted from some corrupt motive or other." Canady observed: "You will note there is nothing in Iredell's comments to suggest that a president who engaged in a corrupt course of conduct by obstructing justice and committing perjury would be immune from impeachment and removal."

Then Canady turned to Alexander Hamilton's words on the subject:

In the Federalist, Hamilton writes of the Senate:

> The subjects of its jurisdiction are those offenses which proceed from the misconduct of public men, or in other words from the abuse or violation of some public trust. They are of a nature which may with peculiar propriety be denominated political, as they relate chiefly to injuries done immediately to the society itself.

... Despite the claims of the president's lawyers, the comments of Hamilton do not support the view that a president can be impeached and removed only for an abuse of power.... The "misconduct of public men" encompasses a whole range of wrongful deeds committed by those who hold office when those offenses are committed. The "public trust" is violated whenever a public officer breaches any duty he has to the public. "Injuries done ... to the society itself" similarly may occur as the result of misconduct that does not involve the misuse of the powers of office.

... The theme running through all these background sources is that the impeachment process is designed to provide a remedy for the corrupt and lawless acts of public officials. Not surprisingly, those who have been on the receiving end of impeachment proceedings have been quick to argue for a restrictive meaning of "high crimes and misdemeanors." President Clinton's lawyers follow in that well-established tradition.

... In essence, they argue that treason and bribery are the prototypical high crimes and misdemeanors, and that the crimes charged against the president are insufficiently similar in both their nature and seriousness to treason and bribery.

But, as the comments of my fellow manager, Mr. Buyer, have made clear, the crimes set forth in the articles of impeachment are indeed serious offenses against our system of justice....

Moreover, perjury and obstruction of justice are by their very nature akin to bribery. When the crime of bribery is committed, money is given and received to corruptly alter the course of official action. When justice is obstructed, action is undertaken to corruptly thwart the due administration of justice. When perjury occurs, false testimony is given in order to deceive judges and juries and to prevent the just determination of causes pending in the courts. The fundamental purpose and the fundamental effect of each of these offenses...is to defeat the proper administration of government. They all are crimes of corruption aimed at substituting private advantage for the public interest....

There has been a great deal of comment on the report on "Constitutional Grounds for Presidential Impeachment" prepared in February 1974 by the staff of the Nixon impeachment inquiry. Those who assert that the charges against the president do not rise to the level of "high crimes and misdemeanors" have pulled some phrases from that report out of context to support their position. In fact, the general principles concerning grounds for impeachment and removal set forth in that report indicate that perjury and obstruction of justice are high crimes and misdemeanors.

Consider this key language from the staff report describing the type of conduct which gives rise to the proper use of the impeachment and removal power:...:

> The emphasis has been on the significant effects of the conduct—undermining the integrity of office, disregard of constitutional duties and oath of office, arrogation of power, abuse of the governmental process, adverse impact on the system of government.

The report goes on to state:

> Because impeachment of a president is a grave step for the nation, it is to be predicated only upon conduct seriously incompatible with either the constitutional form and principles of our government or the proper performance of constitutional duties of the presidential office.

Perjury and obstruction of justice, I submit to you, clearly "undermine the integrity of office." I ask you, if these offenses do not undermine the integrity of office, what offenses would? Their unavoidable consequence is to erode respect for the office of the president and to interfere with the integrity of the administration of justice. Such offenses are "seriously incompatible" with the president's "constitutional duties and oath of office," and with the principles of our government establishing the rule of law. Moreover, they are offenses which have a direct and serious "adverse impact on the system of government." Obstruction of justice is by definition an assault on the due administration of justice—which is a core function of our system of government. Perjury has the same purpose and effect....

This power—the awesome power of removal vested in the Senate—carries with it an awesome responsibility. This power imposes on the Senate the responsibility to exercise its judgment in establishing the standards of conduct that are necessary to preserve, protect, and strengthen the Constitution which has served the people of the United States so well for more than two centuries.

Thus, the crucial issue before the Senate is what standard will be set for the conduct of the president of the United States.... And make no mistake about it: the choice the Senate makes in this case will have consequences reverberating far into the future of our Republic. Will a president who has committed serious offenses against the system of justice be called to account for his crimes, or will his offenses be regarded as of no constitutional consequence? Will a standard be established that such crimes by a president will not be tolerated, or will the standard be that—at least in some cases—a president may "remain in office with all his infamy" after lying under oath and obstructing justice?...

The Constitution contains wise safeguards against the misuse of the impeachment and removal power. As a practical matter, as we all know, the requirement of a two-thirds vote for conviction virtually ensures that a president will only be removed when a compelling case for removal has been made. And the periodic accountability to the people of Members of both the House and the Senate serves as a check on the improvident use of the impeachment power for unworthy or insubstantial reasons....

But, of course, the ultimate safeguard against the abuse of this power is in the sober deliberation and sound judgment of the Senate itself. The framers of the Constitution vested the removal power and responsibility in the Senate because, as Hamilton observed, they "thought the Senate the most fit depositary of this important trust."...

Ladies and gentlemen of the Senate, this is the great trust which the Constitution has reposed in you.... As you carry out this trust, we do not suggest that you hold this president or any president to a standard of perfection. We do not assert that this president or any president be called to account before the Senate for his personal failings or his sins.... Nor do we suggest that this president or any president should be removed from office for offenses that are not serious and grave.

But we do submit that when this president, or any president, has committed serious offenses against the system of justice—offenses involving the stubborn and calculated choice to place personal interest ahead of the public interest—he must not be allowed to act with impunity....

The chief justice recognized Mr. Manager Gekas.

Mr. Gekas: ... When the record of the independent counsel... reached our doorsteps... and we first read the details and allegations contained therein, we did not... adopt 100 percent of what the independent counsel said were the allegations and accept them as fact... and skip from September to this moment, not having used our intellect, our sympathies, our sense of right, our sense of wrong, our sense of fairness, our elements of truth, our experience, our own intellect, and our own consciences.... Everyone should know that. But it is not recognized. We have been pilloried many times over the course of these proceedings on the notion that we simply adopted that referral and walked with it into the Senate Chamber.

... When I saw one allegation of the independent counsel... that the assertion by President Clinton of executive privilege in the context of all that had transpired in this case constituted an abuse of power, I must tell you that that hit me right between the eyes.... [W]e acted on that feeling—that executive privilege is something that is owed to the president, and that we cannot fairly strip that away from him or in any way diminish the power.... We felt pretty strongly about it, and we... decided that we were going to remove that from the allegations in any of the articles of impeachment....

But here is the point.... We respect the office of the presidency. The presidency is we. The presidency is America. The presidency is the banner under which we all work and live and strive in this nation. We revere the presidency. Any innuendo, or any kind of impulse that anyone has to attribute any kind of motivation on the part of these men of honor who have prepared this case for you today on any whim on their part other than to do their constitutional duty should be rebuffed at every conversation, at every meeting, at every writing that will ultimately flow from the proceedings that we have embarked upon. We revere the presidency. As a matter of fact, when next week we face the prospect of the president of the United States entering the House of Representatives to deliver his State of the Union message, we will greet the president. We will accord him the respect for the office which he holds. He is our president. He occupies the presidency. And we will honor that. And so should we all....

...All we can do is to do the job that was thrust upon us, that was placed in our hands by a statute that this Congress created—that independent counsel statute. The Congress said that we had to listen to the referral, to accept the referral. The Congress said that we must look towards whatever recommendations might be contained in that. It was the Congress, our Congress—many of you who voted for that statute—which mandated that we consider all of this. We did not simply walk around one day and seize upon a moment of deep thought and say let's impeach the president; let's find something upon which we can base a full six months inquiry into the president's actions in front of a court.

This was a duty, much as it is your duty to stay here and listen to what I am saying. The duty that I have of presenting it to you and speaking to you is born of the same statute and of the same process and of the same constitutional background that we all share.

So it worries me and us that any awkward motivation would be attributed to any one of us or collectively to us. And once you render your vote, I am not going to question whether it was done out of blind loyalty or enmity or friendship with the president, or enmity with the president; I am going to judge it as an American citizen, a Member of the House of Representatives, a Member of Congress, an interested community leader, and, last but not least, as a pure American citizen eager to do one's duty....

The chief justice recognized Mr. Manager Hyde.

Mr. Hyde:... [D]espite massive and relentless efforts to change the subject, the case before you Senators is not about sexual misconduct, infidelity or adultery—those are private acts and none of our business. It is not even a question of lying about sex. The matter before this body is a question of lying under oath. This is a public act.

The matter before you is a question of the willful, premeditated deliberate corruption of the nation's system of justice, through perjury and obstruction of justice. These are public acts, and when committed by the chief law enforcement officer of the land, the one who appoints every United States district attorney, every federal judge, every member of the Supreme Court, the attorney general—they do become the concern of Congress.

That is why your judgment, respectfully, should rise above politics, above partisanship, above polling data. This case is a test of whether what the Founding Fathers described as "sacred honor" still has meaning in our time: two hundred twenty-two years after those two words—sacred honor—were inscribed in our country's birth certificate, our national charter of freedom, our Declaration of Independence.

Every school child in the United States has an intuitive sense of the "sacred honor" that is one of the foundation stones of the American house of freedom. For every day, in every classroom in America, our children and grandchildren pledge allegiance to a nation, "under God." That statement is not a prideful or arrogant claim. It is a statement of humility: all of us, as individuals, stand under the judgment of God, or the transcendent truths by which we hope, finally, to be judged. So does our country.

The presidency is an office of trust. Every public office is a public trust, but the Office of president is a very special public trust. The president is the trustee of the national conscience. No one owns the Office of president, the people do. The president is elected by the people and their representatives in the electoral college. And in accepting the burdens of that great office, the president, in his inaugural oath, enters into a covenant—a binding agreement of mutual trust and obligation—with the American people.

Shortly after his election and during his first months in office, President Clinton spoke with some frequency about a "new covenant" in America. In this instance, let us take the president at his word: that his office is a covenant—a solemn pact of mutual trust and obligation—with the American people. Let us take the president seriously when he speaks of covenants: because a covenant is about promise-making and promise-keeping. For it is because the president has defaulted on the promises he made—it is because he has violated the oaths he has sworn—that he has been impeached.

The debate about impeachment during the Constitutional Convention of 1787 makes it clear that the Framers of the Constitution regarded impeachment and removal from office on conviction as a remedy for a fundamental betrayal of trust by the president. The Framers had invested the presidential office with great powers. They knew that those powers could be—and would be—abused if any president were to violate, in a fundamental way, the oath he had sworn to faithfully execute the nation's laws.

For if the president did so violate his oath of office, the covenant of trust between himself and the American people would be broken.

Today, we see something else: that the fundamental trust between America and the world can be broken, if a presidential perjurer represents our country in world affairs. If the president calculatedly and repeatedly violates his oath, if the president breaks the covenant of trust he has made with the American people, he can no longer be trusted. And, because the executive plays so large a role in representing the country to the world, America can no longer be trusted.

It is often said that we live in an age of increasing interdependence. If that is true, and the evidence for it is all around us, then the future will require an even stronger bond of trust between the president and the nation: because with increasing interdependence comes an increased necessity of trust.

This is one of the basic lessons of life. Parents and children know this. Husbands and wives know it. Teachers and students know it, as do doctors and patients, suppliers and customers, lawyers and clients, clergy and parishioners: the greater the interdependence, the greater the necessity of trust; the greater the interdependence, the greater the imperative of promise-keeping.

Trust, not what James Madison called the "parchment barriers" of laws, is the fundamental bond between the people and their elected representatives, between those who govern and those who are governed. Trust is the mortar that secures the foundations of the American house of freedom. And the Senate of the United States, sitting in judgment in this impeachment trial, should not ignore, or minimize, or dismiss the fact that the bond of trust has been broken, because the president has violated both his oaths of office and the oath he took before his grand jury testimony.

In recent months, it has often been asked—so what? What is the harm done by this lying under oath, by this perjury? Well, what is an oath? An oath is an asking almighty God to witness to the truth of what you are saying. Truth telling—truth telling is the heart and soul of our justice system.

I think the answer would have been clear to those who once pledged their sacred honor to the cause of liberty. The answer would have been clear to those who crafted the world's most enduring written constitution. No greater harm can be done than breaking the covenant of trust between the president and the people; among the three branches of our government; and between the country and the world.

For to break that covenant of trust is to dissolve the mortar that binds the foundation stones of our freedom into a secure and solid edifice. And to break that covenant of trust by violating one's oath is to do grave damage to the rule of law among us.

That none of us is above the law is a bedrock principle of democracy. To erode that bedrock is to risk even further injustice. To erode that bedrock is to subscribe to a "divine right of kings" theory of governance, in which those who govern are absolved from adhering to the basic moral standards to which the governed are accountable. We must never tolerate one law for the ruler, and another for the ruled. If we do, we break faith with our ancestors from Bunker Hill, Lexington and Concord to Flanders Field, Normandy, Iwo Jima, Panmunjom, Saigon and Desert Storm.

Let us be clear: The vote that you are asked to cast is, in the final analysis, a vote about the rule of law.

The rule of law is one of the great achievements of our civilization. For the alternative to the rule of law is the rule of raw power. We here today are the heirs of three thousand years of history in which humanity slowly, painfully and at great cost, evolved a form of politics in which law, not brute force, is the arbiter of our public destinies.

We are the heirs of the Ten Commandments and the Mosaic law: a moral code for a free people who, having been liberated from bondage, saw in law a means to avoid falling back into the habit of slaves. We are the heirs of Roman law: the first legal system by which peoples of different cultures, languages, races, and religions came to live together in a form of political community. We are the heirs of the Magna Carta, by which the freeman of England began to break the arbitrary and unchecked power of royal absolutism. We are the heirs of a long tradition of parliamentary development, in which the rule of law gradually came to replace royal prerogative as the means for governing a society of free men and women. Yes, we are the heirs of 1776, and of an epic moment in human affairs when the founders of this Republic pledged their lives, fortunes and, yes, their sacred honor, to the defense of the rule of law. We are the heirs of a tragic civil war, which vindicated the rule of law over the appetites of some for owning others. We are the heirs of the 20th century's great struggles against totalitarianism, in which the rule of law was defended at immense cost against the worst tyrannies in human history.

The "rule of law" is no pious aspiration from a civics textbook. The rule of law is what stands between all of us and the arbitrary exercise of power by the state. The rule of law is the safeguard of our liberties. The rule of law is what allows us to live our freedom in ways that honor the freedom of others while strengthening the common good.

Lying under oath is an abuse of freedom. Obstruction of justice is a degradation of law. There are people in prison for just such offenses. What in the world do we say to them about equal justice if we overlook this conduct in the president? . . .

In doing this, the Office of President of the United States has been debased and the justice system jeopardized.

In doing this, he has broken his covenant of trust with the American people.

The framers also knew that the Office of President of the United States could be gravely damaged if it continued to be unworthily occupied. That is why they devised the process of impeachment by the House and trial by the Senate. It is, in truth, a direct process. If, on impeachment, the president is convicted, he is removed from office—and the office itself suffers no permanent damage. If, on impeachment, the president is acquitted, the issue is resolved once and for all, and the office is similarly protected from permanent damage.

But if, on impeachment, the president is not convicted and removed from office despite the fact that numerous Senators are convinced that he has, in the words of one proposed resolution of censure, "egregiously failed" the test of his oath of office, "violated the trust of the American people," and "dishonored the office which they entrusted to him," then the Office of the presidency has been deeply, and perhaps permanently damaged.

And that is a further reason why President Clinton must be convicted of the charges brought before you by the House and removed from office. To fail to do so, while conceding that the president has engaged in egregious and dishonorable behavior that has broken the covenant of trust between himself and the American people, is to diminish the Office of President of the United States in an unprecedented and unacceptable way. . . .

Ｎone of us comes to this Chamber today without a profound sense of our own responsibilities in life, and of the many ways in which we have failed to meet those responsibilities, to one degree or another. None of us comes before you claiming to be a perfect man or a perfect citizen, just as none of you imagines yourself perfect. All of us, Members of the House and Senate, know that we come to this difficult task as flawed human beings, under judgment.

That is the way of this world: flawed human beings must, according to the rule of law, judge other flawed human beings.

But the issue before the Senate of the United States is not the question of its own Members' personal moral condition. Nor is the issue before the Senate the question of the personal moral condition of the members of the House of Representatives. The issue here is whether the president has violated the rule of law and thereby broken his covenant of trust with the American people. This is a public issue, involving the gravest matter of the public interest. And it is not affected, one way or another, by the personal moral condition of any member of either House of Congress, or by whatever expressions of personal chagrin the president has managed to express.

Senators, we of the House do not come before you today lightly. And, if you will permit me, it is a disservice to the House to suggest that it has brought these articles of impeachment before you in a mean-spirited or irresponsible way. That is not true. We have brought these articles of impeachment because we are convinced, in conscience, that the president of the United States lied under oath; that the president committed perjury on several occasions before a federal grand jury. We have brought these articles of impeachment because we are convinced, in conscience, that the president willfully obstructed justice and thereby threatened the legal system he swore a solemn oath to protect and defend.

These are not trivial matters. These are not partisan matters. These are matters of justice, the justice that each of you has taken a solemn oath to serve in this trial. . . .

Senators, this trial is being watched around the world. Some of those watching, thinking themselves superior in their cynicism, wonder what it is all about. But others know.

Political prisoners know that this is about the rule of law—the great alternative to arbitrary and unchecked state power.

The families of executed dissidents know that this is about the rule of law—the great alternative to the lethal abuse of power by the state.

Those yearning for freedom know that this is about the rule of law—the hard-won structure by which men and women can live by their God-given dignity and secure their God-given rights in ways that serve the common good.

If they know this, can we not know it?

If, across the river in Arlington Cemetery, there are American heroes who died in defense of the rule of law, can we give less than the full measure of our devotion to that great cause? . . .

Hyde then read from a letter from a third-grader in Chicago, William Preston Summers, who suggested a punishment for the president. He "should write a 100 word essay by hand. I have to write an essay when I lie. It is bad to lie because it just gets you in more trouble." William went on: "If you can not believe the president who can you believe. . . . I do not believe the president tells the truth anymore right now. . . ." William's father had added a P.S., explaining: "I made my son either write you a letter or an essay as a punishment for lying. Part of his defense for his lying was the president lied. He is still having difficulty understanding why the president can lie and not be punished."

Mr. Chief Justice and Senators, on June 6, 1994, it was the 50th anniversary of the Americans landing at Normandy. I went ashore at Normandy, walked up to the cemetery area, where as far as the eye could see there were white crosses, Stars of David. And the British had a bagpipe band scattered among the crucifixes, the crosses, playing "Amazing Grace" with that peaceful, mournful sound that only the bagpipe can make. If you could keep your eyes dry you were better than I.

But I walked to one of these crosses marking a grave because I wanted to personalize the experience. I was looking for a name but there was no name. It said, "Here lies in Honored Glory a Comrade in Arms Known but to God."

How do we keep faith with that comrade in arms? Well, go to the Vietnam Memorial on the National Mall and press your hands against a few of the 58,000 names carved into that wall, and ask yourself, How can we redeem the debt we owe all those who purchased our freedom with their lives? How do we keep faith with them? I think I know. We work to make this country the kind of America they were willing to die for. That is an America where the idea of sacred honor still has the power to stir men's souls. My solitary—solitary—hope is that 100 years from today people will look back at what we have done and say, "They kept the faith." . . .

The Senate adjourned, to reconvene on Tuesday, January 19.

THE PRESIDENT'S DEFENSE

On Tuesday, January 19, the chief justice recognized Charles Ruff, to begin the president's defense.

Mr. Ruff: Mr. Chief Justice, Members of the Senate, distinguished managers, William Jefferson Clinton is not guilty of the charges that have been preferred against him. He did not commit perjury; he did not obstruct justice; he must not be removed from office.

...On May 6, 1994, Paula Jones sued President Clinton in the U.S. District Court for the Eastern District of Arkansas. She claimed that then-Governor Clinton had made, in 1991, some unwelcomed overture to her in an Arkansas hotel room and that she suffered adverse employment consequences and was subsequently defamed.

After the Supreme Court decided in May 1997 that civil litigation against the president could go forward while he was in office, the case was remanded to the district court, and over the fall and winter of 1997, the *Jones* lawyers deposed numerous witnesses....

The principal focus of the discovery being conducted by the *Jones* lawyers during this period was...the personal life of the president. Mr. Bennett, the president's counsel, objected to those efforts on the grounds they had no relevance to Ms. Jones' claims...The *Jones* lawyers, however, pursued their efforts...and on December 11, 1997, Judge Wright issued an order allowing questioning regarding only "any individuals with whom the president had sexual relations or proposed or sought to have sexual relations and who were during the relevant time frame a State or federal employee."

Then on December 5, 1997, the *Jones* lawyers placed on their witness list the name of Monica Lewinsky. And on December 19, she was served with a subpoena for her deposition....

Consistent with rulings issued by Judge Wright in connection with the *Jones* lawyers' efforts to secure the testimony of a number of other women, some have sought to avoid testifying by submitting affidavits to the effect that they had no knowledge relevant to Ms. Jones' lawsuit, or that they otherwise do not meet the test that Judge Wright had established before permitting this invasive discovery to go forward. On January 7, 1998, Ms. Lewinsky did execute such an affidavit, and her lawyer provided copies to the lawyers for Ms. Jones and for the president on January 15.

The *Jones* lawyers deposed the president on January 17, 1998. They began the deposition by proffering to him a multi-paragraph definition of the term "sexual relations" that they intended to use in questioning him. There followed an extended debate among counsel and the court concerning the propriety and the clarity of that definition. Mr. Bennett objected to its use, arguing that it was unclear, that it would encompass conduct wholly irrelevant to the case....

Judge Wright acknowledged the overbreadth of the definition, but she ultimately determined that the *Jones* lawyers could use the heavily edited version of the definition.... Immediately after the extended legal skirmishing, the *Jones* lawyers began asking him about Monica Lewinsky.

Mr. Bennett objected, questioning whether counsel had a legitimate basis for their inquiry in light of Ms. Lewinsky's affidavit denying a relationship with the president. Judge Wright overruled that objection and permitted the *Jones* lawyers to pursue their inquiry. Four days later, the independent counsel's investigation became a public matter.

On January 29...Judge Wright ruled that evidence relating to [Ms. Lewinsky's] relationship with the president would be excluded from the trial. She reaffirmed this ruling on March 9 stating that the evidence was not "essential to the core issues in this case of whether the plaintiff herself was the victim of sexual harassment...." On April 1, 1998, Judge Wright...granted summary judgment in favor of President Clinton dismissing the *Jones* suit in its entirety....

Ms. Jones appealed Judge Wright's decision to the Eighth Circuit.... [O]n November 13, 1998, before the decision was rendered, Ms. Jones and the president settled the case.

Briefly then, to... the independent counsel's office, in mid-January 1998, Linda Tripp had brought to the independent counsel information that she had been gathering surreptitiously for months about Ms. Lewinsky's relationship with the president....

Independent counsel met with Ms. Tripp.... On January 13, Ms. Tripp agreed to tape a conversation with Ms. Lewinsky under FBI auspices. And on January 15, armed with that tape, the independent counsel's office first contacted the Department of Justice to seek permission from the attorney general to expand its jurisdiction to cover the investigation that had already begun. On January 16, that permission was granted....

Now, the president's deposition was scheduled to take place the very next day—Saturday, January 17. On the 16th, Ms. Tripp invited Ms. Lewinsky to have lunch with her at the Pentagon City Mall. There she was greeted by four FBI agents and independent counsel lawyers and taken to a hotel room where she spent the next several hours. Ms. Tripp was in the room next door for much of that time. When she left that evening, she went home to meet with the *Jones* lawyers... to brief them about... the relationship between Ms. Lewinsky and the president so that they, in turn, could question the president the next morning....

The existence of the OIC investigation was made public on January 21 in an edition of the *Washington Post*....

On August 17, the president's deposition was taken by the independent counsel for use by the grand jury, and on September 9, there was delivered to the House of Representatives a referral of Independent Counsel Starr containing what purported to be the information concerning acts "that may constitute grounds for impeachment."...

The referral was made public by the House on September 11. On September 21, additional materials were released, along with the president's grand jury videotape that was then played virtually nonstop on every television station in the country during that day.

Here Ruff summarized the proceedings in the House, stressing that the Judiciary Committee had called no fact witnesses. He said that despite "numerous efforts" by the defense to obtain specific charges, they materialized as Ruff was completing his testimony before the committee—in the form of draft articles of impeachment. On December 19, said Ruff, "the House completed its action. And so we are here."

He continued:

[T]he managers spent much of their time last week explaining to you why, if only witnesses could be called, you would be able to resolve all of the supposed conflicts in the evidence. Tell me, then, how is it that the managers can be so certain of the strength of their case? They didn't hear any of these witnesses. The only witness they called, the independent counsel himself, acknowledged that he had not even met any of the witnesses who testified before the grand jury. Yet, they appeared before you to tell you that they are convinced of the president's guilt and that they are prepared to demand his removal from office.

Well, the managers would have you believe that the Judiciary Committee of the House were really nothing more than grand jurors, serving as some routine screening device to sort out impeachment chaff from impeachment wheat. Thus, as they would have it, there was no need for anything more than a review of the cold record prepared by the independent counsel....

...I suggest that what you have before you is...the product of nothing more than a rush to judgment.

And so how should you respond to the managers' belated plea that more is needed to do justice? You should reject it. You have before you all that you need to reach this conclusion: There was no basis for the House to impeach, and there is no, and never will be any, basis for the Senate to convict.

... [T]he president may be removed from office only upon impeachment for and conviction of treason, bribery or other high crimes and misdemeanors. The offenses charged here, even if supported by the evidence, do not meet that lofty standard.... Listen to the words of 10 Republican Members of the 1974 Judiciary Committee.... After President Nixon's resignation, in an effort to articulate a measured and a careful assessment of the issues they had confronted, they reviewed the historical origins of the impeachment clause and wrote:

It is our judgment, based upon this constitutional history, that the framers of the United States Constitution intended that the president should be removable by the legislative branch only for serious misconduct, dangerous to the system of government established by the Constitution. Absent the element of danger to the State, we believe the delegates to the federal convention of 1787, in providing that the president should serve for a fixed elective term rather than during good behavior or popularity, struck the balance in favor of stability in the executive branch.

Where did this lesson in constitutional history come from? It came directly from the words of the framers in 1787. Impeachment was... was familiar to them as part of English constitutional practice and was part of many state constitutions. It is therefore not surprising that whether to make provision for impeachment of the president became the focus of contention, especially in the context of concern whether in our new republican form of government the legislature ought to be entrusted with such a power. On this latter point... Benjamin Franklin noted that it at least had the merit of being a peaceful alternative to revolution.

Gouvernor Morris, one of the principal moving forces behind the language that ultimately emerged from the convention, believed that provision for impeachment should be made but that the offenses must be limited and carefully defined...

Drafts... moved through one that authorized impeachment for treason or bribery or corruption, and then the more limited treason or bribery, until the critical debate of December 8, 1787, when... George Mason moved to add the word "maladministration".... It was in the face of objections from James Madison and Morris, however, that this term was too vague.... that Mason withdrew his proposal and the convention then adopted the language "other high crimes and misdemeanors against the State."...

... To argue, then, as the managers do, that the phrase "other crimes and misdemeanors" was really meant to encompass a wide range of offenses that one might find in a compendium of English criminal law simply flies in the face of the clear intent of the framers, who carefully chose their language... and knew exactly what risks they intended to protect against....

[T]he central premise of the managers' argument appears to be this: Perjury is an impeachable offense no matter the forum or the circumstances in which it is committed. Second, judges have recently been convicted and removed on the basis of articles charging that they committed perjury. The president committed perjury, therefore the president must be removed as well.

That premise is simple but wrong. The first leg on which it rests was removed by the House itself when it voted to defeat Article II, alleging perjury in a civil deposition, and the House thus rejected the committee's core argument that perjury in a civil deposition warrants impeachment as much as perjury in any other setting....

And as to the committee's view that it makes no difference whether perjury occurs in one forum or another, in a private or an official proceeding, again the House said no, and properly so.

What, then, of the managers' argument that the Senate's recent conviction of three judges requires a conviction on the articles before you today?... Surely the managers recognize that the Senate here faces a far different question, a far different constitutional issue than it did, for example, when it asked whether Judge Nixon, convicted and imprisoned for perjury, should be permitted to retain his office; or whether Judge Hastings, who lied about taking a bribe to fix a case before him, should remain on the bench....

... [W]hether weighing the constitutional or governmental implications of removal or asking whether the accused can be expected to perform his duties, the Senate has always recognized that the test will be different depending on the office that the accused holds. This analysis is wholly consistent with the framers' intent in drafting the impeachment clause that removal of a president by the legislature must be an act of last resort when the political process can no longer protect the nation....

The managers...speak of perjury and obstruction of justice in general terms and they argue that they are offenses inimical to the system of justice.

No one here would dispute that simplistic proposition. But the managers will not walk with you down the difficult path. They will not speak of facts, of differing circumstances and differing societal interests. They will not because they do not appear to recognize that those questions must be asked....

The principle that guides your deliberations, I suggest, must not only be faithful to the intent of the framers, it must be consistent with the governmental structure that they gave us and the delicate relationship between the legislative branch and the executive branch that is the hallmark of that structure. It must, above all, reflect the recognition that removal from office is an act of extraordinary proportions, to be taken only when no other response is adequate to preserve the integrity and viability of our democracy....

Ruff now addressed "what standard the evidence must meet to justify a vote of guilty." The Senate, he suggested, should "ask whether the House has established guilt beyond

284 THE IMPEACHMENT AND TRIAL OF PRESIDENT CLINTON

a reasonable doubt." No matter, he said, that the Senate had used the "clear and con-
vincing" standard in judicial trials: "[W]hen a president is on trial, the balance is
very different. Here you are asking, in effect, to overturn the will of the electorate."

Next, Ruff turned to the "constitutional deficiency" of the articles of impeach-
ment. First, he said, there was the absence of specified perjurious words in Article I,
in violation of the Sixth Amendment's guarantee that the accused has the right to be
informed of the nature and cause of the accusation against him. The vague lan-
guage Ruff argued, allowed the House managers to treat them as "empty vessels, to be
filled with some witches' brew of charges considered, charges considered and aban-
doned and charges never considered at all."

In addition, Ruff said, each article combined multiple offenses, creating a risk
"that a verdict may be based not on a unanimous finding of guilt as to any partic-
ular charge. . . ." This problem had come up before, Ruff noted, in the trial of Judge
Nixon. At that time, Democratic Senator Herbert Kohl of Wisconsin had protested:
"Please do not bunch up your allegations. . . . Charge each act of wrongdoing in a
separate count . . . and allow for a cleaner vote on guilt or innocence."

After a brief recess, Ruff moved to the articles of impeachment themselves:

Let me begin with Article I.

Our system of justice recognizes the difficulties inherent in testifying
under oath, and it affords important protections for the witness who may be
charged with perjury, and thus the Judiciary Committee's dissatisfaction with
the president's answers because they thought they were narrow, or even hair-
splitting, in some sense reflect dissatisfaction with the rules that have been applied for centuries. . . .

The defendant must have had a subjective intent to lie. The testimony that
is provided as a result of confusion, mistake, faulty memory, or carelessness, or
misunderstanding is not perjury. . . .

Any assessment of the president's testimony must begin with one im-
mutable fact. He admitted that he had, in his words, "inappropriate, intimate
contact" with Monica Lewinsky. No one who was present for that testimony,
has read the transcript, or watched the videotape could come away believing
anything other than that the president and Ms. Lewinsky engaged in sexual
conduct. . . . [T]he managers . . . have searched every nook and cranny of the
grand jury transcript and sent forward to you a shopping list of alleged misstatements, obviously in the hope that among them you will find one with
which you disagree. But . . . the record simply will not support a finding that
the president perjured himself before the grand jury.

Now, much of the questioning by the prosecutors and much of the grand jury testimony about which the House now complains so vociferously dealt with the president's efforts to explain why his answers in the *Jones* deposition, certainly not pretty, were, in his mind, truthful, albeit narrowly and artfully constructed. We are not here to talk to you today about the president's testimony in the *Jones* deposition. We do seek to convince you that before the grand jury the president was open, candid, truthful.

...Before the president actually began his testimony, his lawyer, Mr. Kendall, spoke to Mr. Starr and told him that at the first moment at which there was an inquiry concerning the detailed nature of the relationship with Ms. Lewinsky, he wished to make a prepared statement.... That statement acknowledged the existence of an intimate relationship, but it did not discuss the specific physical details.... [T]he House has charged that this statement was somehow a "premeditated effort to thwart the OIC's investigation." That is arrant nonsense....

[T]he managers advance the baseless charge that the president intentionally placed the beginning of his relationship with Ms. Lewinsky in 1996 rather than 1995 as she testified. Interestingly, they don't even purport to offer any support for this charge....

Next, the managers assert that the president's admission that he engaged in wrongful conduct "on certain occasions" was false because the president actually engaged in such conduct some 11 times, and...that when the president admitted he had occasional telephone conversations that included inappropriate discussions, that was false because they had actually had 17 such phone conversations.... Assuming that the majority is correct in its assumption that there were 11 or 17, can anyone imagine a trial...in which the issue of whether "certain occasions" by definition could not mean 17 and "occasionally" could not refer to 11 would be the issue being litigated?

...So, thus, the perjury charge in Article I again comes down to the same allegations contained in the independent counsel's referral, that the president lied to the grand jury about two things—his...personal subjective understanding of the definition used in the *Jones* deposition and, second, he lied when he denied that he engaged in certain details of inappropriate conduct.

Now, to conclude that the president lied to the grand jury about his relationship with Ms. Lewinsky, you must determine—forgive me—that he touched certain parts of her body, but for proof you have only her oath against his oath.

Those among you who have been prosecutors or criminal defense lawyers know that perjury prosecutions, as rare as they are, would never be pursued under evidence available here....

Common sense also is enough to tell you that there cannot be any basis for charging a witness with perjury on the ground that you disbelieve his testimony about his own subjective belief in a definition of a term used in a civil deposition....

Now, undeterred in its search for some ground on which to base the charge that the president lied to the grand jury, Article I abandons even the modest level of specificity found in the independent counsel's referral and advances the claim: "The president gave perjurious, false and misleading testimony regarding prior statements of the same nature he made in his deposition."

... To the extent one can determine what the Judiciary Committee had in mind when it drafted this clause, it appears that they intended to charge the president with perjury before the grand jury because he testified that he believed—believed—that he had... "worked through the minefield of the *Jones* deposition without violating the law." And that they hoped to support that charge by reference to various allegedly false statements in his deposition as charged in Article II. Unhappily for the managers, however, the House rejected Article II.... Moreover, there is not a single suggestion in the committee debate—or, more importantly, in the House debate—that those voting to impeach the president believed that this one line that I have quoted to you from the president's grand jury testimony, somehow absorbed into Article I his entire deposition testimony.... [T]he managers cannot be allowed to rely on what the Judiciary Committee thought were false statements encompassed in a rejected Article II to flesh out the unconstitutionally nonspecific charges of Article I....

Now, Article I next alleges that the president lied to the grand jury about the events surrounding certain statements made by Mr. Bennett during the *Jones* deposition....

Now, as we noted earlier, Mr. Bennett argued to Judge Wright that, in light of Ms. Lewinsky's affidavit denying a relationship, the *Jones* lawyers had no good-faith basis for questioning the president about her. The president was not involved in the lengthy back and forth among the judge, the *Jones* lawyers, and Mr. Bennett. He said nothing. When he was asked in the grand jury about Mr. Bennett's statement, he said, "I'm not even sure I paid much attention to what Mr. Bennett was saying."

Now, the managers assert that this is false because the videotape shows that the president was in fact paying attention. But a fairer view of the videotape,

I suggest to you, shows the president... giving no sign that he was following the discussion. ...

I move, now, to the allegations in Article II charging the president with obstruction of justice in the *Jones* lawsuit and in the grand jury investigation. ...

The managers, as was true of the majority report—and the independent counsel role before that—build their theory in this case not on any pillars of obstruction but on shifting sand castles of speculation. Monica Lewinsky met with the president on December 28, 1997, sometime shortly before 8 a.m. to exchange Christmas presents. According to Ms. Lewinsky, they briefly discussed the subject of gifts she had received from the president in connection with her receipt some days earlier of the subpoena in the *Jones* case, and this was the first and the only time, she says, in which the subject was ever discussed. Now, the managers quote one conversation of Ms. Lewinsky's description of that December 28 version as follows:

At some point I said to him, well, you know, should I—maybe I should put the gifts away outside my house somewhere or give them to someone, maybe Betty. And he sort of said—I think he responded "I don't know," or "let me think about that," and left that topic.

But the Senate should know that in fact Ms. Lewinsky has discussed this very exchange on at least 10 different occasions and... in many of her versions she said, among other things, there really was no response... that she didn't have a clear image in her mind what to do next.... And, most importantly, in not a single one of her multiple versions... did she say that the president ever initiated any discussion about the gifts, nor did he ever suggest to her that she conceal them.

Now, there being no evidence of obstruction in that conversation, the managers would have you believe that after Ms. Lewinsky left the White House that day, the president must have told Betty Currie to retrieve the gifts from Ms. Lewinsky. But there is absolutely no evidence that that discussion ever occurred. The only two parties who would have knowledge of it, the president and Ms. Currie, both denied it. ...

[I]n the absence of any such evidence, the managers have relied on Ms. Lewinsky's testimony that Ms. Currie placed a call to her and told her... either that the president had said to Betty Ms. Lewinsky had something for her or merely that she, Ms. Currie, understood that Ms. Lewinsky had something for her.

In this regard, it is important to remember that Ms. Lewinsky herself testified that she was the one who first raised with the president the notion that Ms. Currie could hold the gifts. And it is important to recognize that, contrary to the managers' suggestion to you that Ms. Lewinsky's memory of this event has always been consistent ... she herself acknowledged at her last grand jury appearance that her memory of the crucial conversation is less than crystal clear. To wit:

A Juror: Do you remember Betty Currie saying that the president had told her to call?

Ms. Lewinsky: Right now, I don't remember.

Ruff now turned to his first example of what he called prosecutorial "fudge." He stated the managers' version of the gift exchange. In their view, Ruff said, Currie must be wrong in saying that Lewinsky instigated the exchange, because a cell phone record showed Currie calling Lewinsky at 3:32 P.M. that day. But, Ruff argued, there was a problem: Lewinsky had testified three times that Betty Currie had actually picked up the gifts at 2 P.M. In addition, said Ruff, "the only reasonable explanation" for the fact that the president had given her new gifts on the day he was supposedly conspiring to conceal the old ones was precisely what the president had told the grand jury: "He was simply not concerned about gifts."

Ruff continued:

The next point I want to discuss with you is the statements the president made to Betty Currie on the day after the *Jones* deposition, January 18 of last year. ...

The managers [say] ... that the president attempted to influence the testimony of a "witness" by pressuring Ms. Currie to agree with an inaccurate version of the facts surrounding his relationship with Ms. Lewinsky.

President Clinton has adamantly denied that he had any such intention, and that denial is fortified by the indisputable factual record establishing that Betty Currie neither was an actual or a contemplated witness in the *Jones* litigation, nor did she perceive that she was being pressured in any respect. ...

First ... in the only proceeding the president knew about at that moment, the *Jones* case, Ms. Currie was neither an actual nor a prospective witness. ... In the entire history of the *Jones* case, Ms. Currie's name had not appeared on any of the witness lists. ...

Despite the prosecutor's best efforts to coax Ms. Currie into saying she was pressured to agree with the president, Ms. Currie adamantly denied it.

Now, to understand on a human level why the president reached out to Betty Currie on the day after his deposition, you need only to understand that he had just faced unexpected detailed questions about his worst nightmare. As he candidly admitted to the grand jury, he had long feared that his relationship with Ms. Lewinsky would ultimately become public. Now, with questioning about her in the *Jones* case, publication of the first Internet article, the day of reckoning had arrived. The president knew that a media storm was about to erupt. And it did....

The president of the United States did not tamper with a witness.

Now next, the managers argue that Mr. Clinton corruptly encouraged Ms. Lewinsky to submit a false affidavit to the *Jones* lawyers and to lie if she were ever deposed. But the uncontroverted evidence refutes that charge. Indeed, Ms. Lewinsky herself has repeatedly and forcefully denied that anyone ever asked her to lie....

Left with this record, the managers resort to arguing that Ms. Lewinsky understood that the president wanted her to lie, that he could not have wanted her to file an affidavit detailing their relationship. But the only factual support for this theory recited by the majority is the testimony of Ms. Lewinsky that, while the president never encouraged her to lie, he remained silent about what she should have to say or do, and by such silence she said, "I knew what he meant."...

So to bolster their flawed...theory, the managers assert that the president knew the affidavit would have to be false in order for Ms. Lewinsky to avoid testifying. But the evidence here, too, is that the president repeatedly testified that Ms. Lewinsky could and would file a truthful affidavit. And, of course, Ms. Lewinsky herself has made it clear that her definition of the critical term that might be used in such an affidavit was consistent with the president's....

Further testimony from Ms. Lewinsky herself repudiates any suggestion that she was ever encouraged by anyone to lie if she were deposed in the *Jones* case. In a colloquy with a grand juror, she explicitly and unequivocally rejected the notion that President Clinton encouraged her to deny the relationship after she learned she was a witness. Referring to discussions about the so-called cover stories...a grand juror asked her:

It is possible that you had these discussions after you learned that you were a witness in the *Paula Jones* case?
Answer: I don't believe so, no.
Question: Can you exclude that possibility?
Answer: I pretty much can.

The managers would have you conclude the contrary from a brief snippet of the conversation on December 17 in which Ms. Lewinsky said that at some point, "I don't know if it was before or after the subject of the affidavit came up, the president sort of said, 'Well, you know, you can always say you were coming to see Betty or that you were bringing me letters.' "

But Ms. Lewinsky told the FBI when she was interviewed... "To the best of Miss Lewinsky's memory, she does not believe they discussed"—in this December 17 conversation—"the content of any deposition that Miss Lewinsky might be involved in at a later date." And she told the grand jury the same thing....

... Fourth, Article II alleges that the president obstructed justice by denying to his closest aides he had a sexual relationship with Monica Lewinsky.... These allegedly impeachable denials took place in the immediate aftermath of the public revelation of the Lewinsky matter, at the very time that the president was denying that relationship to the entire country on national television. Having made the announcement to the whole country, it is simply absurd, I suggest to you, to believe that he was somehow attempting corruptly to influence his senior staff when he told them virtually the same thing at the same time....

Now we come to the last of the obstruction charges. The managers ask you to find that the president of the United States employed his friend, Vernon Jordan, to get Monica Lewinsky a job in New York, to influence her testimony, or perhaps in a somewhat forlorn effort... to hide from the *Jones* lawyers...

There is, of course, absolutely no evidence to support this conclusion, and so the managers have constructed out of sealing wax and string and spiders' webs a theory that would lend to a series of otherwise innocuous and, indeed, exculpatory events, a dark and sinister past.

The undisputed record establishes the following: One, that Lewinsky's job search began on her own initiative; two, the search began long before her involvement in the *Jones* case; three, the search had no connection to the *Jones* case; four, Vernon Jordan agreed to help her, not at the direction of the president but at the request of Ms. Currie, Mr. Jordan's long-time friend; five, the idea to solicit Mr. Jordan's assistance again came not from the president, but from Ms. Tripp.

... Both Ms. Lewinsky and Mr. Jordan have repeatedly testified that there was never an agreement, a suggestion, an implication, that Ms. Lewinsky would be rewarded with a job for her silence or her false testimony. As Mr. Jordan succinctly put it, "Unequivocally, indubitably, no."

It was only to appease Ms. Tripp that Ms. Lewinsky ultimately told her that she had told Mr. Jordan she wouldn't sign the affidavit until she had a job....

Now while the managers dismiss as irrelevant Ms. Lewinsky's job search before December, the fact is, Ms. Lewinsky contemplated looking for a job in New York as early as July 1997, and her interest was strengthened in early October when Ms. Tripp told her it was unlikely she would ever get another job in the White House. It was then Ms. Tripp and Ms. Lewinsky discussed the prospect of having Vernon Jordan help her get a job in New York and Ms. Lewinsky mentioned that idea to the president.

Later in October, ... Ambassador Richardson agreed to interview Ms. Lewinsky at the suggestion of then-Deputy Chief of Staff Podesta who had been asked to help by Ms. Currie. And Ambassador Richardson offered her a job and she ... didn't actually turn it down until early January....

Meanwhile, now we come to what, for the managers, is the very heart of the case. On November 5, Ms. Lewinsky had a preliminary meeting with Mr. Jordan and they discussed a list of potential employers. And although the managers then contend that nothing happened from November 5, that first meeting, until December 11, signifying, as they see it, that it must have been Ms. Lewinsky's appearance on the witness list that galvanized Mr. Jordan into action, that is simply false.

Ms. Lewinsky had a follow-up telephone conversation with Mr. Jordan around Thanksgiving in which he told her he was working on the job search and he asked her to call him in the first week of December. The president learned Ms. Lewinsky was on the *Jones* witness list sometime on December 6. He met with Mr. Jordan the very next day, December 7. But oddly, if one adopts the managers' view, there was no discussion of Ms. Lewinsky or the *Jones* case, much less job searches. Then on December 8, Ms. Lewinsky called Mr. Jordan's office and made her appointment to meet with him on December 11.

[T]he president absolutely had nothing to do with that ... and Mr. Jordan denies that there was any intensified effort to find Ms. Lewinsky a job. He said,

"Oh, no, I do not recall any heightened sense of urgency in December, but what I do recall is that I dealt with it when I had time to do it."

Now for my second example of prosecutorial fudging. The managers have devoted much attention to the magic date of December 11, arguing vigorously that it was on that day that getting the job for Ms. Lewinsky suddenly became a matter of high priority for the president and hence to Mr. Jordan. Why is that so? Well, again, I will let the majority counsel for the Judiciary Committee tell you in his own words...:

> ...On the morning of December 11, 1997, Judge Susan Webber Wright ordered that Paula Jones was entitled to information regarding any state or federal employee with whom the president had sexual relations or proposed or sought to have sexual relations. To keep Monica on the team was now of critical importance....

That same theme was picked up last week by Mr. Manager Hutchinson....

Let me show you the official report of the judge's discussion with the lawyers in the *Jones* case on that date.... There's a conference call between the judge and the lawyers, which is memorialized in a formal document prepared by a clerk.... It notes that the conference call began at 5:33 p.m. central standard time. If I have my calculations right, that is 6:33 p.m. in Washington.

I want to stop here for a second so that you know where Mr. Jordan was when that happened....

> I was actually on a plane for Amsterdam by the time the judge issued her order.... I left on United flight 946 at 5:55 from Dulles Airport and landed in Amsterdam the next morning.

So the conference call begins at 6:33 eastern standard time. The...judge didn't even tell the lawyers that she was going to issue an order on the motion to compel these various depositions until the very end of the call, around 7:45 eastern standard time....

...To summarize, let me show you...what the real sequence of events was on December 11. Vernon Jordan makes a possible job call at 9:45, and another at 12:49, and another at 1:07; he meets with Ms. Lewinsky from 1:15 to 1:45; he gets on his plane at 5:55 in the afternoon, and an hour or so later the lawyers are informed that the judge had issued her order....

Ruff then summarized the sinister link the managers purported to see between the signing of the false affidavit and the job offer Lewinsky received from Revlon. No such link, he said: Lewinsky was well on her way to winning the Revlon job before Jordan's phone call on her behalf to the CEO of Revlon's parent company. "So much for obstruction by job search," said Ruff.

Let me be very clear. We do not believe that president Clinton committed any of the offenses charged by the managers....

But suppose we are wrong. Suppose that you find that the president committed one or more of the offenses charged. Then there remains only one issue before you. Whatever your feelings may be about William Clinton, the man, or William Clinton, the political ally or opponent, or William Clinton, the father and husband, ask only this: Should William Clinton, the president, be removed from office? Are we at that horrific moment in our history when our Union could be preserved only by taking the step that the framers saw as the last resort?...

I close as I opened.... William Jefferson Clinton is not guilty of the charges that have been brought against him of committing perjury. He didn't obstruct justice. He must not be removed from office....

The Senate adjourned. That evening, the president gave his State of the Union address to a joint session of Congress. Henry Hyde and Bob Barr did not attend, although the rest of the House managers did.
On Wednesday, January 20, Chief Justice Rehnquist recognized Gregory Craig.

Mr. Craig: ... Article I accuses the president of having given perjurious, false, and misleading testimony to the grand jury concerning one or more of four different subject areas. It is noteworthy that the second and third subject areas are attempts to revisit the president's deposition testimony in the *Jones* case. There was an article that was proposed alleging that the president also committed perjury in the... *Jones* deposition. That article was rejected by the House of Representatives.... Those allegations have been dismissed, and you must not allow the managers to revive them....

You will notice that the third and the fourth subject areas correspond to, coincide, and overlap with many of the allegations of obstruction of justice in Article II. This represents a kind of double charging.... One, the defendant is charged with the core offense; second, the defendant is charged with denying the core offense under oath.... [I]t is a dubious prosecutorial practice that is frowned upon by most courts.

The upshot, though ... is that if you conclude, as I trust you will, that the evidence that the president engaged in obstruction of justice is insufficient to support that charge, it would follow logically that the president's denial that he engaged in any such activity would be respected. ...

Craig then turned to Article I. By failing to specify what the alleged perjury was, he argued, it "violated the president's right to due process." In addition, Craig said, failing to be specific meant that the House had "effectively and unconstitutionally" ceded its authority to the managers, giving them enormous power over just what the president would be charged with.

Craig summed up the "moving target" history of the charges since the original referral, which had suggested three "moderately specific" incidents of perjury, through the presentation of the majority counsel in the Judiciary Committee, which specified different claims, to the drafting of the four proposed articles of impeachment.

Then, said Craig, just three days before the vote in the full House, the committee majority released its report, which argued that the president had made "a whole host of perjurious statements before the grand jury, some statements that ... had never been identified, charged, discussed or debated." And now in the Senate, said Craig, the allegations were "still changing, still expanding, still increasing in number."

Finally, said Craig, the House managers continued to try to "stretch the scope of Article I" to cover the allegations of perjury in the Jones deposition that had been rejected by the House. This case, Craig insisted, "is about the grand jury and the grand jury alone." But the managers' tactic had created great confusion about what the president had actually said to the grand jury.

Craig pleaded with the Senate to "look at the real record" of the grand jury testimony. He continued:

Now, it is timely, I think, to talk a little bit about legalisms and technicalities and hairsplitting because those who have engaged in this process over the past months in this enterprise of defending the president have also been the subject of much criticism. The majority counsel ... urged the Members of the Senate and the House to pay no attention to the "obfuscations and legalistic pyrotechnics of the president's defenders." ...

To the extent that we have relied on overly legal or technical arguments to defend the president from his attackers, we apologize to him, to you, and to the American public. We do the president no earthly good if, in the course of defending him, we offend both the judges, the jurors, and the American public. ...

Allegations of legal crimes invite, indeed they call out for legal defenses.... In fact...the mere act of alleging perjury invites precisely the kind of hair-splitting everyone seems to deplore....

Courts have concluded that no one should be convicted of perjury without demonstrating that the testimony in question was, in fact, false; that the person testifying knew it to be false; and that the testimony involved an issue that is material to the case, one that could influence the outcome of the matter one way or another. In addition, courts and prosecutors are in general agreement that prosecutions for perjury should not be brought on the basis of an oath against an oath....

Ladies and gentlemen of the Senate, when we presented our case to the Judiciary Committee last December, we invited five experienced prosecutors to examine the record of this case and to give us their views as to whether they would bring charges of perjury and obstruction of justice...based on that record.... All were in agreement that no responsible prosecutor would bring this case against President Clinton....

I would like to make one additional point about the...Starr prosecutors. They, as you know, have had a long and difficult relationship with the White House.... Their standard for making a referral is presumably much lower than the standard you would expect from the managers in making a case for the removal of the president in an article of impeachment....

But these lawyers, Mr. Starr and his fellow prosecutors, did not see fit to allege most of the charges that we are discussing today....

This should cause the Members of the Senate some concern and some additional reason to give very careful scrutiny to these charges. When you do, you will find the following: The allegations are frequently trivial, almost always technical, often immaterial and always insubstantial. Certainly not a good or justifiable basis for removing any president from office....

Subpart 1 has to do with testimony about the nature and details of the relationship with Monica Lewinsky.

I begin with what is identified in the majority report as "direct lies." First, the managers claim that the president perjured himself before the grand jury, that he told a direct lie and should be removed from office because in his prepared statement he acknowledged having inappropriate contact with Ms. Lewinsky on "certain occasions." This was a "direct lie," say the managers, because, according to Ms. Lewinsky, between November 15, 1995, and December 28, 1997, they were alone at least 20 times and had, she says, 11 sexual encounters. . . .

The managers also say that the president lied to the grand jury . . . because the president acknowledged that "on occasion" he had telephone conversations that included sexual banter . . . when the managers say the president and Ms. Lewinsky had 17 such . . . telephone conversations over a two-year period of time. . . .

Now, there are 774 days in the time span between November 1995 and December 1997. I submit that it is not . . . dishonest to describe their activity, which Ms. Lewinsky claims occurred on 11 different days . . . as having occurred "on certain occasions." . . . And the same could be said for the use of the words "on occasion" . . . to describe 17 telephone conversations that included explicit sexual language. . . .

There is simply no way . . . that a reasonable person can look at this testimony and conclude—or agree with the managers—that it is a "direct lie." . . . Does anyone here really believe that Members of the House of Representatives would have voted to approve these allegations as the basis for impeaching and removing this president if they had been given the chance with specific, identified perjurious testimony in a proposed article of impeachment? . . .

The president is also accused of lying before the grand jury . . . because, in the prepared statement that he read to the grand jury in August, he acknowledged that he engaged in inappropriate conduct with Ms. Lewinsky "on certain occasions in early 1996 and once in 1997." The managers call this a "direct lie" because the president did not mention 1995. . . ."

This allegation involves an utterly meaningless disparity in testimony. . . . The most likely explanation here is that there was an honest difference in recollection. There is no dispute about the critical facts that Ms. Lewinsky was young, very young, too young, when she got involved with President Clinton. But her age didn't change between November 1995 and January 1996. Her birthday is in July. She was 22 years old in November and 22 years old in January. . . . Nothing of any importance in the case took place between December 1995 and January 1996. She was an intern in the early stage of that period, and she became a Government employee. So it did not change the relationship that she had with the president. It modified her title. . . .

It is unreasonable to argue, as we heard from the House managers last week, that if you believe Ms. Lewinsky and disbelieve the president on this issue as to which date was the date that they began the relationship . . . that you must convict the president and remove him from office. . . .

Craig now turned to the president's grand jury testimony that his encounters with Lewinsky did not constitute "sexual relations." It was important to understand, he said, that the president was dealing with two definitions. There was his own, in which the phrase meant only sexual intercourse; that definition, said Craig, matched both dictionary definitions and Monica Lewinsky's, as shown on one of the Linda Tripp tapes. Then there was the second, the one supplied by Paula Jones' lawyers at his deposition. Craig showed a videotape of the discussion between the lawyers and Judge Wright on the definition; in it, Robert Bennett, the president's attorney, urges the Jones lawyers to scrap the "confusing" definition and simply ask the president straightforward questions. They refuse. The judge then tries to simplify the definition by striking out certain elements. Craig called to the senators' attention that one part she struck out "more closely approximates what went on between Ms. Lewinsky and the president" than the slimmed-down definition the president had to deal with.

The bottom line, Craig argued, was this: "To contend that he is committing perjury when he told the grand jury that he genuinely believed his interpretation of the definition—that is just speculation about what is in his mind and it is not the stuff or fuel of a perjury prosecution." And he played another excerpt from Tom Sullivan's committee testimony, in which Sullivan called the president's interpretation "reasonable" and repeated that no responsible prosecutor would try to convict him on such a matter.

He continued:

The managers place great emphasis and weight on the conflict in the testimony between President Clinton and Ms. Lewinsky over some specific intimate details related to their activity…. What do they disagree about? Not about whether the president and Ms. Lewinsky had a wrongful relationship—the president admitted that before the grand jury. Not about whether the president and Ms. Lewinsky were alone together—the president admitted that before the grand jury. Not about whether, when they were alone together, their relationship included inappropriate, intimate contact—the president admitted that before the grand jury…. Not about whether the president and Ms. Lewinsky wanted to keep their wrongful relationship a secret—the president admitted that before the grand jury.

The difference in their testimony about their relationship is limited to some very specific, very intimate details…. The true nub of the managers' allegation that the president committed perjury is that he described some of the contact one way and she describes it another….

298 THE IMPEACHMENT AND TRIAL OF PRESIDENT CLINTON

According to those experienced prosecutors who testified before the Judiciary Committee, there are two more points to be made about this. First, this is a classic oath on oath—he says, she says—swearing match, that, under ordinary custom and practice at the Department of Justice, never would be prosecuted without substantial corroborative proof....

... The allegations of perjury here have to do with testimony that [the president] gave at the grand jury about his deposition in the *Jones* case. And I begin by repeating a point that I made a little earlier, that the House of Representatives did not vote to approve the article that alleged that President Clinton committed perjury during his deposition in the *Jones* case....

But...in subpart 2 of Article I, the managers seek to reintroduce the issue of the president's testimony in the case by alleging that when the president testified before the grand jury, he testified falsely when he said that he tried to testify truthfully in the *Jones* deposition.... Mr. Manager Rogan has claimed that the president's answers ratified and reaffirmed and put into issue all of his answers in the *Jones* deposition....

But, in fact, President Clinton did not ratify, he did not reaffirm his *Jones* testimony when he testified before the grand jury.... If you look at that transcript carefully, you will find that without admitting wrongdoing, the president elaborated, he modified, he amended and he clarified his testimony in *Jones*....

But actually the specific wording of subpart 2 ... is not illuminating, and we turn to the managers' trial brief to ascertain precisely what the argument is. There the managers allege that the president falsely testified that he answered questions truthfully at his deposition concerning, among other things, whether he had been alone with Ms. Lewinsky....

... The prosecutors asked the president many questions about being alone with Ms. Lewinsky, but they never asked him about the *Jones* testimony....

"When I was alone with Ms. Lewinsky on certain occasions," it says right there—"When I was alone ..." And then you will see over two or three pages of testimony he tries to recall times and incidents when he was alone with Ms. Lewinsky....

This is not a man denying that he was alone with Ms. Lewinsky, but he was not asked about his testimony on that topic when he testified in the *Jones* case.

Now, the managers further allege that the president's testimony before the grand jury that he testified truthfully at his deposition was a lie. In fact, his testimony there that they quote as being false was this: "My goal in this deposition was to be truthful but not particularly helpful.... I was determined to walk through the minefield of this deposition without violating the law, and I believe I did." His statement that "I believe I did," they say, means that everything that he said in the *Jones* deposition was true....

...By claiming that the president's assertions in the grand jury were false when he described his state of mind...the managers seek to put out all of the president's evasive and misleading testimony in the *Jones* deposition in issue. That effort, I submit, should be rejected....

Subpart 3...has to do with the president's testimony about statements he allowed his attorney to make to a federal judge in the *Jones* case....

According to the trial memorandum, the president remained silent during the *Jones* deposition at a time when his counsel, Mr. Bennett, made false and misleading representations to the court about Ms. Lewinsky's affidavit.... [W]hen asked by the independent counsel about this moment before the grand jury, the president testified that he hadn't paid much attention, that he was thinking about his testimony....

Now, in support of their claim that the president lied when he said he was not paying attention, the House managers point to the videotape record of the president's testimony which shows, they argue, that the president was "looking directly at Mr. Bennett, [and] paying close attention to his argument to Judge Wright."...While the videotape shows that the president was looking in Bennett's direction, there is nothing that can be read in his face or in his body language to show that he is listening to, understanding, or affirming Mr. Bennett's statement—no nod of the head, no movement at all, no comment, nothing....

It is hard to believe that the House managers...believe that the Senate should conclude that the president committed perjury and should be removed from his office on the basis of his silence, his failure to speak.

Now, there is a second allegation associated with this incident.... This has to do with the president's now famous testimony about Mr. Bennett's statement about Ms. Lewinsky's affidavit. "It depends what the meaning of 'is' is."...

While raising questions about the good faith of the *Jones* attorney in asking questions about Ms. Lewinsky...Mr. Bennett said, referring to the *Jones* lawyers, "Counsel is fully aware that [Ms. Lewinsky] has filed an affidavit saying that there is absolutely no sex...of any kind in any manner, shape or form with President Clinton."

Now, during his grand jury testimony, the independent counsel reads that statement to the president.... And here is what the independent counsel says to President Clinton ...:

> That statement is a completely false statement. Whether or not Mr. Bennett knew of your relationship with Ms. Lewinsky, the statement that there is "no sex of any kind, manner shape or form with President Clinton" was an utterly false statement.

And he asks the president, "Is that correct?" At that point, pausing just a moment for reflection, President Clinton gives his opinion and explains that opinion....

Now, the president makes a political mistake here and gives in to his instinct to play his own lawyer, to be his own advocate. You may find it frustrating, you may find it irritating...but he is not committing perjury; he is committing the offense of nit-picking.... He is arguing a point.... Mr. Bennett's statement is true if "is" means an ongoing relationship, but Mr. Bennett's statement is false if "is" means at any time ever in time....

There is one final point...because, again, I think there was a mischaracterization of what the president actually said in the grand jury. He didn't say that at the time Mr. Bennett made that statement in the *Jones* deposition, he caught the word "is" and recognized, "Ah-ha, I've got an exit. That makes it accurate." Quite the contrary. He is clear in front of the grand jury when he says that he didn't even notice this issue until he was reviewing the transcript in preparation for his grand jury testimony....

Subpart 4 of this article has to do with false and misleading testimony about the president's efforts, allegedly, to influence witnesses and to impede discovery in *Jones*....

According to the managers, the general language of this provision of subpart 4 is supposed to include a wide range of allegations.... All of these allegations are more properly part of our defense on the obstruction of justice allegation. But I will try to respond briefly to the allegation of perjury, his testimony about Monica Lewinsky's false affidavit. This grows out of the president's conversation with Ms. Lewinsky, allegedly, on December 17, in which he is said to have corruptly encouraged Ms. Lewinsky to execute a sworn affidavit that he knew to be perjurious, false, and misleading.

In that famous late-night telephone conversation, Ms. Lewinsky asked the president what she could do if she were subpoenaed in the *Jones* case. According to Ms. Lewinsky, the president responded, "Well, maybe you can sign an affidavit." That is what Ms. Lewinsky's recollection is.

Now, in the grand jury, the president was repeatedly questioned about this conversation and he repeatedly answered emphatically.... He truly thought, he said, that she could have sworn out an honest affidavit. The managers claim that when he said that—that he thought that she could swear out an honest affidavit—the president perjured himself....

Now, the heart of the managers' argument is that there was no way that an honest affidavit can achieve what the president and Ms. Lewinsky both wanted to have achieved, which was to avoid her having to testify. And so the managers claim the president's statement that he thought she could make out an honest affidavit and avoid testifying in the *Jones* case about her relationship with the president is perjury....

Now, Ms. Lewinsky's inappropriate contact with the president was consensual. An affidavit being sought in a case involving allegations of sexual harassment that says there was no harassment, no effort to impose unwanted sexual overtures, would have been an affidavit that Ms. Lewinsky could honestly execute—an affidavit stating that she had never been on the receiving end of any unwanted sexual overtures from the president and that she had never been harassed.

Second, both Ms. Lewinsky and the president had a definition of "sexual relations" that would have allowed Ms. Lewinsky ... honestly and accurately, in their view, to swear an affidavit that she had never had sexual relations ... with the president....

The second element is the president's testimony about the gifts. The managers' trial brief says that the president committed perjury when he testified that he told Ms. Lewinsky that if the *Jones* lawyers requested the gifts that he had given to her, she should provide them....

Now, the only evidence offered to support the allegation that the president testified falsely before the grand jury on this topic is, A, that Ms. Lewinsky raised a question with the president as to what she should do with the gifts. You have heard a lot of testimony about that, which only establishes one thing—that the topic came up. That is totally consistent with the president's testimony.... The second piece of evidence is that Ms. Currie ended up picking up the gifts and taking them home with her, which ... simply cannot be construed as evidence showing that the president perjured himself when he told the grand jury that he had given this advice to Ms. Lewinsky....

This allegation is all conjecture and there is no evidence. It is really astonishing that the managers would seriously include it in their case....

... The president's meeting and conversation with Betty Currie on Sunday, January 18.... And so, once again, we begin with a question: What is it precisely that the president said that is at the heart of this allegation of perjury? In his presentation last Thursday, Congressman Rogan quoted lengthy passages from a number of President Clinton's answers on the subject but failed to identify anything specific. Finally Congressman Rogan said this:

> When [the president] testified he was only making statements to Ms. Currie to ascertain what the facts were, trying to ascertain what Betty's perception was, this statement was false, and it was perjurious. We know it was perjury because the president called Ms. Currie into the White House the day after his deposition to tell her—not to ask her, to tell her—that he was never alone with Monica Lewinsky. To tell her that Ms. Currie could always hear or see them, and to tell her that he never touched Monica Lewinsky. These were false statements, and he knew that the statements were false at the time he made them to Betty Currie.

... I confess to some confusion about what perjury Congressman Rogan is really alleging here. It seems to me that he has moved from the world of perjury in Article I to the world of obstruction....

The trial brief is more specific. They claim that the testimony was false when the president went in and said that he was "trying to refresh [his] memory about what the facts were"; when he said that he wanted to "know what Betty's memory was about what she heard"; and when he said he was "trying to get as much information as he could." The purpose of the meeting and the conversation, according to the Trial Brief, was to influence Betty Currie's testimony, not to gather information.

In truth, the president gave a number of different reasons to the grand jury for seeking out Betty Currie and talking to her about Monica Lewinsky, and it is totally plausible to conclude that the last thing on the president's mind at that particular moment was Betty Currie's potential role as a witness in a federal court....

Finally, the...allegation is that when the president testified in front of the grand jury and denied that he misled his aides or told them false things, that it was "perjurious, false and misleading testimony" because he was really trying to use them to obstruct justice and influence the grand jury....

In fact, if you look at that testimony...the president acknowledged that he misled an aide and he apologized for it. And he testified that actually he couldn't remember much of what he told his aide. He never challenged or denied what John Podesta said that he told him....And he never challenged Sidney Blumenthal's version of what he said to Mr. Blumenthal. There is absolutely no evidence to suggest that the president intended to deceive the grand jury on this matter because he never denied saying what they said he told them about his relationship....

He did not give the testimony that Congressman Rogan claims that he gave. He did not say that he did not mislead his aides. He said that he had, in fact, misled his aide. He does say that he tried to tell true things, but he does not conceal the nature of the true things he is talking about....He described them for all to see and understand. For example, he says that he told his aides, "I never had sex with her," as it was defined in his mind. You may disagree with his characterization...but he certainly doesn't conceal the basis of his belief that it is true. He also said that he was not involved with Ms. Lewinsky in any sexual way. And he explains by use of the present tense he thought that was a true thing.

But the materiality of this alleged perjury is really a mystery....The only issue here is whether the president, when he discussed Monica Lewinsky with these aides, was seeking to influence the grand jury's proceedings by giving his aides false information. This is not a perjury challenge. This is a subject to be dealt with in the context of Article II and obstruction of justice.

...One of the arguments most frequently employed to urge the president's removal is that in the United States of America no one is above the law; that if the Senate does not take action against the president and convict him and remove him from office, we will not be keeping faith with that principle.

Members of the Senate, I could not disagree more with that formulation of this issue. The principle that "No one is above the Law" is sacred. The idea that the wealthy or the powerful or the famous should receive preferential treatment under the law—treatment that is different from that accorded to the poor and the weak—is anathema to everything that is great and good and special about the United States....

But the framers, in their genius, did not design or intend the awesome power of impeachment and removal for the purpose of vindicating the rule of law. They believed that the power of impeachment and removal should be used for a different purpose—to protect the body politic, to protect the Government itself from a president whose conduct was so abusive as to constitute...a threat to the entire system....

Ladies and gentlemen of the Senate, you must do your duty as you see it..., But, truly, these articles do not justify the nullification of the American people's free choice in a national election.... Do not let this case and these charges, as flawed and as unfair as they are, destroy a fundamental underpinning of American democracy, the right of the people, and no one else, to select the president of the United States.

William Jefferson Clinton is not guilty of obstruction of justice. He is not guilty of perjury. He must not be removed....

After a brief recess, the chief justice recognized White House deputy counsel Cheryl Mills.

Ms. Mills: ... So let's talk about the allegation of obstruction of justice, about the box of gifts that Ms. Currie received from Ms. Lewinsky....

To be fair, the House managers acknowledged up front that their case is largely circumstantial. They are right....

Now, let's go through their story piece by piece. On December 19, Monica Lewinsky was served with a subpoena in the *Jones* case. The subpoena required her to testify at a deposition in January 1998, and also to produce each and every gift given to her by the president. This statement is factually accurate. It does not, however, convey the entire state of affairs. Ms. Lewinsky told the FBI that when she got the subpoena she wanted the gifts out of her apartment. Why? Because she suspected that lawyers for *Jones* would break into her apartment looking for gifts.... The managers entirely disregarded Ms. Lewinsky's own independent motivations for wanting to move the gifts.

Let's continue. On December 28, 1997, Ms. Lewinsky and the president met in the Oval Office to exchange Christmas gifts, at which time they discussed the fact that the lawyers in the *Jones* case had subpoenaed all of the gifts from the president to Ms. Lewinsky.... Ms. Lewinsky asked the president whether she should put away the gifts out of her house some place, or give them to someone, maybe Betty. At that time, according to Ms. Lewinsky, the president said, "Let me think about it."

The House managers have consistently described the December 28 meeting exactly this way, as did the majority counsel for the House Judiciary, as did the Office of Independent Counsel.... But it is not the whole truth. It is not the full record. Ms. Lewinsky actually gave 10 renditions of her conversation with the president.... Invariably, the one most cited is the one least favorable to the president. But even in that version...no one claims he ordered, suggested, or even hinted that anyone obstruct justice....

But what about the nine other versions?... You may have never heard, for example, this version of their conversation. This is Ms. Lewinsky speaking.

It was December 28th and I was there to get my Christmas gifts from him...and we spent maybe about five minutes or so, not very long, talking about the case. And I said to him, "Well, do you think"...and I don't think I said get rid of, but I said, "Do you think I should put away or maybe give to Betty or give someone the gifts?" And he—I don't remember his response. It was something like, "I don't know," or "hmm" or there was really no response.

Mills produced two more versions of Lewinsky's testimony concerning the gifts. In both, the president's response was very vague; in one, Lewinsky said "he really didn't discuss it."

Why haven't we heard these versions? Because they weaken an already fragile circumstantial case. If Ms. Lewinsky says that the president doesn't respond at all, then there is absolutely no evidence for the House managers' obstruction of justice theory.... It is those facts, those stubborn facts, that just don't fit.

But the most significant detail the managers disregard because it doesn't fit is the president's testimony. The president testified that he told Ms. Lewinsky that she had to give the *Jones* lawyers whatever gifts she had.... [W]hy would the president give Ms. Lewinsky gifts if he wanted her to give them right back? The only real explanation is he truly was, as he testified, unconcerned about the gifts. The House managers want you to believe that this gift giving was a show of confidence; that he knew Ms. Lewinsky would conceal them. But then why, under their theory, ask Ms. Currie to go pick them up? Why not know that Ms. Lewinsky is just going to conceal them? Better still, why not just show her the gifts and tell her to come by after the subpoena date has passed?

It simply doesn't make sense....

But let's continue with their version of events.... In telling their story, the managers do concede that there is a conflict in the testimony between Ms.

Lewinsky and Ms. Currie, but they strive mightily to get you to disregard Ms. Currie's testimony by telling you that her memory on the issue of how she came to pick up the gifts was "fuzzy"—fuzzy....

... That is not playing fair by Ms. Currie.... Why? Because Ms. Currie was asked about who initiated the gift pick-up five times. Her answer each time was unequivocal—five times. From the first FBI interview just days after the story broke in the media, to her last grand jury appearance, Ms. Currie repeatedly and unwaveringly testified that it was Ms. Lewinsky who contacted her about the gifts....

... What, then, are the managers talking about when they say that Ms. Currie concedes that Ms. Lewinsky might have a better memory than herself on this issue? They are talking about something a little different; that was whether she, Ms. Currie, had told the president that she had picked up the box of gifts from Ms. Lewinsky. Let's put it in context. After being asked the same question for the fourth time and reiterating for the fourth time that Ms. Lewinsky contacted her about the gifts, the prosecutor asked Ms. Currie:

Well, what if Ms. Lewinsky said that Ms. Currie spoke to the president about receiving the gifts from Ms. Lewinsky?

Ms. Currie responds:

Then she may remember better than I. I don't remember.

... They are asking you to make one of the most awesome decisions the Constitution contemplates. They owe you, they owe the president, they owe the Constitution, and they owe Betty Currie an accurate presentation of the facts.

But what about that supposedly corroborating cell phone call from Betty Currie to Monica Lewinsky on December 28?...

What the managers downplay, as Mr. Ruff discussed yesterday, is the fact that this call to arrange the pickup of the gifts comes after the time Ms. Lewinsky repeatedly testified that the gifts were picked up by Ms. Currie. In citing the cell phone record as corroboration, they also disregard Ms. Currie's testimony that she picked up the gifts leaving from work on her way home; that would have been from Washington to Arlington. That is inconsistent with the call from Arlington....

What next? The House managers...posit this question: Why would Ms. Currie pick up the gifts from Ms. Lewinsky?...Their answer: She must have been ordered to pick up the gifts by the president....

Well, the record before you offers the answer. As Ms. Currie told the FBI during her first interview in January of 1998, Ms. Lewinsky was a friend. She had been helpful and supportive when she was dealing with some very painful personal tragedies. Ms. Currie enjoyed what she saw as a motherly relationship with Ms. Lewinsky.... Why does she agree to hold the box of gifts for Ms. Lewinsky? Because she is a friend. And that is not obstruction of justice....

...The facts clearly do not support their version of events. To believe the managers' version of events, you must not only disbelieve the president, you must also disbelieve Ms. Currie.

Ms. Currie has said that the president did not ask her to pick up the gifts. Ms. Currie has said that Ms. Lewinsky asked her to pick up the gifts. The managers have downplayed Ms. Currie's credibility in this incident. They have urged you to think of her as acting as "a loyal secretary to the president."

Of course she is loyal.... And loyalty and honesty are not mutually exclusive. Betty Currie is a loyal person, and Betty Currie is an honest person.

These are the facts. That is not obstruction of justice....

On January 18, the president talked to Ms. Currie about the *Jones* deposition and in particular about his surprise at some of the questions the *Jones* lawyers had asked about Ms. Lewinsky. In the course of their conversation, the president asked Ms. Currie a series of questions and made some statements about his relationship with Ms. Lewinsky....

The managers' theory is that the president, by his comments, corruptly tried to influence Ms. Currie's potential testimony in the *Jones* case in violation of the obstruction of justice law.... Ms. Currie was not scheduled to be a witness in that case. And, as you will see, the president had other things on his mind.

...I want to begin by focusing on the "corruptly persuade" elements of witness tampering. What does it mean to corruptly persuade?...The U.S. Attorneys' Manual gives some guidance. A prosecution under 1512 would require the Government to prove beyond a reasonable doubt, one, an effort to threaten, force or intimidate another person and; two, an intent to influence the person's testimony. Thus, "corruptly persuade" for career prosecutors requires some element of threat or intimidation or pressure.

Keeping that overview in mind, let's look at the facts. On January 17, 1998, the president called Ms. Currie after his deposition and asked her to meet with him the following day. On January 18, the president and Ms. Currie met.... In the course of their conversation... the president posed a series of questions and made statements...

Our analysis of this issue could stop here. There is no case for obstruction of justice. Why? There is no evidence whatsoever of any kind of threat or intimidation.... But the evidence reveals much more.... [T]he record specifically contains Ms. Currie's undisputed testimony which exonerates the president of this charge....

Question to Ms. Currie:

Now, back again to the four statements that you testified the president made to you that were presented as statements, did you feel you were pressured when he told you those statements?

Ms. Currie: None whatsoever.

Question: What did you think, or what was going through your mind about what he was doing?

Ms. Currie: At the time I felt that he was—I want to use the word shocked or surprised that this was an issue, and he was just talking.

Question: That was your impression, that he wanted you to say—because he would end each of the statements with "Right?"—with a question.

Ms. Currie: I do not remember that he wanted me to say "Right." He would say, "Right?" and I could have said, "Wrong."

Question: But he would end each of these questions with a "Right?" and you could either say whether it was true or not true.

Ms. Currie: Correct.

Question: Did you feel any pressure to agree with your boss?

Ms. Currie: None.

... But let's not stop there. Let's look at the intent element of the obstruction of justice laws—in other words, whether the president had the intent to influence Ms. Currie's supposed testimony, or potential testimony.

... They argue that, based upon the way he answered the questions in the *Jones* deposition, he purposely referred to Ms. Currie in the hopes that the *Jones* lawyers would call her as a corroborating witness. Therefore, according to their theory, he had the specific intent.

... A review of the transcript, however, shows that the president's few references to Ms. Currie were neither forced nor needlessly interposed. They were natural, appropriate; they were responsive. Indeed, the only occasion when he suggested the *Jones* lawyers speak to Ms. Currie is when they asked if it was typical for Ms. Currie to be in the White House after midnight. He understandably said, "You have to ask her." Hardly a challenge....

The managers' conjecture about the president's state of mind, however, fails on an even more basic level. If you believe...that the president went to great lengths to hide his relationship with Ms. Lewinsky, then why on Earth would he want Ms. Currie to be a witness in the *Jones* case? If there was one person who knew the extent of his contact with Ms. Lewinsky, it was Ms. Currie....

So why would the president want her to testify? The answer is simple. He didn't....

The president was not thinking about Ms. Currie becoming a witness in the *Jones* case. So what was the president thinking? The president explained to the grand jury why he spoke to Ms. Currie after the deposition.... The president was concerned that his secret was going to be exposed and the media would relentlessly inquire until the entire story and every shameful detail was public. The president's concern was heightened by an Internet report that morning...which alluded to Ms. Lewinsky and to Ms. Currie and to issues that the *Jones* lawyers had raised....

In trying to prepare for what he saw as the inevitable media attention, he talked to Ms. Currie to see what her perceptions were and what she recalled....

Remember, some of the questions that the *Jones* lawyers asked the president were so off base. For example, they asked him about visits from Ms. Lewinsky between midnight and 6 a.m. where Ms. Currie supposedly cleared her in. The president wanted to know whether or not Ms. Currie agreed with this perception or whether she had a different view, whether she agreed that Ms. Lewinsky was cleared in when he was present or had there been other occasions that he didn't know about. He also wanted to assess Ms. Currie's perception of the relationship. He knew the first person who would be questioned about media accounts, particularly given that she was in the Internet report, was going to be Ms. Currie....

Before I close, I do want to take a moment to address a theme that the House managers sounded throughout their presentation last week—civil rights.... Some managers suggested that we all should be concerned should the Senate fail to convict the president, because it would send a message that our civil rights laws and our sexual harassment laws are unimportant.

I can't let their comments go unchallenged....

... I am not worried about the future of civil rights. I am not worried because Ms. Jones had her day in court and Judge Wright determined that all of the matters we are discussing here today were not material to her case and ultimately decided that Ms. Jones, based on the facts and the law in that case, did not have a case against the president. I am not worried, because we have had imperfect leaders in the past and will have imperfect leaders in the future, but their imperfections did not roll back, nor did they stop, the march for civil rights and equal opportunity for all of our citizens....

Thomas Jefferson, Frederick Douglass, Abraham Lincoln, John F. Kennedy, Martin Luther King, Jr.—we revere these men. We should. But they were not perfect men. They made human errors, but they struggled to do humanity good. I am not worried about civil rights because this president's record on civil rights, on women's rights, on all of our rights is unimpeachable.

Ladies and gentlemen of the Senate, you have an enormous decision to make. And in truth, there is little more I can do to lighten that burden. But I can do this: I can assure you that your decision to follow the facts and the law and the Constitution and acquit this president will not shake the foundation of the house of civil rights....

It would be wrong to convict him on this record. You should acquit him on this record. And you must not let imagined harms to the house of civil rights persuade you otherwise. The president did not obstruct justice. The president did not commit perjury. The president must not be removed from office.

The Senate adjourned for the evening.

The next day, Thursday, January 21, the chief justice recognized David Kendall, the president's private attorney.

Before turning to Article II, Kendall discussed the differences between direct and circumstantial evidence. Direct evidence, from a witness's own five senses, was more probative; from the House managers' case, Kendall argued, it would not be apparent that there was a "large amount" of direct evidence contradicting the obstruction-of-justice allegations. Circumstantial evidence was certainly admissible, he explained, but its value "depends upon the strength of the inference you can logically draw from it." The circumstantial case being presented by the managers, he suggested, is "at best profoundly ambiguous."

Then he turned to Article II:

Mr. Kendall: ... Subpart 1 of Article II alleges that the president encouraged Ms. Lewinsky to execute an affidavit in the *Paula Jones* case "that he knew to be perjurious, false and misleading." The House managers allege that during a December 17 telephone conversation Ms. Lewinsky asked the president what she could do if she were subpoenaed in the *Jones* case and the president responded, "Well, maybe you could sign an affidavit." ...

It is hard to believe, but this statement of the president to Ms. Lewinsky, advising her of the possibility of totally lawful conduct, is the House managers' entire factual basis for supporting the first allegation in subpart 1. The managers don't claim that the president advised her to file a false affidavit.... And there is no evidence in the record anywhere to support such an allegation. Nor do the managers allege he even told her, advised her, urged her, or suggested to her what to put in her affidavit. The charge which the managers have spun out of this single statement by the president is refuted by the direct evidence.

First of all, Ms. Lewinsky has repeatedly and forcefully denied any and all suggestion that the president ever asked her to lie....

It is interesting to see how the House managers try to establish that somehow the president asked Ms. Lewinsky to file a false affidavit.... They argue that the president in fact somehow encouraged her to lie because both parties knew the affidavit would have to be false and misleading to accomplish the desired result.

But ... both Ms. Lewinsky and the president have testified repeatedly that, given the particular claims being made in the *Jones* case, they both honestly believed that a truthful, albeit limited, affidavit might—"might"—establish that Ms. Lewinsky had nothing relevant to offer in the way of testimony in the *Jones* case....

It is important to bear in mind that the *Paula Jones* case was a sexual harassment case, although it turned out to be legally groundless, and it involved allegations of nonconsensual sexual solicitations. Ms. Lewinsky's relationship to the president had been consensual....

It is not disputed that the president showed no interest in viewing a draft of Ms. Lewinsky's affidavit, did not review it, and, according to Ms. Lewinsky, said he did not need to see it. This fact is obviously exculpatory. If the president were truly concerned about what was going into Ms. Lewinsky's affidavit, surely he would have wanted to review it prior to his summation.

Now, to counter this inference, the House managers offer speculation. Mr. Manager McCollum tried to downplay the significance of this fact by asking you to engage in sheer surmise. He said on Friday:

I doubt seriously [the president] was talking about 15 other affidavits of somebody else and didn't like looking at affidavits anymore. I suspect and I would suggest to you that he was talking about 15 other drafts of this proposed affidavit since it had been around the Horn a lot of rounds.

Well, as the able House manager himself stated, this suggestion is mere suspicion, speculation; it flies in the face of Ms. Lewinsky's direct testimony. There is evidence of only a few drafts, and there is no evidence that the president ever saw any draft. . . .

There is another part of the chronology here . . . that the House managers simply ignore in their attempt to fit some of the facts into a sinister pattern. Ms. Lewinsky's name appeared on the *Paula Jones* witness list which, the managers tell us accurately, the president's lawyers reviewed with him on Saturday, December 6. . . .

Now, if the president's concern was so intense about the appearance of her name on the list, would he have waited until December 17 to talk to her? . . . [I]nsofar as you want to draw inferences from the chronology of events in December, this long delay is circumstantial evidence that the president felt no particular urgency either to alert Ms. Lewinsky that her name was on the witness list or make any suggestions to her about an affidavit. . . .

Now, subpart 2 of Article II alleges that the president obstructed justice by encouraging Ms. Lewinsky, in that same late night telephone call . . . to give perjurious, false and misleading testimony if and when she was called to testify personally in the *Jones* litigation. . . .

Well, let's look at the allegations here. . . . I think you logically begin with the direct evidence, and the direct evidence is the testimony of the two people involved in the telephone conversation, Ms. Lewinsky and the president. Ms. Lewinsky has repeatedly stated that no one ever urged her to lie and that this plainly applies to this December 17 conversation. . . .

It is interesting to hear all the ways that the House managers . . . try to minimize the importance of this direct evidence. You would think Ms. Lewinsky's statements under oath were irrelevant to this case. She gave this testimony, for the most part, when she was subject to prosecution for perjury. It simply cannot be blandly dismissed because it was given under this threat. . . .

Likewise, the president has consistently insisted he never asked Ms. Lewinsky to lie. In his grand jury testimony last August, he said that he and Ms. Lewinsky "might have talked about what to do in a non-legal context at some point in the past," if anybody inquired about their relationship, although he had no specific memory of such a conversation. And he testified that they did not talk about this in connection with Ms. Lewinsky's testimony in the *Jones* case....

There is, thus, no direct testimony from anybody that on December 17 the president asked Ms. Lewinsky to lie if called to testify in the *Jones* case. Here the House managers don't really even rely on circumstantial evidence to refute the direct testimony of the two relevant witnesses. They rely, instead, on what they assert is logic....

Their claim boils down...to the inferences to be drawn from the uncontested fact that in the past, before this time, before this December 17 phone call, the president and Ms. Lewinsky had discussions about what she should say if asked about the visits to the Oval Office. Both have acknowledged that....

...Here again, I want to go to the direct evidence...[M]s. Lewinsky's handwritten proffer to the independent counsel on February 1...makes it clear that she does recall having a discussion with the president in which he said that if anyone questioned her about visiting him, she should say she was either bringing him letters or visiting Betty Currie. But Ms. Lewinsky states, "there is truth to both of these statements."...

She also went out of her way in this proffer to emphasize that, while she did not recall precisely when the discussions about cover stories occurred, they occurred "prior to the subpoena in the *Paula Jones* case."...[A]lso...Ms. Lewinsky wrote that to the best of her recollection she did not believe she discussed the content of any deposition during the December 17 conversation with the president....

...Again, despite Ms. Lewinsky's direct and unrefuted testimony about the December 17 telephone call, the House managers asked you to conclude that the president must have asked her to testify falsely, because she had, by her own account, on prior occasions, assured the president that she would deny the relationship.

Think for a moment about that: They ask you to accept their speculation, in the face of contradictory evidence from both parties, and use that as a basis on which to remove the president....

...Subpart 5 alleges that at the deposition, the president allowed his attorney to make false and misleading statements to a federal judge characterizing an affidavit in order to prevent questioning deemed relevant by the judge....

This claim, which also is presented in the perjury section...is deficient as an allegation of obstruction, both as a matter of fact and as a matter of law.

But I will say one thing. The direct evidence on this point is uniquely available because there is only one witness who can testify about what was in his thoughts at a given moment, and the president has testified at great length in his grand jury testimony about what he was thinking at this point.

The president told the grand jury that he was simply not focusing closely on the exchange between the lawyers, but was instead concentrating on his own testimony....

And let's be clear about one other thing.... Judge Wright, in fact, interrupted Mr. Bennett in mid-sentence as he was describing Ms. Jones' affidavit.... She quickly interjected...and said, "No, just a moment, let me make my ruling." And then she proceeded to allow the very line of questioning that Mr. Bennett was trying to prevent. So the president's silence, whatever motivated it, had absolutely no impact on the conduct of the *Jones* deposition....

After a brief recess, Mr. Kendall resumed his presentation:

Subpart 7 of Article II alleges that the president obstructed justice when he relayed or told certain White House officials things about his relationship with Ms. Lewinsky that were false and misleading.... Yesterday, Mr. Craig explained why these statements didn't constitute perjury, and I would like to take just a few minutes...to explain why they don't constitute an obstruction of justice, either....

The statements...were statements that the president made very shortly after the Lewinsky publicity had broken to Mr. Bowles, Mr. Podesta, Mr. Blumenthal and Mr. Ickes, none of whom were witnesses in the *Paula Jones* case...and they had no evidence at all relevant to the *Paula Jones* case....

These allegedly impeachable denials to the four aides occurred, as I said, right after the publicity broke.... This was at the very time the president denied he had had sexual relations with Ms. Lewinsky in nearly identical terms on national television...

Having made this denial to the entire country, it simply is absurd to regard it any differently when made to four aides in the White House directly...rather than through the medium of television. The president talked to these individuals about the Lewinsky matter because of his personal relationship and his direct professional exposure to them on a daily basis. He spoke to them, however, misleadingly in an attempt to allay their concern once the allegations about Ms. Lewinsky become public.

... None of these aides had any independent knowledge of the relationship between the president and Ms. Lewinsky and, therefore, the only evidence they do offer would be a hearsay repetition of what the president had told them. And that was the same public denial that he had told everyone, including, presumably, any member of the grand jury who had his or her television set on on that Monday, January 26....

Let me turn to subpart 4. This subpart alleges that the president obstructed justice when he intensified and succeeded in an effort to secure job assistance for Ms. Lewinsky in order to corruptly prevent her truthful testimony. The claim here is of a quid pro quo, a "this for that." His job assistance was allegedly in order to prevent her truthful testimony....

Now, the proof that is in the record is that there was no corrupt linkage ... nothing which tied the job assistance to what was going on in the *Jones* case. Mr. Jordan did help open doors, and Ms. Lewinsky went through those doors, and she either succeeded or failed on her own merits. Two of the companies declined to offer her a job, and at the third she did get an entry-level job....

There was no fix, no quid pro quo, no link to the *Jones* case. And also there was no urgency to Mr. Jordan's assistance to her. He started assisting her well before she showed up on the *Jones* witness list, and he helped her whenever he could, consistent with his own heavy travel schedule....

What the House managers have tried to do ... they have tried to juxtapose unrelated events and, by a selective chronology, tried to establish causation between two wholly unrelated sets of events....

Let's start with Ms. Lewinsky.... Moving to New York was her own idea, and it was one she raised in July of 1997. This geographical move did not affect in any way her exposure to a subpoena in the Paula *Jones* case....

Now, Ms. Lewinsky testified: "I was never promised a job for my silence." You can't get any plainer than that....

Now, Mr. Jordan ... took care of that claim in his own grand jury testimony. He was asked about any connection between the job search and the affidavit. He said there was absolutely none. He said on March 5 as far as he was concerned these were two entirely separate matters. And in his grand jury appearance on May 5 he was asked whether the two were connected, and Mr. Jordan said, "Unequivocally, indubitably, no."

The president has likewise testified that there was no connection between the *Jones* case and Ms. Lewinsky's job search. He told the grand jury:

I was not trying to buy her silence or get Vernon Jordan to buy her silence. I thought she was a good person. She had not been involved with me for a long time in any improper way, several months, and I wanted to help her get on with her life. It is just as simple as that.

Quid pro quo? No. The uncontested facts bear out these categorical denials of the three most involved people. Ms. Lewinsky began looking for a job in July of 1997, and the event which hardened her resolve to move to New York was a report by her ostensible good friend, Ms. Linda Tripp, on or about October 6 that one of Ms. Tripp's friends at the national Security Council said that Ms. Lewinsky would never ever get a job in the White House again....

Ms. Lewinsky testified that she had discussed with Linda Tripp sometime in late September or early October the idea of asking for Mr. Jordan's assistance.... Mr. Jordan became involved sometime later at the direction not of the president but of Ms. Currie, who was a long-time friend of Mr. Jordan.... Ms. Lewinsky's first meeting was with Mr. Jordan on November 5, and Ms. Lewinsky testified that the meeting lasted about 20 minutes....

Now, Mr. Jordan testified unequivocally that he never, at any time, felt any particular pressure to get Ms. Lewinsky a job.... He was asked in the grand jury if you recall any "kind of a heightened sense of urgency by Ms. Currie or anyone at the White House" about helping Ms. Lewinsky during the first half of December?

And he replied, "Oh, no, I do not recall any heightened sense of urgency. What I do recall is that I dealt with it as I had time to do it."

Now, let me just pause here and observe that... it would have been extremely easy for the president to have arranged for her to be hired at the White House.... But, while she was interviewed a couple of times by White House officials in the summer of 1997, those interviews never resulted in a job offer. The fix was not in....

Now, there is a lot of further direct evidence concerning her job search... in grand jury transcripts from the people at the various New York firms Mr. Jordan contacted on Ms. Lewinsky's behalf. Again, there is simply no direct evidence whatsoever from any of these people of any kind of quid pro quo treatment. While Mr. Jordan made the contacts on her behalf, there was no urgency about them....

Mr. Jordan was able to open some doors, but once open, there was no inappropriate pressure. He really opened three doors for her: at American Express, at Young & Rubicam, and at Revlon. And she batted one for three....

Here Kendall reviewed OIC interviews with executives at the firms where Lewin-sky had interviews. All reported that there had been no pressure on them to hire her. None found Jordan's request that they take a look at her out of the ordinary, and none noticed any urgency.

After her interview with MacAndrews & Forbes, the parent company of Revlon, Lewinsky had called Jordan to apologize, because she thought it had gone badly. In fact, the person who interviewed her had had a favorable impression and forwarded her résumé to Revlon. At that point, Jordan called CEO Ronald Perelman on her be-half. But Revlon was already well on its way to offering Lewinsky a job.

...Now, let's look at the...alleged circumstantial evidence. The quid pro quo theory rests on assumptions about why things happened and on the facts about when things happened. The former requires logic, but the second is a matter of fact....

The managers have argued that what brought Mr. Jordan into action to help Ms. Lewinsky find a job, what really jump-started the process, was Judge Wright's December 11 order....

Now, Mr. Manager Hutchinson...told you that the president's attitude suddenly changed, and what started out as a favor for Betty Currie in finding Ms. Lewinsky a job dramatically changed into something sinister after Ms. Lewinsky became a witness....

Mr. Manager Hutchinson presented...a chart.... I have taken the liberty of borrowing it for our own purposes. You see the key is outlined in detail what happened on December 11. The very first item is that "Judge Susan Webber [Wright] issues order allowing testimony on Lewinsky." The second meeting between Lewinsky and Jordan, "leads provided/recommendation calls placed," and then, later, the "president and Jordan talk about a job for Lewinsky."

Kendall then walked through the facts. Lewinsky had met Jordan in the early af-ternoon of December 11—a meeting scheduled three days earlier. Judge Wright's order was entered sometime after 7:50 P.M. that evening. And by 7:50 P.M. Jordan was on an airplane over the Atlantic Ocean, having taken off before the judge even started the conference call that ended with the entering of her discovery order. "This claim of a causal relationship totally collapses," said Kendall.

He also demonstrated some errors in other charts the managers had used to show the supposed links between the affidavit and the job search. One chart, for example purported to show that Lewinsky obtained a draft affidavit from her lawyer, Frank Carter, on January 5, then offered to show it to the president later that day. But, said

Kendall, Carter drafted the affidavit on the morning of January 6. "Unsupported speculation," said Kendall. "Even worse, it is speculation demolished by fact."
   Kendall continued:

I want to say a final thing about all the charts involving circumstantial evidence. You remember how many telephone calls were up on these charts. . . . It is pretty easy to get telephone call records and to identify telephone calls. . . . No matter how many telephone calls are listed on the chart, you don't know, without testimony, what was happening in that phone call. . . .

The uncontroverted evidence shows that, in fact, Mr. Jordan spoke to the president on many, many, many occasions. He . . . has been a friend of the president since 1973, and a call between them was a common occurrence. When asked in the grand jury if Mr. Jordan believed that the pattern of telephone calls to the president was "striking," Mr. Jordan replied, "It depends on your point of view. I talk to the president of the United States all the time, and so it's not striking to me." . . .

   . . . The managers, in the absence of evidence that anyone endeavored to obtain Ms. Lewinsky a job in exchange for her silence, indeed, in the face of direct testimony of all of those involved that this did not happen, ask you to simply speculate. . . . And they ask you to speculate that a lot of those phone calls must have been about Ms. Lewinsky, and they ask you to speculate further that in one of those unidentified, unknown phone calls, somebody must have said, "Let's get Ms. Lewinsky a job in exchange for her silence."

The simple fact is that there is no evidence indirectly to support the allegation that the president obstructed justice in his December 17 telephone call with Ms. Lewinsky in his statements to his aides, in his statements to Betty Currie with relation to gifts, or the job search. . . .

The president did not commit perjury. He did not obstruct justice, and there are no grounds to remove him from office.

After a recess, the chief justice recognized the last member of the president's defense team, former Arkansas Senator Dale Bumpers.

Mr. Bumpers: . . . Colleagues, I come here with some sense of reluctance. . . . The reason I came here today with some reluctance . . . is because [the president and I] are from the same State, and we are long friends. I know that necessarily diminishes to some extent the effectiveness of my words. So if Bill Clinton, the man, Bill Clinton, the friend, were the issue here, I am quite sure

I would not be doing this. But it is the weight of history on all of us, and it is my reverence for that great document... that we call our Constitution, the most sacred document to me next to the Holy Bible.

These proceedings go right to the heart of our Constitution where it deals with impeachment, the part that provides the gravest punishment for just about anybody—the president—even though the framers said we are putting this in to protect the public, not to punish the president....

Well, colleagues, I have heard so many adjectives to describe this gallery and these proceedings—historic, memorable, unprecedented, awesome. All of those words, all of those descriptions are apt. And to those, I would add the word "dangerous,"... dangerous to the political process. And it is dangerous to the unique mix of pure democracy and republican government Madison and his colleagues so brilliantly crafted and which has sustained us for 210 years....

[T]he danger, as I say, is to the political process, and dangerous for reasons feared by the framers about legislative control of the Executive. That single issue and how to deal with impeachment was debated off and on for the entire four months of the Constitutional Convention. But the word "dangerous" is not mine. It is Alexander Hamilton's.... Mr. Ruff quoted extensively on Tuesday afternoon in his brilliant statement here. He quoted Alexander Hamilton precisely, and it is a little arcane. It isn't easy to understand.

So if I may, at the expense of being slightly repetitious, let me paraphrase what Hamilton said. He said the Senate had a unique role in participating with the executive branch in appointments; and, two, it had a role... in participating with the executive in the character of a court for the trial of impeachments. But he said... it would be difficult to get a, what he called, well-constituted court from wholly elected Members. He said: Passions would agitate the whole community and divide it between those who were friendly and those who had inimical interests to the accused; namely, the president. Then he said...: The greatest danger was that the decision would be based on the comparative strength of the parties rather than the innocence or guilt of the president....

This is the only caustic thing I will say in these remarks this afternoon, but the question is, How do we come to be here? We are here because of a five-year, relentless, unending investigation of the president, $50 million, hundreds of FBI agents fanning across the nation, examining in detail the microscopic lives of people—maybe the most intense investigation not only of a president, but of anybody ever.

I feel strongly about this because of my state and what we have endured. So you will have to excuse me, but that investigation has also shown that the judicial system in this country can and does get out of kilter unless it is controlled. Because there are innocent people—innocent people—who have been financially and mentally bankrupt....

Javert's pursuit of Jean Valjean in *Les Miserables* pales by comparison. I doubt there are few people—maybe nobody in this body—who could withstand such scrutiny. And in this case those summoned were terrified, not because of their guilt, but because they felt guilt or innocence was not really relevant. But after all of those years, and $50 million of Whitewater, Travelgate, Filegate—you name it—nothing, nothing. The president was found guilty of nothing—official or personal.

We are here today because the president suffered a terrible moral lapse of marital infidelity—not a breach of the public trust, not a crime against society, the two things Hamilton talked about in Federalist Paper No. 65 ... but it was a breach of his marriage vows. It was a breach of his family trust. It is a sex scandal. H. L. Mencken one time said, "When you hear somebody say, 'This is not about money,' it's about money." And when you hear somebody say, "This is not about sex," it's about sex.

You pick your own adjective to describe the president's conduct. Here are some that I would use: indefensible, outrageous, unforgivable, shameless. I promise you the president would not contest any of those or any others.

But there is a human element in this case that has not even been mentioned. That is, the president and Hillary and Chelsea are human beings. This is intended only as a mild criticism of our distinguished friends from the House. But as I listened to the presenters, to the managers, make their opening statements, they were remarkably well prepared and they spoke eloquently—more eloquently than I really had hoped.

But when I talk about the human element, I talk about what I thought was, on occasion, an unnecessarily harsh, pejorative description of the president. I thought that the language should have been tempered somewhat to acknowledge that he is the president. To say constantly that the president lied about this and lied about that—as I say, I thought that was too much for a family that has already been about as decimated as a family can get. The relationship between husband and wife, father and child, has been incredibly strained, if not destroyed. There has been nothing but sleepless nights, mental agony, for this family, for almost five years, day after day, from accusations of having Vince Foster assassinated, on down. It has been bizarre.

I didn't sense any compassion. And perhaps none is deserved. The president has said for all to hear that he misled, he deceived, he did not want to be helpful to the prosecution, and he did all of those things to his family, to his friends, to his staff, to his Cabinet, and to the American people. Why would he do that? Well, he knew this whole affair was about to bring unspeakable embarrassment and humiliation on himself, his wife whom he adored, and a child that he worshipped with every fiber of his body and for whom he would happily have died to spare her or to ameliorate her shame and her grief.

The House managers have said shame, an embarrassment is no excuse for lying. The question about lying—that is your decision. But I can tell you, put yourself in his position—and you have already had this big moral lapse—as to what you would do. We are, none of us, perfect. Sure, you say, he should have thought of all that beforehand. And indeed he should, just as Adam and Eve should have, just as you and you and you and you and millions of other people who have been caught in similar circumstances should have thought of it before....

Make no mistake about it: Removal from office is punishment. It is unbelievable punishment, even though the framers didn't quite see it that way. Again, they said—and it bears repeating over and over again—they said they wanted to protect the people. But I can tell you this: The punishment of removing Bill Clinton from office would pale compared to the punishment he has already inflicted on himself. There is a feeling in this country that somehow or another Bill Clinton has gotten away with something. Mr. Leader, I can tell you, he hasn't gotten away with anything. And the people are saying: "Please don't protect us from this man." Seventy-six percent of us think he is doing a fine job; 65 to 70 percent of us don't want him removed from office.

Some have said we are not respected on the world scene. The truth of the matter is, this nation has never enjoyed greater prestige in the world than we do right now. I saw Carlos Menem, president of Argentina, a guest here recently, who said to the president, "Mr. President, the world needs you." The war in Bosnia is under control; the president has been as tenacious as anybody could be about Middle East peace; and in Ireland, actual peace; and maybe the Middle East will make it; and he has the Indians and the Pakistanis talking to each other as they have never talked to each other in recent times.

Vaclav Havel said, "Mr. President, for the enlargement of the North Atlantic Treaty Organization, there is no doubt in my mind that it was your personal leadership that made this historic development possible." King Hussein: "Mr. President, I've had the privilege of being a friend of the United States and presidents since the late President Eisenhower, and throughout all the years in the past I have kept in touch, but on the subject of peace, the peace we are seeking, I have never, with all due respect and all the affection I held for your predecessors, known someone with your dedication, clear-headedness, focus, and determination to help resolve this issue in the best way possible."

I have Nelson Mandela and other world leaders who have said similar things in the last six months. Our prestige, I promise you, in the world, is as high as it has ever been.

Bumpers turned, briefly, to the charges against the president "You know," he said, there is perjury and then there is perjury. He then quoted from Monica Lewinsky's grand jury testimony in which she was asked about the carved bear the president had given her on December 28, 1997. Lewinsky said the president said the bear was "maybe an Indian symbol for strength." Did she interpret that "to be strong in your decision to continue to conceal the relationship?" "No," Lewinsky replied. But the House, Bumpers observed, in trying to explain why the president had given her more gifts even though his gifts to her were being subpoenaed, argued—he quoted from the majority report and the brief: "The only logical inference is that the gifts, including the bear symbolizing strength, were a tacit reminder to Ms. Lewinsky that they would deny the relationship even in the face of a federal subpoena."

Bumpers continued:

Is it perjury to say the only logical inference is something when the only shred of testimony in the record is, "No, that was not my interpretation. I didn't infer that." Yet, here you have it in the committee report and you have it in the brief. Of course, that is not perjury.

First of all, it is not under oath. But I am a trial lawyer and I will tell you what it is; it is wanting to win too badly...

There is a total lack of proportionality, a total lack of balance in this thing. The charge and the punishment are totally out of sync. All of you have heard or read the testimony of the five prosecutors who testified before the House Judiciary Committee—five seasoned prosecutors. Each one of them, veterans, said that under the identical circumstances of this case, they would never charge anybody because they would know they couldn't get a conviction....

How do you reconcile what the prosecutors said with what we are doing here? Impeachment was debated off and on in Philadelphia for the entire four months, as I said. The key players were Gouvernor Morris, a brilliant Pennsylvanian; George Mason, the only man reputed to be so brilliant that Thomas Jefferson actually deferred to him; he refused to sign the Constitution, incidentally, even though he was a delegate because they didn't deal with slavery and he was a strict abolitionist. Then there was Charles Pinckney from South Carolina, a youngster at 29 years old; Edmund Randolph from Virginia, who had a big role in the Constitution in the beginning; and then, of course, James Madison, the craftsman. They were all key players in drafting this impeachment provision.

Uppermost in their minds...was that they did not want any kings. They had lived under despots, under kings, and under autocrats, and they didn't want any more of that. And they succeeded very admirably. We have had 46 presidents and no kings. But they kept talking about corruption. Maybe that ought to be the reason for impeachment, because they feared some president would corrupt the political process. That is what the debate was about—corrupting the political process and ensconcing one's self through a phony election; maybe that is something close to a king.

They followed the British rule on impeachment, because the British said the House of Commons may impeach and the House of Lords must convict.... In all fairness, Alexander Hamilton was not very keen on the House participating. But here were the sequence of events in Philadelphia that brought us here today. They started out with maladministration and Madison said, "That is too vague; what does that mean?" So they dropped that. They went from that to corruption, and they dropped that. Then they went to malpractice, and they decided that was not definitive enough. And they went to treason, bribery, and corruption. They decided that still didn't suit them.

Bear in mind one thing: During this entire process, they are narrowing the things you can impeach a president for. They were making it tougher. Madison said, "If we aren't careful, the president will serve at the pleasure of the Senate." And then they went to treason and bribery.... And George Mason added, "or other high crimes and misdemeanors against the United States." They voted on it, and on September 10 they sent the entire Constitution to a committee they called the Committee on Style and Arrangement, which was the committee that would draft the language in a way that everybody would understand—that is, well crafted from a grammatical standpoint. But that committee, which was dominated by Madison and Hamilton, dropped "against the United States." And the stories will tell you that the reason they did that was because they were redundant....

... We are not debating treason and bribery here in this Chamber. We are talking about other high crimes and misdemeanors. And where did "high crimes and misdemeanors" come from? It came from the English law. And they found it in English law under a category which said distinctly "political' offenses against the state....

So, colleagues, please, for just one moment, forget the complexities of the facts and the tortured legalisms.... But ponder this: If high crimes and misdemeanors was taken from English law by George Madison, which listed high crimes and misdemeanors as "political" offenses against the state, what are we doing here? If, as Hamilton said, it had to be a crime against society or a breach of the public trust, what are we doing here? Even perjury, concealing, or deceiving an unfaithful relationship does not even come close to being an impeachable offense. Nobody has suggested that Bill Clinton committed a political crime against the state.

So, colleagues, if you are to honor the Constitution, you must look at the history of the Constitution and how we got to the impeachment clause. And, if you do that, and you do that honestly, according to the oath you took, you cannot—you can censor Bill Clinton, you can hand him over to the prosecutor for him to be prosecuted, but you cannot convict him....

There has been a suggestion that a vote to acquit would be something of a breach of faith with those who lie in Flanders field, Anzio, Bunker Hill, Gettysburg, and wherever.... I think it was Chairman Hyde who alluded to this and said those men fought and died for the rule of law.

I can remember a cold November 3 morning in my little hometown of Charleston, Arkansas. I was 18 years old. I had just gotten one semester in at the university when I went into the Marine Corps. So I was to report to Little Rock to be inducted.... And I had to catch the bus down at the drugstore at 3 o'clock in the morning. So my mother and father and I got up at 2 o'clock, got dressed, and went down there.... And the bus came over the hill. I was rather frightened anyway about going. I was quite sure I was going to be killed, only slightly less frightened that Betty would find somebody else when I was gone.

The bus came over the schoolhouse hill and my parents started crying. I had never seen my father cry. I knew I was in some difficulty.... You know that scene. It was repeated across this nation millions of times. Then, happily, I survived that war, saw no combat, was on my way to Japan when it all ended....

But I came home to a generous government which provided me under the GI bill an education in a fairly prestigious law school.... I practiced law in this

little town for 18 years, loved every minute of it. But I didn't practice constitutional law. And I knew very little about the Constitution. But when I went into
law school, I did study constitutional law, Mr. Chief Justice. It was very arcane
to me. And trying to read the Federalist Papers, Tocqueville, all of those things
that law students are expected to do, that was tough for me. I confess.

So after 18 years of law practice, I jumped up and ran for Governor. I
served as Governor for four years. I guess I knew what the rule of law was,
but I still didn't really have much reverence for the Constitution. I just did
not understand any of the things I am discussing and telling you. No. My
love for that document came day after day and debate after debate right here
in this Chamber....

The reason I developed this love of it is because I saw Madison's magic
working time and time again, keeping bullies from running over weak people,
keeping majorities from running over minorities, and I thought about all of
the unfettered freedoms we had. The oldest organic law in existence made us
the envy of the world.

Mr. Chairman, we have also learned that the rule of law includes presidential elections. That is a part of the rule of law in this country. We have an event,
a quadrennial event, in this country which we call a presidential election, and
that is the day when we reach across this aisle and hold hands, Democrats and
Republicans, and we say, win or lose, we will abide by the decision. It is a
solemn event, a presidential election, and it should not be undone lightly or
just because one side has the clout and the other one doesn't....

The American people are now and for some time have been asking to be allowed a good night's sleep. They are asking for an end to this nightmare. It is
a legitimate request. I am not suggesting that you vote for or against the polls.
I understand that. Nobody should vote against the polls just to show their
mettle and their courage. I have cast plenty of votes against the polls, and it
has cost me politically a lot of times. This has been going on for a year, though.

In that same op-ed piece, I talked about meeting Harry Truman my first
year as Governor of Arkansas. I spent an hour with him—an indelible experience.... I will never forget what he said: "Put your faith in the people. Trust
the people. They can handle it." They have shown conclusively time and time
again that they can handle it.

Colleagues, this is easily the most important vote you will ever cast. If you
have difficulty because of an intense dislike of the president...rise above it.
He is not the issue. He will be gone. You won't. So don't leave a precedent
from which we may never recover and almost surely will regret.

If you vote to acquit, Mr. Leader, you know exactly what is going to happen. You are going to go back to your committees. You are going to get on with this legislative agenda. You are going to start dealing with Medicare, Social Security, tax cuts, and all those things which the people of this country have a non-negotiable demand that you do. If you vote to acquit, you go immediately to the people's agenda. But if you vote to convict, you can't be sure what is going to happen.

James G. Blaine was a Member of the Senate when Andrew Johnson was tried in 1868, and 20 years later he recanted. He said, "I made a bad mistake." And he said, "As I reflect back on it, all I can think about is that having convicted Andrew Johnson would have caused much more chaos and confusion in this country than Andrew Johnson could ever conceivably have created."

And so it is with William Jefferson Clinton. If you vote to convict, in my opinion, you are going to be creating more havoc than he could ever possibly create. After all, he has only got two years left. So don't, for God sakes, heighten the people's alienation, which is at an all-time high, toward their Government. The people...are calling on you to rise above politics, rise above partisanship. They are calling on you to do your solemn duty, and I pray you will.

QUESTIONS AND ANSWERS

Majority Leader Trent Lott explained the process: There would be sixteen hours for questions, which the senators would submit to Chief Justice Rehnquist; Rehnquist would then direct each question either to the House managers or to the president's defense team. The Republicans would start the questioning, and then they would alternate back and forth.

The Chief Justice: Senators Allard, Bunning, Coverdell and Craig ask... "Is it the opinion of the House Managers that the president's defense team, in the presentation, mischaracterized any factual or legal issue in this case? If so, please explain."

Ed Bryant took the first question. First he addressed Gregory Craig's argument that much of the perjury case rested on "oath versus oath" allegations. The president's defenders, said Bryant, had ignored considerable corroborating evidence, particularly of Lewinsky's testimony about her relationship with the president, including phone logs, Secret Service testimony placing her inside the Oval Office, contemporaneous statements to friends and counselors, and the DNA-tested blue dress. He also cited Lewinsky's transfer to the Pentagon as "indication that efforts had been made to ... relocate her away from the president."

Then Bryant turned to Charles Ruff's charges that the managers' case was misleading, mentioning that before the House Judiciary Committee, Ruff himself had said reasonable people could disagree about how close to the line of perjury the president had gotten:

Mr. Bryant: ... White House Counsel Cheryl Mills spoke in a similar manner and tone to this House about inconvenient and stubborn facts—oh, those stubborn facts.... As carefully as she tried to make innocent the wrongful effort of the president to tamper with [Betty Currie], she just as carefully skirted the entire similar episode two or three days after the first one where he again tampered with her testimony....

Likewise, in her review of witness tampering, she mischaracterized the law—the law—stating that a threat—an actual threat was required. 18 U.S.C. 1503 states that obstruction of justice occurs when a person corruptly endeavors to influence the testimony of another person. And "corruptly" has been interpreted by the District Court here in D.C. to mean acting for an improper purpose....

Mr. Ruff stated the president gave the same denial to his aides that he gave to his country and family.... Well, that's not right.... [T]his is Mr. Podesta talking—"He told me that he never had sex with her and that he never asked—you know, he repeated the denial. But he was extremely explicit in saying he never had sex with her in any way whatsoever, that they had not had oral sex."

And ... he told Mr. Blumenthal an entirely different story, that "Monica Lewinsky came at me and made a sexual demand on me. And I, [the president,] rebuffed her." ... That is not the story that he told the American people and that he told his family. These are embellishments that are very important, because he anticipated that they would go into the grand jury and repeat those misstatements.

And finally, the affidavit of Monica Lewinsky. White House defense lawyers spoke so eloquently about ... how the president believed that Monica Lewinsky could have filed a truthful affidavit while still skirting their sexual relationship sufficiently to ... avoid testifying in the *Paula Jones* case.

... [T]hat is an incredible statement that you can do the twister enough to go into a deposition where the purpose of being there is to discover this type of information, who you might have had an affair with, and have her tell a truthful affidavit and still not to be able to testify. Had she told a truthful affidavit, she would have been immediately called....

The Chief Justice: Senator Sarbanes asks [of the president's team]: "Would you please comment on any of the legal or factual assertions made by the managers in their response to the previous question ...?"

Mr. Ruff:...Mr. Manager Bryant began by suggesting that there really is corroboration on...the nature of the specific details of the relationship between the president and Ms. Lewinsky.... [But] nobody disputes the fact that Ms. Lewinsky was in the White House engaged in inappropriate conduct with the president on a particular day.

The only point that I think the manager raises that is new...is this notion that contemporary, consistent statements made to third parties about these events are somehow corroborative of Ms. Lewinsky's testimony in this regard.... [T]he law rejects the notion that merely because you tell the same story many times it is corroborative of the underlying credibility of the witness's version....

[L]et me go back to his reference to my earlier testimony before the House Judiciary Committee in which I did, indeed...comment that the president may well have walked up to the line believing he didn't cross it, but that reasonable people might conclude otherwise.

The only problem with that example...is that I was talking there...about his testimony in the *Jones* deposition which, as everyone in this room will fully understand, is not before you because the House of Representatives specifically decided that the president's testimony in the *Jones* deposition was not a basis for impeachment....

Cheryl Mills then reiterated that of the two obstruction-of-justice statutes, 1512 "does require a threat or intimidation," and the case law surrounding 1503 required "a nexus between the actual conduct and the official proceeding that would be going forward." There was no suggestion that Betty Currie was going to be a witness in the Jones case, and no one yet knew about the independent counsel's investigation.

A question from Senators Enzi and Coverdell allowed the managers to respond:

Mr. Hutchinson:...Betty Currie testified that two days later she was called into the office, the same series of statements, declarations, coaching was made to her, and the only possible explanation for that is that the president was trying to make a very clear statement to her—"This is what I remember; this is what I want you to do."...

...[I]f you look at the facts in the *Jones* case...on January 22, within five days of the deposition, a subpoena was issued for Betty Currie...and, in fact, on the 23rd, there was a supplement to the witness list by the *Jones* lawyers, which included Betty Currie's name.... In fact, it is clear that the subpoena was issued; it was served.

Whenever that deposition was over of the president, both the president left there and the *Jones* lawyers left there knowing immediately that Betty Currie was going to be a witness.... That is why the president came back and had to deal with Betty Currie being a witness, and the *Jones* lawyers went out and immediately amended the witness list....

The Chief Justice: Senator Levin asks White House counsel: "Would you please comment on any of the legal or factual assertions made by the managers in their response to the previous question?

Ruff acknowledged that after the Washington Post *broke the story of the OIC investigation on January 21, the Jones lawyers did "attempt to track the entire independent counsel investigation," and did subpoena Betty Currie. But what was important, he argued, was the fact that when the president made his statements to Currie, he "had no reason to believe" she was going to be a witness—and that, said Ruff, was critical because "that's what's on his mind, and that is what you have to ask if you are talking about obstruction of justice or witness tampering."*

The Chief Justice: Senators Thurmond, Grassley, Chafee and Craig direct to the House managers: "President Clinton has raised concerns about whether the articles of impeachment are overly vague and whether they charge more than one offense in the same article. How do you respond...?"

Mr. Canady: ... With respect to the first claim, it is clear in the president's trial memorandum and his presentation here that President Clinton and his counsel know exactly what he is being charged with. And I submit to you that if President Clinton had suffered from any lack of specificity in the articles, he could have filed a motion for a bill of particulars. He did not choose to do so.

Moreover, articles of impeachment have never been required to be drafted with the specificity of indictments. After all, this proceeding is not a criminal trial. If it were, then we, as the prosecutors, would not only be entitled to call witnesses, but would be required to call them to prove our case....

... I also point out that unlike the judicial impeachments in the 1980s, President Clinton has not committed a handful of specific misdeeds that can be easily listed in separate articles of impeachment. In order to encompass the whole assortment of misdeeds that caused the House of Representatives to impeach the president, the Judiciary Committee looked to the more analogous case, that of President Nixon....

The articles did not—I repeat "did not"—list each false or misleading statement, did not list each misuse of the CIA, and did not list each respective defendant and what they were promised. That is the record....

I will do my best to briefly address the second claim ... against the form of the articles of impeachment; that is, that they are invalid, charging multiple offenses in one article....

Once again, these articles are modeled after the articles adopted by the House Committee on the Judiciary against President Nixon and were drafted with the rules of the Senate specifically in mind....

Canady addressed Rule 23 of the Senate's impeachment procedures, which had been amended in 1986. The committee that amended it explained: "The portion of the amendment effectively enjoining the division of an article into separate specifications is proposed to permit the most judicious and efficacious handling of the final question." The explanation invoked the Nixon articles of impeachment, which "set out broadly based charges alleging constitutional improprieties followed by a recital of transactions illustrative or supportive of such charges." Canady concluded: "I would submit ... that the articles of impeachment against President Clinton ... are not constitutionally deficient."

A question from Senators Dodd and Leahy allowed the president's lawyers to comment.

Mr. Craig: In our case, we are talking about an allegation of perjury.... I think our argument was that perjury is a different kind of thing. You have to be very specific in what you charge....

Craig reviewed, once again, the history of the perjury charge, from the three allegations in the Starr referral to the eight in the file brief for the Senate trial. Then he turned to how the lack of specificity was playing out in the trial:

... The precise statement that the president is accused of testifying falsely in front of a grand jury was that he was lying when he said that the reason that he was seeing Betty Currie was to refresh his recollection. In the trial brief ... he lied when he said he was going to refresh his recollection. That is not even mentioned in Mr. Rogan's presentation. He changes it. And he says he lied when he said he wanted to ascertain what the facts were, trying to ascertain what Betty's perception was—a very different statement requiring a very different defense....

Mr. Ruff: ... I want to talk briefly about just two aspects of Manager Canady's presentation.

First of all, he asks why didn't we seek a bill of particulars. Well, let me all remind the Senators, ... here that the managers do not have the authority to rewrite the articles, though they certainly have, I suggest, attempted to do so on the fly, but that it would have required a remand to the House of Representatives in order to have a bill of particulars to judge what they themselves meant when they had passed these articles.

Second, just very briefly, I spoke to the issue of multiplicity, duplicity, the other day, and the question of whether the rule 23 revision makes any difference. As I pointed out ... one Member of this body spoke at length about the importance of not loading up multiple offenses into one count well after the revision of rule 23, clearly with no sense that this body had been precluded from dealing with the critical issue of whether a two-thirds vote can sensibly be taken on an article that contains multiple and, particularly as my colleague, Mr. Craig, indicated, multiple nonspecific violations.

The Chief Justice: Senators Thompson and Grassley, Thurmond, Allard, Frist, Burns, and Inhofe direct this question to the president's counsel: "If the president were a federal judge accused of committing the same acts of perjury and obstruction of justice and the Senate found sufficient evidence that the acts alleged were committed, should the Senate vote to convict?"

Mr. Ruff: ... It is absolutely crystal clear from the history of the drafting of the impeachment clause that the concern of the framers was, is there such action as to subvert our Government that we can no longer persist in permitting, in their case, the president of the United States to remain in office. That question must be dramatically different when you ask it about the conduct of 1 of 1,000 judges. ...

That question for Judge Nixon, convicted and imprisoned, has got to be different from—"different" is much too mild a word—stunningly different from the question you ask against the backdrop of our history when you ask whether the president of the United States should be removed and the will of the electorate overturned.

A question from Senators Dorgan, Baucus, and Schumer asked the president's counsel to comment on the fact that after Ruff had "undermined" their theory that the December 11 judge's discovery order had caused the Lewinsky job search to inten-

sify, the House managers had issued a press release asserting that it was the December 5 witness list, not the judge's order, that had caused the intensification.

Mr. Kendall: ... Well, there are a number of things to be said about that. One of them is that they have very clearly said that there was no urgency at all after the witness list arrived to help Ms. Lewinsky. They have said that Mr. Jordan met with the president on December 5 but that meeting had nothing to do with Ms. Lewinsky. This was in the majority report at page 11. They said that very clearly.

So they have now suddenly—because it has been clear that the December 11 order was entered at a time when Mr. Jordan was flying to Europe, he could not have known about it....

A question from Senators Ashcroft and Hatch allowed the managers to respond.

Mr. Hutchinson: ... [T]here are two things that I am pointing to as the trigger mechanisms for the job search intensification. One of them is the witness list that comes in on December 5, the president knows about, at the latest, on December 6. The other ... was the judge's order on December 11....

[W]e say that the judge's order of the 11th ... triggered additional action down the road. The job search was not over; the activity continued into January. And, so, that all put pressure on the ultimate fact, in January when the job was obtained, the false affidavit was filed.

Now let me just point to a couple of other things along that line.... [L]ook at the testimony of Vernon Jordan ... on March 3 of 1998 ...:

Counselor, the lady comes to me with a subpoena in the *Paula Jones* case that I know, as I have testified here today was about sexual harassment.... you didn't have to be an Einstein to know that that was a question that had to be asked by me at that particular time because heretofore this discussion was about a job.

... And, so, Mr. Jordan himself makes the connection, the job search was one thing but whenever she became a witness in the *Jones* case, that changed everything....

And, so, we have to take this picture, that they were related as they were going two tracks, they became interconnected and became one track....

The Chief Justice: This question from Senator Boxer, and it is to counsel for the president: "In light of the concession of Manager Hutchinson that Judge Wright's order had no bearing on the "intensity" of the job search, can you comment on the balance of his claim on the previous question?"

Hutchinson asked the chief justice if he could object to the form of the question: "That was not proper characterizing what I just stated." The parliamentarian said he could object to an answer, but not to a question. Hutchinson withdrew his objection.

Mr. Ruff: ... Let me just respond briefly to Mr. Manager Hutchinson's argument. And let me focus, first, on another portion of his presentation in which he states, and there—and he is referring now to Ms. Lewinsky—she is referring to a December 6 meeting with the president in which, as you will recall, she has testified that there was a brief discussion about her efforts to get a job through Mr. Jordan and the president sort of vaguely said, "Yes, I'll do something about that." And this is Mr. Manager Hutchinson's characterization of that moment. December 6, you will recall, is the day after the witness list comes out. ...

So you can see from that that it was not a high priority for the president either. It was, "Sure, I'll get to that, I will do that." But then the president's attitude suddenly changed. What started out as a favor for Betty Currie dramatically changed after Ms. Lewinsky became a witness and the judge's order was issued again on December 11.

... "The first" their words, page 11, majority brief, majority report—"The first activity calculated to help Ms. Lewinsky actually get a job took place on December 11. There was no urgency." ...

A question from six Republican senators asked the managers to discuss Cheryl Mills's contention that witness tampering required some element of threat or coercion.

Bob Barr replied that this was not so. Mills was relying, he said, on the Supreme Court ruling in United States v. Aguilar. *The court's decision in that case, he said, "was based on a specific finding . . . that the evidence was insufficient to prove that the defendant could have even thought that the investigator was a potential witness at the time that he lied to him." That, said Barr, was not applicable here.*

Senator Byrd then asked the president's lawyers how the president could defend against the charge that giving false and misleading statements under oath violated some public trust. Ruff replied:

Mr. Ruff: ... Let us assume for a moment ... that this body were to conclude that the president lied in the grand jury about his relationship with Ms. Lewinsky. That in and of itself does not lead to the judgment, and in our view must not lead to the judgment, that he needs to be removed from office....

If we have not convinced you on the facts, I hope we will convince you that the framers would have asked: Is our system so endangered that we must not only turn the president over to the same rule of law that any other citizen would be put under, after he leaves office, but must we cut short his term and overturn the will of the nation? And in our view, in the worst case scenario, you can find the answer to that question must still be no.

The Chief Justice: Senator Lott asks the House managers: "Do the managers wish to respond to the answer just given by the president's counsel?"

Mr. Canady: ... We believe that the response and the position taken by the counsel for the president here really involves two great errors. One error is in establishing a standard of conduct for the presidency that is too low. The other error is in attempting to minimize the significance of the offenses that this president has been charged with and which we submit to you the evidence supports the charges....

A president should not be impeached and removed from office for a mistake of judgment. He should not be impeached and removed for a momentary lapse. Instead, he should be impeached and removed if he engages in a conscious and deliberate and settled choice to do wrong, a conscious and deliberate and settled choice to violate the laws of this land....

In response to a question from Senators Torricelli and Rockefeller, Ruff addressed the question of whether private conduct could ever be impeachable. Of course it could, Ruff said, if the conduct were so egregious that "the people simply could not contemplate the notion of a president remaining in office." But apart from such an offense, Ruff argued, "the focus of attention must be ... on the public character of the man, the political, in a broader sense, character of the man and of his acts." The conduct they were considering, he argued, came nowhere near an impeachable standard.

The Chief Justice: Senator Nickles asks the House managers: "President's counsel stated the president did not commit perjury. Please respond."

Mr. Rogan: ... If anybody wants a lesson in legal schizophrenia, please read the president's trial brief on this very subject. They skirt the issue by saying nowhere in the president's grand jury deposition did he ever affirm the truth of his civil deposition testimony.... [T]hey try to ignore the actual fact of when the president was asked questions about his oath that he took during the grand jury. I read, therefrom:

> **Question:** You understand the oath required you to give the whole truth that is a complete answer to each question, sir.
> **Answer:** I will answer each question as accurately and fully as I can.
> **Question:** Now, you took the same oath to tell the truth, the whole truth, and nothing but the truth, on January 17, 1998, in a deposition in the *Paula Jones* litigation, is that correct, sir?
> **Answer:** I did take an oath there.
> **Question:** Did the oath you took on that occasion mean the same to you then as it does today?
> **Answer:** I believed then that I had to answer the questions truthfully, that's correct.

... They attempt to say that that somehow inoculates the president from having to admit that he perjured himself during the *Paula Jones* deposition.

Rogan then read from the president's deposition testimony, in which he denied ever having an affair with Monica Lewinsky under the definition supplied by the Jones lawyers, said he saw her "on two or three occasions" during the government shutdown, when "the whole White House staff was being run by interns," and said he did not believe they had ever been in the hallway between the Oval Office and the kitchen area "unless we were walking back to the dining room with pizzas."

He clearly was giving answers that were false.... He wasn't doing it to protect himself from embarrassment; he was doing it to defeat Paula Jones's sexual harassment case. When the president testified in August before the grand jury, he never denied the truth of those testimonies. He refused to admit he lied during the deposition. He reiterated the truth of those because he knew he would be subject to perjury....

The Chief Justice: To the president's counsel from Senators Conrad and Torricelli: "The House of Representatives rejected two proposed articles of impeachment, including an article of alleged perjury in the *Jones* deposition. Do you believe that the Senate may, consistent with its constitutional role, convict and remove the president based on the allegations under the rejected articles…?"

Mr. Craig: … Article II was defeated. But more importantly, Article I specifically incorporates by reference, or tries to incorporate by reference, all the elements of Article II. And the House of Representatives, when they voted to reject Article II, I think, voted also to eliminate these issues that you have just heard about.…

Now, I have testified, as did Mr. Ruff, before the Judiciary Committee on this issue. I said that the president's responses in the *Jones* deposition were surely evasive, that they surely were incomplete, that they surely were intended to mislead; and it was wrong for him to do all that. But they were not perjurious.

… You cannot impeach the president on the issues that are included in Article II. He was not impeached; you cannot remove.

The Chief Justice: This is a question from Senator Santorum, Smith of Oregon, and Thomas to the House managers: "Please respond to the presentation made by counsel to the president… to the effect that the rejection of Article II had the effect of eliminating that portion of Article I. Did the House conclude that lying in a civil deposition is not impeachable, but that lying to the grand jury about whether the witness lied in a civil deposition is impeachable?"

Mr. Rogan: … [I]f Mr. Craig would read Article I, he would see that one of the allegations of perjury is that the president committed perjury in the grand jury when he referenced his civil deposition answers and reiterated those to the grand jury. And so the House made a decision not to use a separate stand-alone article. But I would respectfully submit to this body that that is the only inference that can be drawn.

The other thing that I want to mention briefly about Mr. Craig's presentation on that issue is what I found to be a startling admission on his part. Assuming, of course, that the Senate is going to look at Article I as it was drafted and passed by the House and is presented to you dealing with civil deposition perjury, Mr. Craig said that the president's testimony in the *Jones* case was evasive and incomplete.

He goes even further in his testimony, or statement to the Senate a couple days ago.... He said, "The president's testimony in the *Jones* case, the president was evasive, misleading, incomplete in his answers."

That begs the question. What kind of oath did the president take in the civil deposition? Did he ... raise his hand and swear to tell the truth, the evasive truth, and nothing but the evasive truth? Did he take an oath to tell the truth, the misleading truth, and nothing but the misleading truth? Did he take an oath to tell the truth, the incomplete truth, and nothing but the incomplete truth? ...

A question from Senator Reed of Rhode Island allowed the White House counsel to reply:

Mr. Ruff: The problem with Mr. Manager Rogan's analysis is twofold: One, he and his colleagues in the House on the Judiciary Committee drafted these four articles. They believed ... that it should be an impeachable offense, as he now puts it: did he fulfill, did the president fulfill his obligation in the *Jones* deposition? You don't need to make a lot of assumptions to understand merely on the face of the action that was taken that the full House said, no, it is not ...

Now, they try to hook onto a statement ... which the president said, I tried to walk through the minefield of the *Jones* deposition without violating the law and think I did. And, on that frail hook—which is clearly a statement of the president's state of mind about whether he succeeded or didn't succeed in testifying without violating the law in the *Jones* case—on that hook they hang every single item ... that the House rejected out of hand in Article II....

... I defy anybody in this Chamber, including the managers, to justify asking the president of the United States to defend against a reference from one page of a brief to another in order to tell the charges that he has been accused of.

If you read his grand jury testimony, you see he addressed a number of issues that he addressed in the *Jones* deposition. He clarified. He elaborated. He told the truth in the grand jury. Not once was he ever asked by the independent counsel and all his lawyers there who had been pursuing this investigation for seven months when they had him in the grand jury—not once did they ask him this simple question: Is everything you testified to in the *Jones* deposition true? Or, go down the list and say: Is what you testified to on page 6, or page 8, or page 87 true? ...

The Chief Justice: Senators Grassley, Smith of New Hampshire, Bunning and Craig ask the House managers: "In your presentation, you made the case that the Senate should call witnesses. In light of the White House's response to this argument, do you still hold this position?..."

Mr. McCollum: Mr. Chief Justice and Senators, the House definitely holds to the position that we should call witnesses....

In any criminal trial, you are going to call witnesses; you need to judge their credibility. I want to walk through what else they have said to you in the last couple of days that makes that point very clear with regard to...judging who you believe or who you don't believe and how important that is....

So let's take, for example, the gift-exchange discussion counsel had out here a couple of days ago with us.... The counsel said, well, let's go back and look at 10 different times where [Lewinsky] said about that subject all kinds of different ways. I submit to you that her grand jury testimony, after she got the immunity to testify, is clearly the most credible. We presented that to you, and that is what the president said....

The reality of this is that when you look at it, you have to question her testimony; you have to question her believability.... She should be brought out here, if they are going to challenge her like this, and give an opportunity for us to examine her on both sides and determine what is her best testimony about that, if that is important to you, and apparently it is to White House counsel.

The same thing is true of the questions with regard to Ms. Currie and the phone call dealing with the question of coming over to get the gifts.... White House counsel is saying, in essence, Ms. Lewinsky is not telling the truth; Ms. Currie is. If you don't have them here to listen to, who are you going to believe?...

The Chief Justice: The question from Senator Bryan to the White House counsel: "Would you please comment on any of the legal or factual assertions made by the managers in their response to the previous question...?"

Mr. Kendall: Mr. Chief Justice, the first question to ask about the need to call witnesses is, What would the witnesses add?... And the answer to that is, they would add nothing to what is not already there.

Yesterday, I held up the five volumes of testimony, thousands and thousands of pages.... Now, those five volumes represent eight or nine months of activity by the independent counsel. The independent counsel called many, many, many witnesses, many, many, many times.... And they repeatedly—I think abusively—but they repeatedly called witnesses—like Ms. Currie, Mr. Jordan, Ms. Lewinsky—back to the grand jury for repeated interviews. It is all right there. And the managers have really told you nothing that could be added to this record....

Now, in response to the question of how long it will take, I must tell you, we have never had a chance to call witnesses ourselves, to examine them, to cross-examine them, to subpoena documentary evidence—at no point in this process. It would be malpractice for any lawyer to try even a small civil case, let alone represent the president of the United States when the issue is his removal from office, without an adequate opportunity for discovery.

And I think if they are going to begin calling witnesses, and going outside the record, which we have right now—I think the record is complete; and we are dealing with it as best we can without having had an ability ourselves to subpoena people and cross-examine them and depose them—but I think you are looking realistically at a process of many months to have a fair discovery process.

> *A question from Senator Chafee asked the House managers to expand on the timing of the gift exchange and Betty Currie's cell phone call to Monica Lewinsky.*
>
> *Asa Hutchinson replied. He cited three separate Currie versions of when she had picked up the gifts, including "sometime in the last six months" and "a couple of weeks" after the December 28 meeting. Hutchinson contrasted that to Lewinsky's testimony, which during various interviews and testimony included "later that afternoon," "later in the day," "several hours" after she left the White House and "about 2 o'clock."*
>
> *The cell phone call came at about 3:30. "Now, does this destroy her credibility, particularly in contrast to that of Betty Currie?" Hutchinson asked. "I think it corroborates her." In addition, he observed, the White House team had made much of the fact that the cell phone call lasted only one minute. "It doesn't take a minute to say 'The president indicated you had something for me'—Monica knows what she is talking about—'Come over'—and that is the end of the conversation."*

> *A question from Senators Leahy, Schumer, and Wyden gave the president's lawyers a chance to respond. Ruff argued that Lewinsky had said on three occasions that Currie had picked up the gifts at 2. "So if you are going to ask, consistency, good*

memory . . . you have to ask, if it really happened at 2 o'clock as she recalled, what is the meaning of the 3:32 call?"

Ruff continued: "[T]here are only two people present at the moment in which . . . the managers would have that the president urged Betty Currie to go off and pick up the gifts. The president of the United States and Betty Currie, they both testified, flatly, that such a conversation did not occur." And Ruff dismissed as "wishful thinking" the managers' argument that the president had given Lewinsky more gifts "on the very day when he is conspiring with her to hide them"—their theory that "somehow it is a . . . message being sent, that because of these gifts she is . . . being roped into a conspiracy of silence." There was, he said, "not one single iota of evidence" to back that notion.

A question from Senators Snowe, Ashcroft, Enzi, Burns, Smith of New Hampshire, and Craig then turned the subject to the president's series of statements to Betty Currie after his deposition. Mr. Rogan reviewed the by now familiar scene and repeated the president's testimony eight months later, when asked what he had been trying to accomplish: "I was just trying to figure out what the facts were. I was trying to remember." Rogan then repeated the House managers' contention that this grand jury testimony was false; that in fact, after repeatedly invoking Betty Currie at the deposition as someone who could answer many questions, he was certain she would be called as a witness and was trying to influence her testimony.

Hutchinson added that although the president's lawyers had stressed Currie's testimony that she did not feel threatened during that session, that was beside the point. "The question is the president's intent, not how Betty Currie felt," he argued.

A question from Senator Kennedy allowed the White House counsel to respond. Ruff repeated the arguments made by Cheryl Mills about "the essential human dynamic . . . with the president, who had just gone through a deposition in which his worst fears were being realized. . . . He could see the press coming at him. They were already on the Internet. . . ." He repeated the White House contention that Betty Currie, who knew the most about his relationship with Lewinsky, was the last person he would want to have testify.

The Chief Justice: This is from Senator Feingold to the House managers: ". . . Should a Senator vote to convict the president based on his allegedly committing these federal statutory crimes if each of the elements of the crimes have not been proven beyond a reasonable doubt?"

Mr. Buyer:... [T]he Constitution does not discuss the standard of proof for impeachment trials. It simply states that the Senate shall have the power to try all impeachments....

Historically, the Senate has never set a standard of proof for impeachment trials. In the final analysis to the question, one which historically has been answered by individual Senators guided by your individual conscience.... White House counsel...like to talk to you about criminal statutes and cite that it requires the proof beyond a reasonable doubt. That is not so. This argument has been rejected by the Senate historically....

The criminal standard of proof again is inappropriate for impeachment trials. The result of conviction in an impeachment trial is removal from office, not punishment....

In addition, the House argued in the Claiborne trial the criminal standard is inappropriate because impeachment is, by its nature, a proceeding where the public interest weights more heavily than the interest of the individual....

The Chief Justice: The president's counsel are asked by Senators Thompson, Snowe, Enzi, Frist, Craig, DeWine, and Hatch: "... why would Dick Morris conduct a poll on whether the American people would forgive the president for committing perjury and obstruction of justice?"

Mr. Ruff:... You know, I think the honest answer has two pieces to it. I don't have a clue...But if you look at the record...it seems to me of absolutely no relevance whatsoever because...if the conversation occurred, there is nothing in this record that suggests that it had any impact on the conduct of the president or any other person....

I am not sure what a conversation with Mr. Morris, if it occurred, or a poll, if it was asked for, or what the motivation behind that poll means once you come to grips with the fact that the president of the United States was deceiving his family, his child, his wife, his colleagues, and the American people in that period in January....

The Chief Justice: Senator Lieberman asks the House managers: "... Given that any criminal act would arguably be at odds with the president's duty to execute the law, is it your position that the president may be impeached and removed for committing any criminal act, regardless of the type of crime it is?..."

Mr. Graham:... The answer is no, I would not want my president removed for any criminal wrongdoing. I would want my president removed only when there was a clear case that points to the right decision for the future of the country.... I would not want my president removed for trivial offenses, and that is the heart of the matter here.

I think I know why he took a poll. I think I know very well what he was up to: That his political and legal interests were so paramount in his mind, The law be damned and anybody who got in his way be damned.

Those are strong statements, but I think they are borne out by the facts in this case, and that is what I would look for....

My belief is that this president did not trust the American legal system to vindicate his interest without cheating. My belief is that when he went back to his secretary, it is not reasonable that he was trying to refresh his memory and get his thoughts together. My belief is that he tried to set up a scenario that was going to make a young lady pay a price if she ever decided to cooperate with the other side. I believe he did not need to refresh his memory whether or not Monica Lewinsky wanted to have sex with him....

I believe that you should only remove a president who, in a calculated fashion, puts the legal and political interests of himself over the good of the nation in a selfish way, that you only should remove a president who, after being begged by everybody in the country, don't go into a grand jury and lie, and he in fact lied. Nothing trivial should remove my president....

...A question from Senators Schumer and Kerrey of Nebraska allowed the president's lawyers to repeat their complaint that the perjury charges against the president had been changing, in Gregory Craig's words, "right up until...the very first day of this trial." What Rogan said in his presentation, Craig argued, was different from what had been in the trial brief. And before that, at almost every stage, he said, "there were allegations added, there were allegations subtracted."

Craig also took the opportunity to repeat the defense team's explanation of the grand jury testimony about the Lewinsky affidavit. The president's answer had been clear, he said: He had not been focused on what Bennett was saying. Craig continued: "Then, at the grand jury some seven months later, he was read that statement by the special prosecutor. The question was, 'And this statement was false, isn't that true?' The answer the president gave was that, well, in fact, it depends on the meaning of the word 'is.' He didn't claim that that was what he was thinking at the time in the Jones deposition."

A question from Senator Lott allowed Rogan to reply. "Try as they might, the facts are clear," he said. "The president, in his August deposition, attempted to justify away, attempted to explain away his perjurious conduct on January 17 when he

was deposed." As for the larger allegation that the president had been un-
fairly by never being presented with the charges against him, Rogan said: "He would
be an ostrich with his neck so far down in the sand" not to know. The preceding fall,
the independent counsel had filed a 445-page report, he said; within it "are all of
the allegations, are all of the facts and all of the circumstances that were forwarded
to the House of Representatives for review." And, said Rogan, "Not only did the
president have the benefit of Judge Starr's report, he also has the benefit of the writ-
ten report from the House Judiciary Committee—same facts, same circumstances,
nothing changed." It couldn't all have come as a surprise, Rogan noted, since some-
how the president's "army of lawyers" had been able to respond to the Starr report
almost as quickly as it appeared.

Ruff took advantage of a rhetorical question from three senators to get in a last
word: "It does seem mildly odd to me that the answer to the question your charges
aren't known or vague is, 'Look at that pile. You will find them right in there. You
fellows . . . did a good job responding to what you could. So you must be perfectly
well prepared to defend against whatever charges we bring.' I don't think there is
a judge anywhere in the United States . . . who would accept either explanation
from a prosecutor. . . ."

The Chief Justice: This is from Senator Kerry of Massachusetts to the counsel for the president: "Is it fair to say that the articles and manager presentations stress the *Jones* perjury allegations rejected by the House, because they
cannot credibly, on the law, satisfy the elements and argue perjury in the
grand jury investigation?"

Mr. Ruff: . . . I do not want to suggest in any way that the motivation of the
managers is less than professional and appropriate. But I do think that, indeed,
they know . . . that the president of the United States, when he began his grand
jury testimony by making the most painful admission a human being could
ever make, and thereafter did his best—albeit in the face of tough and probing and repetitive questioning for 4 hours—did his best to tell the truth.
    That they had a very difficult, indeed virtually impossible, task to persuade
any dispassionate trier of fact and law that he had intentionally given false testimony, and you can see that evidenced, I think most clearly, if you look at
some of the first allegations made as to what constitutes perjury—things like
the use of the words "on certain occasions" or "occasionally" to describe a battle over whether 11 or 20 or 17 fit within that description. It does seem fair to

say that they would not be fighting those battles in this Chamber if they had any real confidence in their cause on Article I, and thus they do seek, for whatever tactical or other purpose, to try to bring in those things which so many of their colleagues rejected out of hand in the House of Representatives.

The Chief Justice: Senators Specter, Helms, Abraham, Ashcroft, and Stevens direct this question to the president's counsel: "President Clinton testified before the grand jury that he was merely trying to "refresh" his memory when he made these statements to Betty Currie. How can someone "refresh" their recollection by making statements they know are false?"

Ms. Mills: [O]bviously he was understandably concerned about the media attention that he knew was impending. And in particular, as he walked through the questions, he was thinking about his own thoughts and seeking, as I think I talked about, concurrence or input or some type of reaction from Ms. Currie.

I think in making those statements, he was asking questions to see what her understanding was based on some of the questions that had been posed to him by the *Jones* lawyers, because some of them were so off base. And so he was asking from Ms. Currie essentially what her perception was, what her thoughts were.

I think as you walk through each one of those questions, he was expressing what his own thoughts and feelings were with regard to this and was seeking some concurrence or affirmation from her. I think he was agitated. I think he was concerned. He knew what was going to happen, and I think that is why he posed the question in the way that he did.

The next morning, Saturday, January 23, the Senate reassembled for more questions and answers.

The first question, from Senator Reid of Nevada, challenged the House managers on the fact that they had asked the independent counsel to intervene to get Monica Lewinsky to submit to an informal interview with them—something her lawyers had previously refused. Reid wanted to know whether they had informed the White House lawyers of this move, and if not, why not.

Ed Bryant responded. No, he said, he was not aware of any such notice to the president's counsel. He went on to explain that since the question of whether witnesses would be called was still up in the air, the managers wanted to interview Lewinsky, who was potentially "very important." Most of the other potential wit-

nesses "are in essence in the White House control," Bryant explained. But Lewinsky was in a "unique" position, he said, and they had asked the OIC, which had jurisdiction over her immunity agreement, to intervene on their behalf.

Senator Leahy wanted to know whether the managers had consulted with the Senate before asking Starr to help them interview Lewinsky; it might, he suggested, violate the Senate's rules on trial procedure.

McCollum answered that they had not consulted any senators because they didn't think their desire to speak with Lewinsky "had anything to do with the rule you passed." He added: "If you have a witness that you are going to produce, you have a right to prepare that witness. It is as plain and simple as that." The managers, he argued, would have been derelict in their duty if they had not tried to interview Lewinsky.

The Chief Justice: This question is from Senators Lott and Thurmond to the House managers: "Please give specific examples of conflicting testimony or an incomplete record where the calling of witnesses would prove beneficial to the Senate."

Mr. Hutchinson:... The White House counselors, the president of the United States, has denied each and every allegation under the two articles that have been submitted to this body. I focused on the obstruction of justice, and each of the seven elements of the obstruction of justice has been denied by the president. This puts it all in issue.

For example, let's start with the issue of lying to the aides. The president said he was truthful with his aides, Mr. Podesta and Sidney Blumenthal. Yet, if you look at the testimony of John Podesta, where he says the president came in and denied having sex of any kind with Ms. Lewinsky and goes into the details of that, that is in direct conflict with the testimony of the president of the United States. The same thing is true of the testimony of Mr. Blumenthal versus the testimony of the president of the United States.

Then Hutchinson reviewed the conflicts between the testimony of Lewinsky and the president: on whether he had told her she had to turn over the gifts, on whether they had talked about their cover stories in regard to the affidavit. Lewinsky's and Jordan's testimony conflicted, too, on whether she had told him details about the relationship (she said yes, he said no); on whether he had advised her to get rid of notes she had been keeping (she said yes, he said no); on whether he assisted in correcting

the affidavit (he did not recall that). And there were differences between Betty Cur-
rie and the president on what Hutchinson called "the coaching incident." Finally,
Hutchinson said there was conflict between the president and a witness at the de-
position over whether the president had been paying attention to Robert Bennett
when he invoked the false affidavit. All this, he argued, cried out for testimony.

The Chief Justice: This is a question from Senator Abraham to the president's counsel: "Is it your position that Ms. Lewinsky was lying in her grand jury testimony, her grand jury deposition, and her FBI interviews when she said that the president engaged in conduct with her that constituted "sexual relations" even under his narrow interpretation of the term in the *Jones* deposition? Is it your position that she was also lying when she gave essentially the same account contemporaneously with the occurrence of the events to her friends and counselors?"

Mr. Craig: ... In my presentation to the Senate, I acknowledged that there was a disparity between what the president had recounted and what Ms. Lewinsky said happened when it came to recalling and reporting these specific rather graphic and intimate details concerning their activities.... But I also suggested—and I suggest to you today—that not every disagreement, not every discrepancy, is the foodstuff or the subject of a perjury charge....

I said also that I thought that this disagreement, this disparity, was of questionable materiality. Let me explain why. On January 29, Judge Wright ruled that Ms. Lewinsky's testimony about her relationship with President Clinton was unnecessary and maybe even inadmissible; that she had had no information relating to the core issues of the case. She made that ruling after all the allegations about that relationship had been made public.... In truth, Ms. Lewinsky was ... a peripheral witness on issues not having to do with the core issues of the case, and the case had no legal merit.

... The House managers ... argue that if you believe Monica Lewinsky on this issue, you must disbelieve Bill Clinton, and if you disbelieve Bill Clinton, you must conclude that he knowingly perjured himself when he denied under oath having this kind of contact with Ms. Lewinsky.

Now, this direct issue was addressed by the panel of expert prosecutors that we brought to testify before the Judiciary Committee.... They talked about the oath-on-oath issue ... and they concluded that no reasonable, though responsible, prosecutor would bring this kind of case based on that kind of an issue....

In response to a question from Senators Voinovich, Jeffords, and Chafee, McCollum addressed the question of what the president had meant when he told Lewinsky he did not need to see her affidavit because he had seen "15 others." McCollum said that "the most logical conclusion is that he had seen 15 other drafts" of her affidavit. He explained this "in the context of everything else this president was intent on . . . and the interest that he had already shown from all the conversations that he had had with Vernon Jordan and others to make sure that this affidavit was on track, and knowing that he was going to testify in a few days himself in the Jones case, and rely on it. . . ."

A question from Senator Leahy allowed David Kendall to respond. There was simply no evidence at all, he said, that the president saw any affidavit draft. In fact, he said, there was nothing in the record indicating "that there were more than one or two drafts of Ms. Lewinsky's affidavit."

The Chief Justice: This question is from Senators DeWine, Santorum, and Fitzgerald to the president's counsel: ". . . [I]s it your contention that if the president tampered with witnesses, encouraged the hiding of evidence, and corruptly influenced the filing of a false affidavit by a witness, that these acts do not rise to the level of an impeachable offense?

Mr. Ruff: . . . [A]ll I can do, I suppose, is to remind you, as I have too frequently, I am sure, that if you try to put yourself in the minds and the hearts of the men who created our system of Government, they wanted to know only really one answer to one question, as framed in many different ways, but the essence remains the same: Is there a sufficient danger to the state—danger to the state—to warrant what my colleagues across the aisle here have called the political death penalty. And I think the answer to that is no.

Then, in answer to a question from Senator Wellstone, Ruff turned to the subject of how much weight public opinion should have in the Senate's decision:

. . . I think that the answer to that question is not the polls that you read in the newspapers or that you see on your evening news. . . . But surely one way to test the ultimate question that I just described in response to the last inquiry . . . is to ask yourself, on the basis of experience over the last year . . . what the people are saying to you and what your sense of their needs is: Do they need the kind of cleansing that Manager Buyer spoke about?

I think the answer to that, if you look within the body of people you are most familiar with, must be no. This isn't to say that it is a popularity contest, that we ought to go out and have a referendum or another poll before you all decide on this. But surely the sense of the people, the will of the people, the belief of the people in this president's ability to govern must educate each of you, not mandate a result, but surely guide the result that you reach in this proceeding.

Asked by Senator Lott whether the managers wished to respond, Hyde spoke of the Congress's responsibilities in a representative democracy. "We are not delegates who are sent here to weigh our mail every day and then to vote accordingly," he said. "We are elected to bring our judgment, our experience and our consciences with us here." There were certain principles, he said, over which he would be prepared to lose his job. "Despite all the polls and all the hostile editorials, America is hungry for people who believe in something. You may disagree with us, but we believe in something."

After a recess, the trial recommenced. The first question came from Senator Biden: "If a Senator believes that the president may have lied to the American people, his family and his aides, and that some of his answers before the grand jury were misleading or half-truths, but that he could not be convicted in a court of law for either perjury or obstruction of justice, is it the opinion of the House managers that his actions still justify removing the president from office?"

Bob Barr took the floor:

Mr. Barr: ... [The] Criminal Code does not include the offenses of lying to one's family. That is not what brings us here today. What brings us here today is the belief by the House of Representatives in lawful public vote that this president violated, in numerous respects, his oath of office and the Criminal Code of the United States of America—in particular, that he committed perjury and obstruction of justice....

We respectfully submit ... that these are prosecutable cases....

The Chief Justice: This is a question from Senators Snowe, Mack, Chafee, Burns, and Craig to the House managers: "Before Ms. Lewinsky was subpoenaed in the *Jones* case, the president refused on five separate occasions ... to produce information about gifts from Lewinsky. The president's counsel argued the president was unconcerned about these gifts. If that is the case, why didn't he produce these gifts in November and December?"

Mr. Rogan: ... Every piece of this puzzle, when put together, demonstrates a very clear pattern of obstructing justice, not to cover up personal affairs, not to cover up an indiscretion, but to destroy Paula Jones's rights under the sexual harassment laws of this country to have her day in court. That is the ultimate question that this body is going to have to address.

Yes, reasonable minds can differ on this case as to whether the president should be removed from office. But reasonable minds can only differ if those reasonable minds come to the conclusion that enforcement of the sexual harassment laws in this country are less important than the preservation of this man in the office of the presidency. And that is the ultimate question that this body is going to have to answer. What is more important—the survival of Bill Clinton's presidency in the face of perjury and obstruction of justice, or the protection of the sexual harassment laws in this country? ...

The Chief Justice: This is from Senator Daschle to the House managers: "Will you agree to arrange to have prepared a verbatim, unedited transcript of any debriefing which may occur with Ms. Lewinsky for immediate distribution to the Senate? And will you agree also to provide for the inclusion of any such debriefing of representatives of the Senate, one selected by the majority and one by the minority?"

Mr. McCollum: Mr. Chief Justice and Members of the Senate, it is not our intent to be doing a deposition, a formal presentation, a preparation for the Senate, if we talk to Ms. Lewinsky. It is our intent to do what any good attorney would do in preparing to go to trial, presuming ... we are going to be able to depose and have witnesses, and that is to meet with the witness, talk with the witness, and prepare the witness. And any good attorney who does that is going to meet his or her witness in their own confidences, in their own quiet respite. We discover things that way. We are not prepared. No. The answer to your question is no, we are not prepared to say we are going to give you our work product, which is what that would be....

I think it was Mr. Hutchinson who said earlier—this is an adversarial position. The White House counsel will have their chance to talk to witnesses that they are going to present; we will have our chance to talk to ours. Then there is the opportunity for the depositions, which is what comes next, which is the formal proceedings when we both have a chance to talk with them. Then, of course, if you let us call them as witnesses here, they will be here, and they will get cross-examined, and examined, and all the questions you can imagine will be asked. That is the traditional American system of justice....

Senator Hatch submitted a question noting that Chief Federal District Judge Johnson had ruled that Monica Lewinsky's immunity agreement required her to submit to an interview with the House. What light did that shed on the earlier debate, Hatch asked the House managers?

Bryant responded. "What we have seen this morning is a completely innocent standard practice of sitting down with a potential witness ... and deciding whether or not you want to use her," he said. "Judge Johnson clearly vindicated this right to do that." If the managers had offended the senators in any way, he apologized, "We certainly didn't intend to break any rules about this, and we don't think we did."

The Chief Justice: This question is from Senators Thurmond and Bunning to the counsel for the president: "If there was no case and the White House accepted the results of the justice system, why then did the president pay nearly $1 million to Paula Jones?"

Mr. Ruff: ... As I think everyone knows in this Chamber, and outside this Chamber, who has practiced law, litigated difficult cases, the judgment of a defendant to settle a case, to pay whatever sum may be required to settle it, is ... not reflective of any belief that he was wrong, that the other side was right. It reflects in this case, very candidly, a judgment by the president, which he has stated publicly, that in the midst of the many matters that he is responsible for ... he could no longer spend any of that time and any of that energy on the *Jones* case....

After a lunch break, the session resumed with a question from Senator Bingaman for the president's lawyers: "When Samuel Dash resigned as adviser to the independent counsel, he wrote ... that he was doing so because the independent counsel had become an advocate and had 'unlawfully intruded on the power of impeachment which the Constitution gives solely to the House.' In using his power to assist one party to the pending impeaching trial ... do you believe he has unlawfully intruded on the power of the Senate to try impeachments?"

Mr. Ruff: ... We were, obviously, dismayed at the role that the independent counsel chose to follow rather than simply sending information to the House that might bear on possible impeachable offenses but, rather, to drive his van up to the building and unload unscreened, undiluted boxes of information which thereafter made their way, at least in part, into the public domain.

But surely it was a shock to all of us, at least on this side, to learn yesterday evening that playing a role in the House proceedings had now become a role in this Chamber, that the independent counsel was using not only his powers of coercion but calling on the U.S. district court to assist him and, in turn, enabling the managers not simply, as they would have it, to do a little work product, to do a little meeting and greeting ... but, rather, saying to this witness: I hold your life in my hands and I'm going to transfer that power to the managers for the House of Representatives.

The managers have said we are engaged in an adversary process here, and they themselves have talked long and loud today about letting them play out the process that any lawyer would play out preparing for trial. Well, no other lawyer that I know of gets to have a prosecutor sitting in a room with him and saying to the witness: Talk to these people or your immunity deal is gone and you may go to jail. ...

The Chief Justice: This is a question from Senators Specter, Frist, Smith of New Hampshire, Inhofe, Lugar, Brownback, Roth, and Crapo to counsel for the president: "In arguing that an impeachable offense involves only a public duty, what is your best argument that a public duty is not involved in the president's constitutional duty to execute the laws? At a minimum, doesn't the president have a duty not to violate the laws under the constitutional responsibility to execute the laws?"

Mr. Ruff: It can't be. It can't be that if the president violates the law and thus violates his duty faithfully to carry out the laws, he is removed from office. Because that would literally encompass virtually every law, every regulation, every policy, every guideline that you could imagine that he is responsible for carrying out in the executive branch. If that were so, it would have been very simple for the framers to say the president shall be impeached for treason, bribery and failure to carry out his oath faithfully to execute the laws. ...

Senator Graham asked the president's lawyers to comment on whether, if the Senate decided not to remove the president, there were constitutional impediments to lesser measures, including some form of censure of a motion requiring the president to promise never to accept a pardon for any previous criminal activities.

Ruff replied that he had "stated formally on behalf of the president... that he would not... seek or accept a pardon." As for lesser measures, he said he saw no constitutional barriers to the Senate's doing pretty much anything it chose to do.

The Chief Justice: This is a question from Senator Thompson to the House managers: "Do you have any comment on the answer given by the president's counsel with regard to the Office of Independent Counsel?"

Mr. McCollum: ... It is our judgment—and I think a fair judgment—that we should be allowed and are permitted, under any of the rules normal to this, to request of the Office of Independent Counsel the opportunity to talk to Monica Lewinsky, which we otherwise apparently were not going to be able to have as a normal course of preparation.

It makes me wonder—with all of the complaints that are going on here from the White House attorneys about this and their desire not to have witnesses—what they are afraid of. Are they afraid of our talking to Monica Lewinsky?... Are they afraid of what she might say out here? I don't think they should be, but they appear to be.

We are not doing anything abnormal. We are exercising our privileges, our rights. If it were a prosecutor and you had a prosecutorial arm, which you do in the case of the Independent Counsel Office, that had an immunity agreement... you certainly would not hesitate if you had a recalcitrant witness who you needed to call to utilize that immunity agreement... and you certainly would not hesitate if you needed to use that immunity agreement to assure truthful testimony in any proceeding that was going on....

The Chief Justice: This is a question from Senator Bond to the House managers: "When Ms. Mills described the president's testimony before the *Jones* grand jury, she said the president was "surprised" by questions about Ms. Lewinsky. What evidence is there of the president's knowledge that Lewinsky questions would be asked? Is there evidence that he knew in advance the details of the Lewinsky affidavit which his counsel presented at the *Jones* deposition?

Mr. Hutchinson: ... There are numerous evidences in the record to show that the president was not surprised about the questions pertaining to Monica Lewinsky at the January 17 deposition. First of all, in regard to the affidavit testimony of Monica Lewinsky—I believe it was January 6—5th or 6th—is that she discussed that with the president, signing that affidavit, and the content of the affidavit. That is whenever he made his statement, "I don't need to see it. I have seen 15 of them."... Also, circumstantially, there is a conversation between Mr. Jordan and the president during this time.

But in addition... a few days before the president's deposition testimony... Michael Isikoff of a national publication called Betty Currie and asked about courier records on the gifts. This startled Betty Currie, obviously, because the gifts at that point were under her bed. As she recalled, she probably told the president that.

And then second, she went to see Vernon Jordan about that issue. All of that leads you to believe, clearly, that the president fully knew that when he went into the deposition on January 17, that he would be asked time and time again about the specifics of his relationship with Monica Lewinsky....

The Chief Justice: This question is from Senators Bond, Brownback, Campbell, Hagel, Lugar, Hutchison of Texas, Roth and Stevens. It is directed to the House managers: "After everything you have heard over the last several weeks from the president's counsel, do you still believe that the facts support the charges of obstruction of justice alleged in the articles of impeachment? Specifically, what allegations of improper conduct has the president's counsel failed to undermine?..."

Mr. Hutchinson:... The question is, Where has the president attacked, counselors attacked credibly the allegations of obstruction? The first one is that the president personally encouraged a witness, Monica Lewinsky, to lie. This is on December 17 at 2 a.m. in the morning when the president calls Monica to tell her that she is a witness on the list.... At that time, of course, she is nervous, she is a witness and asked, "Well, what am I going to say?" And the president offers, according to Monica Lewinsky, you can always say you came to see Betty or you came to deliver papers.

The president's counselor attacked this by saying, "Well, remember what Monica said, 'I was never told to lie.' " I refer you to a Tenth Circuit case, *United States v. Tranakos,* Tenth Circuit, 1990. The law is that the request to lie need not be a direct statement. As the court held: "The statute prohibits elliptical suggestions as much as it does direct commands....

The second one is the jobs and the false affidavit. They say there is absolutely no connection in these two, none whatsoever. Of course, I pointed out the testimony of Vernon Jordan who testified it doesn't take an Einstein to know that whenever he found out she was a witness, she was under subpoena, that the subpoena changed the circumstances.... Of course, Vernon Jordan also indicated the president's personal involvement when he testified before the grand jury in June. He said he was interested in this matter: "He ... was the source of it coming to my attention in the first place." ...

The third area of obstruction is tampering with the witness, Betty Currie, on January 18 and January 20 when the questions were posed after the deposition. The president's counselor challenged this and said, Well, she wasn't a witness. Even the *Jones* lawyers never had any clue that she was going to be a witness in this case.... [B]ut we found the subpoena. We found the subpoena that was actually issued a few days after the deposition for Betty Currie. She was a witness; she was not just a prospective witness. She was there, she had to be ready to go and the president knew this and the *Jones* lawyer knew it. So that stands. The pillar of obstruction stands....

Another area of obstruction was December 28 when the gifts were retrieved, and this has been challenged. I will admit, as I always have, that there is a dispute in the testimony. But I believe the case is made through the circumstances, the motivation, the testimony of Monica Lewinsky as to what Betty Currie said when she called and the corroborating evidence. I don't believe they have poked a hole in that. I believe it stands. We would like to hear the witnesses to make you feel more comfortable in resolving that conflict and determine the credibility of those witnesses.

But the gifts that were subpoenaed were evidence in a trial; they were needed in a civil rights case. The president knew they were under subpoena; he had the most to gain, and they were retrieved....

There are other areas of obstruction, including the president allowing his attorney, Robert Bennett, to make false representations to the Federal district judge in the deposition. The president's defense is that there is no proof whatsoever that he was paying any attention. We offered the videotape that shows he is believed to be looking at the attorney, but we would offer a witness in that regard to show that he was attentive. That is simply something that can be substantiated....

The Chief Justice: ... This question from Senator Harkin is to counsel for the president: "There are three contradictions in the record: One, who touched whom on what parts of the body; two, when the relationship began; three, who called whom to get the gifts, Ms. Currie or Ms. Lewinsky. How will these witnesses clear up the contradiction?"

Mr. Craig: ... The House managers have argued that they need to call witnesses for the purposes of resolving inconsistencies, conflicts, and discrepancies in testimony. And they have, in fact, identified Monica Lewinsky in particular as having given testimony in conflict with the testimony of the president, with Betty Currie and Vernon Jordan....

I would suspect that one of the reasons they want to inquire of Ms. Lewinsky is not to resolve discrepancies and disputes, it is to perhaps challenge her testimony when it is helpful to the president and perhaps bolster her testimony when it is not helpful to the president....

I suggest ... they seek to do nothing more than to attack, attack, attack the best friend of the United States, the president of the United States, and his personal secretary. That is the reason they want to talk to these people. I think it is an improper reason. It is wanting to win too much. I don't think the U.S. Senate should be part of it.

The majority leader announced that the Senate would adjourn, to resume work on Monday, January 25.

DEBATING THE MOTIONS

On Monday, January 25, the first order of business was the White House's motion to dismiss the case against President Clinton. Each side had one hour to present its arguments.

Making the arguments for dismissal on behalf of the White House was Nicole Seligman. "We submit to you that the moment has arrived where the best interests of the nation, the wise prescription of the framers and the failure of the managers' proof all point to dismissal," she said. "You have listened. You have heard. The case cannot be made." There, were, said Seligman, four grounds for the White House's argument.

Ms. Seligman: ... The first ground is the core constitutional issue before you, the failure of the articles to charge impeachable offenses. They do not do so. They do not allege conduct that, if proven, violated the public trust in the manner the framers intended when they wrote the words "treason, bribery or other high crimes and misdemeanors." For absent an element of immediate danger to the state, a danger of such magnitude that it cannot await resolution by the electorate in the normal cycle, the framers intended restraint. There is no such danger to the state here. ...

The second and third grounds we offer to you relate to the deeply flawed drafting of the articles by the House of Representatives. They have left the House managers free to fill what Mr. Ruff described as "an empty vessel," to define for the House of Representatives what it really had in mind when it impeached the president. But that is not a role that the Constitution allows to be delegated to the House managers.... It is a role that is explicitly and uniquely reserved to the full House of Representatives which, under our Constitution, has the sole power to impeach.

The articles also are unconstitutionally defective for yet another reason, because each article combines a menu of charges, and the managers invite the Members of this body to convict on one or more of the charges they list. The result is the deeply troubling prospect that the president might be convicted and removed from office without two-thirds of the Senate agreeing on what the president actually did....

The fourth ground for the motion is based on the facts.... Recognizing that each Senator is free to choose the standard of proof that his or her conscience dictates, we submit that if the question is, as the managers would have it, whether the president has committed a crime, that standard should be proof beyond a reasonable doubt. And it is clear that such a standard, that is, proof to the level of certainty necessary to make the most significant decisions you face in life, cannot possibly be met here. The presentations last week demonstrated that the record is full of exculpatory facts and deeply ambiguous circumstantial evidence that will make it impossible for the managers to meet this standard...

Now, the managers have with great ingenuity spun out theories of wrongdoing that they have advanced repeatedly, persistently, passionately. But mere repetition, no matter how dogged, cannot create a reality where there is none. The factual record is before you. We submit that it does not approach the kind of case that you would need to justify the conviction and removal of the president from office. And calling witnesses is not the answer. All the evidence you need to make your decision is before you....

Seligman elaborated on each of the grounds for dismissal, ending with the facts of the case. "The managers cannot possibly meet their burden of proof here," she said. She continued:

Look briefly at Article I. Much of it challenges the president's assertions of his own state of mind, his understanding of the definition given to him, ... his legal opinion of his *Jones* testimony, his mindset during statements of his lawyer, Robert Bennett. The managers offer speculation and theories about these matters, but you are not here to try speculation and theories. You are here to try facts....

Other claims in Article I are so insubstantial as to be frivolous.... Certain answers about the particulars of the admitted intimate relationship between the president and Ms. Lewinsky—whether their admitted inappropriate encounters were properly characterized as occurring on "certain occasions" is but one example—could not possibly have had any bearing on the Starr investigation....

Remember, in the grand jury the president admitted to the relationship, admitted it was improper, admitted it occurs over time, admitted he had sought to hide it, admitted he had misled his wife, his staff, his friends, the country. But how it began, exactly when it began, how many intimate encounters there were, whether there were 11 or 17 or some other number and with what frequency, these are details irrelevant to the Starr investigation, and I must say, irrelevant to your decision whether to remove the freely elected president of the United States.

The president did not obstruct justice. The president did not commit perjury. The president must not be removed. The facts do not permit it....

If you don't believe this body should remove the president, or if you... simply have heard enough to make up your mind, then the time to end this is now.

Asa Hutchinson had stated the House managers' general argument against dismissal even before Seligman spoke:

Mr. Hutchinson: ... In this case of impeachment, the House of Representatives found that there was substantial evidence to support these articles. And the Senate should not summarily dismiss the charges.

... [T]o dismiss the case would be unprecedented from a historical standpoint...; it would be damaging to the constitution, because the Senate would fail to try the case; it would be harmful to the body politic, because there is no resolution of the issues of the case; but, most importantly, it would show willful blindness to the evidentiary record....

After Seligman's presentation, Hutchinson spoke briefly, emphasizing what Seligman's presentation had not addressed: the president's second interview with Betty Currie, repeating the false statements about the relationship, and the "mission accomplished" message from Vernon Jordan. Both of these, he contended, were comprehensible only in terms of the managers' obstruction-of-justice case.

Then it was Lindsey Graham's turn.

Mr. Graham: ... Take this case to a conclusion, so America will not be confused as to whether or not their president committed crimes. There will be people watching what we do here, and they will be confused as to whether or not the conversation between President Clinton and Ms. Currie was illegal or not. Let us know. That is so important. Let us know—when he went to Monica Lewinsky and talked about a cover story—if that is what we want to go on here every day. And a trial 20 months from now does us no good, because this happened when he was president, ladies and gentlemen. This happened when he raised the defense, "You can't sue me because I'm president." ...

Graham pressed through the details of the managers' case, stressing what he called its "subtleties." He concluded:

You pick the lie, but it is there. And if you can reconcile that, you are better than I am. That is up to you all. And does it really matter? So what? I think it matters a great deal if you are suing for sexually harassing somebody, and they are on to the fact that you can't control yourself enough to stop it four or five years after you are sued, and you are doing it in the White House with somebody half your age. I think that would matter. Maybe that is the difference between getting bamboozled in court and having to pay $850,000.

People are going to be confused if we don't bring this case to a conclusion. I suggest to you, it matters a great deal, that any major CEO, any low-level employee of any business in the country, would have been tossed out for something like that. But I know he is the president. Electing somebody should not distance them from common decency and the rule of law to the point that, when it is all over with, you don't know what you have got left in this country....

Finally, it was Henry Hyde's turn.

Mr. Hyde: ... Mr. Ruff, and counsel, and distinguished Senators, I want to be very candid with you, and that may involve diplomatic breaches because I am parliamentarily illiterate. But nonetheless, I looked at this motion to dismiss and I was astounded, really....

I ... looked in the thesaurus about "dismiss" and I came up with "disregard, ignore, brush off." I just was surprised that this motion is here now before we conclude the case....

The most salient reason for defeating this motion is Article I, section 3 of the Constitution which says that the Senate shall have the sole power to try—

to try—all impeachments. Now, a trial, as I understand it, is a search for truth, and it should not be trumped by a search for an exit strategy.

It seems to me this motion elevates convenience over constitutional process and by implication ratifies an unusual extension of sovereign immunity. If these articles are dismissed, all inferences in support of the respondents, in support of us, the managers, should be allowed; and if you allow all reasonable inferences in our favor, what kind of a message does it send to America to dismiss the articles of impeachment? Charges of perjury, obstruction of justice are summarily dismissed—disregarded, ignored, brushed off. These are charges that send ordinary folk to jail every day of the week and remove Federal judges. But I can see this president is different. But if the double standard is to flourish on Capitol Hill, I don't think we have accomplished a great deal.... That is an awful lot to dismiss with a brush-off, to ignore with a mere "so what."

... It may be routine to file a motion to dismiss. But I take very seriously a motion to dismiss, especially when it is offered by the very distinguished Senator[1] who did that. But I hope in a bipartisan way, I would hope some Democrats would support the rejection of this motion, as difficult as it is, because I don't think this whole sad, sad, drama will end. We will never get it behind us until you vote up or down on the articles. And when you do, however you vote, we will all collect our papers, bow from the waist, thank you for your courtesy, and leave and go gently into the night. But let us finish our job.

After the managers concluded, Sen. Tom Harkin of Iowa introduced a motion to suspend the Senate rules to allow open debate on the motion to dismiss. It failed to pass, and the Senate closed its doors for debate.

The next day, Tuesday, January 26, the topic was whether to call witnesses. On behalf of the House managers, Ed Bryant presented the motion. It requested depositions of Monica Lewinsky, Vernon Jordan, and Sidney Blumenthal, and asked the Senate to admit into evidence certain documents not already included.

McCollum began the debate by saying the managers had wanted to call ten or twelve witnesses for deposition and had hoped that two or three might actually testify live in the Senate chamber, but they had been told to keep their deposition list to just two or three.

[1] The motion had been introduced by Sen. Robert Byrd of West Virginia.

If allowed these witnesses, McCollum said, they would ask no questions of Monica Lewinsky about explicit sexual relations. And they thought the entire process of deposing and calling all the witnesses could be accomplished in two to five days.

For some of the charges, McCollum said, "it is our judgment that the president's guilt is so clear . . . that we don't think that any witnesses are needed." One was the perjury charge about where the president had touched Lewinsky; Lewinsky's testimony—corroborated by people she told—put what had happened between them squarely within the definition of sexual relations in the Jones case.

McCollum also said no witnesses were needed to establish perjury when the president "told the grand jury it was his goal to be truthful in the Jones deposition." None were needed on the obstruction and witness-tampering charge about the statements to Betty Currie, either, nor on the obstruction and perjury charges related to the president's allowing his lawyer to make false statements about Lewinsky's affidavit.

McCollum continued:

On the other hand, we believe that . . . we need to bring in witnesses to resolve conflicting testimony to give you a true picture of the president's scheme to lie and conceal evidence for the other obstruction of justice charges and certainly for the last perjury charge. They are more complex. They are more dependent on circumstantial evidence and inferences you logically have to draw. And that is why you need to hear from Monica Lewinsky, Vernon Jordan and Sidney Blumenthal, to tell you about these things themselves.

When you do, you are just plain going to get a different flavor; you are going to feel the sense of this. We believe you will find at the end of the day, once you have done that . . . the president is guilty of the entire scheme we presented to you in every detail beyond a reasonable doubt. . . .

I am not going to be the one describing what Monica Lewinsky is going to show you if she comes in here. I am going to tell you, even if we depose her, having had the opportunity to talk with this intelligent and very impressionable young woman the other day, I can tell you that she herself will convey this story to you in a way that it cannot be conveyed off a piece of paper. . . .

I suppose that is why the White House counselors are so afraid of our calling any witnesses. They don't want you to have the opportunity to see that, an opportunity you can only get the full flavor of if not only you let us take the depositions, but you at least let us call her live here on the floor. . . .

They know that the written record conceals this. There is no way to lift that out. There is no way for you to see the relationship, how she responds to the questions, how she answers, how she conducts herself in making it very apparent what the president's true meaning and intent was.…

McCollum then turned to three additional pieces of new evidence the managers wanted to admit. First was an affidavit from Barry W. Ward, a law clerk to Judge Susan Webber Wright during the Jones case. In it, said McCollum, Ward testified that the president had been observant during the exchanges between Robert Bennett and the judge over Monica Lewinsky's false affidavit. The second piece of new evidence was a copy of the Jones subpoena to Betty Currie, dated January 22, a copy of the witness list on which she appeared, and a declaration from Jones lawyer T. Wesley Holmes that Currie had been subpoenaed because the lawyers had good information that she had facilitated Lewinsky's meetings with the president and was central to their "cover story." Finally, the managers wanted to admit evidence about a fifty-six-minute telephone conversation on December 6 between the president and Lewinsky.

Ed Bryant then argued that it was critical for the Senate to hear and see Monica Lewinsky, in particular, on the factual disputes over the affidavit, the gift exchange, and the job search.

Asa Hutchinson argued the case for calling Vernon Jordan, whose testimony, he noted, "goes to the heart of one of the elements of obstruction of justice—that is, the job search and the false affidavit and the interconnection between those." Jordan would help resolve many of the conflicts in the testimony, Hutchinson contended, including Lewinsky's testimony that he had told her about the notes to the president she had in her apartment, "Go home and make sure they're not there."

James Rogan explained the case for Sidney Blumenthal, whose "testimony puts him in direct conflict with the claims of the president and shatters the myth of the president's truthful but misleading answers." All his testimony, Rogan pointed out, had been given before the truth about the Lewinsky-Clinton relationship had been learned; it would be helpful to question him in light of what everyone now knew.

Next, it was the defense team's turn. The chief justice recognized David Kendall to argue the White House's case.

Mr. Kendall:…I am duty-bound to observe that it is, in fact, a dereliction of duty to have come this far in the process…and not to have talked to the witnesses on whom they purport to rely. How can they have come this far and now tell you: Oh, yes, we now need to meet face to face with the witnesses? We don't know what they sound like, how credible they will be, but we have rested our judgment on this. We need to see them personally.

This procedure, I submit to you, is just backward. First, they filed the charges, which have been spoon fed by Mr. Starr. They don't bother to check these out; they take them at face value, and now they finally want to talk to the witnesses, and they again use Mr. Starr to threaten Ms. Lewinsky with imprisonment unless she cooperates...

This has been a partisan process on the part of the House managers. In the House, they had the votes. They didn't think they needed to talk to witnesses. When you have the votes and the independent counsel on your side, you don't need to independently develop the evidence....

Now, they are trying to take a different track, and I think it comes from desperation. You have had the case analyzed before you; you have had the evidence in the case assessed. I think it has been demolished in an adversary proceeding....

Kendall then addressed each of the proposed witnesses in turn. By every account, he said, the managers' weekend visit with Monica Lewinsky had produced no new information. Vernon Jordan's testimony already ran to 900 pages, he pointed out; and as for the alleged remark about the notes, even if true, it simply "doesn't concern the president." On Sidney Blumenthal: First, there was no conflict at all between his testimony and the president's; second, any statements to him had no impact whatsoever on the Paula Jones case, which was precisely the justice the alleged obstruction would have been aimed at.

Kendall briefly discussed the new evidence the managers wanted admitted. The Ward affidavit, he contended, could not amount to much since even though he might have observed the president during the deposition, "he is not a mindreader." Similarly with Holmes, although Kendall did say an opportunity to depose him "would provide a great deal of information about what really motivated the events of January 1998"—especially the connections among the independent counsel, Linda Tripp, and the Jones lawyers. As for the phone records, he said, "they really are inscrutable" in the absence of explanations from the people involved in the conversation. Then Kendall turned to how witnesses would affect the trial process:

Finally, I want to be candid with you. I don't want to be alarmist, I want to be honest, though, about what opening the door for discovery will mean for this process.... Should the Senate decide to authorize the House managers to call additional witnesses live in this proceeding or have the depositions taken, we will be faced with a critical need for the discovery of evidence useful to our defense.

I made the point that the discovery of evidence in the Office of the Independent Counsel proceeding was—not to put too fine a point on it—not aimed at getting us exculpatory or helpful evidence. We need to be able to do that. We have never had the kind of compulsory process, the kind of ability to subpoena documents and witnesses that you will have in a garden variety civil case. We have not had access to a great deal, many thousands of pages of evidence which is, first of all, in the hands of the House managers that they got from the Office of Independent Counsel, but did not put into the public record....

Our dilemma is this: We do not know what we do not know. That is what discovery means. You have to get discovery so you can find out what is available. It may not necessarily prolong a trial, but it makes you available to defend your client in the way you have to be able to do as a lawyer. It doesn't turn on the number of witnesses.

The calling of these witnesses produces a need in us to be ready to examine them, to cross-examine them. It initiates a process that leaves us unprepared and exposed unless we have adequate discovery. This is a proceeding, I need not remind you—I know everyone recognizes its gravity—to remove the president of the United States. You have to give us, and I believe you will, the discovery that will enable us to represent the president adequately, competently and effectively.

The sequence of discovery is also important. I want to be clear about that. It is all very well and I recognize how it happens for one side to say, "Well, we are going to put on three witnesses and they can put on three witnesses." Ladies and gentlemen of the Senate, we don't know right now how to make a reasoned choice because we haven't had the discovery you would normally have to do that. We would first need to obtain and review the relevant documents. I have indicated where those are. We would then need to be able to depose relevant witnesses. We need to know whether the witness depositions that the House managers had taken would need to lead to other depositions there. Only at that point when we have had discovery of our witnesses will we be able to identify the witnesses we might want to call....

But let me conclude by saying that I don't think, and I respectfully submit to you, that there is a need to prolong this process. We hope that you will render your decision in a manner that is speedy, and we are confident that you will decide to make that decision in a manner that is fair, and that this body will, as so often it has done in past times of crisis, be able to bring to the country both the closure and reconciliation that the country wants so very much. Thank you.

Now the House managers had time for rebuttal. First, Bryant addressed the "selective" way Kendall had used quotes, and argued that that in itself was an excellent argument for calling witnesses. In their absence, said Bryant, both sides had been picking and choosing quotes from the voluminous record, and it would be helpful to hear from the witnesses themselves. Bryant objected to Kendall's characterization of the managers' meeting with Lewinsky. She had been very ably represented by attorneys, he noted, and had not been imposed upon.

Asa Hutchinson observed that Kendall had used film of Vernon Jordan in order to make his points; that, he said, spoke directly to why actually seeing and hearing a witness told more than simply reading their words in type.

Bill McCollum stressed, again, "the need for witnesses out here to determine their credibility, to check their demeanor, to see how they respond to questioning."

Then the chief justice recognized James Rogan.

Mr. Rogan: ... Now, in the words of Yogi Berra, "I fear that we are going through déjà vu all over again" with Mr. Kendall's able proceeding, because what he has accentuated in this presentation has been accentuated by White House counsel ever since they first rose to address this body at the lectern, and that is the complaint that no witnesses were called before the House Judiciary Committee, and how wrong it is for members of the House managers now to assert the need and the right to have witnesses before this body. ...

Once again, he mistakes the function of the two Houses. But I would invite the Members of this body, if that is an issue concerning them, to go back and review the voluminous transcripts during the Judiciary Committee where Chairman Hyde did everything but get on his knees and beg the members of the president's defense team, beg our colleagues on the other side of the aisle, to identify for us which witnesses they wished to dispute, what facts they wanted to challenge, let us know who the witnesses are where there is a contention in the evidence, and despite their complaining ... they never once identified in the factual record whose testimony they wished to challenge. ...

Rogan reviewed a bit of the history of the House Judiciary Committee discussions about witnesses, including the fact that when the president's defense team finally supplied the names of witnesses it wanted to call, all fifteen were allowed to testify, but none testified about the facts of the case. "The complaints of unfairness," said Rogan, "are unfair." He concluded:

Members of this body, it is the job of the House of Representatives, it is the constitutional obligation of the House of Representatives, to act as the accusatory body in an impeachment proceeding. The Constitution gives the authority to this body the right to try that case. This is the place for trial. This is the place to determine guilt. This is the place to determine credibility. This is the place for witnesses.

The chief justice recognized Henry Hyde.

Mr. Hyde: ... [W]itnesses help you. They won't help me. I know the record. I am satisfied a compelling case is here for removal of the president. But they will help you. And we aren't dragging this out. We have been as swift as decency will let us be throughout this entire situation.

Their defense has never been on the facts.... Their defense has been to demonize Mr. Starr to a fare-thee-well and then yell about the process. That is their defense....

We have a good case. We have an excellent case without the witnesses. But the witnesses help you. We have narrowed it down to three—a pitiful three. I should think you would want to proceed with that minimum testimony, and Mr. Kendall can try his cross-examination skills on them, and that I want to watch.

On Wednesday, January 27, the senators voted on both the motion to dismiss and on the deposing of witnesses.

On the motion to dismiss, the results were: yes 44, no 56.

On the question of subpoenaing witnesses, the results were: yes 56, no 44.

Both votes were along strictly partisan lines, with one exception: Democrat Russ Feingold of Wisconsin voted with the Republicans on both matters.

On Thursday, January 28, after a day of behind-the-scenes negotiations, the senators voted on how to proceed with the trial. A Democratic version would have barred Monica Lewinsky from testifying on the Senate floor. But on a strict par-

tisan vote, the Republican plan won, 54–44. Republicans—again joined by Fein-gold—also defeated a Democratic attempt to move immediately to a final decision on impeachment.

The depositions of Lewinsky, Jordan, and Blumenthal were scheduled for Monday, February 1 through Wednesday, February 3. One senator from each party would be present for the depositions, and two House managers and two of the president's attorneys would take the depositions.

THE DEPOSITIONS

On Thursday, February 4, the Senate convened to consider the new depositions of Monica Lewinsky, Vernon Jordan, and Sidney Blumenthal. On behalf of the House managers, Bill McCollum offered a motion that included three parts: (1) that transcriptions and videotapes of the depositions be admitted into evidence; (2) that the Senate issue a subpoena for the appearance of Monica Lewinsky before the Senate; (3) that both sides be permitted to use videotapes of all the depositions in a six-hour presentation equally divided between them.

The Senate voted separately on each of the three parts of the managers' motion. The motion to admit the transcripts and videotapes into evidence passed, 100 to 0. The motion to subpoena Lewinsky to testify in person failed by a vote of 70 to 30. The senators rejected, 73 to 27, an amendment introduced by Senator Patty Murray of Washington, which would have barred the use of videotapes during the deposition presentations. The motion to allow such presentations then passed, 62 to 38.

Minority Leader Tom Daschle introduced a motion to proceed directly to closing arguments. It failed by a vote of 56 to 44, with Democrat Russ Feingold once again voting with the Republican majority.

Finally, Charles Ruff presented a motion for the White House that would require the managers to specify ahead of time, in writing, what parts of videos they would use in presenting the depositions. James Rogan objected to the idea, quoting a late justice of the California Supreme Court: "I believe the appropriate response to your request is that it is none of your damn business what the other side is going to put on."

The vote on Ruff's motion: yeas 46, nays 54.

When the senators reassembled on February 6, the chief justice recognized the House managers to begin their presentations of the depositions of Lewinsky, Jordan, and Blumenthal. James Rogan took the floor.

Mr. Rogan: ... Today ... you will have your only opportunity to hear from the one person whose testimony invariably leads to the conclusion that the president of the United States committed perjury and obstructed justice in a federal civil rights action.... There is only one judgment the Senate must make for history about Monica Lewinsky: Do you believe her? ...

To justify a vote of not guilty for the president, you certainly have the right to reject Monica Lewinsky's testimony as untruthful.... If you believe her, you will see this morning how the president wove the web of perjury and obstruction of justice. You will see why he was impeached by the House of Representatives....

Consider, for example, Ms. Lewinsky's testimony regarding witness tampering, one element of the obstruction of justice charge against the president....

Q: We're at that point that we've got a telephone conversation in the morning with you and the president, and he has ... mentioned to you that your name is on the Jones witness list. He has also mentioned to you that perhaps you could file an affidavit to avoid possible testifying in that case. Is that right?

A: Correct.

Q: And he has also, I think ... referenced the cover story that you and he had had, that perhaps you could say that you were coming to my office to deliver papers or to see Betty Currie; is that right?

A: Correct. It was from the entire relationship, that story.

Q: Now, when he alluded to that cover story, was that instantly familiar to you?

A: Yes....

... During Ms. Lewinsky's testimony ... she further elaborated on this critical piece of evidence.

Q: Did you discuss anything else that night in terms of—I would draw your attention to the cover stories. I have alluded to that earlier, but, uh, did you talk about cover story that night?

A: Yes, sir.

Q: And what was said?

A: Uh, I believe that, uh, the president said something—you can always say you were coming to see Betty or bringing me papers.

Q: I think you've testified that you're sure he said that that night. You are sure he said that that night?

A: Yes.

Consider also Ms. Lewinsky's testimony regarding concealing subpoenaed evidence; namely, the gifts he gave her.... Did he do this? Remember, on the morning of December 28, 1997, a few days after Ms. Lewinsky received a subpoena directing her to turn over any gifts she had received from the president, the president met with Ms. Lewinsky. She suggested to him that she could give the gifts he gave her to Betty Currie, the president's personal secretary. The president said that he would think about it. Listen to what Monica Lewinsky said happened next.

Q: Did you later that day receive a call from Betty Currie?

A: Yes, I did.

Q: Tell us about that.

A: I received a call from—Betty, and to the best of my memory, she said something like I understand you have something for me or I know—I know I've testified to saying that—that I remember her saying either I know you have something for me or the president said you have something for me. And to me, it's a—she said—I mean, this is not a direct quote, but the gist of the conversation was that she was going to go visit her mom in the hospital and she'd stop by and get whatever it was.

Q: Did you question Ms. Currie or ask her, what are you talking about or what do you mean?

A: No.

Q: Why didn't you?

A: Because I assumed that it meant the gifts.

Then Rogan turned to the job search, playing an excerpt from Lewinsky's testimony in which she confirmed that before December 11, although she had spoken with Ver-

*non Jordan about getting a job in New York, there hadn't been much progress—but
that by early January she had an offer from Revlon with Jordan's help.*

*Rogan now reviewed the managers' version of the entire case. He listed a number
of "bad choices" on the part of the president, starting with whatever happened in
1991 to inspire Paula Jones's allegations of sexual harassment, continuing through
his physical relationship with a 22-year-old White House intern and through the
aftermath of Judge Wright's order that he answer questions about any intimate relationships with subordinate government employees while he was governor or president. He recounted how Lewinsky had been transferred to the Pentagon, but
continued to see the president with the help of Betty Currie, how she finally decided
to look for a job in New York, and how Currie enlisted the help of Vernon Jordan.*

Rogan continued:

Nothing happened on her job search through the month of November, because Mr. Jordan was either gone or he simply wasn't returning Monica's
phone calls. All that changed on December 5, 1997. That was the day Monica
Lewinsky's name appeared on the Paula Jones witness list.

Members of the Senate, this is how the whole thing started. A lone woman
in Arkansas felt that she had been wronged by the president of the United
States. The law said that she had a right to have her claim heard in a court of
law. At each stage the president could have chosen to uphold the law. Instead,
he chose to obstruct justice and to commit perjury....

In his presentation, Mr. Manager Hutchinson will show you, through
videotape words of the key witnesses, how the president used his position to
obstruct justice as set forth in the articles of impeachment. I will then return
to make the same showing respecting the allegations of perjury in the articles.
Throughout all of this, throughout this presentation, it is important to keep in
mind that we seek no congressional punishment for a man who chose to cheat
on his wife. However, we have a legal obligation to expect constitutional accountability for a president who chooses to cheat the law.

*The chief justice recognized Asa Hutchinson. Hutchinson told the senators to
watch, as the depositions were presented, for the fact that only the president "had all
the facts, and he did not always share those facts with others." He also emphasized
that it did not necessarily matter whether, say, Vernon Jordan thought there was an
integral connection between the signing of the affidavit and getting Lewinsky a job.
"There is only one issue," said Hutchinson, "and that is whether the president
viewed that there was a connection."*

Hutchinson then went through the managers' case on the job search, from the moment Betty Currie contacted Vernon Jordan to help Lewinsky to the day the job at Revlon came through. He used clips from the president's testimony and from Jordan's and Lewinsky's new depositions to illustrate the managers' theory: that the president was using Jordan to make sure Lewinsky filed an affidavit that would keep her from testifying in the Paula Jones case and also to secure her a job so that she would cooperate in keeping their relationship quiet, and that Jordan was keeping the president informed every step of the way.

Like Rogan, Hutchinson made use of an excerpt from Lewinsky's testimony about her early-morning telephone call from the president on December 17, 1997:

Mr. Hutchinson: ... And now, let's go to the 17th, because now the president is ready to share some additional information with Ms. Lewinsky. Now that he has got the job search moving, perhaps she is in a more receptive mood so that she can handle the news that she is on the witness list. So let's listen to Ms. Lewinsky's testimony....

Q: ... At that point we got a telephone conversation in the morning with you and the president. And he has, among other things, mentioned to you that your name is on the Jones witness list. He has also mentioned to you that perhaps you could file an affidavit to avoid possible testifying in that case. Is that right?

A: Correct.

Q: And he's also, I think, now at the point that we were in our questioning in reference to the cover story that you and he had, that perhaps you could say that you were coming to my office to deliver papers or to see Betty Currie. Is that right?

A: Correct. It was from the entire relationship. That's correct.

Q: Now, when he alluded to that cover story, was that instantly familiar to you.

A: Yes.

Q: You knew what he was talking about.

A: Yes.

Q: And why was this familiar to you.

A: Because it was part of the pattern of the relationship.

Q: As I understand your testimony, too, the cover stories were reiterated to you by the president that night on the telephone—

A: Correct.

Q: ... And did you understand that since your name was on the witness list that there would be a possibility that you could be subpoenaed to testify in the Paula Jones case?

A: I think I understood that I could be subpoenaed, and there was a possibility of testifying. ...

Q: Were you in fact subpoenaed to testify?

A: Yes.

Q: ... Did you understand in the context of the telephone conversation with the president that early morning of December the 17th—did you understand that you would deny your relationship with the president to the Jones lawyers through use of these cover stories?

A: From what I learned in that—oh, through those cover stories, I don't know, but from what I learned in that conversation, I thought to myself I knew I would deny the relationship.

Q: And you would deny the relationship to the Jones lawyer?

A: Yes, correct.

... The news is broken to her that she is on the witness list. It puts it in a legal context. This is a 24-year-old ex-intern. She might not have the legal sophistication of the president, but the president certainly knows the legal consequences as to his actions. What he is telling a witness in a case that is adverse to him is that: You do not have to tell the truth. You can use the cover stories that we used before. And that might have been in a nonlegal context, but now we are in a different arena and he says: Continue the same lies, even though you are in a court of law. Continue the same pattern.

Ladies and gentlemen of the Senate, in my book that is illegal, and I hate to say it, but that is obstruction of justice by the president of the United States. And, if you believe Ms. Lewinsky, then you have to accept that fact. ...

Hutchinson continued to walk through the managers' case: How Jordan asked the president directly whether he had had sexual relations with Lewinsky and the president denied it ("I believed him," said Jordan); how he had arranged for lawyer Frank Carter to be Lewinsky's lawyer; how the affidavit came to be signed and the job at Revlon came through. He ended his presentation by playing several excerpts from Lewinsky's testimony, concluding with the now famous quote: "... no one asked or encouraged me to lie, but no one discouraged me, either."

He continued:

It is very important to understand that we want you to know very clearly that Ms. Lewinsky says that the president never told her to lie. There is no question about that.... What the president did suggest to her was to use an affidavit to avoid truthful testimony, to stick with the cover stories under legal context....

It is not Ms. Lewinsky's viewpoint that is important. It is what the president intended. What did the president intend by this conversation when he told her on December 17, "Guess what, bad news; you're a witness"? Then he proceeded to suggest to her ways to avoid truthful testimony.

After a brief recess, the chief justice recognized James Rogan to discuss the perjury aspects of the managers' case. Much as Hutchinson had done, Rogan used clips from the deposition videotapes as illustration as he walked through the allegations against the president.

First, said Rogan, "the president's testimony that he said things that were misleading but true to his aides was perjury." Several of those aides, said Rogan, were called to testify before the grand jury and duly passed along the untruths the president had told them. But the "most glaring example" of using an aid as a "messenger of lies," said Rogan, was the case of Sidney Blumenthal. He showed a clip from Blumenthal's deposition, in which the president's aide recounted how on December 21, 1997, the day the Lewinsky story broke in the press, the First Lady had told Blumenthal the president just couldn't resist trying to help "troubled people." Later, the president called him in and Blumenthal told him about the conversation with Mrs. Clinton. Rogan continued:

Mr. Rogan: ... Following this conversation where Mr. Blumenthal told the president about his conversation with the First Lady that day, the president told Mr. Blumenthal about the president's own conversation he had earlier that day with his pollster, Dick Morris.

Q: What was the substance of that conversation, as the president related it to you?

A: He said that he had spoken to Dick Morris earlier that day, and that Dick Morris had told him that if Nixon, Richard Nixon, had given a nationally televised speech at the beginning of the Watergate affair, acknowledging everything he had done wrong, he may well have survived it, and that was the conversation that Dick Morris—that's what Dick Morris said to the president.

Q: Did it sound to you like the president was suggesting perhaps he would go on television and give a national speech?

A: Well, I don't know. I didn't know.

Q: When the president related the substance of his conversation with Dick Morris to you, how did you respond to that?

A: I said to the president, "Well, what have you done wrong?"

Q: Did he reply?

A: He did.

Q: What did he say?

A: He said, "I haven't done anything wrong."

Q: And what did you say to that response?

A: Well, I said, as I recall, "That's one of the stupidest ideas I ever heard. If you haven't done anything wrong, why would you do that?"

After denying to Mr. Blumenthal any wrongdoing with Monica Lewinsky, the president then struck the harshest of blows against her. He launched a preemptive strike against her name and her character to an aide who he expected would be, and very shortly became, a witness before a Federal grand jury investigation.

Q: Did the president then give you his account of what happened between him and Monica Lewinsky?

A: As I recall, he did.

Q: What did the president tell you?

A: He, uh—he spoke, uh, fairly rapidly, as I recall, at that point and said that she had come on to him and made a demand for sex, that he had rebuffed her, turned her down, and that she, uh, threatened him. And, uh, he said that she said to him, uh, that she was called "the stalker" by her peers and that she hated the term, and that she would claim that they had had an affair whether they had or they hadn't....

Q: Can you describe for us the president's demeanor when he shared this information with you?

A: Yes. He was, uh, very upset. I thought he was, a man in anguish.

Q: Do you remember the president also saying something about being like a character in a novel?

A: I do.... Uh, he felt like somebody, uh, surrounded by, uh, an oppressive environment that was creating a lie about him. He said he felt like, uh, the character in the novel Darkness at Noon.

Q: Did he also say he felt like he can't get the truth out?

A: Yes, I—I believe he said that....

Q: Did you understand what the president was trying to communicate when he related his situation to the character in that novel?

A: I think he felt that the world was against him.

The president continued to pass along false information to Mr. Blumenthal with regard to the substance of his relationship with Monica Lewinsky.

A: I asked him a number of questions that appeared in the press that day. I asked him, uh, if he were alone, and he said that, uh, he was within eyesight or earshot of someone when he was with her....

Q: You had asked him about a press account that said there were potentially a number of telephone messages left by the president for Monica Lewinsky. And he relayed to you that he called her. Did he tell you how many times he called her?

A: He—he did. He said he called once. He said he called when, uh, Betty Currie's brother had died, to tell her that.

Q: And other than that ... he shared no other information respecting additional calls?

A: No....

Q: Based on the president's response to your question at that time, would it have surprised you to have been told or to have later learned that there were over 50 recorded—50 conversations between the president and Ms. Lewinsky?

A: I did later learn that, uh, as the whole country did, uh, and I was surprised....

Q: This conversation that you had with the president on January the 21st, 1998, how did that conversation conclude?

A: Uh, I believe we, uh—well, I believe after that, I said to the president that, uh—who was—seemed to me to be upset, that you needed to find some sure footing and to be confident. And, uh, we went on, I believe, to discuss the State of the Union.

Q: You went on to other business?

A: Yes, we went on to talk about public policy.

Q: When this conversation with the president concluded as it related to Monica Lewinsky, what were your feelings toward the president's statement?

A: Uh, well, they were complex. Uh, I believed him, uh, but I was also, uh—I thought he was very upset. That troubled me. And I also was troubled by his association with troubled people and thought this was not a good story and thought he shouldn't be doing this.

Q: Do you remember also testifying before the grand jury that you felt that the president's story was a very heartfelt story and that "he was pouring out his heart, and I believed him"?

A: Yes, that's what I told the grand jury, I believe; right....

Q: He never described to you any intimate physical activity he may have had with Monica Lewinsky?

A: Oh, no.

Q: Did the president ever tell you that he gave any gifts to Monica Lewinsky?

A: No.

Q: Did he tell you that Monica Lewinsky gave him any gifts?

A: No.

Q: Based on the president's story as he related on January 21st, would it have surprised you to know at that time that there was a repeated gift exchange between Monica Lewinsky and the president?

A: Well, I learned later about that, and I was surprised.

Q: The president never told you that he engaged in occasional sexual banter with her on the telephone?

A: No.

Q: He never told you about any cover stories that he and Monica Lewinsky may have developed to disguise a relationship?

A: No.

Q: He never suggested to you that there might be some physical evidence pointing to a physical relationship between he—between himself and Monica Lewinsky?

A: No.

Q: ... Did the president ever discuss his deposition testimony with you in the Paula Jones case on that date?

A: Oh, no.

Q: Did he ever tell you that he denied under oath in his Paula Jones deposition that he had an affair with Monica Lewinsky?

A: No....

Mr. Rogan: ... Remember, the date of this conversation that Sidney Blumenthal just related to you was January 21, the day the Monica Lewinsky story broke. About a month later, Sidney Blumenthal was called to testify as a witness before the grand jury. That was the first time.

... Four months later Sidney Blumenthal was called back to testify to the grand jury—not once, but two more times. From January 21 until the end of June 1998, the president had almost six months in which to tell Sidney Blumenthal, after he was subpoenaed, but before he testified, not to tell the grand jury information that was false. The president had the opportunity to not use his aide as a conduit of false information....

The president of the United States used a special assistant, one of his aides, as a conduit to go before a Federal grand jury and present false and misleading information and precluded the grand jury from being able to make an honest determination in their investigation. He obstructed justice when he did it, and when he denied that testimony he committed the offense of perjury.

In response to a question from Mr. Manager Graham, Mr. Blumenthal candidly addressed the president's claim under oath that he was truthful with his aides that he knew would be future grand jury witnesses:

Q: Knowing what you know now, do you believe the president lied to you about his relationship with Ms. Lewinsky?

A: I do.

Q: I appreciate your honesty....

Q: ... Is it a fair statement, given your previous testimony concerning your 30-minute conversation, that the president was trying to portray himself as a victim of a relationship with Monica Lewinsky?

A: I think that's the import of his whole story.

Rogan concluded by saying that the president did not want to play by the same rules that his Justice Department enforced against other American citizens. He played, from the House Judiciary hearings, testimony from Dr. Barbara Battolino, a former Veterans Administration psychiatrist, about her conviction for perjury—in a civil case that was later dismissed—for lying under oath about a consensual sexual relationship. Dr. Battolino had lost her job and her license. Rogan concluded: "That is how the Clinton administration defines proportionality in punishment."

Now it was the turn of the White House. The chief justice recognized Nicole Seligman, who addressed Monica Lewinsky's deposition.

Ms. Seligman: ... As those of you who watched the entire video are well aware, the managers have cleverly snipped here and there in an effort to present their story even if, as a result, the story they are telling you is not Ms. Lewinsky's story. They have distorted, they have omitted, and they have created a profoundly erroneous impression....

In her deposition this week, Ms. Lewinsky reaffirmed her previous testimony and provided extremely useful supplements to that testimony. We asked her no questions. Why? Because there was no need. Her testimony exonerated the president....

Let's begin with the December 17 phone call between the president and Ms. Lewinsky, which is at the heart of Article II's first two subparts.... It is critically important. And we are showing it to you unvarnished, not in snippets, because the snippets you have seen are terribly misleading. The tape you will hear establishes beyond doubt that she and the president did not discuss the content of the affidavit in that call, or ever. It establishes beyond doubt that what happened is not obstruction of justice.

Q: Sometime back in December of 1997, in the morning of December the 17th, did you receive a call from the president?

A: Yes.

Q: What was the purpose of that call? What did you talk about?

A: It was threefold—first, to tell me that Ms. Currie's brother had been killed in a car accident; second, to tell me that my name was on a witness list for the Paula Jones case; and thirdly, he mentioned the Christmas present he had for me.

Q: This telephone call was somewhere in the early morning hours of 2 o'clock to 2:30.

A: Correct.

Q: Did it surprise you that he called you so late?

A: No.

Q: Was this your first notice of your name being on the Paula Jones witness list?

A: Yes....

Q: Did he say anything to you about how he felt concerning this witness list?

A: He said it broke his heart that, well, that my name was on the witness list....

Q: He expressed to you that your name—you know, again, you talked about some other things—but he told you your name was on the list.

A: Correct.

Q: What was your reaction to that?

A: I was scared.

Q: What other discussion did you have in regard to the fact that your name was on the list? You were scared; he was disappointed, or it broke his heart. What other discussion did you have?

A: Uh, I believe he said that, uh—and these are not necessarily direct quotes, but to the best of my memory, that he said something about that, uh, just because my name was on the list didn't necessarily mean I'd be subpoenaed; and at some point, I asked him what I should do if I received a subpoena. He said I should, uh, I should let Ms. Currie know. Uh—

Q: Did he say anything about an affidavit?

A: Yes.

Q: What did he say?

A: He said that, uh, that I could possibly file an affidavit if I—if I were subpoenaed, that I could possibly file an affidavit maybe to avoid being deposed.

Q: How did he tell you you would avoid being deposed by filing an affidavit?

A: I don't think he did.

Q: You just accepted that statement?

A: Yes. . . .

Q: Are you, uh—strike that. Did he make any representation to you about what you could say in that affidavit or—

A: No.

Q: What did you understand you would be saying in that affidavit to avoid testifying?

A: Uh, I believe I've testified to this in the grand jury. To the best of my recollection, it was, uh—to my mind came—it was a range of things. I mean, it could either be, uh, something innocuous or could go as far as having to deny the relationship. Not being a lawyer nor having gone to law school, I thought it could be anything.

Q: Did he at that point suggest one version or the other version?

A: No. I didn't even mention that, so there, there wasn't a further discussion—there was no discussion of what would be in an affidavit.

Q: When you say, uh, it would be—it could have been something where the relationship was denied, what was your thinking at that point?

A: I—I—I think I don't understand what you're asking me. I'm sorry.

Q: Well, based on prior relations with the president, the concocted stories and those things like that, did this come to mind? Was there some discussion about that, or did it come to your mind about these stories—the cover stories?

A: Not in connection with the—not in connection with the affidavit.

Q: How would—was there any discussion of how you would accomplish preparing or filing an affidavit at that point?

A: No.

Q: Why—why didn't you want to testify? Why would not you—why would you have wanted to avoid testifying?

A: First of all, I thought it was nobody's business. Second of all, I didn't want to have anything to do with Paula Jones or her case. And—I guess those two reasons.

Q: You—you have already mentioned that you were not a lawyer and you had not been to law school, those kinds of things. Did, uh, did you understand when you—the potential legal problems that you could have caused yourself by allowing a false affidavit to be filed with the court, in a court proceeding?

A: . . . Are you—are you still referring to December 17th?

Q: The night of the phone call, he's suggesting you could file an affidavit. Did you appreciate the implications of filing a false affidavit with the court?

A: I don't think I necessarily thought at that point it would have to be false, so, no, probably not. I don't—I don't remember having any thoughts like that, so I imagine I would remember something like that, and I don't, but—

Q: Did you know what an affidavit was?

A: Sort of.

Q: Of course, you're talking at that time by telephone to the president, and he's—and he is a lawyer, and he taught law school—I don't know—did you know that? Did you know he was a lawyer?

A: I—I think I knew it, but it wasn't something that was present in my, in my thoughts, as in he's a lawyer, he's telling me, you know, something.

Q: Did the, did the president ever tell you, caution you, that you had to tell the truth in an affidavit?

A: Not that I recall.

Q: It would have been against his interest in that lawsuit for you to have told the truth, would it not?

A: I'm not really comfortable—I mean, I can tell you what would have been in my best interest, but I—

Q: But you didn't file the affidavit for your best interest, did you?

A: Uh, actually, I did.

Q: To avoid testifying.

A: Yes.

Q: But had you testified truthfully, you would have had no—certainly, no legal implications—it may have been embarrassing, but you would have not had any legal problems, would you?

A: That's true.

Q: Did you discuss anything else that night in terms of—I would draw your attention to the cover stories. I have alluded to that earlier, but, uh, did you talk about cover story that night?

A: Yes, sir.

Q: And what was said?

A: Uh, I believe that, uh, the president said something—you can always say you were coming to see Betty or bringing me papers.

Q: I think you've testified that you're sure he said that that night. You are sure he said that that night?

A: Yes.

Q: Now, was that in connection with the affidavit?

A: I don't believe so, no.

Q: Why would he have told you you could always say that?

A: I don't know.

Q: We're at that point that we've got a telephone conversation in the morning with you and the president, and he has among other things mentioned to you that your name is on the Jones witness list. He has also mentioned to you that perhaps you could file an affidavit to avoid possible testifying in that case. Is that right?

A: Correct.

Q: And he has also, I think, now at the point that we were in our questioning, referenced the cover story that you and he had had, that perhaps you could say that you were coming to my office to deliver papers or to see Betty Currie; is that right?

A: Correct. It was from the entire relationship, that story.

Q: Now, when he alluded to that cover story, was that instantly familiar to you?

A: Yes.

Q: You knew what he was talking about?

A: Yes.

Q: And why was this familiar to you?

A: Because it was part of the pattern of the relationship.

Q: Had you actually had to use elements of this cover story in the past?

A: I think so, yes.

Q: Okay. Now let me go back again to the December 11th date—I'm sorry—the 17th. This is the conversation in the morning. What else—was there anything else you talked about in terms of—other than your name being on the list and the affidavit and the cover story?

A: Yes. I had—I had had my own thoughts on why and how he should settle the case, and I expressed those thoughts to him. And at some point, he mentioned that he still had this Christmas present for me and that maybe he would ask Mrs. Currie to come in that weekend, and I said not to because she was obviously going to be in mourning because of her brother.

Q: As I understand your testimony, too, the cover stories were reiterated to you by the president that night on the telephone—

A: Correct.

Q: —and after he told you you would be a witness—or your name was on the witness list, I should say?

A: Correct.

Q: And did you understand that since your name was on the witness list that there would be a possibility that you could be subpoenaed to testify in the Paula Jones case?

A: I think I understood that I could be subpoenaed, and there was a possibility of testifying. I don't know if I necessarily thought it was a subpoena to testify, but—

Q: Were you in fact subpoenaed to testify?

A: Yes.

Q: And that was what—

A: December 19th, 1997.

Q: December 19th. Now, you have testified in the grand jury. I think your closing comments was that no one ever asked you to lie, but yet in that very conversation of December the 17th, 1997 when the president told you that you were on the witness list, he also suggested that you could sign an affidavit and use misleading cover stories. Isn't that correct?

A: Uh—well, I—I guess in my mind, I separate necessarily signing affidavit and using misleading cover stories. So, does—

Q: Well, those two—

A: Those three events occurred, but they don't—they weren't linked for me.

Q: But they were in the same conversation, were they not?

A: Yes, they were.

Q: Did you understand in the context of the conversation that you would deny the—the president and your relationship to the Jones lawyers?

A: Do you mean from what was said to me or—

Q: In the context of that—in the context of that conversation, December the 17th—

A: I—I don't—I didn't—

Q: Okay. Let me ask it. Did you understand in the context of the telephone conversation with the president that early morning of December the 17th—did you understand that you would deny your relationship with the president to the Jones lawyers through use of these cover stories?

A: From what I learned in that—oh, through those cover stories, I don't know, but from what I learned in that conversation, I thought to myself I knew I would deny the relationship.

Q: And you would deny the relationship to the Jones lawyers?

A: Yes, correct.

Q: Good.

A: If—if that's what it came to.

Q: And in fact you did deny the relationship to the Jones lawyers in the affidavit that you signed under penalty of perjury; is that right?

A: I denied a sexual relationship.

Q: The president did not in that conversation on December the 17th of 1997 or any other conversation, for that matter, instruct you to tell the truth; is that correct?

A: That's correct.

Q: And prior to being on the witness list, you—you both spoke—

A: Well, I guess any conversation in relation to the *Paula Jones* case. I can't say that any conversation from the—the entire relationship that he didn't ever say, you know, "Are you mad? Tell me the truth." So—

Q: And prior to being on the witness list, you both spoke about denying this relationship if asked?

A: Yes. That was discussed.

Q: He would say something to the effect that—or you would say that—you—you would deny anything if it ever came up, and he would nod or say that's good, something to that effect; is that right?

A: Yes, I believe I testified to that.

Q: In his answer to this proceeding in the Senate, he has indicated that he thought he had—might have had a way that he could have you—get you to file a—basically a true affidavit, but yet still skirt these issues enough that you wouldn't be called as a witness. Did he offer you any of these suggestions at this time?

A: He didn't discuss the content of my affidavit with me at all, ever.

Ms. Seligman: ... First, let's be very clear, as you saw, Ms. Lewinsky repeatedly told Mr. Manager Bryant that she and the president did not discuss the content of the affidavit in that phone call. ...

Now, where does this leave us? Ms. Lewinsky described a brief conversation in which the president mentioned the possibility that an affidavit might enable her to avoid testifying if the need for it arose, and they left the subject. No discussion of content. No discussion of logistics. No discussion of timing. Virtually no discussion at all. And that very brief exchange is the heart of the case. ...

Now, the managers contend that because Ms. Lewinsky also recalls a reference to cover stories in that call, it is clear beyond doubt that the president instructed her to file a false affidavit.

But for at least two reasons, this claim fails also. First, Ms. Lewinsky repeatedly told Mr. Manager Bryant that the mention of cover stories in that call was not connected to the mention of a possible affidavit—a position, I must note, that she had taken with the independent counsel for a very long time.

Second, Ms. Lewinsky has insisted for more than a year that the cover stories were not, in any event, false—a position she reasserted this week ...

As Seligman put it, "The truth is that she didn't tell the story that the managers wanted to hear." The same was true, she argued, about the testimony about the gift exchange. "Perhaps most notably," said Seligman, "her testimony also provides corroboration for the president's testimony that he told her she had to turn over to the Jones lawyers what gifts she had." Again, she turned to the Lewinsky videotape:

Q: Okay. Now, were you ever under the impression from anything that the president said that you should turn over all the gifts to the Jones lawyers?

A: No, but where this is a little tricky ... I had an occasion in an interview with one of the—with the OIC—where I was asked a series of statements, if the president had made those, and there was one statement that Agent Fallon said to me—I—there were—other people, they asked me these statements—this is after the president testified and they asked me some statements, did you say this, did you say this, and I said, no, no, no. And Agent Fallon said something, and I think it was, "Well, you have to turn over whatever you have." And I said to you, "You know, that sounds a little bit familiar to me." So that's what I can tell you on that.

Q: That's in the 302 exam?

A: I don't know if it's in the 302 or not, but that's what happened.

Q: Uh-huh.

This is extraordinary testimony. Why? Because Ms. Lewinsky apparently corroborated the president. She recognized those words when she heard them. She didn't refute the president. And the OIC never told us that that was what she said.... We had no idea about Ms. Lewinsky's recollection until we heard her testimony. We can only wonder—in troubled disbelief—how much more we still don't know. The president did not obstruct justice....

Then Seligman turned to the job search. Lewinsky's deposition, she said, confirmed what they already knew: that Lewinsky had started her job search long before there was any question of affidavits or testimony, and that she was insistent that no one had asked her to lie or promised a job for her silence.

The House managers repeatedly have tried to suggest that these words must mean something else. But at no time in their hours of questioning Ms. Lewinsky did they question her about this pivotal assertion regarding the job search allegation. They did not ask her to explain it, to amend it, to qualify it. They did not challenge it. They did not confront it. They didn't dare. They knew the answer. They knew there was no quid pro quo....

After a brief recess, the chief justice recognized David Kendall, who addressed Vernon Jordan's deposition.

Mr. Kendall:... The most critical thing about this deposition is it contained no evidence of any kind which supports the central allegation of article II, the obstruction of justice article, that Mr. Jordan's job search assistance was tied to Ms. Lewinsky testifying in a certain way or that the president intended Mr. Jordan's assistance to corruptly influence her testimony. Mr. Jordan was unequivocal about the fact that he had frequently helped other people and that here there was no quid pro quo, no tie-in of any kind....

> **Q:** Was your assistance to Ms. Lewinsky which you have described in any way dependent upon her doing anything whatsoever in the Paula Jones case?
>
> **A:** No.

That is direct evidence. That is not circumstantial evidence. That is unimpugned direct evidence.... Let's listen to the full context and listen for any evidence of a quid pro quo.

> **Q:** Mr. Jordan, let me go back to that meeting on December 11th. I believe we were discussing that. My question would be: How did the meeting on December 11 of 1997 with Ms. Lewinsky come about?
>
> **A:** Ms. Lewinsky called my office and asked if she could come to see me.
>
> **Q:** And was that preceded by a call from Betty Currie?
>
> **A:** At some point in time, Betty Currie had called me, and Ms. Lewinsky followed up on that call, and she came to my office, and we had a visit.
>
> **Q:** Ms. Lewinsky called, set up a meeting, and at some point sent you a resume, I believe.
>
> **A:** I believe so.
>
> **Q:** And did you receive that prior to the meeting on December 11th?
>
> **A:** I—I have to assume that I did, but I—I do not know whether she brought it with her or whether—it was at some point that she brought with her or sent to me—somehow it came into my possession—a list of various companies in New York with which she had—which were her preferences, by the way—most of which I did not know well enough to make any calls for.
>
> **Q:** All right. And I want to come back to that, but I believe—would you dispute if the record shows that you received the resume of Ms. Lewinsky on December 8th?
>
> **A:** I would not.
>
> **Q:** And presumably, the meeting on December 11th was set up somewhere around December 8th by the call from Ms. Lewinsky?
>
> **A:** I—I would not dispute that, sir.
>
> **Q:** All right. Now, you mentioned that she had sent you a—I guess some people refer to it—a wish list, or a list of jobs that she—

A: Not jobs—companies.

Q: —companies that she would be interested in seeking employment with.

A: That's correct.

Q: And you looked at that, and you determined that you wanted to go with your own list of friends and companies that you had better contacts with.

A: I'm sure, Congressman, that you too have been in this business, and you do know that you can only call people that you know or feel comfortable in calling.

Q: Absolutely. No question about it. And let me just comment and ask your response to this, but many times I will be listed as a reference, and they can take that to any company. You might be listed as a reference and the name "Vernon Jordan" would be a good reference anywhere, would it not?

A: I would hope so.

Q: And so, even though it was a company that you might not have the best contact with, you could have been helpful in that regard?

A: Well, the fact is I was running the job search, not Ms. Lewinsky, and therefore, the companies that she brought or listed were not of interest to me. I knew where I would need to call.

Q: And that is exactly the point, that you looked at getting Ms. Lewinsky a job as an assignment rather than just something that you were going to be a reference for.

A: I don't know whether I looked upon it as an assignment. Getting jobs for people is not unusual for me, so I don't view it as an assignment. I just view it as something that is part of what I do.

Q: You're acting in behalf of the president when you are trying to get Ms. Lewinsky a job, and you were in control of the job search?

A: Yes.

Q: Now, going back—going to your meeting that we're talking about on December 11th, prior to the meeting did you make any calls to prospective employers in behalf of Ms. Lewinsky?

A: I don't think so. I think not. I think I wanted to see her before I made any calls.

Q: And so if they were not before, after you met with her, you made some calls on December 11th?

A: I—I believe that's correct.

Q: And you called Mr. Richard Halperin of MacAndrews & Forbes?

A: That's right.

Q: You called Mr. Peter—

A: Georgescu.

Q: —Georgescu. And he is with what company?

A: He is chairman and chief executive officer of Young & Rubicam, a leading advertising agency on Madison Avenue.

Q: And did you make one other call?

A: Yes. I called Ursie Fairbairn, who runs Human Resources at American Express, at the American Express Company, where I am the senior director.

Q: And what did you basically communicate to each of these officials in behalf of Ms. Lewinsky?

A: I essentially said that you're going to hear from Ms. Lewinsky, and I hope that you will afford her an opportunity to come in and be interviewed and look favorably upon her if she meets your qualifications and your needs for work.

Q: Okay. And at what level did you try to communicate this information?

A: By—what do you mean by "what level"?

Q: In the company that you were calling, did you call the chairman of human resources, did you call the CEO—who did you call, or what level were you seeking to talk to?

A: Richard Halperin is sort of the utility man, he does everything at MacAndrews & Forbes. He is very close to the chairman, he is very close to Mr. Gittis. And so at MacAndrews & Forbes, I called Halperin. As I said to you, and as my grand jury testimony shows, I called Young & Rubicam, Peter Georgescu as its chairman and CEO. I have had a long-term relationship with Young & Rubicam going back to three of its CEOs, the first being Edward Ney, who was chairman of Young & Rubicam when I was head of the United Negro College Fund, and it was during that time that we developed the great theme, "A mind is a terrible thing to waste." So I have had a long-term relationship with Young & Rubicam and with Peter Georgescu, so I called the chairman in that instance.

At American Express, I called Ms. Ursie Fairbairn who is, as I said before, in charge of Human Resources. So that is the level—in one instance, the chairman; in one instance a utilitarian person; and in another instance, the head of the Human Resources Department.

Q: And the utilitarian connection, Mr. Richard Halperin, was sort of an assistant to Mr. Ron Perelman?

A: That's correct. He's a lawyer.

Q: Now, going to your meeting on December 11th with Ms. Lewinsky, about how long of a meeting was that?

A: I don't—I don't remember. You have a record of it, Congressman.

Q: And actually, I think you've testified it was about 15 to 20 minutes, but don't hold me to that, either. During the course of the meeting with Ms. Lewinsky, what did you learn about her?

A: Uh, enthusiastic, quite taken with herself and her experience, uh, bubbly, effervescent, bouncy, confident, uh—actually, I sort of had the same impression that you House Managers had of her when you met with her. You came out and said she was impressive, and so we come out about the same place.

Q: And did she relate to you the fact that she liked being an intern because it put her close to the president?

A: I have never seen a White House intern who did not like being a White House intern, and so her enthusiasm for being a White House intern was about like the enthusiasm of White House interns—they liked it. She was not happy about not being there anymore—she did not like being at the Defense Department—and I think she actually had some desire to go back. But when she actually talked to me, she wanted to go to New York for a job in the private sector, and she thought that I could be helpful in that process.

Q: Did she make reference to someone in the White House being uncomfortable when she was an intern, and she thought that people did not want her there?

A: She felt unwanted—there is no question about that. As to who did not want her there and why they did not want her there, that was not my business.

Q: And she related that—

A: She talked about it.

Q: —experience or feeling to you?

A: Yes.

Q: Now, your meeting with Ms. Lewinsky was on December 11th, and I believe that Ms. Lewinsky has testified that she met with the president on December 5—excuse me, on December 6—at the White House and complained that her job search was not going anywhere, and the president then talked to Mr. Jordan. Do you recall the president talking to you about that after that meeting?

A: I do not have a specific recollection of the president saying to me anything about having met with Ms. Lewinsky. The president has never told me that he met with Ms. Lewinsky, as best as I can recollect. I—I am aware that she was in a state of anxiety about going to work. She was in a state of anxiety in addition because her lease at Watergate, at the Watergate, was to expire December 31st. And there was a part of Ms. Lewinsky, I think, that thought that because she was coming to me, that she could come today and that she would have a job tomorrow. That is not an unusual misapprehension, and it's not limited to White House interns.

Q: I mentioned her meeting with the president on the same day, December 6th. I believe the record shows the president met with his lawyers and learned that Ms. Lewinsky was on the Jones witness list. Now, did you subsequently meet with the president on the next day, December 7th?

A: I may have met with the president. I'd have to—I mean, I'd have to look. I'd have to look. I don't know whether I did or not.

Q: If you would like to confer—I believe the record shows that, but I'd like to establish that through your testimony.... All right. So you met with the president on December 7th. And was it the next day after that, December 8th, that Ms. Lewinsky called to set up the job meeting with you on December 11th?

A: I believe that is correct.

Q: And sometime after your meeting on December 11th with Ms. Lewinsky, did you have another conversation with the president?

A: Uh, you do understand that conversations between me and the president, uh, was not an unusual circumstance.

Q: And I understand that—

A: All right.

Q: —and so let me be more specific. I believe your previous testimony has been that sometime after the 11th, you spoke with the president about Ms. Lewinsky.

A: I stand on that testimony.

Q: All right. And so there's two conversations after the witness list came out—one that you had with the president on December 7th, and then a subsequent conversation with him after you met with Ms. Lewinsky on the 11th. Now, in your subsequent conversation after the 11th, did you discuss with the president of the United States Monica Lewinsky, and if so, can you tell us what that discussion was?

A: If there was a discussion subsequent to Monica Lewinsky's visit to me on December the 11th with the president of the United States, it was about the job search.

Q: All right. And during that, did he indicate that he knew about the fact that she had lost her job in the White House, and she wanted to get a job in New York?

A: He was aware that—he was obviously aware that she had lost her job in the White House, because she was working at the Pentagon. He was also aware that she wanted to work in New York, in the private sector, and understood that that is why she was having conversations with me. There is no doubt about that.

Q: And he thanked you for helping her?

A: There's no question about that, either.

Q: And on either of these conversations that I've referenced that you had with the president after the witness list came out, your conversation on December 7th, and your conversation sometime after the 11th, did the president tell you that Ms. Monica Lewinsky was on the witness list in the Jones case?

A: He did not.

Q: And did you consider this information to be important in your efforts to be helpful to Ms. Lewinsky?

A: I never thought about it.

Mr. Kendall:... Mr. Jordan found out about Ms. Lewinsky's subpoena on December 19 when a weeping Ms. Lewinsky telephoned him and came to his office.... Mr. Jordan then did what I think is best called due diligence. He talked to Ms. Lewinsky, got her a lawyer, asked her whether there was any sexual relationship with the president, and was assured that there was not. That same evening, he went to the White House and made a similar inquiry of the president and he received a similar response.... So I think it is absolutely clear that there is no conflict between the president's testimony and Mr. Jordan's testimony about this. Mr. Jordan had recommended Ms. Lewinsky and took her to the lawyer's office, to a lawyer, a Mr. Frank Carter, a respected Washington, DC, lawyer, to whom Mr. Jordan had recommended other clients....

Next, Kendall said he wanted to correct the record. Two days before, he said, the managers had displayed a chart that purported to show "interconnection between job help and testimony." On it was a question—"[so you] talk to her both about the job and her concerns about parts of the affidavit"—and an answer: "That is correct."

But Jordan's real testimony, said Kendall, was rather different. He played a long clip, which contained the portion the managers had excerpted:

Q: In your conversation with Ms. Lewinsky prior to the affidavit being signed, did you in fact talk to her about both the job and her concerns about parts of the affidavit?

A: I have never in any conversation with Ms. Lewinsky talked to her about the job, on one hand, or job being interrelated with the conversation about the affidavit. The affidavit was over here. The job was over here.

Q: But the—in the same conversations, both her interest in a job and her discussions about the affidavit were contained in the same conversation?

A: As I said to you before, Counselor, she was always interested in the job.

Q: Okay. And she was always interested in the job, and so, if she brought up the affidavit, very likely it was in the same conversation?

A: No doubt.

Q: And that would be consistent with your previous grand jury testimony when you expressed that you talked to her both about the job and her concerns about parts of the affidavit?

A: That is correct.

Q: Now, on January 7th, the affidavit was signed. Subsequent to this, did you notify anyone in the White House that the affidavit in the *Jones* case had been signed by Ms. Lewinsky?

A: Yeah. I'm certain I told Betty Currie, and I'm fairly certain that I told the president.

Q: And why did you tell Betty Currie?

A: I'm—I kept them informed about everybody else that was—everything else. There was no reason not to tell them about that she had signed the affidavit.

Q: And why did you tell the president?

A: The president was obviously interested in her job search. We had talked about the affidavit. He knew that she had a lawyer. It was in the due course of a conversation. I would say, "Mr. President, she signed the affidavit. She signed the affidavit."

Q: And what was his response when you informed him that she had signed the affidavit?

A: "Thank you very much."

Q: All right. And would you also have been giving him a report on the status of the job search at the same time?

A: He may have asked about that, and—and part of her problem was that, you know, she was—there was a great deal of anxiety about the job. She wanted the job. She was unemployed, and she wanted to work.

Q: Now, I think you indicated that he was obviously concerned about—was it her representation and the affidavit?

A: I told him that I had found counsel for her, and I told him that she had signed the affidavit.

Q: Okay. You indicated that he was concerned, obviously, about something. What was he obviously concerned about in your conversations with him?

A: Throughout, he had been concerned about her getting employment in New York, period.

Q: And he was also concerned about the affidavit?

A: I don't know that that was concern. I did tell him that the affidavit was signed. He knew that she had counsel, and he knew that I had arranged the counsel.

...In his presentation, Mr. Manager Hutchinson discussed the breakfast with Ms. Lewinsky, which Mr. Jordan now concedes he had, on December 31....

There is plainly a conflict in the testimony between Ms. Lewinsky and Mr. Jordan; although Mr. Jordan, as you will recall, vehemently denies ever giving that instruction, saying in the videotape played this morning: "I'm a lawyer and I'm a loyal friend, but I'm not a fool. That's ridiculous. I never did that."

...[This] was not presented as a separate ground for impeachment by the independent counsel. It was identified—the fact of the conflicted testimony was identified, but it was not urged as a separate ground, despite the very, very energetic investigation of Mr. Starr. We have heard a lot in this case about "dogs that won't hunt." In my mind, this is like a Sherlock Holmes story about the dog that didn't bark. If the independent counsel didn't raise it, that is significant. Finally, it has nothing whatsoever to do with the president, by anybody's contention.

The House managers now had time for rebuttal. The chief justice recognized Ed Bryant.

Mr. Bryant:...Let's not throw away all of our common sense here.

She gets a phone call in the middle of the night with a message that you are on the witness list, and she says three things occurred: You are on the witness list, you can file an affidavit, and you can use a cover story. Why else would the president raise the issue of a cover story at 2:30 in the morning if he didn't intend for her to use that?

But keep in mind, too, it really doesn't matter how she appreciated this. It really matters what the president intended. And he intended to let her know that she was on the list, she could be subpoenaed, she could file an affidavit, and she could use the cover story.

And in fact she did use that cover story. She went to her lawyer, Mr. Carter, and told him that. And it was incorporated into the draft affidavit that she went to take papers to the president to sign, and in those cases she may have been alone. But they didn't like the specter of her being alone. So they struck that provision out of the final affidavit....

But keep in mind also that it is the president's intent. And his intent was to interfere with justice in the *Paula Jones* case and to have her give a false affidavit....

On the gifts to people, is it really an issue?...Ms. Lewinsky testified that there was no doubt in her mind that Ms. Currie initiated the call.... The fact that there were other calls in the day, the fact that one of the other calls may have been at 3:30, really are moot points. The issue is, if Betty Currie initiated that phone call, the only impetus for her to initiate that call had to come from the president. She was not in that conversation that morning. The president had to tell her, and apparently did so, because she made the call....

I ask you to consider each of these seven pillars of obstruction that Mr. Hutchinson raised, and look at the end results of those acts, and look at who benefited from those results. And what I believe you...find is that each case resulted in impeding justice in the *Paula Jones* case in some way that favored the president....

I guess if you...accept each and every argument of these extremely fine defense counsel that the president wasn't behind any of this, then I guess you just have to reach the conclusion that the president was the luckiest man in the world, that people would commit crimes by filing false affidavits, by hiding evidence, by going out and possibly trashing the witnesses and giving false testimony in grand jury proceedings.... But I suggest to you that the facts of this case are really not in contest....

The chief justice recognized Asa Hutchinson, who played a clip of Lewinsky telling the story about her breakfast with Vernon Jordan on December 31, 1997. In it, she testified that she had told Jordan about the drafts of notes to the president at her apartment. His response: "I believe he said something like, well, go home and make sure they're not there." She then "got rid of some of the notes." Hutchinson ended: "This goes to the overall pattern of obstruction. It goes to credibility. I believe it is relevant in this case."

The chief justice recognized Lindsey Graham, who had the final word of rebuttal. He wanted, he said, to "refocus." For instance, he wondered, was it really credible that the president had told Monica Lewinsky that she should turn over all the gifts if the Jones lawyers asked? He went on:

Mr. Graham: ... If you believe that, that is the only time he really embraced the law in this case, as I can see. Everything about him, in the way he behaved, was 180 degrees out from that statement. ... The truth is that a reasonable person should conclude that when Ms. Lewinsky approached him about what to do with the gifts, he said, "I'll have to think about that." And you know what, ladies and gentlemen, he thought about it. And do you know what he did after he thought about it? "Betty, go get those gifts." ...

Affidavit—where I come from, you call somebody at 2:30 in the morning, you are up to no good. That will be borne out, if you listen to the testimony and use your common sense. He was up to no good. He told her, "My heart is breaking because you are on this witness list and maybe here's a way to get out of it." That is the God's truth. That is what he did and that is wrong and that is a crime. ...

This affidavit was false for a reason—because the president and Ms. Lewinsky wanted it to be false.

The job search? "Mission accomplished," says it all. ... It went from being no big deal to the biggest deal in the world with a telephone bill—I don't know what the telephone bill was to get this job, but it was huge. "Mission accomplished."

All these are crimes. ... But you can say this about the president: He was trying to get her a job and he was trying to just get her to file a false affidavit so this would go away. And he was trying to hide the gifts. And that is bad but that is not nearly as bad as what was to come.

After the deposition, said Graham, "when it was clear that Ms. Lewinsky may have been talking ... the alarm bells went off." He reviewed the statements to Betty Currie, then continued:

... But here is where it gets to be nasty. Here is where it gets to be mean: "Monica came on to me and I never touched her, right? She wanted to have sex with me and I couldn't do that." He didn't say it once, he said it twice, just to make sure Ms. Currie would get the point.

Now that Ms. Lewinsky may be a problem, let me tell you how the discussion goes. ...

Conversation with Mr. Morris, after they did the poll about what to do here, and "We just have to win." The president had a follow-up conversation with Mr. Morris during the evening of January 22, 1998, the day after the story broke, when Mr. Morris was considering holding a press conference to blast Ms. Lewinsky out of the water, the president told Mr. Morris to be careful.... According to Mr. Morris, the president warned him not to be too hard on Ms. Lewinsky because "there is some slight chance that she may not be cooperating with Mr. Starr and we don't want to alienate her by anything we are going to put out." In other words, don't blast her now, she may not be a problem to us.

During this period of time, it went from concealing to redefining. When he knew he had to win, what did he do? He went to his secretary and he made her a sexual predator and him an innocent victim, and he did it twice. But did he do it to anybody else? Did he redefine his relationship to anybody else?

I now would like to have a clip from Mr. Blumenthal, please.

Q: You have a conversation with the president on the same day the article comes out, and the conversation includes a discussion about the relationship between him and Ms. Lewinsky, is that correct?

A: Yes.

Next tape:

Q: Now, you stated, I think very honestly, and I appreciate that, you were lied to by the president. Is it a fair statement, given your previous testimony concerning your 30-minute conversation, that the president was trying to portray himself as a victim of a relationship with Monica Lewinsky?

A: I think that's the import of his whole story.

Ladies and gentlemen, that is the import of his whole story. That story was told on the day this broke in the press, and it goes on. That story is very detailed. It makes him the victim of a sexual predator called Ms. Lewinsky. He had to rebuff her.... She threatened him.... And it goes on and on and on. And I have always wondered, how did that story make it to the grand jury and how did it make it into the press? We know how it made it to the grand jury, because Mr. Blumenthal told it and the president told him and they claimed executive privilege and the president never straightened it out. Your president redefined this relationship, and your president let that lie be passed to a grand jury. Your president obstructed justice in a mean way.

Next statement.

Q: That's where you start talking about the story that the president told you. Knowing what you know now, do you believe the president lied to you about his relationship with Ms. Lewinsky?

A: I do.

Next statement.

Q: Okay. Do you have any idea how White House sources are associated with statements such as "She's known as 'Elvira'," "She's obsessed with the president," "She's known as a flirt," "She's the product of a troubled home, divorced parents," "She's known as 'The Stalker'"? Do you have any idea how that got in the press?...

A: I have no idea how anything came to be attributed to a White House source.

...Let me quietly, if I can, for God's sakes, get to the truth. For God's sakes, figure out what kind of person we have here in the White House. For God's sakes, spend some time to fulfill your constitutional duty so that we can get it right, not just for our political moment but for the future of this Nation....

The final thing is that our president, in my opinion, and for you to judge, in August of last year, after being begged not to by many Members of this body and prominent Americans, appeared before a Federal grand jury to answer for the conduct in this case.... We have alleged that with forewarning and knowledge on his part, that instead of clearing it up...instead of fulfilling his role as the chief law enforcement officer of the land to do honor to the law, instead of taking this burden off all Americans' backs, he told a story that defies common sense....

He went on and told an elaborate farce to a federal grand jury that they just didn't ask the right question and really the sexual relationship did include one thing but not another. And he says he never lied to his aide and he says he never lied to the grand jury. Well, God knows he lied to somebody, and he lied to that grand jury, and this whole story is a fraud and a farce. The last people in the United States to straighten it out is the U.S. Senate. God bless you in your endeavors.

THE CLOSING ARGUMENTS

The chief justice recognized James Sensenbrenner to lead off the managers' last arguments.

Mr. Sensenbrenner: ... Regardless of what some may say, this constitutional crisis was caused by William Jefferson Clinton and by no one else. President Clinton's actions, and his actions alone, have caused the national agenda for the past year to be almost exclusively concentrated on those actions and what consequences the president, and the president alone, must suffer for them.

This trial is not about the president's affair with Monica Lewinsky. It is about the perjury and obstruction of justice he committed during the course of the civil rights lawsuit filed against him, and the subsequent independent counsel investigation authorized by Attorney General Janet Reno. ...

Sensenbrenner outlined what he called "four glaring examples" of the president's "perjurious, false and misleading statements to the grand jury": his testimony about his lawyer's use of Lewinsky's affidavit at his deposition; his testimony about his conversations with Betty Currie; his testimony about what he told his aides about his relationship with Lewinsky, and his testimony about "the nature" of that relationship.

He continued:

The decision each Senator must make with respect to Article I is whether the president is to pay a price for his perjury, just like any citizen must....

Senators, don't be fooled by the president's excuses and spin control. The facts and the evidence clearly show that he knew what he was doing was to deceive everyone, including the grand jury. He and his defenders are still in denial. They will not accept the consequences of his repeated and criminal attempts to defeat the judicial process. His lies to the grand jury were not to protect his family or the dignity of his office but to protect himself from criminal liability for his perjury and obstruction of justice in the *Jones* case.

To justify the president's criminal behavior by demonizing those who seek to hold him accountable ignores the fact that President Clinton's actions, and those actions alone, precipitated the investigations which have brought us here today. To keep a president in office whose gross misconduct and criminal actions are a well-established fact will weaken the authority of the presidency, undermine the rule of law, and cheapen those words which have made America different from most other nations on the Earth: Equal justice under law....

The chief justice recognized Christopher Cannon.

Cannon outlined a number of ways this trial had differed from past impeachment proceedings. In an ordinary trial, he noted, "each side typically takes the time necessary to establish its case or undermine the witness through cross-examination. After the moving party has made its case, the responding party makes its case.... The case develops tested piece by tested piece." But in this proceeding, he said, "We had a limited number of witnesses limited to videotaped appearances limited to fit an arbitrary three-hour rule." The rules, including the form of the question-and-answer sessions, he argued, had made the proceeding awkward and incomplete.

He continued:

Mr. Cannon: ... As the Senate deliberates this case I would ask that a few key facts never be forgotten: One, that the president committed perjury when he lied under oath; two, the Senate has historically impeached judges for perjury...; three, any American watching these proceedings who commits perjury would also be punished by the law; four, if the Senate follows our nation's precedents of punishing perjurers, and if the Senate follows its own precedents of convicting perjurers, then there is only one clear conclusion in this matter: conviction.

Senators, we as Americans and legislators have never supported a legal system which has one set of laws for the ruler, and another for the ruled.

After all, our very own pledge of allegiance binds us together with the language of "liberty and justice for all." If that is the case, if we intend to live up to the oaths and pledges we take, then our very own president must be subject to the precedents our nation's judicial system and this Senate body have heretofore set....

The chief justice recognized George Gekas.

Mr. Gekas: ... It all swoops down the telescope to one issue: Did the president utter falsehoods under oath? Everyone understands that. Everyone comes to the conclusion that that is a serious allegation that has been made through the impeachment, and one which you must judge in the final vote that you will be casting....

This is, to me, proof positive that the president uttered falsehoods under oath in all of his public stances. On December 23, the president, under oath, answered interrogatories that were sent to him by the court in the *Jones* case ... Have you ever had sexual relations with anyone in a subordinate role while you were governor of Arkansas, or president of the United States? ... At that time there was no definition in front of him, no gaggle of attorneys trying to dispute what word meant what, no judge there to interpose the legal standard that should be employed, but rather the boldfaced, naked phrase of "sexual relations" that everyone in the whole world understands to be what it is—and the president answered under oath "None."

I submit to the Members of the Senate ... you can refer back to December 23 and see a starting point of a pattern of conduct on the part of the president that proves beyond all doubt that he committed a pattern and actual falsehoods under oath time and time again.

If that is not enough, on January 15, as the record will disclose, he answered under oath requests for documents in which the question is asked under oath ... Have you ever received any gifts or documents from—and it mentioned among others Monica Lewinsky—and the president under oath said "No" or "None." ...

I submit to you that if you are confused about that, because of the great presentation made by the counsel for the president about the murkiness and cloudiness of the *Jones* deposition, the maddening consequences of the president's testimony ... then you can refer back to January 15 before the deposition, and December 23, and find proof positive in the documents already a part of the case that you have to decide that, indeed, a pattern of falsehoods under oath was initiated and conducted by the president of the United States.... Those allegations, by the way, have gone completely uncontradicted by the president of the United States....

I have a witness. I call a witness to bolster my part of this summation. The witness is the American people.

Mr. Craig, in his last appearance on this podium, was delighted to be able to quote a poll that showed that 75 percent of the people of our country felt that there was no need to present videotapes to the Senate in the trial—75 percent, he said with great gusto, of the American people....

I now call the American people's poll on whether or not they believe that the president committed falsehoods under oath—80 percent of the American people—I call them to my side here at the podium to verify to you that the president committed falsehoods under oath.

The chief justice recognized Steve Chabot.

Mr. Chabot: ... At the beginning of this trial, I predicted in my presentation that they would use legal smokescreens to mask the law and the facts. To their credit, they produced smoke so thick that it continues to cloud this debate. But if you look through the smoke and the mirrors employed by these very able lawyers, you will see the truth. The truth is that President Clinton lied to a federal grand jury....

In my opening statement before this body, I outlined the four elements of perjury: An oath, intent, falsity, materiality. In this case, all those elements have been met.

President Clinton also obstructed justice and encouraged others to lie in judicial proceedings. He sought to influence the testimony of a potentially adverse witness with job assistance, and he attempted to conceal evidence that was under subpoena.

These truths cannot be ignored, distorted, or swept under the rug. Some of the president's partisan defenders want you to do just that. But it would be wrong. It would be wrong for you to send the message to every American that it is acceptable to lie under oath and obstruct justice. It would be wrong for you to tell America's children that some lies are all right. It would be wrong to show the rest of the world that some of our laws don't really matter....

The chief justice recognized Bob Barr.

Mr. Barr: ... In the past month, you have heard much about the Constitution; and about the law. Probably more than you'd prefer; in a dizzying recitation of the U.S. Criminal Code. ... Tampering. Perjury. Obstruction. That is a lot to digest, but these are real laws and they are applicable to these proceedings and to this president. Evidence and law, you have seen it and you have heard it.

You've also seen and heard about straw men raised up by the White House lawyers, and then stricken down mightily. You've heard them essentially describe the president alternately as victim or saint. You've heard even his staunchest allies describe his conduct as "reprehensible." Even some of you, on the president's side of the aisle, have concluded, "there's no question about his having given false testimony under oath and he did that more than once."

There has also been much smoke churned up by the defense.

Men and women of the Senate, Monica Lewinsky is not on trial. Her conduct and her intentions are not at issue here. Vernon Jordan is not on trial and his conduct and his intentions are not at issue here. William Jefferson Clinton is on trial here. His behavior, his intentions, his actions—these and only these are the issues here. When the White House lawyers raise up as a straw man that Vernon Jordan may have had no improper motive in seeking a job for Ms. Lewinsky; or that there was no formal "conspiracy" proved between the president and Vernon Jordan; or that Ms. Lewinsky says she did not draw a direct link between the president's raising the issue of a false affidavit and the cover stories, keep in mind, these are irrelevant issues. When the White House lawyers strike these theories down, even if you were to conclude they did, they are striking down nothing more than irrelevant straw men.

What stands today, as it has throughout these proceedings, are facts—a false affidavit that benefits the president, the coaching of witnesses by the president, the secreting of subpoenaed evidence that would have harmed the president, lies under oath by the president. These reflect President Clinton's behavior; President Clinton's intentions; President Clinton's actions; and President Clinton's benefit. Not through the eyes of false theories; but by the evidence through the lens of common sense. ...

The chief justice recognized Stephen Buyer.

Mr. Buyer: ... I assure you, the House managers would not have prosecuted the articles of impeachment before the bar of the Senate had we not had the highest degree of faith, belief and confidence that, based on the evidence, the president committed high crimes and misdemeanors which warrant his removal from office....

I have...heard some Senators from both sides of the aisle state publicly, "I think these offenses rise to the level of high crimes and misdemeanors." To state publicly that you believe that high crimes and misdemeanors have occurred, but for some reason you have this desire not to remove the president, that desire, though, does not square with the law, the Constitution, and the Senate's precedents for removing federal judges for similar offenses.

So long as William Jefferson Clinton is president, the only mechanism to hold him accountable for his high crimes and misdemeanors is the power of impeachment and removal. The Constitution is very clear. You cannot vindicate the rule of law by stating high crimes and misdemeanors have occurred, but leave the president in office subject to future prosecution after his term is expired....

The president is answerable for his alleged crimes to the Senate here and now....

I have asked myself many times how allowing a president to remain in office while having committed perjury and obstruction of justice is fair to those across the country who are sitting in jail for having committed the same crimes....

Fairness is important. Fairness is something that is simple in its nature and is powerful in the statement that it makes. A statement which you send carries us into tomorrow and becomes our future legacy....

Alexander Hamilton, writing not long after the Constitution was adopted, well expressed the harm that would come to our Republic from those who, by example, undermine respect for the law. In a statement that bears repeating, Hamilton wrote:

> If it were to be asked, What is the most sacred duty and the greatest source of security in a Republic? The answer would be, an inviolable respect for the Constitution and Laws—the first growing out of the last...Those, therefore, who...set examples, which undermine or subvert the authority of the laws, lead us from freedom to slavery; they incapacitate us from a government of laws....

President Clinton, by his persistent and calculated misconduct and illegal acts, has set a pernicious example of lawlessness, an example which, by its very nature, subverts respect for the law. His perverse example inevitably undermines the integrity of both the office of the president and the judicial process....

After a ten-minute recess, the chief justice recognized Charles Ruff.

Ruff began by addressing, once again, the question of whether perjury and obstruction of justice "should be treated as the equivalent of treason and bribery," and whether the arguments of the House managers had proven that they should. True, he said, Blackstone had ranked perjury among twenty-one offenses against public justice. But it was number 15 among them, he said, well behind other offenses that today seem quaint (number 1 on the list, for instance, was "vacating records"). Then Ruff turned to McCollum's argument that modern sentencing guidelines make perjury at least as serious as bribery. McCollum, said Ruff, had not explained that a bribe taken by an elected official carried, under the same guidelines, twice the offense level of perjury, "and a prison sentence four to five times longer."

The real question facing the senators was this, said Ruff: "Would it put at risk the liberty of the people to retain the president in office?" If they thought not, they must acquit him.

Ruff continued:

Mr. Ruff: ... I want to focus for just a little while on those aspects of the managers' presentation that merit your special attention....

As we start this discussion, let me offer you a phrase that I hope you will remember as I move through the articles with you. That phrase is "moving targets and empty pots." "Moving targets," ever-shifting theories, each one advanced to replace the last as it has fallen, fallen victim to the facts. "Empty pots," attractive containers, but when you take the lid off you find nothing to sustain them....

Article I, the first moving target. Now, as we have said repeatedly, we have been more than a little puzzled as to the exact nature of the charges advanced by the managers under the rubric of Article I, ... As you look to Article I ... ask yourselves whether you can at this late moment in the trial identify for yourselves with any remote sense of certainty the statements that the managers claim were perjurious....

Now, just to give you an example of how rapidly the target can move, you will recall that in describing the incidents of perjury allegedly committed by the president, the managers made much of the preliminary statement he read to the grand jury, including the use of the words "occasionally," and "on certain occasions" to describe the frequency of certain conduct....

Yet, strangely, when Mr. Manager Rogan was asked about these very charges as late as January 20, he quite clearly abandoned them.... Appearing on television ... with Chris Matthews, this is what transpired:

Matthews: ... now defend these—these elements—one, that the president lied when he said he had had these relationships with her on certain occasions. Is that the language?

Rep. Rogan: That is the ...

Matthews: And—and why is that perjurious—perjurious?

Rep. Rogan: In fact, I'm not—I don't think it's necessarily perjurious. That is—that's one little piece of this answer that he gave at the grand jury....

Matthews: Well, another time he used a phrase with regard to this ridiculous thing called phone sex, he referred to it as occasionally or on occasion. Why do you add them in as part of the perjury indictment?

Rep. Rogan: That's not added in as part of the perjury indictment in Article I. I simply raised that issue when I was addressing the Senate.

Matthews: You better get to those senators because I think they made the mistake I did of thinking that was one of the elements in the perjury charge.

... And so as to Article I's charge, now that this is off the books, that the president perjured himself concerning his relationship with Ms. Lewinsky, we are once again left with the claim that he lied about touching, about his denial that he engaged in conduct that fell within his subjective understanding of the definition used in the *Jones* deposition.... And as any experienced prosecutor ... will tell you, it defies real world experience to charge anyone, president or not, with perjury on the grounds that you disbelieve his testimony about his own subjective belief in the definition of a term used in a civil deposition....

Now, there are three other elements of Article I. First, the allegation that the president lied when he claimed he did not perjure himself in the *Jones* deposition. The president, of course, made no such representation in the grand jury.

And the managers cannot, no matter how they try, resurrect the charges of the article ... that was so clearly rejected by the House of Representatives....

There is literally nothing in the president's grand jury testimony that purports to adopt wholesale his testimony in the *Jones* deposition. If anything, it is evident that he is explaining at length and clarifying and adding to his deposition testimony. Indeed, even if the original Article II had survived, the president's belief that he had "worked through the minefield of the *Jones* deposition without violating the law"—which is a quote from his grand jury testimony—could not allow the managers, somehow, to establish that that statement was independently perjurious. . . .

Now, as to the second and third remaining elements of Article I, that the president lied about Mr. Bennett's statement to Judge Wright at the time of the *Jones* deposition, and that he lied about his own statements to his staff, I will deal with them in my discussion of the obstruction charges in Article II. . . .

Let me move to Article II. Manager Hutchinson told you in his original presentation that Article II rested on—his words—"seven pillars of obstruction." . . . Let's remove one pillar right at the start.

Article II charges that the president engaged in a scheme to obstruct the *Jones* case—the *Jones* case—and alleges as one element of this scheme that in the days following January 21 the president lied to his staff about his relationship with Ms. Lewinsky, conduct that could not possibly have had anything to do with the *Jones* litigation.

. . . I have yet to hear from the managers a single plausible explanation for the inclusion of this charge as part of a scheme to obstruct the *Jones* litigation, and I can think of none. . . . And, so, one pillar gone; a slight list observed.

Next: Ms. Lewinsky's affidavit and the first of the empty pots. The managers charge that the president corruptly encouraged a witness to execute a sworn affidavit that he knew to be perjurious, false, and misleading, and similarly encouraged Ms. Lewinsky to lie if she were ever called as a witness. . . .

Now, it is not in dispute that the president called Ms. Lewinsky in the early morning of December 17 . . . and . . . he told her that she was now listed on the *Jones* witness list. The managers have from the beginning relied on one fact and on one baseless hypothesis stemming from this call which, in the managers' minds, was the beginning and the middle and the end of the scheme to encourage the filing of a false affidavit. . . .

The one fact to which the managers point is Ms. Lewinsky's testimony that the president said that if she were actually subpoenaed, she possibly could file an affidavit to avoid having to testify, and at some point in the call mentioned one of the so-called cover stories that they had used when she was still working at the White House—that is, bringing papers to him. . . .

After you saw Ms. Lewinsky's testimony, there can be nothing left of what was, at best, only conjecture. . . .

Ruff replayed the videotape excerpt culminating in Lewinsky's statement: "He didn't discuss the content of my affidavit with me at all, ever." Then he showed the segment in which she said there had been no discussion of the "cover stories" in connection with the affidavit and which included the following exchange:

Q: ... when the president told you that you were on the witness list, he also suggested that you could sign an affidavit and use misleading cover stories. Isn't that correct?

A: Uh—well, I—I guess in my mind, I separate necessarily signing affidavit and using misleading cover stories. So, does—

Q: Well, those two—

A: Those three events occurred, but they don't—they weren't linked for me.

Finally, he showed the portion of Lewinsky's testimony in which Bryant had asked her whether, after the president suggested she could file an affidavit, she appreciated "the implications of filing a false affidavit." Lewinsky's reply: "I don't think I necessarily thought at that point it would have to be false, so no, probably not...."

Ruff continued:

There was another issue that surfaced early on, although perhaps it has dissipated, and that is whether the president ever saw a draft of Ms. Lewinsky's affidavit.... Early on, Manager McCollum speculated for you ... that when the president told Ms. Lewinsky that he didn't need to see her affidavit because he had seen other affidavits, he really must have meant that he had seen previous drafts of hers.

... Now we know that those drafts didn't exist. They never existed. How do we know? Somewhat belatedly, the managers got around to telling us that. In describing the testimony they would expect to receive from Ms. Lewinsky when they moved for the right to take her deposition, they wrote in their motion:

That same day, January 5, she called President Clinton to ask if the president would like to review her affidavit before it was signed. He declined, saying he had already seen about 15 others. She understood that to mean that he had seen 15 other affidavits rather than 15 prior drafts of her affidavit (which did not exist).

In sum, one, the only reference to an affidavit in the December 17 call was the suggestion of the president that filing one might possibly enable Ms. Lewinsky to avoid being deposed, itself an entirely legitimate and proper suggestion.

Two, the president and Ms. Lewinsky never discussed the content of her affidavit on or after December 17.

Three, the president never saw or read any draft of the affidavit before it was signed.

Four, the president believed that she could file a true affidavit.

Five, Ms. Lewinsky believed that she could file a true affidavit.

Six, there is not one single document or piece of testimony that suggests that the president encouraged her to file a false affidavit.

If there is no proof the president encouraged Ms. Lewinsky to file a false affidavit, surely there must be some proof on the other charge that he encouraged her to give perjurious testimony if she were ever called to testify. Well, there isn't. . . .

But let's put this in the managers' own context. On December 6, the president learned that Ms. Lewinsky was on the *Jones* witness list. According to the managers, that was a source of grave concern and spurred intensified efforts to find her a job—efforts that were still further intensified when, on December 11, Judge Wright issued her order allowing lawyers to inquire into the president's relationships with other women. . . .

Now, as to the charge of subornation, the managers do concede, as they must, that the president and Ms. Lewinsky did not even discuss her deposition on the 17th, logically, I suppose, since she wasn't actually subpoenaed until two days later.

Now, one might think that this would dispose of the matter, since they do not identify a single other moment in time when there was any discussion of Ms. Lewinsky's potential testimony. But once again, having lifted the lid and seen that their pot was empty, they would ask you to find that the same signal that we now know did not encourage the filing of an affidavit was a signal to Ms. Lewinsky to lie if she was ever called to testify. But of course we have long known that there was no such signal. And . . . one of the jurors took it upon him or herself to ask that which the independent counsel chose not to. . . .

A Juror: It is possible that you also had these discussions [about denying the relationship] after you learned that you were a witness in the *Paula Jones* case?

Ms. Lewinsky: I don't believe so. No.

A Juror: Can you exclude that possibility?

Ms. Lewinsky: I pretty much can. I really don't remember it. I mean, it would be very surprising for me to be confronted with something that would show me different, but I—it was 2:30 in the—I mean, the conversation I'm thinking of mainly would have been December 17th, which was—

A Juror: The telephone call.

Ms. Lewinsky: Right. And it was—you know, 2:00, 2:30 in the morning. I remember the gist of it and I—I really don't think so.

A Juror: Thank you.

But all of this is not enough to dissuade the managers.

Now that they know that the only two participants in the relevant conversation denied that there was any discussion of either the affidavit or the testimony, they have created still another theory. As Manager Bryant told you last week—and in essence it was repeated today—"I don't care what was in Ms. Lewinsky's mind."

Well, that is quite extraordinary. The only witness, the supposed victim of the obstruction, the person whose testimony is being influenced, says that it didn't happen. And the managers nonetheless want you to conclude, I assume, that some subliminal message was being conveyed that resulted in the filing of a false affidavit without the affiant knowing that she was being controlled by some unseen and unheard force. . . . Two more pillars lie in the dust.

Next, the gifts. . . .

On the morning of December 28, the president gave Ms. Lewinsky Christmas presents in token of her impending departure for New York. Ms. Lewinsky testified that she raised the subject of her subpoena and said something about getting the gifts out of her apartment, to which she herself has now told you the president either made no response or said something like, "Let me think about it."

Betty Currie testified consistently that Ms. Lewinsky called her to ask her to pick up a box and hold them for her. Ms. Lewinsky has testified equally consistently . . . that it was her recollection that Ms. Currie called her and said that she understood she "had something for her" or perhaps even the president said, "You have something for me." The president denies that he ever spoke to Betty Currie about picking up gifts from Monica Lewinsky. Betty

Currie denies that the president ever asked her to pick up gifts from Monica Lewinsky.

Now, Ms. Lewinsky has stated on three occasions before her most recent deposition that Ms. Currie picked up the gifts at 2 o'clock in the afternoon on the 28th. Having been shown the infamous 3:32 cell phone call, which had previously been trumpeted by the managers as absolute proof that it was Ms. Currie who called Ms. Lewinsky, who initiated the process, Ms. Lewinsky testified on Monday that Ms. Currie came to pick up the gifts sometime during the afternoon and that there had been other calls earlier in the day.

But we learned at least a couple of interesting new things from Ms. Lewinsky on this subject.

First, when she received her subpoena on December 19, nine days ... before she spoke to the president about them, Ms. Lewinsky was frightened at the prospect that the *Jones* lawyers would search her apartment, and she began to think about concealing the gifts that she cared most about that would suggest some special relationship with the president....

Thus, when she arrived to pick up her Christmas gifts from the president on December 28, she had already decided that she would not turn over all the gifts called for by the subpoena.... But she didn't tell the president about that. Instead, as she testified, she broached the question of what to do with the gifts and the possibility of giving them to Betty Currie ... to which the president either made no reply or said something like, "I'll think about it."

This testimony sheds light on one of the issues that has troubled everyone.... Why would the president, if he were really worried about Ms. Lewinsky's turning over gifts pursuant to the subpoena, give her more gifts? From our perspective, the answer has always been an easy one.... he wasn't worried about it.

Now, we know that from Ms. Lewinsky's perspective ... it also made no difference that the president was giving her additional gifts, because she had already decided ... that she would not turn them over.

> *Ruff reminded his listeners of the trial brief allegation that the president had lied in saying to the grand jury that he had told Lewinsky she would have to "turn over whatever she had" if the Jones lawyers asked for the gifts. But in her new testimony, Ruff noted, she said one of the OIC FBI agents had asked whether she recalled the president's saying anything like that, and she replied, "That sounds familiar."*

...As my colleague, Ms. Seligman, pointed out to you on Saturday, this was the first time after all Ms. Lewinsky's recorded versions of the events of De-

cember 28, that we had ever heard that the president's version sounded familiar to her.... If she hadn't been honest enough to tell Manager Bryant about it,
we and you would never have known.

Senators, what else is there in the vaults of the independent counsel or in
the memory of his agents that we don't know about?

Another pillar down.

The job search. It may have become tiresome to hear, but any discussion of
the job search must begin with Ms. Lewinsky's testimony oft repeated that no
one promised her a job to influence her testimony....

Now we know that Monica Lewinsky's job search began in the summer of
1997, well in advance of her being involved in the *Jones* case. In October, she
interviewed with U.N. Ambassador Richardson, was offered a job. She had her
first meeting with Mr. Jordan early in November, well before she appeared in
the *Jones* case. The next contact was actually before Thanksgiving when she
made an effort to set up another meeting with Mr. Jordan and was told to call
back after the holiday. She did, on December 8, and set up a meeting on December 11...

Now, on that date of December 11...Mr. Jordan did open doors for Ms.
Lewinsky in New York, but there was no inappropriate pressure.... As Mr.
Jordan told the grand jury when asked whether there was any connection between his assistance to her and the *Jones* case, his answer was "unequivocally,
indubitably no."

In search of some evidence that Mr. Jordan's efforts were, indeed, trigger-
ing Ms. Lewinsky's status as a witness and therefore inappropriate, the managers focused on his January 8 call to Mr. Perelman, the CEO of MacAndrews
& Forbes.... Ms. Lewinsky had reported that her original interview had not
gone well, although we know it actually had, and that her résumé had already
been sent over from MacAndrews & Forbes to Revlon where she ultimately
was offered a job.

Mr. Jordan was candid stating he went to the top because he wanted to get
action if action could be had, but the record is clear that the woman involved
at Revlon who interviewed Ms. Lewinsky had already made a decision to hire
her. No one put any pressure on her. There was no special urgency. There was
no fix....

Now, other than the managers, there are only two people, as far as I can tell,
who ever tried to create a link between the job search and the affidavit: Linda

Tripp and Kenneth Starr. No one—not Ms. Lewinsky, not Mr. Jordan, not the president, no one—ever said anything to so much as suggest the existence of such a linkage, and the managers can find no proof....

Now, the managers would also have you believe that Mr. Jordan was involved in drafting the affidavit and that he was involved in the deletion of language from the draft that suggested that she had been alone with the president. Ms. Lewinsky's and Mr. Jordan's testimony is essentially the same. They talked, Mr. Jordan listened ... he called Mr. Carter, he transmitted to Mr. Carter some of her concerns, but he made it very clear to Ms. Lewinsky he wasn't her lawyer. And in words that will resonate forever, at least among the legal community, Mr. Jordan said, "I don't do affidavits." ...

Now, recognizing that they would never be able to show that the inception of the job search was linked in any way to the affidavit, the managers developed a theory which they have advanced to you that the president committed obstruction of justice when the job search assistance became, in their words, "totally interconnected, intertwined, interrelated," with the filing of Ms. Lewinsky's affidavit.

The problem the managers have had, however, is that they have not been able to figure out when this occurred, why it occurred, or how it occurred....

> *Ruff turned to a chart Asa Hutchinson had used in his presentation, which bore a list of dates. Each had a notation of something that had happened that day: "December 5th, witness list—Lewinsky!"; "December 6, president meets with attorneys on witness list"; December 7th, president and Jordan meet." It included the events of December 11 (Jordan-Lewinsky meeting; judge's order), the famous phone call of December 17, the serving of Lewinsky's subpoena on December 19, and the December 28 gift exchange.*
>
> *Ruff continued:*

... There is only one problem: Other than what we know to be true on this list, there is nothing other than surmise that links them together in any fashion that one could consider improper or certainly illegal. But that is, in essence, where the managers have brought us in their theorizing, for their fourth theory is that the pressure did not really begin to build until Ms. Lewinsky was actually subpoenaed and began to prepare an affidavit.

On this theory, a call to Mr. Perelman was the final step—going right to the top of MacAndrews & Forbes to make absolutely sure that Ms. Lewinsky stayed on the team. But here there are other facts to deal with. For example, look what happened—or more importantly, didn't happen—on December 19.

On that day, Monica Lewinsky came, weeping, to Mr. Jordan's office carrying with her the dreaded subpoena. Mr. Jordan called the president and visited with him that evening.... Wouldn't one think that if the president was, in fact, engaged in some scheme to use a job in New York to influence Ms. Lewinsky's testimony, this would be the critical moment?.... But what do we find? Mr. Jordan takes no further action on the job front until January 8....

Now, the fact that Ms. Lewinsky ... didn't know she was on the witness list until December 17, and Mr. Jordan didn't know about it until she was subpoenaed on the 19th, and Mr. Perelman never knew it, all are "proof positive" that the president himself was the "mastermind" pulling on unseen strings and influencing the participants in this drama, without their even knowing that they were being influenced.... With all due respect, somebody has been watching too many reruns of "The X-Files."...

And so this pillar returns to the dust from which it came.

Ruff now discussed Bennett's remarks to Judge Wright during the Jones deposition. The affidavit by the judge's clerk just introduced into evidence, which the managers had said would show that the president was paying close attention to Bennett's comments, said nothing of the sort. "Well," said Ruff, "it was not much of a pillar to start with."

Next, Ruff turned to Betty Currie. The new testimony from Jones lawyer Wesley Holmes cited two reasons for putting Ms. Currie's name on the Jones witness list: one, the president's deposition testimony, and two, because they had "reliable information" that Currie had facilitated Lewinsky's meetings with the president and was "central to the cover story." In fact, said Ruff, a close look at the deposition testimony revealed that it had been mostly the Jones lawyers who raised Currie's name. Ruff suggested it was far more likely that the Jones lawyers developed their new witness list by tracking the independent counsel's work.

Ruff then moved to the president's "coaching" sessions with Betty Currie. Once again, he played the clip from her testimony in which, when asked whether she felt pressure by the president, she responded, twice, that she had felt none whatsoever.

Only one pillar left. The managers ask the Senate to find that the president's conversations with Mr. Blumenthal and other aides was an effort to influence their testimony before the grand jury....

Ruff showed the excerpt from the president's grand jury testimony in which the president explained how he had handled his aides. "It's no secret to anybody that I hoped that this relationship would never become public," he said. "It's a matter of fact that it had been many, many months since there had been anything improper about it. . . ." He had not wanted *"to mislead my friends,"* he went on: *"So I said to them things that were true about this relationship. . . . I said there's nothing going on between us. That was true. I said I have not had sex with her as I defined it. That was true. And did I hope that I would never have to be here on this day giving this testimony? Of course. But I also didn't want to do anything to complicate this matter further. So I said things that were true. They may have been misleading, and if they were I have to take responsibility for it and I'm sorry."*

Pressed further, the president added that in the flurry of media attention, everyone was saying *"well, this is not really a story about sex, or this is a story about subornation of perjury."* As a result, he explained, he was trying to give his aides *"something . . . that would be true, even if misleading in the context of this deposition, and keep them out of trouble . . . and deal with what I though was the almost ludicrous suggestion that I had urged someone to lie or tried to suborn perjury."*

Ruff continued:

. . . I find it difficult to figure out how it is that they believe the president intended that his statement to Mr. Blumenthal or his statement to Mr. Podesta would involve their conveying false information to the grand jury, or that he sought in some fashion to send that message to the grand jury when, at the very moment that those aides were first subpoenaed, he asserted executive privilege to prevent them from testifying before the grand jury. For someone who wanted Mr. Blumenthal to serve, as the managers would have it, as his messenger of lies, that is strange behavior indeed.

Now, there is an issue here that I don't really want to get into at length, and I, not having heard the last two hours of the managers' presentation, don't know whether they are going to get into, and that is Manager Graham's favorite issue, the question of whether there was some scheme to smear Monica Lewinsky—early, middle, or late. Other than to say that no such plan ever existed. . . .

Ladies and gentlemen of the Senate, I don't know whether there is a market for used pillars, but they are all lying in the dust. . . .

Now, you have heard the managers tell you very early on in these meetings that we have advanced a "so what" defense; that we are saying that the president's conduct is really nothing to be concerned about; that we should all simply go home and ignore what he has done. And that, of course, to choose a word that would have been familiar to the framers themselves, is balderdash.

If you want to see "so what" in action, look elsewhere. "So what" if the framers reserved impeachment and removal for only those offenses that threaten the state? "So what" if the House Judiciary Committee didn't quite do their constitutional job, if they took the independent counsel's referral and added a few frills and then washed their hands of it? "So what" if the House approved articles that wouldn't pass muster in any court in the land? "So what" if the managers have been creating their own theories of impeachment as they go long? ...

By contrast, what we offer is not "so what," but this: Ask what the framers handed down to us as the standard for removing a president. Ask what impeachment and removal would mean to our system of government in years to come. Ask what you always ask in this Chamber: What is best for the country? No, the president wouldn't allow any of us to say "so what," to so much as suggest that what he has done can simply be forgotten. He has asked for forgiveness from his family and from the American people, and he has asked for the opportunity to earn back their trust. ...

And now our last words to you, which are the words I began with: William Jefferson Clinton is not guilty of the charges that have been brought against him. He did not commit perjury. He did not commit obstruction of justice. He must not be removed from office.

After a fifteen-minute recess, it was the House managers' turn once again. The chief justice recognized Bill McCollum.

Mr. McCollum: ... Having heard all of the evidence over the past few days and weeks, there should be little doubt that beginning in December 1997 William Jefferson Clinton set out on a course of conduct designed to keep from the *Jones* court the true nature of his relationship with Monica Lewinsky. Once he knew he would have to testify, he knew he was going to lie in his deposition. And he knew he was going to have to ... get Monica Lewinsky to lie ... and he was going to have to get his personal secretary to lie about his relationship, and have his aides and others help cover them up. ...

He did all of these things. And then he chose to lie to the grand jury again, because if he did not, he would have not been able to protect himself from the crimes he had already committed.

No amount of arguments by White House counsel can erase one simple fact: If you believe Monica Lewinsky, you cannot believe the president. If you believe Monica Lewinsky, the president committed most of the crimes with which he is charged in these arguments today.

For example, while the president did not directly tell her to lie, he never advised her what to put in her affidavit, she knew from the December 17 telephone conversation with the president that he meant for her to lie about the relationship and file a false affidavit, and he would lie as well....

...Monica Lewinsky was equally clear in her testimony to you Saturday that Betty Currie called her about the gifts, not the other way around. And surely nobody believes that Betty Currie would have called Monica Lewinsky about the gifts on December 28 unless the president had asked her to do so.

And then the day after the president's deposition in the *Jones* case, the president clearly committed the crimes of witness tampering and obstruction of justice when, in logical anticipation of Betty Currie being called as a witness, he said to Betty Currie, "You were always there when she was there, right?..."

I am not going to rehash all of the evidence...but it is my understanding that some of you may be prepared to vote to convict the president on obstruction of justice and not on perjury. I don't know how you can do that.... If you believe Sidney Blumenthal's testimony that the president told him that Monica Lewinsky came at him and made a sexual demand...surely you must conclude that the president committed perjury when he told the grand jury that he told his aides...nothing but the truth, even if misleading....

What he told Sidney Blumenthal was not true. It wasn't just misleading, it was not true. And he knew it was not true and it was perjury in front of the grand jury.

If you believe the president committed the crimes of witness tampering and obstruction of justice when he called Betty Currie to his office the day after his deposition...surely you must also conclude that the president committed perjury before the grand jury when he told the grand jurors his purpose in making these statements.... "I was trying to figure out what the facts were...."

...He knew that was not true.... That was perjury in front of the grand jury.

And then we have heard a lot of talk about the civil deposition.... [T]he president said before the grand jurors: "My goal"—talking about the *Jones* case deposition—"in this deposition was to be truthful....

Does anybody believe, after hearing all of this, that the goal of the president in the *Jones* deposition was to be truthful? He lied to the grand jury and committed perjury.

Last but not least, if you believe Monica Lewinsky about the acts of a sexual nature that they engaged in, how can you not conclude the president committed perjury when he specifically denied those acts?...

If you are going to vote to convict the president on the articles of impeachment regarding obstruction of justice, I urge you in the strongest way to also vote to convict him on the perjury article as well. I...

McCollum briefly discussed the differences between perjury and bribery in the sentencing guidelines, observing that Ruff had been right—"you can get enhancements for aggravating circumstances for bribery in certain cases"—but adding that "so can you get a greater sentence for perjury if there was a significant effort to wrongfully influence the administration of justice."

Then he addressed the consequences of failing to remove the president from office: a "precedent of doubt" about whether perjury and obstruction of justice are high crimes and misdemeanors; a precedent that standards for removal of a president are different from those for other officials. He continued:

To vote to acquit puts the president on a pedestal which says that, as long as he is popular, we are going to treat him differently...than any other person in any other position of public trust in the United States of America. The president is the Commander in Chief; he is the chief law enforcement officer; he is the man who appoints the Cabinet; he appoints the judges.

Are you going to put on the record books the precedent that all who serve under the president and whom he has appointed will be held to a higher standard than the president? What legacy to history is this? What mischief have you wrought to our Constitution, to our system of government, to the values and principles cherished by future generations of Americans?...All this, when it is clear that a vote to convict would amount to nothing more than the peaceful, orderly, and immediate transition of government of the presidency to the vice president?

William Jefferson Clinton is not a king; he is our president. You have the power and the duty to remove him from office for high crimes and misdemeanors.... William Jefferson Clinton has committed high crimes and misdemeanors. Convict him and remove him....

The chief justice recognized Charles Canady.

Mr. Canady: ... Let me refer you once again to a statement from the 1974 report...prepared by the staff of the Nixon impeachment inquiry....

Because impeachment of a president is a grave step for the nation it is to be predicated only upon conduct seriously incompatible with either constitutional form and principles of our government or the proper performance of constitutional duties of the presidential office. For our purposes now, impeachment is to be predicated only upon conduct seriously incompatible with the proper performance of constitutional duties of the presidential office.

That is a standard the managers accept. That is a standard the president's lawyers apparently also accept, and that is a standard I hope all 100 Members of the U.S. Senate could accept.... The problem comes, of course, in applying the standard.... The president's lawyers say that under this standard the case against the president isn't even worth considering. The managers argue on the contrary, that a conscientious application of the standard leads to the firm conclusion that the president should be convicted and removed....

I think we have agreement that obstruction of justice and lying under oath are incompatible with the proper performance of the constitutional duties of the presidential office. A president who has lied under oath and obstructed justice has by definition breached his constitutional duty to take care that the laws be faithfully executed. Such conduct is directly and unambiguously at odds with the duties of this office. So far so good.

But here is the real question. Is that conduct seriously incompatible with the president's constitutional duties? That is the question you all must answer. If you say yes, it is seriously incompatible, you must vote to convict and remove the president. If you say no, you must vote to acquit.

The president's defenders have not offered a clear guide to determining what is serious enough to justify removal. Instead, they have simply sought to minimize the significance of the particular offenses charged against the president.

Today we heard an attempt to minimize the significance of perjury. I was somewhat amazed to hear that. There was no mention made of what the first Chief Justice of the United States, Justice Jay, had to say about perjury, being of all crimes the most pernicious to society. That was omitted from the president's analysis.

... I would like to briefly review the factors advanced at mitigating the seriousness of the president's crimes.

We all know what the leading mitigating factor is. We have all heard this 1,000 times. It goes like this: The offenses are not sufficiently serious because it is all about sex....

It is very common for people to lie under oath and obstruct justice to do so at least in part to avoid personal embarrassment. People engage in such conduct in their efforts to extricate themselves from difficulty and embarrassing situations. To a large extent, the offenses of President Nixon could be attributed to his desire to avoid embarrassing revelations. Did that reduce his culpability? Did that lessen the seriousness of his misconduct? The answer is obvious. It did not.

The desire to avoid embarrassment is not a mitigating factor. Likewise, the nature of the precipitating misconduct of a sexual affair does not mitigate the seriousness of the president's crimes. If you accept the argument that it is just about sex, you will render the law of sexual harassment virtually meaningless. Any defendant guilty of sexual harassment would obviously have an incentive to lie about any sexual misconduct that may have occurred....

I would suggest to you that an objective review of all the circumstances of this case—and you need to look at all of the circumstances, all of the facts in context—if you do that, you will be pointed not to mitigating factors, but to aggravating factors.

The conduct of the president was calculated and sustained. His subtle and determined purpose was corrupt. It was corrupt from start to finish. He knew exactly what he was doing. He knew that it was in violation of the criminal law. He knew that people could go to prison for doing such things. He knew that it was contrary to his oath of office. He knew that it was incompatible with his constitutional duty as president. And he most certainly knew that it was a very serious matter. I am sure he believed he could get away with it, but I am equally sure that he knew just how serious it would be if the truth were known and understood.

He knew all these things. In the midst of it all, he showed not the slightest concern for the honor, the dignity, and the integrity of his high office. When he called Ms. Lewinsky at 2:30 in the morning, he was up to no good, just as my colleague, Mr. Graham, noted. He knew exactly what he was doing. When he called Ms. Currie into his office twice and told her lies about his relationship with Ms. Lewinsky, he knew exactly what he was doing.

When he sent Ms. Currie to retrieve the gifts from Ms. Lewinsky...he knew exactly what he was doing.... He was doing everything he could to make sure that Paula Jones did not get the evidence that a federal district judge had determined and ordered that she was entitled to receive.... That is what he planned to do, and that is what he did. And to cap it all off, he went before the federal grand jury and lied.

Whatever you may think about the president's testimony to the grand jury, one thing is clear. He didn't lie to the grand jury to avoid personal embarrassment. The DNA on the dress had ensured his personal embarrassment.... The stakes were higher before the federal grand jury.... This was a federal criminal investigation concerning crimes against the system of justice. This was about lying under oath and obstructing justice in the *Jones* case.

And what did he do when he testified to the grand jury? He said anything he thought he needed to say to avoid responsibility for his prior crimes.... He swore to God to tell the truth, and then he lied. He planned to lie, and he executed his plan because he believed it was in his personal and political interests to lie....

The chief justice recognized Ed Bryant.

Mr. Bryant:...We have been over the last four weeks...involved in an extraordinary process. It is uniquely thorough. And we have tried to blend the facts of this case with the law of the charges, together with the politics and the polls and the media, and we have had to make some tough decisions.... And what has in large part made this process distinct from past impeachments...has been just, it seems, the media and the daily grind on all of us, the critiques. It is almost as if we are performing, we are in a play, and every day we get a review.... And if that is what you see on TV and that is what you read in the paper, you are going to see the trees and not the forest here and miss the big picture.

That is so important. It is not about the personalities of these people or the personalities here or the politics involved or the polls, but it is about the facts. And ladies and gentlemen of the Senate, there are conclusive facts here that support a conviction....

Take, for instance, the affidavit.... Mr. Ruff, I think, challenged people...well, what do you think the president meant to do that night when he called her at 2:30 in the morning?

Well, what do you think he intended to do in that call at 2:30 in the morning? Do you think he called her to tell her he had a Christmas present for her, or do you think his intent was to tell her, which he did, that you have been listed on the witness list and you could be subpoenaed. And, you know, you might give an affidavit to avoid testifying. He suggested the affidavit, and then he said in that same conversation, well, you know, you can always use that cover story.

Why would he suggest using a cover story that night? Were they even seeing each other then? It belittles all reasonable judgment to accept this type of defense of this conduct, that it was an innocent phone conversation, the president really meant nothing by it, and the fact that Ms. Lewinsky said, well, I didn't connect the two. But look at what she did. She went to her lawyer and used that concocted story in an affidavit that she filed in the case.

Bryant walked through the managers' case on Bennett's use of the false affidavit during the president's deposition and the two conversations with Betty Currie: "Initially, remember, his defense was I was simply trying to recall what happened. And then we brought up the fact: Why did you go the second time? Did you have a short memory? Didn't you get it right the first time?" He mentioned the job search and the president's talks with his aides. Then he continued:

But if you will look carefully, you will see that the president is the only thread that goes from each one of these, from the very beginning, from the point when he met Monica Lewinsky...until they terminated the relationship, this president is involved in each one of these issues of the obstruction of justice.

It is always him, by himself, testifying falsely, sitting there letting his lawyers submit a false affidavit, or it is him and one other person—he and Monica Lewinsky talking about filing a false affidavit; he and Monica Lewinsky talking about a concocted story to testify. He and Betty Currie on two occasions: Betty, you remember the testimony was like this.

He and John Podesta, Sidney Blumenthal, the many aides—talking to them individually, giving them a false story. As Mr. Hutchinson pointed out so well in his argument the other day...no one else knows what is going on. Vernon Jordan didn't know what was happening with the affidavit, necessarily. Betty Currie didn't understand what was happening with the affidavit, or the job search.... Look at and analyze each one of these and you will see that there is a compartmentalization going on with this president. And he is at the center of it each time....

As I close, let me just tell you, too—on the heels of Mr. Canady—that there are law professors who testified in our hearing who have the contrary view to the view that was expressed by...law professors that Mr. Ruff referred to, that it is constitutional to impeach a president for conduct...that might be described as personal, particularly conduct of perjury or obstruction of justice. Professor Turley says: "In my view, serious crimes in office, such as lying under oath before a federal grand jury, have always been *malum in se* conduct for a president and sufficient for impeachment." Professor John McGinnis of

Benjamin Cardozo Law School says that obstruction of justice is clearly within the ambit of high crimes and misdemeanors.

…Given the right type of personal misconduct, it is clearly an impeachable offense.…

The chief justice recognized Asa Hutchinson. Hutchinson began by addressing some of the points Ruff had made in his summation. For example, he acknowledged that the president's lying to his aides did not directly involve the Paula Jones case, but read the article's language specifying the result of those lies: "causing the grand jury to receive false and misleading information." He emphasized that it was Monica Lewinsky, not the managers, who had said Vernon Jordan urged her to get rid of her draft notes to the president. And he said the president's lawyers continued to miss the legal significance of the second "coach episode" with Betty Currie—that it contradicted the president's testimony that he was talking to Currie to get facts, to help in media inquiries. "If that is the case," said Hutchinson, "there is absolutely no reason for it to be done on the second occasion, and clearly she was known to be a witness at that time."

He continued:

Mr. Hutchinson: …Let's look at the direct proof, not circumstantial evidence, but direct testimony.

What did Vernon Jordan testify as to the president's involvement in the job search?

Question to Mr. Jordan: You're acting in behalf of the president when you're trying to get Ms. Lewinsky a job and you were in control of the job search?

His answer: Yes.

He was acting at the direction of the president and he was in control.

What did Vernon Jordan testify he told the president when a job was secured for a key witness and the false affidavit was signed?

Mr. President, she signed the affidavit, she signed the affidavit.

Then the next day, the job is secured and the report to Betty Currie, the report to the president, "Mission accomplished."

Is this circumstantial evidence? This is direct testimony by a friend and confidant of the president, Vernon Jordan.

Who is the one person who clearly knew all of the ingredients to make the job search an obstruction of justice? It was the president who knew he had a dangerous relationship with Ms. Lewinsky. He knew his friend was securing a job at his direction, and he knew that a false affidavit was being procured at his suggestion. He was the one person who knew all the facts.

Fourthly, Ms. Lewinsky, is this circumstantial evidence or direct testimony when she talked about what the president told her on December 17? She was a witness, and immediately following the fact she was a witness, the suggestion that she could use the cover stories, the suggestion that she could use an affidavit.

Direct testimony, was it direct proof about the president's tampering with the testimony of Betty Currie? It was Betty Currie herself who acknowledged this and testified to it. No, this is not circumstantial evidence, it is direct testimony.

The same with Sidney Blumenthal. Direct testimony after direct testimony painting a picture, setting up the pillars of obstruction.

They want you to believe Monica Lewinsky sometimes, but they don't want you to believe her other times, and you have to weight her testimony.

I could go on with the facts, but the truth is that our case on obstruction of justice has been established. Some of you might conclude, "Well, I accept five or six of those pillars of obstruction, but there is one I have a reservation about." If you look at the article, if there is one element of obstruction that you accept and believe and you agree upon, then that is sufficient for conviction....

The next argument is: "Well, yes, the president should be held accountable, but he can always be prosecuted later. In fact, I understand a censure resolution is being circulated emphasizing that the president can be held criminally responsible for his actions when he leaves office. This is not too subtle of a suggestion that the independent counsel go ahead and file criminal charges against the president."

I appreciate Judge Starr, but I do not believe that is what the country has in mind when they say they want to get this matter over. I do not believe your vote on the articles of impeachment should be a signal to the independent counsel to initiate criminal proceedings....

And finally, there are some who consider the politics of this matter. We have proven our case. I entered this body thinking that this was a legal, judicial proceeding and not political. And I have been reminded there are political aspects under the Constitution to a Senate trial. So I concede the point.

. . . I appear before this body as an advocate. I am not paid for this special responsibility. But I am here because I believe the Constitution requires me to make this case. The facts prove overwhelmingly that the president committed obstruction of justice and perjury. Despite this belief, whatever conclusion you reach will not be criticized by me. And I will respect this institution regardless of the outcome.

As the late federal Judge Orin Harris of Arkansas always said from the bench to the jury when I was trying cases—and I hated his instruction because I was the prosecutor—but he would tell the jury, "Remember, the government never wins or loses a case. The government always wins when justice is done." Well, this is the Congress and this is the Senate. And it is your responsibility to determine the facts and to let justice roll down like mighty waters.

The chief justice recognized James Rogan.

Mr. Rogan: ... The mere fact that a person is elected president does not give him the right to become president, no matter how overwhelming his vote margin. Votes alone do not make a person president of the United States. There is a requirement that precedes obtaining the power and authority of obtaining the presidency. It is the oath of office. It is swearing to preserve, protect, and defend the Constitution. It is accepting the obligation that the laws are to be faithfully executed....

The founders did not intend the oath to be an afterthought or a technicality. They viewed it as an absolute requirement before the highest office in the land was entrusted to any person.

The evidence shows the president repeatedly violated his oath of office. Now the focus shifts to your oath of office. The president hopes that in this Chamber the polls will govern. On behalf of the House of Representatives, we entreat you to require the Constitution reign supreme. For if polls matter more than the oath to uphold the law, then yet another chip out of the marble has been struck....

The evidence clearly shows that the president engaged in a repeated and lengthy pattern of felonious conduct—conduct for which ordinary citizens can be and have been jailed and lost their liberty. This simply cannot be wished or censured away.

With his conduct aggravated by a motivation of personal and monetary leverage in the *Paula Jones* lawsuit, the solemnity of our sacred oath obliges us to do what the president regretfully has failed to do: defend the rule of law, defend the concept that no person is above the law.

On the day the House impeached President Clinton, I said that when they are old enough to appreciate the solemnity of that action, I wanted my little girls to know that when the roll was called, their father served with colleagues who counted it a privilege to risk political fortunes in defense of the Constitution.

Today, I am more resolute in that opinion. From the time I was a little boy, it was my dream to one day serve in the Congress of the United States. My dream was fulfilled two years ago. Today, I am a Republican in a district that is heavily Democratic. The pundits keep telling me that my stand on this issue puts my political fortunes in jeopardy. So be it. That revelation produces from me no flinching. There is a simple reason why: I know that in life dreams come and dreams go. But conscience is forever. I can live with the concept of not serving in Congress. I cannot live with the idea of remaining in Congress at the expense of doing what I believe to be right.

I was about 12 years old when a distinguished Member of this body, the late Senator Ralph Yarborough of Texas, gave me this sage advice about elective office: Always put principle above politics; put honor above incumbency.

I now return that sentiment to the body from which it came. Hold fast to it, Senators, and in doing so, you will be faithful both to our founders and to our heirs.

The chief justice recognized Lindsey Graham.

Mr. Graham: . . . Let me tell you what it all comes down to for me. If you can go back and explain to your children and your constituents how you can be truthful and misleading at the same time, good luck. That is the legacy that Bill Clinton has left all of us if we keep him in office—the idea that "I was truthful but misleading." That scenario focuses around whether or not one type of sex occurred versus the other type of sex. He is wanting you to buy into this definition that was allowed to exist because the wording wasn't quite right. That is the essence of it—"I was truthful, but I was misleading."

Mr. Podesta asked a little more questions than the other people did and the president denied any type of sexual relationship to him. Was he truthful there? Was he truthful in his grand jury testimony? How can you be both? It is just absolutely impossible. I want to play two clips for you now. . . .

[Text of Videotape Presentation]

Q. Now, you've stated . . . that you were lied to by the president. Is it a fair statement, given your previous testimony concerning your 30-minute conversation, that the president was trying to portray himself as a victim of a relationship with Monica Lewinsky?

A. I think that's the import of his whole story.

Before you put the other tape in, every Member of this body should need to answer this question: Is that a truthful statement? If you believe that the president of the United States is a victim of Ms. Lewinsky, we all owe him an apology. He is not. He is not.

You ask me why I want this president removed? Not only are they high crimes, not only do they rise to the level of constitutional out-of-bounds behavior, not only are they worse than what you remove judges for, they show a tremendous willingness of a national leader to put himself above anything decent and good. I hope that still matters in America....

... Let me say this about being truthful but misleading. Can you sit back as the president, after you told a lie to a key aide, where you portrayed yourself as a victim, and watch the press stories role out along the lines that "she wears her dresses too tight"; "she comes from a broken home"; "she's a stalker"; "she's sex obsessed"; can you sit back and watch all that happen and still be truthful but misleading?

We have laws against that in this country. We have laws in this country that even high Government officials cannot tell a lie to somebody knowing that lie will be repeated to a grand jury. That is exactly what happened here. He portrayed himself as a victim, which is not a misleading statement; it is a lie because if you knew the truth, you wouldn't consider him a victim. And that lie went to the federal grand jury. And those citizens were trying very hard to get it right, and he was trying very hard to mislead them. At every turn when they tried to get to the truth, he ran the other way, and he took the aura of the White House with him.

If you believe he is a victim, then you ought to acquit him. If you believe he has lied, then he ought not to be our president....

... [W]hen the article came out on January 21, the whole flavor of this case changed. And I don't know how you are going to explain it to yourself or others. But I want to lay out to you what I think happened based on the evidence.

That January 21 when the story broke that she may have been telling what went on, and the president was faced with the idea that the knowledge of their relationship was out in the public forum, what did he do then? There were no more nice jobs using a good friend. There was no more "Let's see if we can hide the gifts and play hide the ball." Do you know what happened then? He turned on her. Not my favorite part of the case—it is the most disgusting part of the case. It is part of the case that history will judge. The crimes change. They become more ominous, because the character traits became more ominous. The young lady who was the stalker, who was sex-obsessed, who wore her skirts too tight, that young lady was being talked about openly in the public. That young lady was being lied about to the federal grand jury. And the truth is that young lady fell in love with him. And probably to this day a 24- or 25-year-old young girl doesn't want to believe what was going to come her way. But you all are adults. You all are leaders of this nation. For you to look at these facts and conclude anything else would be an injustice, because without that threat, ladies and gentlemen, the stories were going to grow in number, and we would have no admissions of "misleading" and "truthful."

The White House is the bully pulpit. But it should never be occupied by a bully....

What we do today will put a burden on the White House and the burden on our future, one way or the other. Is it too much of a burden to say to future presidents, Don't fabricate stories in front of a grand jury, don't parse words, don't mislead, don't lie when you are begged not to? Is it too much to say to a president, If you are ever sued, play it straight; don't hide the gifts under the bed, don't give people false testimony, don't try to trash people who are witnesses against you? If that is too much of a burden to put on the White House, this nation is in hopeless decline. It is not too much of a burden, ladies and gentlemen. It is only common decency being applied to the occupant of the White House....

The chief justice recognized Henry Hyde.

Mr. Hyde: ... [I]n 1946 a British playwright, Terrance Rattigan, wrote a play based on a true experience.... And the story ... involved a young 13-year-old lad who was kicked out of the Royal Naval College for having forged somebody else's signature on a postal money order. Of course, he claimed he was innocent, but he was summarily dismissed.... Sir Edward Carson, the best lawyer of his time ... got interested in the case and took it on pro bono and lost all the way through the courts.

Finally, he had no other place to go, but he dug up an ancient remedy in England called "petition of right." You ask the King for relief. And so Carson wrote out five pages of reasons why a petition of right should be granted.... The King read it, agreed with it, and wrote across the front of the petition, "Let right be done. Edward VII."

I have always been moved by that phrase.... "Let right be done." I hope when you finally vote that will move you, too.

M<small>S</small>. Seligman last Saturday said we want to win too badly. This surprised me because none of the managers has committed perjury nor obstructed justice and claimed false privileges, none has hidden evidence under anyone's bed nor encouraged false testimony before the grand jury. That is what you do if you want to win too badly....

I doubt there are many people on the planet who doubt the president has repeatedly lied under oath and has obstructed justice. The defense spent a lot of time picking lint. There is a saying in the courts, I believe, that equity will not stoop to pick up pins. But that was their case. So the real issue doesn't concern the facts, the stubborn facts, as the defense is fond of saying, but what to do about them.

I am still dumbfounded about the drafts of the censures that are circulating. We aren't half as tough as the president in our impeachment articles as this draft is that was printed in the *New York Times:*

> "An inappropriate relationship with a subordinate employee in the White House which was shameless, reckless and indefensible."

I have a problem with that. It seems they are talking about private acts of consensual sexual misconduct which are really none of our business. But that is the leadoff. Then they say:

> "The president deliberately misled and deceived the American people and officials in all branches of the U.S. Government."

This is not a Republican document. This is coming from here.

> "The president gave false or misleading testimony and impeded discovery of evidence in judicial proceedings."

Isn't that another way of saying obstruction of justice and perjury?

"The president's conduct demeans the Office of the President as well as the president himself and creates disrespect for the laws of the land. Future generations of Americans must know that such behavior is not only unacceptable but bears grave consequences including loss of integrity, trust and respect."

But not loss of job.

"Whereas, William Jefferson Clinton's conduct has brought shame and dishonor to himself and to the Office of the President; whereas, he has violated the trust of the American people—"

See Hamilton Federalist No. 65—

"he should be condemned in the strongest terms."

Well, the next to the strongest terms. The strongest terms would remove him from office....

... There is no denying the fact that what you decide will have a profound effect on our culture, as well as on our politics. A failure to convict will make a statement that lying under oath, while unpleasant and to be avoided, is not all that serious. Perhaps we can explain this to those currently in prison for perjury. We have reduced lying under oath to a breach of etiquette, but only if you are the president....

On the subject of civil rights, it is my belief this issue doesn't belong to anyone; it belongs to everyone.... and one would have to be catatonic not to know that the struggle to keep alive equal protection of the law never ends. The mortal enemy of equal justice is the double standard, and if we permit a double standard, even for the president, we do no favor to the cause of human rights. It has been said that America has nothing to fear from this president on the subject of civil rights. I doubt Paula Jones would subscribe to that endorsement.

If you agree that perjury and obstruction of justice have been committed, and yet you vote down the conviction, you are extending and expanding the boundaries of permissible presidential conduct. You are saying a perjurer and obstructer of justice can be president, in the face of no less than three precedents for conviction of federal judges for perjury. You shred those precedents and you raise the most serious questions of whether the president is in fact subject to the law or whether we are beginning a restoration of the divine right of kings. The issues we are concerned with have consequences far into the future because the real damage is not to the individuals involved, but to the American system of justice and especially the principle that no one is above the law.

Edward Gibbon wrote his magisterial "Decline and Fall of the Roman Empire" in the late 18th century—in fact the first volume was issued in 1776. In his work, he discusses an emperor named Septimius Severus, who died in 211 A.D. after ruling 18 years. And here is what Gibbon wrote about the emperor:

> Severus promised, only to betray; he flattered only to ruin; and however he might occasionally bind himself by oaths and treaties, his conscience, obsequious to his interest, always released him from the inconvenient obligation.

I guess those who believe history repeats itself are really onto something. Horace Mann said:

> You should be ashamed to die unless you have achieved some victory for humanity.

To the House managers, I say your devotion to duty and the Constitution has set an example that is a victory for humanity. Charles de Gaulle once said that France would not be true to herself unless she was engaged in some great enterprise. That is true of us all. Do we spend our short lives as consumers, space occupiers, clock watchers, as spectators, or in the service of some great enterprise?

I believe, being a Senator, being a Congressman, and struggling with all our might for equal justice for all, is a great enterprise. It is our great enterprise. And to my House managers, your great enterprise was not to speak truth to power, but to shout it. And now let us all take our place in history on the side of honor and, oh, yes: Let right be done.

The Senate, sitting as a Court of Impeachment, adjourned until February 9.

THE DEBATE AND THE VOTE

On Tuesday, February 9, fourteen Republicans and all forty-five Democrats voted to open the debate—eight short of the two-thirds vote required to suspend the secrecy rules. Shortly before 2 P.M., reporters, spectators, prosecutors, and defense lawyers were ordered from the chamber, and the senators began their deliberations in private.

Over the course of three days, the debate continued. Participants described it as collegial, sometimes impassioned. And several senators announced publicly how they would vote. Three Republicans—John Chafee of Rhode Island, James Jeffords of Vermont, and Arlen Specter of Pennsylvania—declared that they would reject both articles of impeachment; two more, Slade Gorton of Washington and Ted Stevens of Alaska, said they would oppose the perjury article, but support the obstruction-of-justice article.

On the morning of Friday, February 12, after a final closed session in which the last few debaters finished their remarks, the Senate again opened its doors. The chief justice recognized Majority Leader Lott.

Mr. Lott: Mr. Chief Justice, Members of the Senate, the Senate has met almost exclusively as a Court of Impeachment since January 7, 1999, to consider the articles of impeachment against the president of the United States.

The Senate meets today to conclude this trial by voting on the articles of impeachment, thereby, fulfilling its obligation under the Constitution. I believe we are ready to proceed to the votes on the articles. And I yield the floor.

The Chief Justice: The clerk will now read the first article of impeachment.

Article I, charging President Clinton with perjury, was read aloud. Then the chief justice called for the vote.

The Chief Justice: The question is on the first article of impeachment. Senators, how say you? Is the respondent, William Jefferson Clinton, guilty or not guilty? A roll call vote is required.
The clerk will call the roll.

The results: guilty 45, not guilty 55. Ten Republicans joined the Democrats in voting to acquit.[1]

The Chief Justice: On this article of impeachment, 45 Senators having pronounced William Jefferson Clinton, president of the United States, guilty as charged, 55 Senators having pronounced him not guilty, two-thirds of the Senators present not having pronounced him guilty, the Senate adjudges that the respondent, William Jefferson Clinton, president of the United States, is not guilty as charged in the first article of impeachment.

Article II, charging President Clinton with obstruction of justice, was read aloud.

The Chief Justice: The question is on the second article of impeachment. Senators, how say you? Is the respondent, William Jefferson Clinton, guilty or not guilty?
The clerk will call the roll.

The results: guilty 50, not guilty 50. This time, five Republicans joined the Democrats for acquittal.

The Chief Justice: ... On this article of impeachment, 50 Senators having pronounced William Jefferson Clinton, president of the United States, guilty

[1] For full roll call results, see Appendix VII.

as charged, 50 Senators having pronounced him not guilty, two-thirds of the Senators present not having pronounced him guilty, the Senate adjudges that the respondent, William Jefferson Clinton, president of the United States, is not guilty as charged in the second article of impeachment....

It was almost over. A bipartisan majority did try to force through a resolution censuring the president,[2] but only 56 senators—short of the required two-thirds—voted to suspend the rules.

At 12:43 P.M., the Senate, sitting as a Court of Impeachment, adjourned.

[2] For text of the Censure Resolution, see Appendix VIII.

PART IV

APPENDICES

APPENDIX I

105TH CONGRESS
COMMITTEE ON THE JUDICIARY

Henry J. Hyde (R-Illinois), *Chairman**

Republicans	**Democrats**
F. James Sensenbrenner (Wisconsin)*	John Conyers, Jr. (Michigan), *Ranking*
Bill McCollum (Florida)*	Barney Frank (Massachusetts)
George W. Gekas (Pennsylvania)*	Charles E. Schumer (New York)
Howard Coble (North Carolina)	Howard L. Berman (California)
Lamar S. Smith (Texas)	Rick Boucher (Virginia)
Elton Gallegly (California)	Jerrold Nadler (New York)
Charles T. Canady (Florida)*	Robert C. Scott (Virginia)
Bob Inglis (South Carolina)	Melvin L. Watt (North Carolina)
Robert W. Goodlatte (Virginia)	Zoe Lofgren (California)
Stephen E. Buyer (Indiana)*	Sheila Jackson Lee (Texas)
Ed Bryant (Tennessee)*	Maxine Waters (California)
Steve Chabot (Ohio)*	Martin T. Meehan (Massachusetts)
Bob R. Barr (Georgia)*	William D. Delahunt (Massachusetts)
William L. Jenkins (Tennessee)	Robert Wexler (Florida)

* Managers of the trial in the Senate

(*continued*)

(*continued*)

Republicans	Democrats
Asa Hutchinson (Arkansas)*	Steven R. Rothman (New Jersey)
Edward A. Pease (Indiana)	Thomas M. Barrett (Wisconsin)
Christopher B. Cannon (Utah)*	
James E. Rogan (California)*	
Lindsey O. Graham (South Carolina)*	
Mary Bono (California)	

Chief Investigative Counsel	Minority Chief Investigative Counsel
David P. Schippers	Abbe D. Lowell

* Managers of the trial in the Senate

COUNSEL TO THE PRESIDENT

Williams & Connolly, Washington, D.C.

David E. Kendall   Nicole K. Seligman
Emmet T. Flood   Max Stier
Glen Donath   Alicia L. Marti

Office of the White House Counsel

Charles F. C. Ruff   Gregory B. Craig
Bruce R. Lindsey   Cheryl D. Mills
Lanny A. Breuer

HOUSE RESOLUTION 581

Resolution authorizing and directing the Committee on the Judiciary to investigate whether sufficient grounds exist for the impeachment of William Jefferson Clinton, president of the United States.

Resolved, That the Committee on the Judiciary, acting as a whole or by any subcommittee thereof appointed by the chairman for the purposes hereof and in accordance with the rules of the committee, is authorized and directed to investigate fully and completely whether sufficient grounds exist for the House of Representatives to exercise its constitutional power to impeach William Jefferson Clinton, president of the United States of America. The committee shall report to the House of Representatives such resolutions, articles of impeachment, or other recommendations as it deems proper.

SEC. 2.
(a) For the purpose of making such investigation, the committee is authorized to require—

(1) by subpoena or otherwise—

(A) the attendance and testimony of any person (including at a taking of a deposition by counsel for the committee); and

(B) the production of such things; and

(2) by interrogatory, the furnishing of such information as it deems necessary to such investigation.

(b) Such authority of the committee may be exercised

(1) by the chairman and the ranking minority member acting jointly, or, if either declines to act, by the other acting alone, except that in the event either so declines, either shall have the right to refer to the committee for decision the question whether such authority shall be so exercised and the committee shall be convened promptly to render that decision; or

(2) by the committee acting as a whole or by subcommittee.

Subpoenas and interrogatories so authorized may be issued over the signature of the chairman, or ranking minority member, or any member designated by either of them, and may be served by any person designated by the chairman, or ranking minority member, or any member designated by either of them. The chairman, or ranking minority member, or any member designated by either of them (or, with respect to any deposition, answer to interrogatory, or affidavit, any person authorized by law to administer oaths) may administer oaths to any witness. For the purposes of this section, "things" includes, without limitation, books, records, correspondence, logs, journals, memorandums, papers, documents, writings, drawings, graphs, charts, photographs, reproductions, recordings, tapes, transcripts, printouts, data compilations from which information can be obtained (translated if necessary, through detection devices into reasonably usable form), tangible objects, and other things of any kind.

House Resolution 611*

Resolution impeaching William Jefferson Clinton, president of the United States, for high crimes and misdemeanors.

Resolved, That William Jefferson Clinton, president of the United States, is impeached for high crimes and misdemeanors, and that the following articles of impeachment be exhibited to the United States Senate:

Articles of impeachment exhibited by the House of Representatives of the United States of America in the name of itself and of the people of the United States of America, against William Jefferson Clinton, president of the United States of America, in maintenance and support of its impeachment against him for high crimes and misdemeanors.

Article I

In his conduct while president of the United States, William Jefferson Clinton, in violation of his constitutional oath faithfully to execute the office of president of the United States and, to the best of his ability, preserve, protect, and

* Articles I and III passed the full House and went on to become Articles I and II in the Senate.

defend the Constitution of the United States, and in violation of his constitutional duty to take care that the laws be faithfully executed, has willfully corrupted and manipulated the judicial process of the United States for his personal gain and exoneration, impeding the administration of justice, in that:

On August 17, 1998, William Jefferson Clinton swore to tell the truth, the whole truth, and nothing but the truth before a Federal grand jury of the United States. Contrary to that oath, William Jefferson Clinton willfully provided perjurious, false and misleading testimony to the grand jury concerning one or more of the following: (1) the nature and details of his relationship with a subordinate Government employee; (2) prior perjurious, false and misleading testimony he gave in a Federal civil rights action brought against him; (3) prior false and misleading statements he allowed his attorney to make to a Federal judge in that civil rights action; and (4) his corrupt efforts to influence the testimony of witnesses and to impede the discovery of evidence in that civil rights action.

In doing this, William Jefferson Clinton has undermined the integrity of his office, has brought disrepute on the presidency, has betrayed his trust as president, and has acted in a manner subversive of the rule of law and justice, to the manifest injury of the people of the United States.

Wherefore, William Jefferson Clinton, by such conduct, warrants impeachment and trial, and removal from office and disqualification to hold and enjoy any office of honor, trust or profit under the United States.

Article II

In his conduct while president of the United States, William Jefferson Clinton, in violation of his constitutional oath faithfully to execute the office of president of the United States and, to the best of his ability, preserve, protect, and defend the Constitution of the United States, and in violation of his constitutional duty to take care that the laws be faithfully executed, has willfully corrupted and manipulated the judicial process of the United States for his personal gain and exoneration, impeding the administration of justice, in that:

(1) On December 23, 1997, William Jefferson Clinton, in sworn answers to written questions asked as part of a Federal civil rights action brought

against him, willfully provided perjurious, false and misleading testimony in response to questions deemed relevant by a Federal judge concerning conduct and proposed conduct with subordinate employees.

(2) On January 17, 1998, William Jefferson Clinton swore under oath to tell the truth, the whole truth, and nothing but the truth in a deposition given as part of a Federal civil rights action brought against him. Contrary to that oath, William Jefferson Clinton willfully provided perjurious, false and misleading testimony in response to questions deemed relevant by a Federal judge concerning the nature and details of his relationship with a subordinate Government employee, his knowledge of that employee's involvement and participation in the civil rights action brought against him, and his corrupt efforts to influence the testimony of that employee.

In all of this, William Jefferson Clinton has undermined the integrity of his office, has brought disrepute on the presidency, has betrayed his trust as president, and has acted in a manner subversive of the rule of law and justice, to the manifest injury of the people of the United States.

Wherefore, William Jefferson Clinton, by such conduct, warrants impeachment and trial, and removal from office and disqualification to hold and enjoy any office of honor, trust or profit under the United States.

Article III

In his conduct while president of the United States, William Jefferson Clinton, in violation of his constitutional oath faithfully to execute the office of president of the United States and, to the best of his ability, preserve, protect, and defend the Constitution of the United States, and in violation of his constitutional duty to take care that the laws be faithfully executed, has prevented, obstructed, and impeded the administration of justice, and has to that end engaged personally, and through his subordinates and agents, in a course of conduct or scheme designed to delay, impede, cover up, and conceal the existence of evidence and testimony related to a Federal civil rights action brought against him in a duly instituted judicial proceeding.

The means used to implement this course of conduct or scheme included one or more of the following acts:

(1) On or about December 17, 1997, William Jefferson Clinton corruptly encouraged a witness in a Federal civil rights action brought against him to execute a sworn affidavit in that proceeding that he knew to be perjurious, false and misleading.

(2) On or about December 17, 1997, William Jefferson Clinton corruptly encouraged a witness in a Federal civil rights action brought against him to give perjurious, false and misleading testimony if and when called to testify personally in that proceeding.

(3) On or about December 28, 1997, William Jefferson Clinton corruptly engaged in, encouraged, or supported a scheme to conceal evidence that had been subpoenaed in a Federal civil rights action brought against him.

(4) Beginning on or about December 7, 1997, and continuing through and including January 14, 1998, William Jefferson Clinton intensified and succeeded in an effort to secure job assistance to a witness in a Federal civil rights action brought against him in order to corruptly prevent the truthful testimony of that witness in that proceeding at a time when the truthful testimony of that witness would have been harmful to him.

(5) On January 17, 1998, at his deposition in a Federal civil rights action brought against him, William Jefferson Clinton corruptly allowed his attorney to make false and misleading statements to a Federal judge characterizing an affidavit, in order to prevent questioning deemed relevant by the judge. Such false and misleading statements were subsequently acknowledged by his attorney in a communication to that judge.

(6) On or about January 18 and January 20–21, 1998, William Jefferson Clinton related a false and misleading account of events relevant to a Federal civil rights action brought against him to a potential witness in that proceeding, in order to corruptly influence the testimony of that witness.

(7) On or about January 21, 23 and 26, 1998, William Jefferson Clinton made false and misleading statements to potential witnesses in a Federal grand jury proceeding in order to corruptly influence the testimony of those witnesses. The false and misleading statements made by William Jef-

ferson Clinton were repeated by the witnesses to the grand jury, causing the grand jury to receive false and misleading information.

In all of this, William Jefferson Clinton has undermined the integrity of his office, has brought disrepute on the presidency, has betrayed his trust as president, and has acted in a manner subversive of the rule of law and justice, to the manifest injury of the people of the United States.

Wherefore, William Jefferson Clinton, by such conduct, warrants impeachment and trial, and removal from office and disqualification to hold and enjoy any office of honor, trust or profit under the United States.

Article IV

Using the powers and influence of the office of president of the United States, William Jefferson Clinton, in violation of his constitutional oath faithfully to execute the office of president of the United States and, to the best of his ability, preserve, protect, and defend the Constitution of the United States, and in disregard of his constitutional duty to take care that the laws be faithfully executed, has engaged in conduct that resulted in misuse and abuse of his high office, impaired the due and proper administration of justice and the conduct of lawful inquiries, and contravened the authority of the legislative branch and the truth-seeking purpose of a coordinate investigative proceeding in that, as president, William Jefferson Clinton, refused and failed to respond to certain written requests for admission and willfully made perjurious, false and misleading sworn statements in response to certain written requests for admission propounded to him as part of the impeachment inquiry authorized by the House of Representatives of the Congress of the United States.

William Jefferson Clinton, in refusing and failing to respond, and in making perjurious, false and misleading statements, assumed to himself functions and judgments necessary to the exercise of the sole power of impeachment vested by the Constitution in the House of Representatives and exhibited contempt for the inquiry.

In doing this, William Jefferson Clinton has undermined the integrity of his office, has brought disrepute on the presidency, has betrayed his trust as president, and has acted in a manner subversive of the rule of law and justice, to the manifest injury of the people of the United States.

Wherefore, William Jefferson Clinton, by such conduct, warrants impeachment and trial, and removal from office and disqualification to hold and enjoy any office of honor, trust, or profit under the United States.

APPENDIX V

PROPOSED HOUSE CENSURE RESOLUTION

In the House of Representatives, Mr. Boucher (for himself, Mr. Delahunt, Mr. Barrett, and Ms. Jackson Lee) introduced the following joint resolution . . . expressing the sense of Congress with respect to the censure of William Jefferson Clinton.

Resolved by the Senate and House of Representatives of the United States of America in Congress assembled, That it is the sense of Congress that:

(1) On January 20, 1993, William Jefferson Clinton took the oath prescribed by the Constitution of the United States faithfully to execute the office of president; implicit in that oath is the obligation that the president set an example of high moral standards and conduct himself in a manner that fosters respect for the truth; and William Jefferson Clinton has egregiously failed in this obligation, and through his actions violated the trust of the American people, lessened their esteem for the office of president, and dishonored the office which they have entrusted to him;

(2) (A) William Jefferson Clinton made false statements concerning his reprehensible conduct with a subordinate;
(B) William Jefferson Clinton wrongly took steps to delay discovery of the truth; and

(C) inasmuch as no person is above the law, William Jefferson Clinton remains subject to criminal and civil penalties; and

(3) William Jefferson Clinton, president of the United States, by his conduct has brought upon himself, and fully deserves, the censure and condemnation of the American people and the Congress; and by his signature on this joint resolution, William Jefferson Clinton acknowledges this censure and condemnation.

APPENDIX VI

HOUSE ROLL CALL ON ARTICLES OF IMPEACHMENT

ROLL CALLS 543–546, RECORDED DECEMBER 19, 1998

Overview

Article	I	II	III	IV
For	228	205	221	148
Against	206	229	212	285
Not Voting	1	1	2	2

District	DEMOCRATS	Article I	Article II	Article III	Article IV
	ALABAMA				
5	Robert E. (Bud) Cramer				
7	Earl F. Hilliard				
	ARIZONA				
2	Ed Pastor				
	ARKANSAS				
1	Marion Berry				
2	Vic Snyder				

District	REPUBLICANS	Article I	Article II	Article III	Article IV
	ALABAMA				
1	Sonny Callahan	•	•	•	•
2	Terry Everett	•	•	•	•
3	Bob Riley	•	•	•	•
4	Robert B. Aderholt	•	•	•	•
6	Spencer Bachus	•	•	•	•
	ALASKA				
	Don Young	•	•	•	•

• indicates vote FOR article of impeachment
x indicates did not vote

(*continued*)

454 THE IMPEACHMENT AND TRIAL OF PRESIDENT CLINTON

(*continued*)

District	DEMOCRATS	Article I	Article II	Article III	Article IV
	CALIFORNIA				
3	Vic Fazio				
5	Robert T. Matsui				
6	Lynn Woolsey				
7	George Miller	x	x	x	x
8	Nancy Pelosi				
9	Barbara Lee				
10	Ellen O. Tauscher				
12	Tom Lantos				
13	Fortney Pete Stark				
14	Anna G. Eshoo				
16	Zoe Lofgren				
17	Sam Farr				
18	Gary A. Condit				
20	Calvin Dooley				
22	Lois Capps				
24	Brad Sherman				
26	Howard L. Berman				
29	Henry A. Waxman				
30	Xavier Becerra				
31	Matthew G. Martinez				
32	Julian C. Dixon				
33	Lucille Roybal-Allard				
34	Esteban Torres				
35	Maxine Waters				
36	Jane Harman				
37	Juanita Millender-McDonald				
42	George E. Brown Jr.				
46	Loretta Sanchez				
50	Bob Filner				
	COLORADO				
1	Diana DeGette				
2	David E. Skaggs				
	CONNECTICUT				
1	Barbara B. Kennelly				
2	Sam Gejdenson				

District	REPUBLICANS	Article I	Article II	Article III	Article IV
	ARIZONA				
1	Matt Salmon	•	•	•	•
3	Bob Stump	•	•	•	•
4	John Shadegg	•	•	•	
5	Jim Kolbe	•	•	•	
6	J. D. Hayworth	•	•	•	•
	ARKANSAS				
3	Asa Hutchinson	•	•	•	•
4	Jay Dickey	•		•	
	CALIFORNIA				
1	Frank Riggs	•	•	•	
2	Wally Herger	•	•	•	•
4	John T. Doolittle	•	•	•	•
11	Richard W. Pombo	•	•	•	•
15	Tom Campbell	•		•	
19	George P. Radanovich	•	•	•	•
21	Bill Thomas	•	•	•	•
23	Elton Gallegly	•	•	•	•
25	Howard P. (Buck) McKeon	•	•	•	•
27	James E. Rogan	•	•	•	•
28	David Dreier	•	•	•	•
38	Steve Horn	•	•	•	•
39	Ed Royce	•	•	•	•
40	Jerry Lewis	•	•	•	•
41	Jay C. Kim	•			
43	Ken Calvert	•	•	•	•
44	Mary Bono	•	•	•	•
45	Dana Rohrabacher	•	•	•	•
47	Christopher Cox	•	•	•	•
48	Ron Packard	•	•	•	•
49	Brian P. Bilbray	•	•	•	•
51	Randy (Duke) Cunningham	•	•	•	•
52	Duncan Hunter	•	•	•	•
	COLORADO				
3	Scott McInnis	•	•	•	

• indicates vote FOR article of impeachment
x indicates did not vote

District	DEMOCRATS	Article I	Article II	Article III	Article IV
3	Rosa DeLauro				
5	Jim Maloney				
	FLORIDA				
2	Allen Boyd				
3	Corrine Brown				
5	Karen L. Thurman				
11	Jim Davis				
17	Carrie P. Meek				
19	Robert Wexler				
20	Peter Deutsch				
23	Alcee L. Hastings				
	GEORGIA				
2	Sanford D. Bishop Jr.				
4	Cynthia A. McKinney				
5	John Lewis				
	HAWAII				
1	Neil Abercrombie				
2	Patsy T. Mink				
	ILLINOIS				
1	Bobby L. Rush				
2	Jesse L. Jackson Jr.				
3	William O. Lipinski				
4	Luis V. Gutierrez				
5	Rod R. Blagojevich				
7	Danny K. Davis				
9	Sidney R. Yates				
12	Jerry F. Costello				
17	Lane Evans				
19	Glenn Poshard				
	INDIANA				
1	Peter J. Visclosky				
3	Tim Roemer				

District	REPUBLICANS	Article I	Article II	Article III	Article IV
4	Bob Schaffer	•	•	•	•
5	Joel Hefley	•	•	•	
6	Dan Schaefer	•	•	•	•
	CONNECTICUT				
4	Christopher Shays				
6	Nancy L. Johnson	•	•		
	DELAWARE				
	Michael N. Castle	•			
	FLORIDA				
1	Joe Scarborough	•		•	
4	Tillie Fowler	•	•	•	•
6	Cliff Stearns	•	•	•	•
7	John L. Mica	•	•	•	•
8	Bill McCollum	•	•	•	•
9	Michael Bilirakis	•	•	•	•
10	C. W. Bill Young	•	•	•	•
12	Charles T. Canady	•	•	•	•
13	Dan Miller	•	•	•	•
14	Porter J. Goss	•	•	•	
15	Dave Weldon	•	•	•	•
16	Mark Foley	•		•	
18	Ileana Ros-Lehtinen	•	•	•	•
21	Lincoln Diaz-Balart	•	•	•	•
22	E. Clay Shaw Jr.	•		•	
	GEORGIA				
1	Jack Kingston	•	•	•	•
3	Mac Collins	•	•	•	•
6	Newt Gingrich*	•	•	•	•
7	Bob Barr	•	•	•	•
8	Saxby Chambliss	•	•	•	•
9	Nathan Deal	•	•	•	•
10	Charlie Norwood	•	•	•	•
11	John Linder	•	•	•	•

• indicates vote FOR article of impeachment
x indicates did not vote

(*continued*)

(*continued*)

District	DEMOCRATS	Article I	Article II	Article III	Article IV
9	Lee H. Hamilton				
10	Julia Carson				
	IOWA				
3	Leonard L. Boswell				
	KENTUCKY				
6	Scotty Baesler				
	LOUISIANA				
2	William J. Jefferson				
7	Christopher John				
	MAINE				
1	Thomas H. Allen	x	x	x	x
2	John Elias Baldacci				
	MARYLAND				
3	Benjamin L. Cardin				
4	Albert Wynn				
5	Steny H. Hoyer				
7	Elijah E. Cummings				
	MASSACHUSETTS				
1	John W. Olver				
2	Richard E. Neal				
3	Jim McGovern				
4	Barney Frank				
5	Martin T. Meehan				
6	John F. Tierney				
7	Edward J. Markey				
8	Joseph P. Kennedy 2d				
9	Joe Moakley				
10	Bill Delahunt				
	MICHIGAN				
1	Bart Stupak				
5	James A. Barcia				

District	REPUBLICANS	Article I	Article II	Article III	Article IV
	IDAHO				
1	Helen Chenoweth	•	•	•	•
2	Michael D. Crapo	•	•	•	•
	ILLINOIS				
6	Henry J. Hyde	•	•	•	•
8	Philip M. Crane	•	•	•	•
10	John Edward Porter	•	•	•	
11	Jerry Weller	•	•	•	
13	Harris W. Fawell	•	•	•	
14	Dennis Hastert	•	•	•	•
15	Thomas W. Ewing	•	•	•	•
16	Donald Manzullo	•	•	•	•
18	Ray LaHood	•	•	•	•
20	John Shimkus	•	•	•	
	INDIANA				
2	David M. McIntosh	•	•	•	
4	Mark Souder			•	
5	Steve Buyer	•	•	•	•
6	Dan Burton	•	•	•	•
7	Ed Pease	•	•	•	•
8	John N. Hostettler	•	•	•	•
	IOWA				
1	Jim Leach	•	•		
2	Jim Nussle	•	•	•	•
4	Greg Ganske	•	•	•	
5	Tom Latham	•	•	•	
	KANSAS				
1	Jerry Moran	•	•	•	
2	Jim Ryun	•	•	•	•
3	Vince Snowbarger	•	•	•	•
4	Todd Tiahrt	•	•	•	•
	KENTUCKY				
1	Edward Whitfield	•	•	•	

• indicates vote FOR article of impeachment
x indicates did not vote

District	DEMOCRATS	Article I	Article II	Article III	Article IV
8	Debbie Stabenow				
9	Dale E. Kildee				
10	David E. Bonior				
12	Sander M. Levin				
13	Lynn Rivers				
14	John Conyers Jr.				
15	Carolyn C. Kilpatrick				
16	John D. Dingell				
	MINNESOTA				
2	David Minge				
4	Bruce F. Vento				
5	Martin O. Sabo				
6	William D. (Bill) Luther				
7	Collin C. Peterson				
8	James L. Oberstar				
	MISSISSIPPI				
2	Bennie Thompson				
5	Gene Taylor	•	•	•	•
	MISSOURI				
	William L. Clay				
3	Richard A. Gephardt				
4	Ike Skelton				
	Karen McCarthy				
	Pat Danner				
	NEW JERSEY				
	Robert E. Andrews				
	Frank Pallone Jr.				
	Bill Pascrell Jr.				
	Steven R. Rothman				
10	Donald M. Payne				
13	Robert Menendez				
	NEW YORK				
	Carolyn McCarthy				
	Gary L. Ackerman				

District	REPUBLICANS	Article I	Article II	Article III	Article IV
2	Ron Lewis	•	•	•	•
3	Anne M. Northup	•	•	•	
4	Jim Bunning	•	•	•	•
5	Harold Rogers	•	•	•	
	LOUISIANA				
1	Robert L. Livingston	•	•	•	•
3	W. J. (Billy) Tauzin	•	•	•	
4	Jim McCrery	•	•	•	
5	John Cooksey	•	•	•	•
6	Richard H. Baker	•	•	•	•
	MARYLAND				
1	Wayne T. Gilchrest	•	•	•	
2	Robert L. Ehrlich Jr.	•	•	•	
6	Roscoe G. Bartlett	•	•	•	•
8	Constance A. Morella				
	MICHIGAN				
2	Peter Hoekstra	•	•	•	•
3	Vernon J. Ehlers	•	•	•	•
4	Dave Camp	•	•	•	•
6	Fred Upton	•	•	•	
7	Nick Smith	•	•	•	•
11	Joe Knollenberg	•	•	•	•
	MINNESOTA				
1	Gil Gutknecht	•	•	•	•
3	Jim Ramstad	•		•	
	MISSISSIPPI				
1	Roger Wicker	•	•	•	•
3	Charles W. (Chip) Pickering Jr.	•	•	•	•
4	Mike Parker	•	•	•	
	MISSOURI				
2	James M. Talent	•	•	•	•
7	Roy Blunt	•	•	•	•
8	Jo Ann Emerson	•	•	•	

• indicates vote FOR article of impeachment
x indicates did not vote

(*continued*)

(*continued*)

District	DEMOCRATS	Article I	Article II	Article III	Article IV
6	Gregory W. Meeks				
7	Thomas J. Manton				
8	Jerrold Nadler				
9	Charles E. Schumer				
10	Edolphus Towns				
11	Major R. Owens				
12	Nydia M. Velazquez				
14	Carolyn B. Maloney				
15	Charles B. Rangel				
16	Jose E. Serrano				
17	Eliot L. Engel				
18	Nita M. Lowey				
21	Michael R. McNulty				
26	Maurice D. Hinchey				
28	Louise M. Slaughter				
29	John J. LaFalce				
	NORTH CAROLINA				
1	Eva Clayton				
2	Bob Etheridge				
4	David E. Price				
7	Mike McIntyre				
8	W. G. (Bill) Hefner				
12	Melvin Watt				
	NORTH DAKOTA				
	Earl Pomeroy				
	OHIO				
3	Tony P. Hall				
6	Ted Strickland				
9	Marcy Kaptur				
10	Dennis J. Kucinich				
11	Louis Stokes				
13	Sherrod Brown				
14	Tom Sawyer				
17	James A. Traficant Jr.				

District	REPUBLICANS	Article I	Article II	Article III	Article IV
9	Kenny Hulshof	•	•		•
	MONTANA				
	Rick Hill	•	•	•	
	NEBRASKA				
1	Doug Bereuter	•	•	•	
2	Jon Christensen	•	•	•	•
3	Bill Barrett	•	•	•	•
	NEVADA				
1	John Ensign	•		•	
2	Jim Gibbons	•		•	•
	NEW HAMPSHIRE				
1	John E. Sununu	•	•	•	•
2	Charles Bass	•	•	•	
	NEW JERSEY				
2	Frank A. LoBiondo	•	•	•	
3	Jim Saxton	•	•	•	
4.	Christopher H. Smith	•	•	•	•
5	Marge Roukema	•	•	•	•
7	Bob Franks	•	•	•	
11	Rodney P. Frelinghuysen	•	•	•	
12	Michael Pappas	•	•	•	•
	NEW MEXICO				
1	Heather A. Wilson	•	•	•	•
2	Joe Skeen	•	•	•	•
3	Bill Redmond	•	•	•	•
	NEW YORK				
1	Michael P. Forbes	•	•	•	•
2	Rick A. Lazio	•		•	

• indicates vote FOR article of impeachment
x indicates did not vote

District	DEMOCRATS	Article I	Article II	Article III	Article IV
	OREGON				
1	Elizabeth Furse				
3	Earl Blumenauer				
4	Peter A. DeFazio				
5	Darlene Hooley				
	PENNSYLVANIA				
1	Robert A. Brady				
2	Chaka Fattah				
3	Robert A. Borski				
4	Ron Klink				
6	Tim Holden				
11	Paul E. Kanjorski				
12	John P. Murtha				
14	William J. Coyne				
15	Paul McHale	•	•	•	
18	Mike Doyle				
20	Frank R. Mascara				
	RHODE ISLAND				
1	Patrick J. Kennedy				
2	Bob Weygand				
	SOUTH CAROLINA				
5	John M. Spratt Jr.				
6	James E. Clyburn				
	TENNESSEE				
5	Bob Clement				
6	Bart Gordon				
8	John Tanner				
9	Harold E. Ford Jr.				
	TEXAS				
1	Max Sandlin				
2	Jim Turner				
4	Ralph M. Hall	•	•	•	
9	Nick Lampson				

District	REPUBLICANS	Article I	Article II	Article III	Article IV
3	Peter T. King				
13	Vito J. Fossella	•	•	•	
19	Sue W. Kelly	•		•	
20	Benjamin A. Gilman	•		•	
22	Gerald B. H. Solomon	•	•	•	•
23	Sherwood L. Boehlert	•	•		
24	John M. McHugh	•	•		
25	James T. Walsh	•	•	•	
27	Bill Paxon	•	•	•	•
30	Jack Quinn	•	•	•	
31	Amo Houghton				
	NORTH CAROLINA				
3	Walter B. Jones Jr.	•	•	•	•
5	Richard M. Burr	•		•	
6	Howard Coble	•	•	•	•
9	Sue Myrick	•	•	•	•
10	Cass Ballenger	•	•	•	•
11	Charles H. Taylor	•	•	•	•
	OHIO				
1	Steve Chabot	•	•	•	•
2	Rob Portman	•	•	•	
4	Michael G. Oxley	•	•	•	•
5	Paul E. Gillmor	•	•	•	
7	David L. Hobson	•		•	
8	John A. Boehner	•	•	•	•
12	John R. Kasich	•	•	•	
15	Deborah Pryce	•		•	
16	Ralph Regula	•	•		
18	Bob Ney	•		•	
19	Steven C. LaTourette	•	•	•	
	OKLAHOMA				
1	Steve Largent	•	•	•	
2	Tom Coburn	•	•	•	•
3	Wes Watkins	•	•	•	•
4	J. C. Watts Jr.	•	•	•	•

• indicates vote FOR article of impeachment
x indicates did not vote

(*continued*)

(*continued*)

District	DEMOCRATS	Article I	Article II	Article III	Article IV
10	Lloyd Doggett				
11	Chet Edwards				
15	Ruben Hinojosa				
16	Silvestre Reyes				
17	Charles W. Stenholm	•	•	•	
18	Sheila Jackson-Lee				
20	Henry B. Gonzalez				
24	Martin Frost				
25	Ken Bentsen				
27	Solomon P. Ortiz				
28	Ciro D. Rodriguez				
29	Gene Green				
30	Eddie Bernice Johnson				
	VIRGINIA				
2	Owen B. Pickett				
3	Robert C. Scott				
4	Norman Sisisky				
5	Virgil H. Goode Jr.	•	•	•	
8	James P. Moran				
9	Rick Boucher				
	WASHINGTON				
6	Norm Dicks				
7	Jim McDermott				
9	Adam Smith				
	WEST VIRGINIA				
1	Alan B. Mollohan				
2	Bob Wise				
3	Nick J. Rahall 2d				
	WISCONSIN				
3	Ron Kind				
4	Gerald D. Kleczka				
5	Thomas M. Barrett				
7	David R. Obey				
8	Jay W. Johnson				

District	REPUBLICANS	Article I	Article II	Article III	Article IV
5	Ernest Istook	•	•	•	•
6	Frank D. Lucas	•	•	•	•
	OREGON				
2	Bob Smith	•	•	•	•
	PENNSYLVANIA				
5	John E. Peterson	•	•	•	•
7	Curt Weldon	•	•	•	
8	James C. Greenwood	•		•	
9	Bud Shuster	•		•	
10	Joseph M. McDade	•	•	•	•
13	Jon D. Fox	•	•	•	•
16	Joseph R. Pitts	•	•	•	•
17	George W. Gekas	•	•	•	•
19	Bill Goodling	•	•	•	•
21	Phil English	•			
	SOUTH CAROLINA				
1	Mark Sanford	•		•	•
2	Floyd D. Spence	•	•	•	•
3	Lindsey Graham	•		•	•
4	Bob Inglis	•	•	•	•
	SOUTH DAKOTA				
	John Thune	•	•	•	
	TENNESSEE				
1	Bill Jenkins	•	•	•	
2	John J. Duncan Jr.	•	•	•	•
3	Zach Wamp	•	•	•	•
4	Van Hilleary	•	•	•	•
7	Ed Bryant	•	•	•	•
	TEXAS				
3	Sam Johnson	•	•	•	•
5	Pete Sessions	•	•	•	•
6	Joe L. Barton	•	•	•	•
7	Bill Archer	•	•	•	•

• indicates vote FOR article of impeachment
x indicates did not vote

District	INDEPENDENT	Article I	Article II	Article III	Article IV
	VERMONT				
	Bernard Sanders				

District	REPUBLICANS	Article I	Article II	Article III	Article IV
8	Kevin Brady	•	•	•	•
12	Kay Granger	•	•	•	
13	William M. (Mac) Thornberry	•	•	•	
14	Ron Paul	•	•	•	•
19	Larry Combest	•	•	•	•
21	Lamar Smith	•	•	•	•
22	Tom DeLay	•	•	•	•
23	Henry Bonilla	•	•	•	
26	Dick Armey	•	•	•	•
	UTAH				
1	James V. Hansen	•	•	•	•
2	Merrill Cook	•	•	•	•
3	Chris Cannon	•	•	•	•
	VIRGINIA				
1	Herbert H. Bateman	•	•	•	•
6	Robert W. Goodlatte	•	•	•	•
7	Thomas J. Bliley Jr.	•	•	•	•
10	Frank R. Wolf	•	•	•	•
11	Thomas M. Davis	•	•	•	
	WASHINGTON				
1	Rick White	•	•	•	
2	Jack Metcalf	•	•	•	•
3	Linda Smith	•	•	•	•
4	Richard (Doc) Hastings	•	•	•	•
5	George R. Nethercutt Jr.	•	•	•	
8	Jennifer Dunn	•	•	•	•
	WISCONSIN				
1	Mark W. Neumann	•	•	•	•
2	Scott L. Klug	•		•	
6	Tom Petri	•	•	•	
9	F. James Sensenbrenner Jr.	•	•	•	•
	WYOMING				
	Barbara Cubin	•	•	•	•

• indicates vote FOR article of impeachment
x indicates did not vote

SENATE VOTE ON ARTICLES OF IMPEACHMENT

VOTES NOS. 17–18, RECORDED FEBRUARY 12, 1999

DEMOCRATS	Article I	II
Daniel Akaka (HI)		
Max Baucus (MT)		
Evan Bayh (IN)		
Joseph Biden Jr (DE)		
Jeff Bingaman (NM)		
Barbara Boxer (CA)		
John Breaux (LA)		
Richard Bryan (NV)		
Robert Byrd (WV)		
Max Cleland (GA)		
Kent Conrad (ND)		
Thomas Daschle (SD)		
Christopher Dodd (CT)		
Byron Dorgan (ND)		
Richard Durbin (IL)		
John Edwards (NC)		

REPUBLICANS	Article I	II
Spencer Abraham (MI)	•	•
Wayne Allard (CO)	•	•
John Ashcroft (MO)	•	•
Robert Bennett (UT)	•	•
Christopher Bond (MO)	•	•
Sam Brownback (KS)	•	•
Jim Bunning (KY)	•	•
Conrad Burns (MT)	•	•
Ben Nighthorse Campbell (CO)	•	•
John Chafee (RI)		
Thad Cochran (MS)	•	•
Susan Collins (ME)		
Paul Coverdell (GA)	•	•
Larry Craig (ID)	•	•
Mike Crapo (ID)	•	•
Mike Dewine (OH)	•	•

• indicates vote for a finding of GUILTY

(*continued*)

(*continued*)

DEMOCRATS	Article 1	Article 2
Russell Feingold (WI)		
Dianne Feinstein (CA)		
Bob Graham (FL)		
Tom Harkin (IA)		
Ernest Hollings (SC)		
Daniel Inouye (HI)		
Tim Johnson (SD)		
Edward Kennedy (MA)		
Robert Kerrey (NE)		
John Kerry (MA)		
Herb Kohl (WI)		
Mary Landrieu (LA)		
Frank Lautenberg (NJ)		
Patrick Leahy (VT)		
Carl Levin (MI)		
Joseph Lieberman (CT)		
Blanche Lincoln (AR)		
Barbara Mikulski (MD)		
Daniel Moynihan (NY)		
Patty Murray (WA)		
Jack Reed (RI)		
Harry Reid (NV)		
Charles Robb (VA)		
John Rockefeller IV (WV)		
Paul Sarbanes (MD)		
Charles Schumer (NY)		
Robert Torricelli (NJ)		
Paul Wellstone (MN)		
Ron Wyden (OR)		
45	0	0

REPUBLICANS	Article I	Article II
Pete Domenici (NM)	•	•
Mike Enzi (WY)	•	•
Peter Fitzgerald (IL)	•	•
William Frist (TN)	•	•
Slade Gorton (WA)		•
Phil Gramm (TX)	•	•
Rod Grams (MN)	•	•
Chuck Grassley (IA)	•	•
Judd Gregg (NH)	•	•
Charles Hagel (NE)	•	•
Orrin Hatch (UT)	•	•
Jesse Helms (NC)	•	•
Tim Hutchinson (AR)	•	•
Kay Bailey Hutchison (TX)	•	•
James Inhofe (OK)	•	•
James Jeffords (VT)		
Jon Kyl (AZ)	•	•
Trent Lott (MS)	•	•
Richard Lugar (IN)	•	•
Connie Mack (FL)	•	•
John McCain (AZ)	•	•
Mitch McConnell (KY)	•	•
Frank Murkowski (AK)	•	•
Don Nickles (OK)	•	•
Pat Roberts (KS)	•	•
William Roth Jr (DE)	•	•
Rick Santorum (PA)	•	•
Jeff Sessions (AL)	•	•
Richard Shelby (AL)		•
Bob Smith (NH)	•	•

• indicates vote for a finding of GUILTY

REPUBLICANS	Article	
	1	2
Gordon Smith (OR)	•	•
Olympia Snowe (ME)		
Arlen Specter (PA)		
Ted Stevens (AK)		•
Craig Thomas (WY)	•	•
Fred Thompson (TN)		•
Strom Thurmond (SC)	•	•
George Voinovich (OH)	•	•
John Warner (VA)		•
55	45	50

• indicates vote for a finding of GUILTY

PROPOSED SENATE
CENSURE RESOLUTION

Relating to the Censure of William Jefferson Clinton, president of the United States (Senate—February 12, 1999)

Mrs. Feinstein (for herself, Mr. Bennett, Mr. Moynihan, Mr. Chafee, Mr. Kohl, Mr. Jeffords, Mr. Lieberman, Mr. Smith of Oregon, Mr. Daschle, Ms. Snowe, Mr. Reid, Mr. Gorton, Mr. Bryan, Mr. McConnell, Mr. Cleland, Mr. Domenici, Mr. Torricelli, Mr. Campbell, Mr. Wyden, Mrs. Lincoln, Mr. Kerry, Mr. Kerrey, Mr. Schumer, Mr. Durbin, Mrs. Murray, Mr. Wellstone, Mr. Breaux, Ms. Mikulski, Mr. Dorgan, Mr. Baucus, Mr. Reed, Ms. Landrieu, Mr. Kennedy, Mr. Levin, Mr. Rockefeller, Mr. Robb, Mr. Inouye, and Mr. Akaka) submitted the following resolution; which was referred to the Committee on Rules and Administration:

WHEREAS William Jefferson Clinton, president of the United States, engaged in an inappropriate relationship with a subordinate employee in the White House, which was shameless, reckless and indefensible;

WHEREAS William Jefferson Clinton, president of the United States, deliberately misled and deceived the American people and officials in all branches of the United States Government;

WHEREAS William Jefferson Clinton, president of the United States, gave false or misleading testimony and impeded discovery of evidence in judicial proceedings;

WHEREAS William Jefferson Clinton's conduct in this matter is unacceptable for a president of the United States, does demean the Office of the president as well as the president himself, and creates disrespect for the laws of the land;

WHEREAS President Clinton fully deserves censure for engaging in such behavior;

WHEREAS future generations of Americans must know that such behavior is not only unacceptable but also bears grave consequences, including loss of integrity, trust and respect;

WHEREAS William Jefferson Clinton remains subject to criminal and civil actions;

WHEREAS William Jefferson Clinton's conduct in this matter has brought shame and dishonor to himself and to the Office of the President; and

WHEREAS William Jefferson Clinton through his conduct in this matter has violated the trust of the American people;

Now therefore, be it resolved that: The United States Senate does hereby censure William Jefferson Clinton, president of the United States, and condemns his conduct in the strongest terms.

APPENDIX IX

OTHER RESOURCES

A remarkable array of information pertaining to the impeachment is available on the World Wide Web at locations too numerous to list individually. Probably the best place to start is Thomas (thomas.loc.gov), a Web site run by the Library of Congress. Its extensive resources include a complete searchable text of the *Congressional Record* and links to dozens of other government sites, including the Government Printing Office. The House also has a useful Web site (www.house.gov) which breaks down by committee and provides the text of all recent legislation, as does the Senate (www.senate.gov).

Following are some of the documents the editor of this volume found useful in understanding the proceedings. As of this writing, all are available on the Web, most in several locations and formats.

The Federalist Papers (Nos. 64–66, *The Powers of the Senate*)

The Independent Counsel Statute (Title 28, U.S. Code, Sections 591–599)

The Starr Report (*Referral to the United States House of Representatives Pursuant to Title 28, United States Code, § 595(c)*, September 9, 1998)

First White House rebuttal of the Starr Report (*Preliminary Memorandum Concerning Referral of Office of Independent Counsel,* September 11, 1998)

Second White House rebuttal of the Starr Report (*Initial Response to Referral of Office of Independent Counsel,* September 12, 1998)

The Judiciary Committee's "Eighty-One Questions" (*Requests for Admission of William J. Clinton, President of the United States, Relating to the Inquiry of Impeachment Authorized Pursuant to H. Res. 581,* November 5, 1998)

Judiciary Committee report to the full House (*House Report 105–830, Impeachment of William Jefferson Clinton, President of the United States,* December 16, 1998)

The president's response to impeachment (*Answer of President William Jefferson Clinton to the Articles of Impeachment,* January 10, 1999)

The House's proposed prosecution in the Senate trial (*Trial Memorandum of the United States House of Representatives,* January 11, 1999)

The president's proposed defense in the Senate trial (*Trial Memorandum of President William Jefferson Clinton,* January 13, 1999)

INDEX